D1557558

I & II THESSALONIANS

THE NEW TESTAMENT LIBRARY

Editorial Advisory Board

M. Eugene Boring

I & II Thessalonians
A Commentary

WESTMINSTER
JOHN KNOX PRESS
LOUISVILLE · KENTUCKY

© 2015 M. Eugene Boring

First edition
Published by Westminster John Knox Press
Louisville, Kentucky

15 16 17 18 19 20 21 22 23 24—10 9 8 7 6 5 4 3 2 1

Book design by Jennifer K. Cox

Library of Congress Cataloging-in-Publication Data

Boring, M. Eugene.
  I & II Thessalonians: a commentary / M. Eugene Boring.—First edition.
    pages cm.—(The New Testament library)
  Includes bibliographical references and index.
  ISBN 978-0-664-22099-0 (alk. paper)
  1. Bible. Thessalonians—Commentaries. I. Title. II. Title: I and II Thessalonians.
  BS2725.53.B67 2015
  227'.8107—dc23

                              2014049525

Most Westminster John Knox Press books are available at special quantity discounts when purchased in bulk by corporations, organizations, and special-interest groups. For more information, please e-mail SpecialSales@wjkbooks.com.

For Karen,
with love, respect, and gratitude

CONTENTS

COMMENTARY ON 1 THESSALONIANS

PREFACE

"Why have you never written a commentary?" Reliable oral tradition has it that a student posed this question to Bishop J. A. T. Robinson, of *Honest to God* fame/notoriety a generation ago. His response: "Whoever writes a commentary must say something about every text, whether they have anything to say or not." The good bishop in fact had a lot to say that was worth listening to. In the midst of his church responsibilities, Robinson continued to be an active New Testament scholar on the Cambridge faculty, lecturing, directing dissertations, writing scholarly monographs and articles. Several of these are still relevant for the would-be interpreter of 1–2 Thessalonians. On the historical development of apocalyptic thought from Jesus to the New Testament, his *Jesus and His Coming: Did the Early Church Misinterpret the Original Teaching of Jesus* (1957) still deserves pondering, and his *In the End, God . . . A Study of the Christian Doctrine of the Last Things* (1968) continues to be a profoundly thoughtful and personal hermeneutical proposal for taking New Testament eschatology seriously in our own theology and life.

Robinson was indeed correct in assuming that a commentary cannot consist of a series of topical essays, even if these are evoked and informed by biblical study, but "must say something about every text." Aye, there's the rub. The question, however, is not whether the commentator has something to say about every text, but whether the biblical text itself has something to say, the commentator's task being to assist the reader (of the Bible, not just the commentary) in coming within hearing distance of the text, in all its nitty-gritty particularity.

First and Second Thessalonians are themselves not topical essays, but letters. We might well reflect on how much we already know about how to read letters. In particular, if we are members of the Christian community, we already know a great deal about how to read and understand 1–2 Thessalonians. Beverly Gaventa has called attention to a paragraph in Mortimer Adler's *How to Read a Book*, in which he claimed that there is one situation in which people do in fact already know how to read:

> When they are in love and are reading a love letter, they read for all they are worth. They read every word three ways; they read between the lines and in the margins;

they read the whole in terms of the parts, and each part in terms of the whole; they grow sensitive to context and ambiguity, to insinuation and implication; they perceive the color of words, the odor of phrases, and the weight of sentences. They might even take the punctuation into account. Then, if never before, they *read*.[1]

All the historical, literary, and theological dimensions of interpretation explored in the following commentary are important, but, as Gaventa points out, the reader who wants to truly hear the text must approach it as a love letter in which Paul pours out his heart to the Thessalonians, in the glad confidence that as members of the household of faith, the family of God, they love him as well, and that their mutual love derives from God's love for all. The letter's first interpreter, the author of 2 Thessalonians, must do the same, and so must we.

Like all the volumes of the New Testament Library, this commentary includes the author's translation, itself, of course, an act of interpretation. The translation here provided is not suggested as a standard translation for liturgical reading, which must take other factors into consideration. The translation attempts to follow the Greek structure even when it is unwieldy or inelegant in English, to facilitate a close reading by the modern student. In contrast to the original, the translation is not designed for oral reading, but for the student who ponders, with pauses, the meaning of the written word and *sees* the text in a particular form on the printed page. Though I have not detailed the process on individual texts, three procedures have been helpful (in addition to the standard tools of historical and literary criticism): (1) discerning the narrative world projected by all the texts in the Pauline corpus; (2) diagramming every sentence in Greek; (3) searching ancient texts facilitated by Accordance biblical software.

I am indebted to the students in numerous classes over the years with whom I have studied the letters of Paul, as I am to several friends and colleagues who have shared their time and wisdom as this project entered its final phase. Steve Fowl read the section of the introduction on canonical criticism. Bill Baird read the final draft of the whole, as did Bobby Cook. Jim Wait checked Scripture references and made suggestions on translation. John Carroll made insightful editorial suggestions, and the editorial and production staff of Westminster John Knox Press did their usual superb job, including especially Marianne Blickenstaff, her successor Bridgett Green, Daniel Braden, and the sharp eyes and detailed knowledge of the copyeditor, S. David Garber. All made a contribution for which I offer my heartfelt gratitude, but the mistakes that remain are my own.

The book is dedicated to Karen, loving and supporting partner for many decades. Words fail me, but she knows.

1. Adler 14. Cited in Gaventa 1998, 9.

ABBREVIATIONS

Ancient Sources

Abbreviations of titles for most ancient sources conform to *The SBL Handbook of Style for Ancient Near Eastern, Biblical, and Early Christian Studies*, edited by P. H. Alexander et al. (Peabody, MA: Hendrickson, 1999). Full titles are in the Index of Ancient Sources (in the back of this volume). Below are abbreviations for other ancient sources:

CD	Cairo Genizah copy of the *Damascus Document*. *See* index under Dead Sea Scrolls
Diodorus (of Sicily), *Hist.*	*Library of History*
Iamblichus, *Vit. Pythag.*	*Life of Pythagoras*
Polybius, *Hist.*	*The Histories*
Q	*Quelle* (source), hypothetical collection of sayings used by Matthew and Luke
4Q521	Sample for a Qumran scroll. *See* index under Dead Sea Scrolls

Journals, Series, Versions, and Common Usage

See also Bibliography: Reference Works and Greek Texts (below)

AB	Anchor Bible
ABRL	Anchor Bible Reference Library
ad loc.	*ad locum*, at the place discussed
AnBib	Analecta biblica
ANTC	Abingdon New Testament Commentaries
ARSHLL	Acta Regiae Societatis humaniorum litterarum Lundensis
ASV	American Standard Version
AT	author's translation
ATANT	Abhandlungen zur Theologie des Alten und Neuen Testaments
ATR	*Anglican Theological Review*
BBC	Blackwell Bible Commentaries
B.C.E.	before the Common Era

BECNT	Baker Exegetical Commentary on the New Testament
BETL	Bibliotheca ephemeridum theologicarum lovaniensium
BEvT	Beiträge zur evangelischen Theologie
BHR	Bibliothéque histoire des religions
BHT	Beiträge zur historischen Theologie
Bib	*Biblica*
BibS	Biblische Studien
BIS	Biblical Interpretation Series
BNTC	Black's New Testament Commentary
BThN	Bibliotheca theologica Norvegica
BU	Biblische Untersuchungen
BZ	*Biblische Zeitschrift*
BZNW	Beihefte zur Zeitschrift für die neutestamentliche Wissenschaft
CBQ	*Catholic Biblical Quarterly*
CBQMS	Catholic Biblical Quarterly Monograph Series
C.E.	Common Era
CEB	Common English Bible
cent.	century
cf.	*confer*, compare
ch(s).	chapter(s)
CNT	Commentaire du Nouveau Testament
ConBNT	Coniectanea biblica: New Testament Series
ÉBib	Études bibliques
ed(s).	edited (by), edition, editor/s
e.g.	*exempli gratia*, for example
EKK	Evangelisch-katholischer Kommentar zum Neuen Testament
esp.	especially
ESV	English Standard Version
ET	English translation/version(s)
et al.	*et alii(ae)*, and others
etc.	*et cetera*, and the rest
ETL	*Ephemerides theologicae lovanienses*
ETS	Erfurter theologische Studien
EvT	*Evangelische Theologie*
ExpTim	*Expository Times*
FAT	Forschungen zum Alten Testament
FBBS	Facet Books, Biblical Series
FRLANT	Forschungen zur Religion und Literatur des Alten und Neuen Testaments
GNS	Good News Studies
GOODSPEED	*The New Testament: An American Translation*. Translated by Edgar J. Goodspeed. Chicago: University of Chicago Press, 1923

GTA	Göttinger theologische Arbeiten
HBT	*Horizons in Biblical Theology*
Hermeneia	Hermeneia: A Critical and Historical Commentary on the Bible
HNT	Handbuch zum Neuen Testament
HTKNT	Herders theologischer Kommentar zum Neuen Testament
HTR	*Harvard Theological Review*
HTS	Harvard Theological Studies
HUT	Hermeneutische Untersuchungen zur Theologie
IBC	Interpretation: A Bible Commentary for Teaching and Preaching
IBT	Interpreting Biblical Texts
ICC	International Critical Commentary
idem	the same (author as just named)
i.e.	id est, that is
IG	*See* Reference Works and Greek Texts
Int	Interpretation
intro	introductions to 1 and 2 Thessalonians in this commentary
ITS	International Theological Studies
IVPNTC	InterVarsity Press New Testament Commentary
JAAR	*Journal of the American Academy of Religion*
JBL	*Journal of Biblical Literature*
JQR	*Jewish Quarterly Review*
JSNT	*Journal for the Study of the New Testament*
JSNTSup	Journal for the Study of the New Testament: Supplement Series
JSOTSup	Journal for the Study of the Old Testament: Supplement Series
KEK	Kritisch-exegetischer Kommentar über das Neue Testament (Meyer-Kommentar)
ktl.	*kai ta loipa,* and the remainder
LCC	Library of Christian Classics. Philadelphia, 1953–
LCL	Loeb Classical Library
LD	Lectio divina
LEC	Library of Early Christianity
lit.	literal, literally
LNTS	Library of New Testament Studies
LW	Luther's Works. St. Louis: Concordia, 1955–
LXX	Septuagint (Greek OT). *See* Reference Works and Greek Texts
M.A.	Master of Arts
mg.	marginal note
MNTC	Moffatt New Testament Commentary. 1922
MOFFATT	*The Bible: A New Translation.* By James Moffatt. New York: Harper, 1922
MS(S)	manuscript(s)

MT	Masoretic Text (of the OT)
NA	Neutestamentliche Abhandlungen
NA²⁸	*See* Reference Works and Greek Texts
NAB	New American Bible
NABRE	New American Bible, Revised Edition. 2011
NAS95	New American Standard Bible, 1995 Update
NCBC	New Century Bible Commentary
NedTT	*Nederlands theologisch tijdschrift*
NETS	*A New English Translation of the Septuagint.* Oxford: Oxford University Press, 2009. Corrected ed., 2014. http://ccat.sas .upenn.edu/nets/edition/
NICNT	New International Commentary on the New Testament
NIGTC	New International Greek Testament Commentary
NIV	New International Version. 1978
NIV11	New International Version, 2011 Update
NJB	New Jerusalem Bible
NKJV	New King James Version
NovT	*Novum Testamentum*
NovTSup	Supplements to Novum Testamentum
NPNF¹	*Nicene and Post-Nicene Fathers*, Series 1
NRSV	New Revised Standard Version
NS	new series
NT	New Testament
NTL	New Testament Library
NTOA	Novum Testamentum et Orbis Antiquus
NTR	New Testament Readings
NTS	*New Testament Studies*
NTTh	New Testament Theology
NTTS	New Testament Tools and Studies
olim	formerly (numbered)
OT	Old Testament
OTL	Old Testament Library
par.	parallel text, //
PG	*See* Reference Works and Greek Texts
PHILLIPS	*The New Testament in Modern English.* Translated by J. B. Phillips. Rev. ed., 1960
PKNT	Papyrologische Kommentare zum Neuen Testament
pl.	plural
PNTC	Pillar New Testament Commentary
Procl	Proclamation Commentaries
QD	Quaestiones disputatae
REB	Revised English Bible

rev. ed.	revised edition
RSV	Revised Standard Version
SBLDS	Society of Biblical Literature Dissertation Series
SBLSBS	Society of Biblical Literature Sources for Biblical Study
SBS	Stuttgarter Bibelstudien
SBT	Studies in Biblical Theology
SCJ	Studies in Christianity and Judaism
sg.	singular
SHCT	Studies in the History of Christian Thought
SNTSMS	Society for New Testament Studies Monograph Series
SNTW	Studies of the New Testament and Its World
SP	Sacra pagina
SPAW	*Sitzungsberichte der preussischen Akademie der Wissenschaften*
STDJ	Studies on the Texts of the Desert of Judah
TEV	Today's English Version = 1992 edition of Good News Bible
THKNT	Theologischer Handkommentar zum Neuen Testament
ThSt	Theologische Studien
TLZ	*Theologische Literaturzeitung*
TNIV	Today's New International Version
trans.	translation (note), translated (by), translator
TU	Texte und Untersuchungen zur Geschichte der altchristlichen Literatur
TZ	*Theologische Zeitschrift*
UBS⁴	*See* Reference Works and Greek Texts
US	Unam sanctam
USA	United States of America
v./vv.	verse/verses
vol(s).	volume(s)
WBC	Word Biblical Commentary
WMANT	Wissenschaftliche Monographien zum Alten und Neuen Testament
WUNT	Wissenschaftliche Untersuchungen zum Neuen Testament
×	times a form occurs (e.g., *oidate*, 9× in 1 Thessalonians)
ZBK	Zürcher Bibelkommentare
ZNW	*Zeitschrift für die neutestamentliche Wissenschaft und die Kunde der älteren Kirche*
ZST	*Zeitschrift für systematische Theologie*
ZTK	*Zeitschrift für Theologie und Kirche*
ZWT	*Zeitschrift für wissenschaftliche Theologie*

BIBLIOGRAPHY

For a virtually complete bibliography for the study of 1–2 Thessalonians to 1998, see

Weima, Jeffrey A. D., and Stanley E. Porter. *An Annotated Bibliography of 1 and 2 Thessalonians*. NTTS. Leiden: Brill, 1998.

For more recent publications, see *New Testament Abstracts*.

Reference Works and Greek Texts

Cited by abbreviation or author(s)

ABD   *The Anchor Bible Dictionary*. Edited by D. N. Freedman. 6 vols. New York: Doubleday, 1992.

ANRW   *Aufstieg und Niedergang der römischen Welt: Geschichte und Kultur Roms im Spiegel der neueren Forschung*. Edited by J. Vogt, H. Temporini, and W. Haase. 37 vols. Berlin: de Gruyter, 1972–.

BDAG   Bauer, W., F. W. Danker, W. F. Arndt, and F. W. Gingrich. *A Greek-English Lexicon of the New Testament and Other Early Christian Literature*. 3d ed. Chicago: University of Chicago Press, 2000.

BDF   Blass, F., and A. Debrunner. *A Greek Grammar of the New Testament and Other Early Christian Literature*. Translated by R. W. Funk. Chicago: University of Chicago Press, 1961.

BGU   *Ägyptische Urkunden aus den Königlichen Staatlichen Museen zu Berlin: Griechische Urkunden*. 15 vols. Berlin, 1895–1983.

Boring, M. Eugene, K. Berger, and C. Colpe, eds. *Hellenistic Commentary to the New Testament*. Nashville: Abingdon, 1995.

DPL   *Dictionary of Paul and His Letters*. Edited by Gerald F. Hawthorne and Ralph P. Martin. Downers Grove, IL: InterVarsity, 1993.

EDNT   *Exegetical Dictionary of the New Testament*. Edited by H. Balz and G. Schneider. ET. Grand Rapids: Eerdmans, 1990–1993.

Ellingworth, P., and E. A. Nida. *A Handbook on Paul's Letters to the Thessalonians*. UBS Translators' Handbooks. New York: American Bible Society, 1975.

IB   *The Interpreter's Bible.* Edited by G. A. Buttrick et al. 12 vols. New
          York, 1951–1957.

IDB   *The Interpreter's Dictionary of the Bible.* Edited by G. A. Buttrick et
          al. 4 vols. Nashville: Abingdon, 1962.

IDBSup *The Interpreter's Dictionary of the Bible: Supplementary Volume.*
          Edited by K. Crim. Nashville: Abingdon, 1976.

IG   *Inscriptiones graecae.* Editio minor. Berlin, 1924–.

LSJM   Liddell, G., and R. Scott. *A Greek-English Lexicon.* Edited by H. S.
          Jones and R. McKenzie. New/9th ed. Oxford: Clarendon Press, 1961.

LXX   *Septuaginta.* Based on editing work of A. Rahlfs. Edited by R. Hanhart.
          2d, rev. ed. Stuttgart: Deutsche Bibelgesellschaft, 2006. http://www
          .academic-bible.com.

Metzger, Bruce M. *A Textual Commentary on the Greek New Testament.* 2d ed.
          Stuttgart: United Bible Societies, 1994.

Moule, C. F. D. *An Idiom-Book of New Testament Greek.* Cambridge: Cam-
          bridge University Press, 1960.

NA²⁸   Nestle, Eberhard, Erwin Nestle, Barbara and Kurt Aland, et al., eds.
          Novum Testament Graece. 28th ed. Stuttgart: Deutsche Bibelgesell-
          schaft, 2012.

NIB   *The New Interpreter's Bible.* Edited by L. E. Keck. 12 vols. + index.
          Nashville, 1994–2004.

NIDB   *The New Interpreter's Dictionary of the Bible.* Edited by K. Doop. 5
          vols. Nashville, 2006–2009.

OCD   Hammond, N. G. L., and H. H. Scullard, eds. *The Oxford Classical
          Dictionary.* 2d ed. Oxford: Clarendon Press, 1970.

OTP   *Old Testament Pseudepigrapha.* Edited by J. H. Charlesworth. 2 vols.
          Garden City, NY: Doubleday, 1983–85.

PG   *Patrologia graeca.* Edited by J.-P. Migne. 162 vols. as 167. Paris,
          1857–86, 1912.

Str-B   Strack, Hermann, and Paul Billerbeck. *Kommentar zum Neuen Testa-
          ment aus Talmud und Midrasch.* 6 vols. Munich: Beck, 1922–1961.

TDNT   *Theological Dictionary of the New Testament.* Edited by G. Kittel and
          G. Friedrichs. Translated by Geoffrey W. Bromiley. 10 vols. Grand
          Rapids: Eerdmans, 1964–1976.

UBS⁴   United Bible Societies. *The Greek New Testament.* Edited by B. Aland,
          K. Aland, J. Karavidopoulos, C. M. Martini, and B. M. Metzger. 4th
          rev. ed. New York, 1983.

Wallace, Daniel B. *Greek Grammar beyond the Basics.* Grand Rapids: Zonder-
          van, 1996.

Weima, Jeffrey A. D., and Stanley E. Porter. *An Annotated Bibliography of
          1 and 2 Thessalonians.* NTTS. Leiden: Brill, 1998.

Commentaries on 1–2 Thessalonians

Cited by author, plus year if needed

Beale, G. K. 2003. *1–2 Thessalonians*. IVPNTC. Downers Grove, IL: InterVarsity.

Best, Ernest. 1979. *A Commentary on the First and Second Epistles to the Thessalonians*. BNTC. London: Adam & Charles Black.

Bruce, F. F. 1982. *1 & 2 Thessalonians*. WBC 45. Waco: Word.

Calvin, Jean. 1960a. *The Epistles of Paul to the Romans and to the Thessalonians*. Vol. 8 of *Calvin's Commentaries*. Edited by David W. Torrance and Thomas F. Torrance. Translated by Ross Mackenzie. Grand Rapids: Eerdmans.

Collins, Raymond F. 1990. "The First Letter to the Thessalonians." Pages 772–79 in *The New Jerome Biblical Commentary*. Edited by Raymond E. Brown, Joseph A. Fitzmyer, and Roland E. Murphy. Englewood Cliffs, NJ: Prentice-Hall.

Dibelius, Martin. 1937. *An die Thessalonicher I, II*. 3d ed. HNT 11. Tübingen: Mohr.

Dobschütz, Ernst von, and W. Bornemann. 1909. *Die Thessalonicher-Briefe*. KEK. 7th ed. Göttingen: Vandenhoeck & Ruprecht.

Fee, Gordon D. 2009. *The First and Second Letters to the Thessalonians*. NICNT. Grand Rapids: Eerdmans.

Frame, James Everett. 1912. *A Critical and Exegetical Commentary on the Epistles of Paul to the Thessalonians*. ICC. New York: Scribners.

Furnish, Victor Paul. 2007. *1 Thessalonians, 2 Thessalonians*. ANTC. Nashville: Abingdon.

Gaventa, Beverly Roberts. 1998. *First and Second Thessalonians*. IBC. Louisville: Westminster John Knox.

Green, Gene L. 2002. *The Letters to the Thessalonians*. PNTC. Grand Rapids: Eerdmans.

Holtz, Traugott. 1986. *Der erste Brief an die Thessalonicher*. EKK 13. Neukirchen-Vluyn: Neukirchener Verlag.

Jewett, Robert. 2003. "1 and 2 Thessalonians." In *Eerdmans Commentary on the Bible*. Edited by James D. G. Dunn and John W. Rogerson. Grand Rapids: Eerdmans.

Keck, Leander E. 1971. "The First Letter of Paul to the Thessalonians." Pages 865–74 in *The Interpreter's One-Volume Commentary on the Bible*. Edited by Charles M. Laymon. New York: Abingdon.

Kreinecker, Christina M. 2010. *2. Thessaloniker*. PKNT 3. Göttingen: Vandenhoeck & Ruprecht.

Malherbe, Abraham J. 2000. *The Letters to the Thessalonians: A New Translation with Introduction and Commentary*. AB 32B. New York: Doubleday.

Marshall, I. Howard. 1983. *1 and 2 Thessalonians: Based on the Revised Standard Version*. NCBC. Grand Rapids: Eerdmans.

Marxsen, Willi. 1982. *Der zweite Brief an die Thessalonicher*. ZBK 11/2. Zurich: Theologischer Verlag.

Masson, Charles. 1957. *Les deux épitres de Saint Paul aux Thessaloniciens*. CNT 11A. Paris: Delachaux & Niestlé.

Menken, Maarten J. J. 1994. *2 Thessalonians*. NTR. London: Routledge.

Milligan, George. 1908. *St. Paul's Epistles to the Thessalonians: The Greek Text with Introduction and Notes*. New York: Macmillan.

Morris, Leon. 1959. *The First and Second Epistles to the Thessalonians: The English Text with Introduction, Exposition, and Notes*. NICNT. Grand Rapids: Eerdmans.

Richard, Earl J. 1995. *First and Second Thessalonians*. SP. Collegeville, MN: Liturgical Press.

Rigaux, Béda. 1956. *Saint Paul: Les épitres aux Thessaloniciens*. ÉBib. Paris: Gabalda.

Smith, Abraham. 2000. "First Letter to the Thessalonians." Pages 671–738 in *2 Corinthians, Galatians, Ephesians, Philippians, Colossians, 1 & 2 Thessalonians, 1 & 2 Timothy, Titus, Philemon*. Vol. 11 of *The New Interpreter's Bible*. Edited by Leander E. Keck. Nashville: Abingdon.

Thiselton, Anthony C. 2011. *1 & 2 Thessalonians: Through the Centuries*. BBC. Malden, MA: Wiley-Blackwell.

Trilling, Wolfgang. 1980. *Der zweite Brief an die Thessalonicher*. EKK 14. Neukirchen-Vluyn: Neukirchener Verlag.

Wanamaker, Charles A. 1990. *The Epistles to the Thessalonians: A Commentary on the Greek Text*. NICNT. Grand Rapids: Eerdmans.

Weima, Jeffrey A. D. 2014. *1–2 Thessalonians*. BECNT. Grand Rapids: Baker Academic.

Witherington, Ben. 2006. *1 and 2 Thessalonians: A Socio-rhetorical Commentary*. Grand Rapids: Eerdmans.

Monographs, Books, Essays

Cited by author, plus year if needed

Achtemeier, Paul J. 1996. *1 Peter: A Commentary on First Peter*. Hermeneia. Minneapolis: Fortress Press.

Adams, Sean A. 2009. "Evaluating 1 Thessalonians: An Outline of Holistic Approaches to 1 Thessalonians in the Last 25 Years." *Currents in Biblical Research* 8, no. 1:51–70.

Adler, Mortimer Jerome. 1940. *How to Read a Book: The Art of Getting a Liberal Education*. New York: Simon & Schuster, 1940.

Allison, Dale C. 1982. "The Pauline Epistles and the Synoptic Gospels: The Pattern of the Parallels." *NTS* 28:1–32.

Ascough, Richard S. 2003. *Paul's Macedonian Associations: The Social Context of Philippians and 1 Thessalonians.* WUNT 2/161. Tübingen: Mohr Siebeck.

———. 2009. "Thessalonians, First Letter to the." *NIDB* 5:569–79.

———. 2014. "Redescribing the Thessalonians' 'Mission' in Light of Graeco-Roman Associations." *NTS* 60:61–82.

Augustine of Hippo. 1965. *Treatises on Various Subjects.* Fathers of the Church 16. Washington, DC: Catholic University of America Press.

Aune, David E. 1983. *Prophecy in Early Christianity and the Ancient Mediterranean World.* Grand Rapids: Eerdmans.

———. 1987. *The New Testament in Its Literary Environment.* LEC. Philadelphia: Westminster.

Aus, Roger D. 1973. "The Liturgical Background of the Necessity and Propriety of Giving Thanks according to 2 Thes 1:3." *JBL* 92:432–38.

Baarda, T. 1985. "1 Thess. 2:14–16: Rodrigues in 'Nestle-Aland.'" *NedTT* 39:186–93.

Bailey, J. A. 1978. "Who Wrote II Thessalonians?" *NTS* 25:131–45.

Baird, William R. 1971. "Pauline Eschatology in Hermeneutical Perspective." *NTS* 17:314–27.

———. 1992–2013. *History of New Testament Research.* 3 vols. Minneapolis: Fortress.

Bammel, Ernst. 1959. "Judenverfolgung und Naherwartung: Zur Eschatologie des ersten Thessalonicherbriefs." *ZTK* 56:294–315.

Barclay, John M. G. 1993. "Conflict in Thessalonica." *CBQ* 55:512–30.

Barr, James. 1962. *Biblical Words for Time.* SBT 33. Naperville, IL: Alec R. Allenson.

———. 1999. *The Concept of Biblical Theology: An Old Testament Perspective.* Minneapolis: Fortress.

Barth, Karl. 1933. *The Epistle to the Romans.* Translated by Edwyn C. Hoskyns. Translated from the 6th German ed. London: Oxford University Press.

———. 1957. "The Strange New World within the Bible." Pages 28–50 in *The Word of God and the Word of Man.* Translated by Douglas Horton. New York: Harper & Brothers.

———. 1958. *The Doctrine of Reconciliation.* Vol. IV/1 of *Church Dogmatics.* Translated by Geoffrey Bromiley. Edinburgh: T&T Clark.

———. 1960. *The Doctrine of Creation.* Vol. III/2 of *Church Dogmatics.* Translated by Geoffrey W. Bromiley, J. K. S. Reid, and Reginald H. Fuller. Edinburgh: T&T Clark.

———. 1962. *The Doctrine of Reconciliation.* Vol. IV/3.2 of *Church Dogmatics.* Translated by Geoffrey Bromiley. Edinburgh: T&T Clark.

Bassler, Jouette M. 1984. "The Enigmatic Sign: 2 Thessalonians 1:5." *CBQ* 46:496–510.

———. 1991. "Peace in All Ways: Theology in the Thessalonian Letters; A Response to R. Jewett, E. Krentz, and E. Richard." Pages 71–85 in *Thessalonians, Philippians, Galatians, Philemon*. Edited by Jouette M. Bassler. Vol. 1 of *Pauline Theology*. Minneapolis: Fortress.

———. 1995. "*Skeuos*: A Modest Proposal for Illuminating Paul's Use of Metaphor in 1 Thessalonians 4:4." Pages 91–100 in *The Social World of the First Christians: Essays in Honor of Wayne A. Meeks*. Edited by Michael L. White and O. Larry Yarbrough. Minneapolis: Augsburg Fortress.

———. 2007. *Navigating Paul: An Introduction to Key Theological Concepts*. Louisville: Westminster John Knox.

Baxter, Brian, Steven LoVullo, and Rex A. Koivisto. 2013. "Diagram of the Greek New Testament (Acts, Epistles, Revelation)." In *Accordance Bible Software*. Altamonte Springs, FL: OakTree Software.

Becker, Jürgen. 1993. *Paul: Apostle to the Gentiles*. Translated by O. C. Dean. Louisville: Westminster John Knox.

Beker, J. Christaan. 1991. *Heirs of Paul: Paul's Legacy in the New Testament and in the Church Today*. Minneapolis: Fortress.

Bengel, Johann Albrecht. 1971. *Gnomon of the New Testament*. A New Translation by Charlton T. Lewis and Marvin R. Vincent. 2 vols. Grand Rapids: Kregel.

Berger, Klaus. 1974. "Apostelbrief und apostolische Rede: Zum Formular frühchristlicher Briefe." *ZNW* 65:190–231.

———. 1994. *Theologiegeschichte des Urchristentums: Theologie des Neuen Testaments*. Tübingen: Francke.

Berger, Peter L., and Thomas Luckmann. 1966. *The Social Construction of Reality: A Treatise in the Sociology of Knowledge*. New York: Random House.

Betz, Hans Dieter. 1967. *Nachfolge und Nachahmung Jesu Christi im Neuen Testament*. BHT 37. Tübingen: Mohr.

———. 1979. *Galatians: A Commentary on Paul's Letter to the Churches in Galatia*. Hermeneia. Philadelphia: Fortress.

Binder, Hermann. 1990. "Paulus und die Thessalonikerbriefe." Pages 87–93 in *The Thessalonian Correspondence*. Edited by Raymond F. Collins and Norbert Baumert. BETL 87. Leuven: Leuven University Press.

Bjerkelund, Carl Johan. 1967. *Parakaleō: Form, Funktion und Sinn der parakaleō-Sätze in den paulinischen Briefen*. BThN 1. Oslo: Universitetsforlaget.

Black, C. Clifton. 2013. *The Rhetoric of the Gospel: Theological Artistry in the Gospels and Acts*. 2d ed. Louisville: Westminster John Knox.

Blumenthal, Christian. 2005. "Was sagt 1 Thess 1.9b–10 über die Adressaten des 1 Thess? Literarische und historische Erfahrungen." *NTS* 51:96–105.

Boring, M. Eugene. 1982. *Sayings of the Risen Jesus: Christian Prophecy in the Synoptic Tradition.* SNTSMS 46. Cambridge: Cambridge University Press.

———. 1984. *Truly Human/Truly Divine: Christological Language and the Gospel Form.* St. Louis: CBP Press.

———. 1986. "The Language of Universal Salvation in Paul." *JBL* 105:269–92.

———. 1989. *Revelation.* IBC. Louisville: John Knox.

———. 1991. *The Continuing Voice of Jesus: Christian Prophecy and the Gospel Tradition.* Louisville: Westminster/John Knox.

———. 1994. "Revelation 19–21: End without Closure." *Princeton Seminary Bulletin,* Supplementary Issue 3:57–77.

———. 2007. "Narrative Dynamics in 1 Peter: The Function of Narrative World." Pages 7–40 in *Reading 1 Peter with New Eyes: Methodological Reassessments of the Letter of First Peter.* Edited by Robert L. Webb and Betsy Bauman-Martin. LNTS. Edinburgh: T&T Clark.

———. 2012. *Introduction to the New Testament: History, Literature, Theology.* Louisville: Westminster John Knox.

Bornkamm, Günther. 1971. *Paul: Paulus.* Translated by D. M. G. Stalker. New York: Harper & Row.

Bosch, Jorge Sanchez. 1991. "La chronologie de la première aux Thessaloniciens et les relations de Paul avec d'autres églises." *NTS* 37:336–47.

Brown, Alexandra R. 2000. "Paul and the Parousia." Pages 47–76 in *The Return of Jesus in Early Christianity.* Edited by John T. Carroll. Peabody, MA: Hendrickson.

Brown, Raymond E. 1994a. *The Death of the Messiah: From Gethsemane to the Grave; A Commentary on the Passion Narratives in the Four Gospels.* ABRL. 2 vols. New York: Doubleday.

———. 1994b. *An Introduction to New Testament Christology.* New York: Paulist Press.

Brown, Raymond E., and Thomas A. Collins. 1990. "Church Pronouncements." Pages 1166–74 in *The New Jerome Biblical Commentary.* Edited by Raymond E. Brown, Joseph A. Fitzmyer, and Roland E. Murphy. Englewood Cliffs, NJ: Prentice-Hall.

Bultmann, Rudolf. 1951–55. *Theology of the New Testament.* Translated by Kendrick Grobel. 2 vols. New York: Scribner.

Burke, Trevor J. 2003. *Family Matters: A Socio-historical Study of Kinship Metaphors in 1 Thessalonians.* JSNTSup 247. London: T&T Clark.

Caird, G. B. 1994. *New Testament Theology.* Oxford: Oxford University Press.

Calvin, Jean. 1960b. *Institutes of the Christian Religion.* Translated by Ford Lewis Battles. 2 vols. LCC 20–21. Philadelphia: Westminster.

Cerfaux, Lucien. 1959. *Christ in the Theology of St. Paul.* Translated by Geoffrey Webb and Adrian Walker. New York: Herder & Herder.

————. 1965. *La théologie de l'église suivant saint Paul.* US. 3d ed. Paris: Éditions du Cerf.

Charlesworth, James H., ed. 1983–85. *The Old Testament Pseudepigrapha.* 2 vols. Garden City, NY: Doubleday.

Childs, Brevard S. 1984. *The New Testament as Canon: An Introduction.* Philadelphia: Fortress.

————. 1992. *Biblical Theology of the Old and New Testaments: Theological Reflection on the Christian Bible.* Minneapolis: Fortress.

Chrysostom, John. 1994. "Homilies on Galatians, Ephesians, Philippians, Colossians, Thessalonians, Timothy, Titus, and Philemon." In vol. 13 of *A Select Library of the Nicene and Post-Nicene Fathers of the Christian Church.* First Series. Edited by Philip Schaff. Peabody, MA: Hendrickson. First published in the USA by the Christian Literature Publishing Co., 1889.

Collins, Adela Yarbro. 1983. "Persecution and Vengeance in the Book of Revelation." Pages 729–49 in *Apocalypticism in the Mediterranean World and the Near East. Proceedings of the International Colloquium on Apocalypticism, Uppsala, August 12–17, 1979.* Edited by David Hellholm. Tübingen: Mohr.

————. 1984. *Crisis and Catharsis: The Power of the Apocalypse.* Philadelphia: Westminster.

Collins, Raymond F. 1984a. "Recent Scholarship on the First Letter to the Thessalonians." Pages 3–75 in *Studies on the First Letter to the Thessalonians.* Edited by Raymond F. Collins. BETL 66. Leuven: Leuven University Press.

————. 1984b. "The Text of the Epistles to the Thessalonians in Nestle-Aland[26]." Pages 79–95 in *Studies on the First Letter to the Thessalonians.* Edited by Raymond F. Collins. BETL 66. Leuven: Leuven University Press.

————. 1988. *Letters That Paul Did Not Write: The Epistle to the Hebrews and the Pauline Pseudepigrapha.* GNS 28. Wilmington, DE: Michael Glazier.

————. 1993. *The Birth of the New Testament. The Origin and Development of the First Christian Generation.* New York: Crossroad.

Collins, Raymond F., and Norbert Baumert, eds. 1990. *The Thessalonian Correspondence.* BETL 87. Leuven: Leuven University Press.

Conzelmann, Hans. 1969. *An Outline of the Theology of the New Testament.* Translated by John Bowden. New York: Harper & Row.

————. 1974. "Paulus und die Weisheit." Pages 177–90 in *Theologie als Schriftauslegung: Aufsätze zum Neuen Testament.* Edited by Hans Conzelmann. BEvT 65. Munich: Kaiser.

————. 1975. *1 Corinthians: A Commentary on the First Epistle to the Corinthians.* Translated by James W. Leitch. Hermeneia. Philadelphia: Fortress.

————. 1979. "Die Schule des Paulus." Pages 85–96 in *Theologia crucis, signum crucis: Festschrift für Erich Dinkler zum 70. Geburtstag.* Edited by Carl Andresen and Günter Klein. Tübingen: Mohr.

Coulot, Claude. 2006. "Paul à Thessalonique (1 Th 2.1–12)." *NTS* 52:377–93.

Crossan, John Dominic, and Jonathan L. Reed. 2004. *In Search of Paul: How Jesus's Apostle Opposed Rome's Empire with God's Kingdom: A New Vision of Paul's Words and World.* New York: HarperSanFrancisco.

Cullmann, Oscar. 1956. "The Tradition." Translated by S. Godman and A. J. B. Higgins. Pages 59–104 in *The Early Church.* Edited by A. J. B. Higgins. London: SCM.

Day, Peter. 1963. "The Practical Purpose of Second Thessalonians." *ATR* 45:203–6.

Deissmann, Adolf. 1927. *Light from the Ancient East: The New Testament Illustrated by Recently Discovered Texts of the Graeco-Roman World.* Translated by Lionel R. M. Strachan. New York: Doran.

———. 1957. *Paul: A Study in Social and Religious History.* Translated by William E. Wilson. New York: Harper.

Dibelius, Martin, and Hans Conzelmann. 1972. *The Pastoral Epistles.* Translated by Philip Buttolph and Adela Yarbro. Hermeneia. Philadelphia: Fortress.

Dodd, C. H. 1928. *The Authority of the Bible.* New York: Harper & Row. Rev. ed., 1960a.

———. 1932. *The Epistle of Paul to the Romans.* MNTC. New York: Harper & Brothers.

———. 1960b. *The Apostolic Preaching and Its Developments.* London: Hodder & Stoughton.

Doering, Lutz. 2012. *Ancient Jewish Letters and the Beginnings of Christian Epistolography.* WUNT 298. Tübingen: Mohr Siebeck.

Donelson, Lewis R. 1986. *Pseudepigraphy and Ethical Argument in the Pastoral Epistles.* HUT. Tübingen: Mohr.

Donfried, Karl P. 1984. "Paul and Judaism: 1 Thessalonians 2:13–16 as a Test Case." *Int* 38:242–53.

———. 1985. "Cults of Thessalonica and the Thessalonian Correspondence." *NTS* 31:336–56.

———. 1990. "1 Thessalonians, Acts, and the Early Paul." Pages 3–26 in *The Thessalonian Correspondence.* Edited by Raymond F. Collins and Norbert Baumert. BETL 87. Leuven: Leuven University Press.

———. 1992. "Chronology, New Testament." Pages 111–22 in vol. 1 of *The Anchor Bible Dictionary.* Edited by David Noel Freedman. New York: Doubleday.

———. 1993a. "The Theology of 1 Thessalonians." Pages 1–80 in *The Theology of the Shorter Pauline Letters.* Edited by Karl P. Donfried and I. Howard Marshall. NTTh. Cambridge: Cambridge University Press.

———. 1993b. "The Theology of 2 Thessalonians." Pages 81–114 in *The Theology of the Shorter Pauline Letters.* Edited by Karl P. Donfried and I. Howard Marshall. NTTh. Cambridge: Cambridge University Press.

————. 2002a. "The Cults of Thessalonica and the Thessalonian Correspondence." Pages 21–48 in *Paul, Thessalonica, and Early Christianity*. Edited by Karl P. Donfried. Grand Rapids: Eerdmans.

————, ed. 2002b. *Paul, Thessalonica, and Early Christianity*. Grand Rapids: Eerdmans.

————. 2002c. "Was Timothy in Athens? Some Exegetical Reflections on 1 Thess. 3:1–3." Pages 209–20 in *Paul, Thessalonica, and Early Christianity*. Edited by Karl P. Donfried. Grand Rapids: Eerdmans.

Donfried, Karl P., and Johannes Beutler, eds. 2000. *The Thessalonians Debate: Methodological Discord or Methodological Synthesis?* Grand Rapids: Eerdmans.

Donfried, Karl P., and I. Howard Marshall. 1993. *The Theology of the Shorter Pauline Letters*. NTTh. Cambridge: Cambridge University Press.

Doty, William G. 1973. *Letters in Primitive Christianity*. Philadelphia: Fortress.

Driver, Daniel R. 2010. *Brevard Childs, Biblical Theologian: For the Church's One Bible*. FAT 2/46. Tübingen: Mohr Siebeck.

du Toit, David. 2013. "Christologische Hoheitstitel." Pages 294–99 in *Paulus Handbuch*. Edited by Friedrich Wilhelm Horn. Tübingen: Mohr Siebeck.

Dunn, James D. G. 2009. *Beginning from Jerusalem*. Vol. 2 of *Christianity in the Making*. Grand Rapids: Eerdmans.

Elgvin, Torlief. 1997. "'To Master His Own Vessel': 1 Thess 4:4 in Light of New Qumran Evidence." *NTS* 43:604–19.

Ellis, E. Earle. 1971. "Paul and His Co-Workers." *NTS* 17:437–52.

Feldmeier, Reinhard, and Hermann Spieckermann. 2011. *God of the Living: A Biblical Theology*. Waco: Baylor University Press.

Fischel, H. A. 1947. "Martyr and Prophet: A Study in Jewish Literature." *JQR*, NS, 37:265–80, 363–86.

Focant, Camille. 1990. "Les fils du jour (1 Thes 5,5)." Pages 348–55 in *The Thessalonian Correspondence*. Edited by Raymond F. Collins and Norbert Baumert. BETL 87. Leuven: University Press.

Forbes, Christopher. 1995. *Prophecy and Inspired Speech in Early Christianity and Its Hellenistic Environment*. Peabody, MA: Hendrickson.

Foster, Paul. 2012. "Who Wrote 2 Thessalonians? A Fresh Look at an Old Problem." *JSNT* 35:150–75.

Fowl, Stephen E. 1990. "A Metaphor in Distress: NHΠIOI in 1 Thessalonians 2.7." *NTS* 36:469–73.

Fowler, Harold North, W. R. M. Lamb, Robert Gregg Bury, and Paul Shorey, eds. 1966. *Plato in Twelve Volumes*. Vol. 7. LCL 7. Cambridge, MA: Harvard University Press.

Frend, W. H. C. 1965. *Martyrdom and Persecution in the Early Church: A Study of a Conflict from the Maccabees to Donatus*. Oxford: Blackwell.

Freyne, Seán. 1985. "Vilifying the Other and Defining the Self: Matthew's and John's Anti-Jewish Polemic in Focus." Pages 117–43 in *"To See Ourselves as Others See Us": Christians, Jews, "Others" in Late Antiquity*. Edited by Jacob Neusner, Ernest S. Frerichs, and Caroline McCracken-Flesher. Scholars Press Studies in the Humanities. Chico, CA: Scholars Press.

Friesen, Steven J. 2010. "Second Thessalonians, the Ideology of Epistles, and the Construction of Authority: Our Debt to the Forger." Pages 189–213 in *From Roman to Early Christian Thessalonikē: Studies in Religion and Archaeology*. Edited by Laura Nasrallah, Charalambos Bakirtzis, and Steven J. Friesen. HTS. Cambridge, MA: Harvard University Press.

Funk, Robert W. 1966. *Language, Hermeneutic, and Word of God*. New York: Harper.

Furnish, Victor Paul. 1984. *II Corinthians*. AB 32A. Garden City, NY: Doubleday.

———. 2004. "The Spirit in 2 Thessalonians." Pages 229–40 in *The Holy Spirit and Christian Origins: Essays in Honor of James D. G. Dunn*. Edited by Graham Stanton, Bruce W. Longenecker, and Stephen C. Barton. Grand Rapids: Eerdmans.

———. 2009a. *The Moral Teaching of Paul: Selected Issues*. 3d ed. Nashville: Abingdon.

———. 2009b. *Theology and Ethics in Paul*. With a new introduction by Richard B. Hays. 2d ed. NTL. Louisville: Westminster John Knox.

Gaventa, Beverly R. 2007. *Our Mother Saint Paul*. Louisville: Westminster John Knox.

Gerber, Christine. 2013. "Das Apostolatsverständnis und die Beziehung von Apostel und Gemeinden zueinander." Pages 416–20 in *Paulus Handbuch*. Edited by Friedrich Wilhelm Horn. Tübingen: Mohr Siebeck.

Friedrich, Gerhard. 1965. "Ein Tauflied hellenistischer Judenchristen: 1. Thess. 1,9f." *TZ* 21:502–16.

Giblin, Charles Homer. 1967. *The Threat to Faith: An Exegetical and Theological Reexamination of 2 Thessalonians 2*. AnBib 31. Rome: Pontifical Biblical Institute.

Gilliard, Frank D. 1989. "The Problem of the Antisemitic Comma between 1 Thessalonians 2.14 and 15." *NTS* 35:481–502.

Goguel, Maurice. 1922–26. *Introduction au Nouveau Testament*. BHR. 4 vols. Paris: Ernest Leroux.

Graafen, Josef. 1930. *Die Echtheit des zweiten Briefes an die Thessalonicher*. NA 14/5. Münster: Aschendorff.

Green, Joel B. 2010. "Discourse Analysis and New Testament Interpretation." Pages 218–239 in *Hearing the New Testament: Strategies for Interpretation*. Edited by Joel B. Green. Grand Rapids: Eerdmans.

Haacker, Klaus. 1988. "Elemente des heidnischen Antijudaismus im Neuen Testament." *EvT* 48:404–18.

Harnack, Adolf von. 1910. "Das Problem des 2. Thessalonicherbriefes." *SPAW: Philosophisch-historische Klasse* 31:560–78.

Harnisch, Wolfgang. 1973. *Eschatologische Existenz: Ein exegetischer Beitrag zum Sachanliegen von 1. Thessalonicher 4, 13–5, 11.* FRLANT 110. Göttingen: Vandenhoeck & Ruprecht.

Harrison, James R. 2011. *Paul and the Imperial Authorities at Thessalonica and Rome: A Study in the Conflict of Ideology.* WUNT 273. Tübingen: Mohr Siebeck.

Haufe, Günter. 1999. *Der erste Brief des Paulus an die Thessalonicher.* THKNT 12.1. Leipzig: Evangelische Verlagsanstalt.

Hays, Richard B. 1996. *The Moral Vision of the New Testament: A Contemporary Vision of New Testament Ethics.* San Francisco: HarperSanFrancisco.

———, ed. 2005a. *The Conversion of the Imagination: Paul as Interpreter of Israel's Scripture.* Grand Rapids: Eerdmans.

———. 2005b. "The Conversion of the Imagination: Scripture and Eschatology in 1 Corinthians." Pages 1–24 in *The Conversion of the Imagination.* Edited by Richard B. Hays. Grand Rapids: Eerdmans.

Hewett, James Allen. 1975. "1 Thessalonians 3:13." *ExpTim* 87:54–55.

Hilgenfeld, A. 1862. "Die beiden Briefe an die Thessalonicher." *ZWT* 5:225–64.

Hock, Ronald F. 1979. "The Workshop as a Social Setting for Paul's Missionary Preaching." *CBQ* 41:438–50.

———. 1980. *The Social Context of Paul's Ministry: Tentmaking and Apostleship.* Philadelphia: Fortress.

Holland, Glenn Stanfield. 1988. *The Tradition That You Received from Us: 2 Thessalonians in the Pauline Tradition.* HUT 24. Tübingen: Mohr.

Holmberg, Bengt. 1978. *Paul and Power: The Structure of Authority in the Primitive Church as Reflected in the Pauline Epistles.* ConBNT 11. Lund: Gleerup.

Holtz, Traugott. 1990. "The Judgment on the Jews and the Salvation of All Israel: 1 Thes 2,15–16 and Rom 11,25–26." Pages 284–94 in *The Thessalonian Correspondence.* Edited by Raymond F. Collins and Norbert Baumert. BETL 87. Leuven: Leuven University Press.

Holtzmann, Heinrich Julius. 1880. *Die Pastoralbriefe.* Leipzig: Wilhelm Engelmann.

———. 1901. "Zum zweiten Thessalonikerbrief." *ZNW* 2:97–108.

Horn, Friedrich Wilhelm, ed. 2013. *Paulus Handbuch.* Tübingen: Mohr Siebeck.

Horrell, David G. 1996. *The Social Ethos of the Corinthian Correspondence: Interests and Ideology from 1 Corinthians to 1 Clement.* SNTW. Edinburgh: T&T Clark.

———. 2005. *Solidarity and Difference: A Contemporary Reading of Paul's Ethics*. Edinburgh: T&T Clark.

Hughes, Frank Witt. 1989. *Early Christian Rhetoric and 2 Thessalonians*. JSNTSup 30. Sheffield: JSOT Press.

———. 1990. "The Rhetoric of 1 Thessalonians." Pages 94–116 in *The Thessalonian Correspondence*. Edited by Raymond F. Collins and Norbert Baumert. BETL 87. Leuven: Leuven University Press.

Hurd, John Coolidge. 1986. "Paul ahead of His Time." Pages 255–69 in *Paul and the Gospels*. Vol. 1 of *Anti-Judaism and Early Christianity*. Edited by Peter Richardson with David Granskou. SCJ 1. Waterloo: Wilfrid Laurier University Press.

Jeremias, Joachim. 1964. *Unknown Sayings of Jesus*. Translated by R. H. Fuller. 2d English ed. London: S.P.C.K.

Jewett, Robert. 1978. "The Redaction of I Corinthians and the Trajectory of the Pauline School." *JAAR* 46:389–444.

———. 1986. *The Thessalonian Correspondence: Pauline Rhetoric and Millenarian Piety*. Philadelphia: Fortress.

———. 1991. "A Matrix of Grace: The Theology of 2 Thessalonians as a Pauline Letter." Pages 63–70 in *Thessalonians, Philippians, Galatians, Philemon*. Vol. 1 of *Pauline Theology*. Edited by Jouette M. Bassler. Minneapolis: Fortress.

Johanson, Bruce C. 1987. *To All the Brethren: A Text-Linguistic and Rhetorical Approach to 1 Thessalonians*. ConBNT. Stockholm: Almqvist & Wiksell International.

———. 1990. "La Composition de 1 Thessaloniciens." Pages 73–86 in *The Thessalonian Correspondence*. Edited by Raymond F. Collins and Norbert Baumert. BETL 87. Leuven: Leuven University Press.

Johnson, Luke Timothy. 1989. "The New Testament's Anti-Jewish Slander and the Conventions of Ancient Polemic." *JBL* 108:419–41.

Karrer, Martin. 1991. *Der Gesalbte: Die Grundlagen des Christustitels*. FRLANT 151. Göttingen: Vandenhoeck & Ruprecht.

Käsemann, Ernst. 1969a. "Beginnings of Christian Theology." Pages 82–107 in *New Testament Questions of Today*. NTL. London: SCM.

———. 1969b. "On the Subject of Primitive Christian Apocalyptic." Pages 108–37 in *New Testament Questions of Today*. NTL. London: SCM.

Kaye, B. N. 1975. "Eschatology and Ethics in 1 and 2 Thessalonians." *NovT* 17:47–57.

Keck, Leander. 1979. *Paul and His Letters*. Procl. Philadelphia: Fortress.

———. 2005. *Romans*. ANTC. Nashville: Abingdon.

Keck, Leander, and Victor Paul Furnish. 1984. *The Pauline Letters*. IBT. Nashville: Abingdon.

Kim, Seyoon. 1993. "Jesus, Sayings of." Pages 474–92 in *Dictionary of Paul and his Letters*. Edited by Gerald F. Hawthorne, Robert P. Martin, and D. G. Reid. Downers Grove: InterVarsity Press.

———. 2002. "The Jesus Tradition in 1 Thess 4:13–5:11." *NTS* 48:225–42.

———. 2005. "Paul's Entry (*eisodos*) and the Thessalonians' Faith (1 Thessalonians 1–3)." *NTS* 51:519–42.

Klassen, William. 1993. "The Sacred Kiss in the New Testament: An Example of Social Boundary Lines." *NTS* 39:122–35.

Klauck, Hans-Josef. 2006. *Ancient Letters and the New Testament: A Guide to Context and Exegesis*. Waco: Baylor University Press.

Kloppenborg, John S. 1993. "*Philadelphia, Theodidaktos* and the Dioscuri: Rhetorical Engagement in 1 Thessalonians 4:9–12." *NTS* 39:265–89.

Knox, John. 1950. *Chapters in a Life of Paul*. London: Adam & Charles Black.

Koch, Dietrich-Alex. 2010. "Die Entwicklung der Ämter in frühchristlichen Gemeinden Kleinasiens." Pages 166–206 in *Neutestamentliche Ämtermodelle im Kontext*. Edited by Thomas Schmeller, Martin Ebner, and Rudolf Hoppe. QD. Freiburg: Herder.

Koester, Helmut. 1979. "Experiment in Christian Writing." Pages 33–44 in *Continuity and Discontinuity in Church History: Essays Presented to George Huntston Williams on the Occasion of His 65th Birthday*. Edited by F. Forrester Church and Timothy George. SHCT. Leiden: Brill.

———. 1990. "From Paul's Eschatology to the Apocalyptic Schemata of 2 Thessalonians." Pages 441–58 in *The Thessalonian Correspondence*. Edited by Raymond F. Collins and Norbert Baumert. BETL 87. Leuven: Leuven University Press.

Konstan, David, and Ilaria Ramelli. 2007. "The Syntax of *en Christō* in 1 Thessalonians 4:16." *JBL* 126:579–93.

Kraus, Wolfgang. 1996. *Das Volk Gottes: Zur Grundlegung der Ekklesiologie bei Paulus*. WUNT 85. Tübingen: Mohr.

———. 2013. "Die Anfänge der Mission und das Selbstverständnis des Paulus als Apostel der Heiden." Pages 227–237 in *Paulus Handbuch*. Edited by Friedrich Wilhelm Horn. Tübingen: Mohr Siebeck.

Krentz, Edgar. 1991. "Through a Lens: Theology and Fidelity in 2 Thessalonians." Pages 53–62 in *Thessalonians, Philippians, Galatians, Philemon*. Vol. 1 of *Pauline Theology*. Edited by Jouette M. Bassler. Minneapolis: Fortress.

Kuhn, Heinz-Wolfgang. "Die Bedeutung der Qumrantexte für das Verständnis des Ersten Thessalonicherbriefes." Pages 339–53 in *The Madrid Qumran Congress: Proceedings of the International Congress on the Dead Sea Scrolls, Madrid, 18–21 March 1991*. Edited by J. T. Barrera and L. V. Montaner. STDJ 11.1. Leiden: Brill, 1992.

Lake, Kirsopp C. 1950. "The Authenticity of 2 Thessalonians." Pages 234–38 in *Contemporary Thinking about Paul*. Edited by Thomas S. Kepler. New York & Nashville: Abingdon-Cokesbury.

Lambrecht, Jan. 2000. "Thanksgivings in 1 Thessalonians 1–3." Pages 135–62 in *The Thessalonians Debate: Methodological Discord or Methodological Synthesis?* Edited by Karl P. Donfried and Johannes Beutler. Grand Rapids: Eerdmans.

Lampe, Peter. 2013. "Epistolographische Grundlagen: Rhetorik und Argumentation." Pages 149–58 in *Paulus Handbuch*. Edited by Friedrich Wilhelm Horn. Tübingen: Mohr Siebeck.

Langlands, Rebecca. 2009. *Sexual Morality in Ancient Rome*. Cambridge: Cambridge University Press.

Laub, Franz. 1973. *Eschatologische Verkündigung und Lebensgestaltung nach Paulus: Eine Untersuchung zum Wirken des Apostels beim Aufbau der Gemeinde in Thessalonike*. BU 10. Regensburg: Pustet.

———. 1990. "Paulinische Autorität in nachpaulinischer Zeit (2 Thes)." Pages 403–17 in *The Thessalonian Correspondence*. Edited by Raymond F. Collins and Norbert Baumert. BETL 87. Leuven: Leuven University Press.

Lewis, Scott M. 2008. "Light and Darkness." *NIDB* 3:662–64.

Lieu, Judith. 1994. "Do God-Fearers Make Good Christians?" Pages 329–45 in *Crossing the Boundaries: Essays in Biblical Interpretation in Honour of Michael D. Goulder*. Edited by Stanley E. Porter, Paul Joyce, and David E. Orton. BIS. Leiden: Brill. Reprinted in Judith Lieu. Pages 31–47 in *Neither Jew nor Greek? Constructing Early Christianity*. London: T&T Clark, 2002.

Lindblom, Johannes. 1962. *Prophecy in Ancient Israel*. Philadelphia: Fortress.

———. 1968. *Gesichte und Offenbarungen: Vorstellungen von göttlichen Weisungen und übernatürlichen Erscheinungen im ältesten Christentum*. ARSHLL 65. Lund: Gleerup.

Lindemann, Andreas. 1977. "Zum Abfassungszweck des zweiten Thessalonicherbriefes." *ZNW* 68:35–47.

Lohse, Eduard. 1996. *Paulus: Eine Biographie*. Munich: Beck.

Longenecker, Bruce W. 2002. "The Narrative Approach to Paul: An Early Retrospective." Pages 88–111 in *Currents in Biblical Research*. Edited by Alan J. Hauser and Scot McKnight. London: Sheffield Academic Press, 2002.

Longenecker, R. W. 1984. *New Testament Social Ethics for Today*. Grand Rapids: Eerdmans.

Lüdemann, Gerd. 1984. *Paul, Apostle to the Gentiles: Studies in Chronology*. Translated by F. Stanley Jones. Philadelphia: Fortress.

———. 2010. *Die gröbste Fälschung des Neuen Testaments: Der zweite Thessalonicherbrief*. Springe: zu Klampen.

———. 2012. *Der älteste christliche Text: Erster Thessalonicherbrief*. Springe: zu Klampen.

Luther, Martin. 1973. *Commentaries on 1 Corinthians 7; 1 Corinthians 15; Lectures on 1 Timothy.* LW 28. St. Louis: Concordia.

―――. 2003. *On Christian Liberty.* Translated by W. A. Lambert. Minneapolis: Fortress.

Luz, Ulrich. 1968. *Das Geschichtsverständnis des Paulus.* BEvT 49. Munich: Kaiser.

MacMullen, Ramsay. 1974. *Roman Social Relations, 50 B.C. to A.D. 284.* New Haven: Yale University Press.

Malherbe, Abraham J. 1977. *The Cynic Epistles: A Study Edition.* SBLSBS 12. Missoula: Scholars Press.

―――. 1983. "Exhortation in 1 Thessalonians." *NovT* 25:238–56.

―――. 1986. *Moral Exhortation: A Greco-Roman Sourcebook.* LEC 4. Philadelphia: Westminster.

―――. 1987. *Paul and the Thessalonians: The Philosophic Tradition of Pastoral Care.* Philadelphia: Fortress.

―――. 1988. *Ancient Epistolary Theorists.* SBLSBS 19. Atlanta: Scholars Press.

Malina, Bruce J. 1993. *Windows on the World of Jesus: Time Travel to Ancient Judea.* Louisville: Westminster/John Knox.

Malina, Bruce J., and John J. Pilch. 2006. *Social-Science Commentary on the Letters of Paul.* Minneapolis: Fortress.

Marshall, I. Howard. 2004. *New Testament Theology: Many Witnesses, One Gospel.* Downers Grove, IL: InterVarsity.

Martyn, J. Louis. 1997. *Galatians: A New Translation with Introduction and Commentary.* AB 33A. New York: Doubleday.

Mearns, C. L. 1981. "Early Eschatological Development in Paul: The Evidence of I and II Thess." *NTS* 27:137–57.

Meeks, Wayne A. 1983. *The First Urban Christians: The Social World of the Apostle Paul.* New Haven: Yale University Press.

―――. 1986. *The Moral World of the First Christians.* Philadelphia: Westminster.

Meeks, Wayne A., and John T. Fitzgerald, eds. 2007. *The Writings of St. Paul.* 2d ed. Norton Critical Edition. New York: Norton.

Menken, Maarten J. J. 1992. "Paradise Regained or Still Lost? Eschatology and Disorderly Behavior in 2 Thessalonians." *NTS* 38:271–89.

Merk, Otto. 2000. "1 Thessalonians 2:1–12: An Exegetical-Theological Study." Pages 89–113 in *The Thessalonians Debate: Methodological Discord or Methodological Synthesis?* Edited by Karl P. Donfried and Johannes Beutler. Grand Rapids: Eerdmans.

Mitchell, Margaret Mary, Frances M. Young, and K. Scott Bowie, eds. 2006. *Origins to Constantine.* Cambridge History of Christianity 1. Cambridge: Cambridge University Press.

Mitton, C. L. 1951. *The Epistle to the Ephesians: Its Authorship, Origin, and Purpose.* Oxford: Oxford University Press.

Moffatt, James. 1949. *An Introduction to the Literature of the New Testament.* ITL. 3d ed. Edinburgh: T&T Clark.

Moss, Candida R. 2013. *The Myth of Persecution: How Early Christians Invented a Story of Martyrdom.* New York: HarperOne.

Moss, Candida R., and Joel S. Baden. 2012. "1 Thessalonians 4.13–18 in Rabbinic Perspective." *NTS* 58:199–212.

Moule, C. F. D. 1963. *The Meaning of Hope.* FBBS 5. Philadelphia: Fortress.

Müller, Peter. 1988. *Anfänge der Paulusschule: Dargestellt am zweiten Thessalonicherbrief und am Kolosserbrief.* ATANT 74. Zurich: Theologischer Verlag.

Nasrallah, Laura. 2003. *An Ecstasy of Folly: Prophecy and Authority in Early Christianity.* HTS 52. Cambridge, MA: Harvard University Press.

———. 2012. "Spatial Perspectives: Space and Archaeology in Roman Philippi." Pages 53–74 in *Studying Paul's Letters: Contemporary Perspectives and Method.* Edited by Joseph A. Marchal. Minneapolis: Fortress.

Neirynck, Frans. 1991. "Paul and the Sayings of Jesus." Pages 511–68 in vol. 2 of *Evangelica: Gospel Studies = Evangelica: Études d'évangile; Collected Essays.* Edited by Frans Neirynck and Frans van Segbroeck. BETL 99. Leuven: Leuven University Press.

Nicholl, Colin R. 2004. *From Hope to Despair in Thessalonica: Situating 1 and 2 Thessalonians.* SNTSMS 126. Cambridge: Cambridge University Press.

Niebuhr, H. Richard. 1937. *The Kingdom of God in America.* New York: Harper & Row.

Niebuhr, Reinhold. 1964. *The Nature and Destiny of Man.* Gifford Lectures. 2 vols. New York: Scribner.

Oakes, Peter S. 2012. "Economic Approaches: Scarce Resources and Interpretive Opportunities." Pages 75–91 in *Studying Paul's Letters: Contemporary Perspectives and Methods.* Edited by Joseph A. Marchal. Minneapolis: Fortress.

O'Brien, Peter Thomas. 1977. *Introductory Thanksgivings in the Letters of Paul.* NovTSup 39. Leiden: Brill. Reprint, Eugene, OR: Wipf & Stock, 2009.

Okeke, George E. 1980. "I Thess. ii. 13–16: The Fate of the Unbelieving Jews." *NTS* 27:127–36.

Olbricht, Thomas H. 1990. "An Aristotelian Rhetorical Analysis of 1 Thessalonians." Pages 216–36 in *Greeks, Romans, and Christians: Essays in Honor of Abraham J. Malherbe.* Edited by David L. Balch, Everett Ferguson, and Wayne A. Meeks. Minneapolis: Fortress.

Oster, Richard E. 1992. "Christianity in Asia Minor [Persecution and Social Harassment]." *ABD* 1:938–54.

Paddison, Angus. 2005. *Theological Hermeneutics and 1 Thessalonians.* SNTSMS 133. Cambridge: Cambridge University Press.

Pahl, Michael W. 2009. *Discerning the "Word of the Lord": The "Word of the Lord" in 1 Thessalonians 4:15.* LNTS 389. London: T&T Clark.

Pearson, Birger. 1971. "1 Thessalonians 2:13–16: A Deutero-Pauline Interpolation." *HTR* 64:79–94.

Perkins, Pheme. 1992. "Ethics, New Testament." *ABD* 2:652–65.

Petersen, Norman R. 1985. *Rediscovering Paul: Philemon and the Sociology of Paul's Narrative World.* Philadelphia: Fortress.

Peterson, Erik. 1929–30. "Die Einholung des Kyrios." *ZST* 7:682–702.

Plevnik, Joseph. 1997. *Paul and the Parousia: An Exegetical and Theological Investigation.* Peabody, MA: Hendrickson, 1997.

———. 1999. "1 Thessalonians 4:17: The Bringing In of the Lord or the Bringing In of the Faithful?" *Bib* 80:537–46.

Pobee, John S. 1985. *Persecution and Martyrdom in the Theology of Paul.* JSNTSup 6. Sheffield: JSOT Press.

Porter, Stanley E. 1999. "Developments in German and French Thessalonians Research: A Survey and Critique." Pages 309–34 in *Currents in Research: Biblical Studies.* Edited by Alan J. Hauser, Philip Sellew, and Duane F. Watson. Sheffield: JSOT Press.

Potter, David S. 1992. "Persecution of the Early Church." *ABD* 5:231–36.

Pregeant, Russell. 2008. *Knowing Truth, Doing Good: Engaging New Testament Ethics.* Minneapolis: Fortress.

Punt, Jeremy. 2012. "Postcolonial Approaches: Negotiating Empires, Then and Now." Pages 191–208 in *Studying Paul's Letters: Contemporary Perspectives and Methods.* Edited by Joseph A. Marchal. Minneapolis: Fortress.

Ramey, William D. 2012. *New Testament Greek in Diagram: The Epistles to the Thessalonians.* 4th ed., online. 5th ed., 2014, https://www.inthebeginning.org/e-diagrams/thessalonians.html.

Reiser, Marius. 1995. "Hat Paulus Heiden Bekehrt?" *BZ* 39:76–91.

Resch, Alfred. 1904. *Der Paulinismus und die Logia Jesu in ihrem gegenseitigen Verhältnis.* TUGAL, NS, 12. Leipzig: J.C. Hinrichs.

Richard, Earl J. 1991. "Early Pauline Thought: An Analysis of 1 Thessalonians." Pages 39–52 in *Thessalonians, Philippians, Galatians, Philemon.* Vol. 1 of *Pauline Theology.* Edited by Jouette M. Bassler. Minneapolis: Fortress.

Robinson, John A. T. 1957. *Jesus and His Coming:Did the Early Church Misinterpret the Original Teaching of Jesus?* London: SCM Press.

Robinson, J. A. T., Robin Parry, and Trevor Hart. 2011. *In the End, God . . . A Study of the Christian Doctrine of the Last Things. Special Edition.* Eugene, OR: Wipf & Stock.

Roetzel, Calvin J. 1999. *Paul: The Man and the Myth.* Minneapolis: Fortress.

————. 2009. *The Letters of Paul: Conversations in Context.* 5th ed. Louisville: Westminster John Knox.

Roh, Taeseong. 2007. *Der zweite Thessalonicherbrief als Erneuerung apokalyptischer Zeitdeutung.* NTOA 62. Göttingen: Vandenhoeck & Ruprecht.

Romaniuk, Kazimierz. 1993. "Les Thessaloniciens étaient-ils des paresseux?" *ETL* 69:142–45.

Russell, David S. 1964. *The Method and Message of Jewish Apocalyptic, 200 BC–AD 100.* OTL. Philadelphia: Westminster.

Russell, Ronald. 1988. "The Idle in 2 Thess 3.6–12: An Eschatological or Social Problem?" *NTS* 34:105–19.

Sanders, E. P. [Ed Parish]. 1977. *Paul and Palestinian Judaism: A Comparison of Patterns of Religion.* Philadelphia: Fortress.

————. 1995. *Paulus: Eine Einführung.* Stuttgart: Reclam.

Sanders, James A. 1987. *From Sacred Story to Sacred Text.* Philadelphia: Fortress.

Sandnes, Karl Olav. 1991. *Paul, One of the Prophets? A Contribution to the Apostle's Self-understanding.* WUNT 2/43. Tübingen: Mohr.

Schenke, Hans-Martin. 1975. "Das Weiterwirken des Paulus und die Pflege seines Erbes durch die Paulusschule." *NTS* 21:505–18.

Schlueter, Carol J. 1994. *Filling Up the Measure: Polemical Hyperbole in 2 Thessalonians 2.14–16.* JSNTSup 98. Sheffield: JSOT Press.

Schmeller, Thomas, and Christian Cebulj. 2001. *Schulen im Neuen Testament? Zur Stellung des Urchristentums in der Bildungswelt seiner Zeit.* Freiburg: Herder.

Schmidt, Daryl Dean. 1983. "1 Thess 2:13–16: Linguistic Evidence for an Interpolation." *JBL* 102:269–79.

Schmithals, Walter. 1972a. "The Historical Situation of the Thessalonian Epistles." Pages 123–218 in *Paul and the Gnostics.* Nashville: Abingdon.

————. 1972b. *Paul and the Gnostics.* Translated by John E. Steely. Nashville: Abingdon.

Schnelle, Udo. 1983. *Gerechtigkeit und Christusgegenwart: Vorpaulinische und paulinische Tauftheologie.* GTA 24. Göttingen: Vandenhoeck & Ruprecht.

————. 1986. "Der erste Thessalonicherbrief und die Entstehung der paulinischen Anthropologie." *NTS* 32:207–24.

————. 1990. "Die Ethik des 1 Thessalonikerbriefes." Pages 295–305 in *The Thessalonian Correspondence.* Edited by Raymond F. Collins and Norbert Baumert. BETL 87. Leuven: Leuven University Press.

————. 2005. *Apostle Paul: His Life and Thought.* Translated by M. Eugene Boring. Grand Rapids: Baker Academic.

————. 2009. *Theology of the New Testament.* Translated by M. Eugene Boring. Grand Rapids: Baker Academic.

Schoeps, Hans Joachim. 1950. "Die jüdischen Prophetenmorde." Pages 126–43 in *Aus frühchristlicher Zeit: Religionsgeschichtliche Untersuchungen.* Edited by Hans Joachim Schoeps. Tübingen: J. C. B. Mohr (Paul Siebeck), 1950.

Schubert, Paul. 1939. *Form and Function of the Pauline Thanksgivings.* BZNW 20. Berlin: Töpelmann.

Schüssler Fiorenza, Elisabeth. 1983. *In Memory of Her: A Feminist Theological Reconstruction of Christian Origins.* New York: Crossroad.

———. 1985. *The Book of Revelation: Justice and Judgment.* Philadelphia: Fortress.

Schweizer, Eduard. 1945. "Der zweite Thessalonicherbrief ein Philipperbrief?" *TZ* 1:90–105.

Sheppard, Gerald T. 1992. "Canonical Criticism." *ABD* 1:861–65.

Simpson, J. W. 1990. "The Problems Posed by 1 Thessalonians 2:15–16 and a Solution." *HBT* 12:42–72.

Söding, Thomas. 1991. "Der Erste Thessalonicherbrief und die frühe paulinische Evangeliumsverkündigung: Zur Frage einer Entwicklung der paulinischen Theologie." *BZ* 35:184–209.

Steck, Odil Hannes. 1967. *Israel und das gewaltsame Geschick der Propheten: Untersuchungen zur Überlieferung des deuteronomistischen Geschichtsbildes im Alten Testament, Spätjudentum und Urchristentum.* WMANT 23. Neukirchen-Vluyn: Neukirchener Verlag. Issued also as thesis, Heidelberg, 1965.

Stendahl, Krister. 1962. "Biblical Theology, Contemporary." *IDB* 1:418–32.

Still, Todd D. 1999. *Conflict at Thessalonica: A Pauline Church and Its Neighbours.* JSNTSup 183. Sheffield: Sheffield Academic Press.

Stowers, Stanley K. 1986. *Letter Writing in Greco-Roman Antiquity.* Philadelphia: Westminster.

Suggs, M. Jack. 1960. "Concerning the Date of Paul's Macedonian Ministry." *NovT* 4:60–68.

Sumney, Jerry L. 1990. "The Bearing of a Pauline Rhetorical Pattern on the Integrity of 2 Thessalonians." *ZNW* 81:192–204.

———. 1999. *"Servants of Satan," "False Brothers" and Other Opponents of Paul.* JSNTSup 188. Sheffield: Sheffield Academic Press.

Thomas, Johannes. 1993. *"Parakaleō, Paraklētos." EDNT* 3:23–27.

Tiwald, Markus. 2010. "Die vielfältigen Entwicklungslinien kirchlichen Amtes im Corpus Paulinum und ihre Relevanz für heutige Theologie." Pages 101–28 in *Neutestamentliche Ämtermodelle im Kontext.* Edited by Thomas Schmeller, Martin Ebner, and Rudolf Hoppe. QD. Freiburg: Herder.

Trilling, Wolfgang. 1972. *Untersuchungen zum zweiten Thessalonicherbrief.* ETS 27. Leipzig: St.-Benno-Verlag.

————. 1987. "Die beiden Briefe des Apostels Paulus an die Thessalonicher: Eine Forschungsübersicht." In *ANRW* 25.4.2:3365–403. Berlin: de Gruyter.

Tuckett, Christopher M. 1990. "Synoptic Tradition in 1 Thessalonians?" Pages 160–82 in *The Thessalonian Correspondence*. Edited by Raymond F. Collins and Norbert Baumert. BETL 87. Leuven: Leuven University Press.

Vegge, Tor. 2006. *Paulus und das antike Schulwesen: Schule und Bildung des Paulus*. BZNW 134. Berlin: de Gruyter.

Verhey, A. 1984. *The Great Reversal: Ethics and the New Testament*. Grand Rapids: Eerdmans.

Verheyden, Joseph. 2013. "Paulus als Heidenmissionar: Die zweite und dritte Missionsreise." Pages 109–16 in *Paulus Handbuch*. Edited by Friedrich Wilhelm Horn. Tübingen: Mohr Siebeck, 2013.

Vom Brocke, Christoph. 2001. *Thessaloniki, Stadt des Kassander und Gemeinde des Paulus: Eine frühe christliche Gemeinde in ihrer heidnischen Umwelt*. WUNT 2/125. Tübingen: Mohr Siebeck.

Walker, William O., Jr. 2001. *Interpolations in the Pauline Letters*. JSNTSup 213. Sheffield: Sheffield Academic Press.

Ware, James P. 1992. "The Thessalonians as a Missionary Congregation: 1 Thessalonians l,5–8." *ZNW* 83:126–31.

Weatherly, Jon Allen. 1991. "The Authenticity of 1 Thessalonians 2.13–16: Additional Evidence." *JSNT* 42:79–98.

Weima, Jeffrey A. D. 2007. "1–2 Thessalonians." Pages 871–90 in *Commentary on the New Testament Use of the Old Testament*. Edited by G. K. Beale and D. A. Carson. Grand Rapids: Baker Academic.

————. 2012. "'Peace and Security' (1 Thess 5.3): Prophetic Warning or Political Propaganda?" *NTS* 58:331–59.

Weiss, Johannes. 1897. "Beiträge zur paulinischen Rhetorik." Pages 165–247 in *Theologische Studien: Herrn Wirklicher Oberkonsistorialrath Professor D. Bernhard Weiss zu seinem 70. Geburtstage dargebracht*. Göttingen: Vandenhoeck & Ruprecht.

————. 1925. *Der erste Korintherbrief*. KEK 5. 9th ed. Göttingen: Vandenhoeck & Ruprecht.

Wengst, K. 1987. *Pax Romana and the Peace of Jesus Christ*. London: SCM.

White, Joel R. 2013. "'Peace and Security' (1 Thessalonians 5:3): Is It Really a Roman Slogan?" *NTS* 59:382–95.

White, John Lee. 1972. *The Form and Function of the Body of the Greek Letter: A Study of the Letter-Body in the Non-literary Papyri and in Paul the Apostle*. SBLDS 2. Missoula: Society of Biblical Literature.

————. 1983. "Saint Paul and the Apostolic Letter Tradition." *CBQ* 45:433–44.

Witmer, Stephen. 2006. "*Theodidaktoi* in 1 Thessalonians: A Pauline Neologism." *NTS* 52:239–50.

Wilder, Amos N. 1971. *Early Christian Rhetoric*. Cambridge, MA: Harvard University Press.

———. 1973. *Theopoetic: Theology and the Religious Imagination*. Philadelphia: Fortress.

Witherington, Ben. 1992. *Jesus, Paul, and the End of the World: A Comparative Study in New Testament Eschatology*. Downers Grove, IL: InterVarsity.

Wrede, William. 1903. *Die Echtheit des zweiten Thessalonicherbriefs*. TU 24. Leipzig: J. C. Hinrichs'sche Buchhandlung.

———. 2002. *Gesammelte theologische Studien*. Edited and introduced by Werner Zager. 2 vols. ThSt 14. Waltrop: Hartmut Spenner. Original, 1897–1907.

Wright, N. T. [Nicholas Thomas]. 2003. *The Resurrection of the Son of God*. Vol. 3 of *Christian Origins and the Question of God*. Minneapolis: Fortress.

———. 2005. *Paul in Fresh Perspective*. Minneapolis: Fortress.

———. 2013. *Paul and the Faithfulness of God*. Vol. 4 of *Christian Origins and the Question of God*. Minneapolis: Fortress.

Wrzoł, Josef. 1916. *Die Echtheit des zweiten Thessalonicherbriefes*. BibS 19.4. Freiburg: Herder.

Wycliffe, John. 1953. *On the Pastoral Office*. Edited and translated by Ford Lewis Battles. Pages 32–60 in *Advocates of Reform: From Wyclif to Erasmus*. Edited by Matthew Spinka. LCC 14. Philadelphia: Westminster.

Yarbrough, O. Larry. 1986. *Not Like the Gentiles: Marriage Rules in the Letters of Paul*. SBLDS 80. Atlanta: Scholars Press.

Zahn, Theodor, John Moore Trout, Melancthon Williams Jacobus, and Charles Snow Thayer. 1909. *Introduction to the New Testament*. 3 vols. Edinburgh: T&T Clark.

Zimmermann, Ruben. 2007. "Jenseits von Indikativ und Imperativ." *TLZ* 132:259–84.

INTRODUCTION TO
1 THESSALONIANS

Reading in Context(s)

All meaning is contextual. "The" context of every biblical text is multidimensional. Four overlapping and interwoven aspects of the context of 1 Thessalonians call for recognition and exploration: (1) the reader's context; (2) the canonical context; (3) the context in the history of interpretation; (4) the original historical context. In the lived experience of interpreting the Bible, these contexts overlap and interpenetrate, but for purposes of clarification and discussion, they may be distinguished—though they cannot be separated.

The Reader's Context

We readers of 1 Thessalonians have no choice but to begin where we are. Each reader's context is different from that of every other—a particular location in time and space, a particular location in social groups with their own history, and within this, the individual reader's unique life story and set of experiences. My context inevitably limits and distorts what I can see, but I may nonetheless see something in the text besides my own reflection and hear more than the echo of my own voice—something that is actually there, before me and apart from me. I may hear something true and important, something the text itself wants to say. While one's own context can be as invisible or unnoticed as water to a fish, it is crucial that every reader be aware of the particular set of eyes with which they peer out at the world, including the words on the pages of the Bible.

As a reader, I bring my agenda to the text, and I cannot do otherwise. While hidden agendas are rightly frowned upon, the word itself has no sinister overtones. The agenda is simply the list of business items that is to be taken care of, that with which we are concerned, what we are about. I need to be aware of the contents and priorities of my agenda, how it influences what I can hear from the text, and acknowledge that I may need to amend it en route, in dialogue with the voice that speaks to me from the text. Hermeneutics can never be neatly settled in advance and then "applied," cookie-cutter-like, to the text; interpretation is always rebuilding the ship at sea.

Each biblical author also has an agenda; every biblical text represents something of this agenda. For the biblical text to get into the discussion, to gain a hearing in the dialogue between text and readers, its agenda must be respected. This involves inquiring what its concerns are, what it is about. Therefore interpreting in context requires the exploration of other contexts besides the reader's own. A principal function of historical criticism is to bring the text's original context into focus, in order to facilitate a hearing of the text in terms of its own agenda. This approach is particularly appropriate in interpreting a letter such as 1 Thessalonians, where the original context is relatively clear. In 2 Thessalonians, if the letter is not by Paul himself, the concept of "original context" becomes more diffuse, and even more so in the interpretation of such texts as the Gospels and the Pentateuch. Even so, such texts do not float above history, and the effort to root them in their historical context cannot be abandoned or considered irrelevant.

The Canonical Context

For every modern reader, the Thessalonian Letters have another context that is immediately perceivable and inescapable: the document is part of the Christian Bible. In the last generation, this fact has been made into the basis for a significant strand of biblical interpretation, *canonical criticism*.[1]

Canonical location. From the viewpoint of canonical criticism, each biblical text has already been integrated into a coherent set of documents, which are more than random clusters. The texts *with which* each text is read—its canonical *con*-text[2]—are theologically important. First Thessalonians, for instance, must be read in relation to the other canonical documents such as 2 Thessalonians, Acts, and the Gospels. Noncanonical texts such as *3 Corinthians*, the *Gospel of Thomas*, and the *Acts of Paul and Thecla* may also provide illuminating historical insights, but receive a different kind of attention than canonical texts.

While each text of Scripture is read in the light of Scripture as a whole, this approach does not mean that texts can be drawn from all over the Bible and fitted into one harmonious scheme, and that this homogenized product can be presented as the "canonical" meaning of a particular text. The varied voices of

---

1. On the "canonical approach" to hermeneutics, see Childs 1984; 1992; J. A. Sanders; Sheppard; Driver; and the bibliographies they provide.

2. Linguistic approaches to the text, such as discourse analysis, distinguish *cotext, intertext,* and *context*. Cotext refers to strings of words, sentences, and paragraphs within which a text is set in a given document, and their relation to the larger structures of that document. *Intertext* refers to relations of a given text to other texts outside the given document, to which it is consciously or unconsciously related (e.g., NT allusions to the OT). *Context* refers to the larger sociohistorical realities within which a text is set. I am using "context" in the conventional broad sense that includes all three. See Green 226.

Scripture retain their differences, including their irreconcilable disagreements. It does mean that, for example, 1 Thessalonians is heard within the whole historical range and theological spectrum of the canonical texts. On almost every topic, the biblical canon contains a spectrum of views, with considerable—but not unlimited—variety. Each text is allowed to speak in its own voice; harmonization does not mean that differences are leveled into a monotone, but rather that each is heard in concert with the other. Dialogue and mutual correction are facilitated when canonical texts are read in relation to each other rather than in isolation. What each distinctive voice has to say is properly heard within the chorus of other voices. Some have used a different image, with canonical location as "conference table."[3] Not just anyone is invited to the table, but a plurality of voices are invited, and all those invited are heard. In the New Testament canon, more than one point of view is acceptable—but not just anything.

To what extent may the modern exegete seek illumination on the meaning of 1 Thessalonians from the other letters in the Pauline corpus, all of which were written later? This is a knotty question, involving the overlapping approaches of historical criticism and a canonical perspective. On the one hand, the new converts in Thessalonica had none of the other letters of Paul, not to speak of the rest of the New Testament, and the later insights of these texts were not available to them, so they could not use them to explicate the meaning of the particular letter addressed to them. Since Paul's Letters are shaped by the particular situation he addresses, these insights may not yet have dawned on him as he writes 1 Thessalonians. On the other hand, Paul writes as one who has been preaching and teaching the basic themes of the faith for more than fifteen years, and he must have already thought through some of the issues that do not explicitly emerge until the later letters. In this commentary, I will mainly attempt to help the modern reader hear 1 Thessalonians as it might have been heard by its first readers, without allowing every occurrence of a key Pauline word ("faith," "church") to trigger the composition of a mini-essay on this theme derived from the whole Pauline corpus. Even so, it is historically impossible, as well as theologically illegitimate, for the modern exegete to pretend that one does not know the later letters, which on occasion are indispensable for clarifying the meaning of the earliest letter. Moreover, the Thessalonians themselves were illuminated by Paul's instruction to them (cf. the repeated "as you know"), instruction that we do not have, but which can to some extent be excavated by what he writes in later letters. While all the insights of later letters must not be read into 1 Thessalonians, there is no way to understand this letter in isolation. Understanding 1 Thessalonians calls for both diachronic and synchronic approaches, attending to the particular text before us yet also seeing it in its canonical context, which includes its comprehensive Pauline context.

3. E.g., Caird.

Authoritative claim. Canonical context signals not only location but also authoritative claim. Reading each text of Scripture in the light of Scripture as a whole means it is being read in the context of the community that accepted this collection of documents as mediating the word of God, the authority for its life and work. The later church reads this constellation of texts together, in the expectation that the word of God that generated them will continue to be heard through them. From the perspective of canonical criticism, canonization by the later church is not seen as the imposition of an external authority on the texts, but as the recognition and acknowledgment of a claim inherent in the texts themselves. When a letter that Paul wrote for a church gathered in a specific time and place became a letter for the whole church around the world and through the centuries, this was in accord with, and the realization of, the text's original impact (cf. 1 Thess 5:27).

What it meant/what it means? In this regard, canonical criticism challenges a two-stage hermeneutical approach that has become conventional for many in the last generation of biblical scholarship. This two-stage line of thought claims to distinguish the original historical meaning ("what it meant") from later theological interpretations and applications ("what it means").[4] In this perspective, contemporary readers of all faiths and none can theoretically agree on the descriptive historical meaning, observing what the text meant to the author and original readers ("what it meant," i.e., "what the historical exegete thinks it meant"). In this view, dissension only arises when this theoretical agreement on the historical meaning is pursued beyond the original context and translated into the conceptuality and terminology of the later reader's own time. This normative sense explicates the meaning and claim of the text for the contemporary reader. In the former reading, the text was "not written to us," and the reader is a more or less interested spectator to a communication event between two other parties. In the latter reading, when readers understand themselves to belong to the same believing community that originally received the canonical documents, "what it means" is or can be a matter of normative theology, existential involvement, and confession of the faith to which the text witnesses and communicates: hence there is a sense in which it is (also) "written to us." This hermeneutical dynamic of "what it meant" // "what it means" and "not written to us" // "written to us" is inherent in affirming historical texts as Holy Scripture.

Advocates of contemporary canonical criticism and theological interpretation have been critical of this two-stage approach to hermeneutics. Some of their objections are well taken, for they are quite right that this meant/means,

---

4. Classically represented by Stendahl, this understanding of the interpreter's task was virtually institutionalized for a generation in the *Interpreter's Bible*'s division of its pages by a firm line that separated historical exegesis, written by a Bible scholar, from contemporary homiletical exposition, written by a preacher. See *IB*.

then/now distinction needs to be nuanced as too quantitative, too partitioned, too diachronic, too assured that both "what it meant" and "what it means" are univocal realities.[5] Such a too-rigid and too-simple view tends to think of the historical "what it meant" as a separate, descriptive task that can be completed without raising normative questions of theological meaning, as though the historical critic could deliver an objective, value-and-ideology-neutral product, the ancient and original meaning uncontaminated by later concerns. Those who have a mind to do so could then take this "objective" meaning and, as an optional additional step, translate it into "meaning for today," in terms of their subjective commitments and/or communities to which they belong. Canonical criticism disputes this sort of partition of the interpreter's task into "then" and "now" components and sees hermeneutics as one dynamic whole.

First Thessalonians was not, in fact, written to isolated individuals in Thessalonica, but to a church. Had the letter been lost en route to the congregation for which it was intended, falling out of the courier's backpack on a street in Thessalonica and found by a casual passer-by, it would not have been understood in the same way the new converts in Thessalonica would have understood it, even though the reader might understand the Greek vocabulary and syntax perfectly. Both author and intended recipients would have considered this understanding to be defective. The letter required the community, and its shared history with the author, in order to understand it rightly. When the letter(s) to the Thessalonians were incorporated into the Scriptures that belong to the whole church, and accompanied it on its journey through history, this original dynamic was not lost. It is the history of the church as the ongoing people of God that binds together the original addressees of 1 Thessalonians and contemporary readers who belong to the same community of faith; this ongoing peoplehood bridges the gap between the historical "what it meant" and theological "what it means."

Canonical criticism vis-à-vis historical criticism. The "canonical" and "historical-critical" approaches to interpretation have sometimes defined themselves in contrast to each other, with occasional touches of caricature from both sides, or have simply stared at each other from across the street. Historians who want to hear biblical texts in their original settings may, in a disdainful tone of voice, refer to canonical groupings artificially imposed on the text centuries later, groupings of which the first readers were completely unaware. Advocates of canonical interpretation may suppose that they are the only ones interested in the "final form of the text," and that historical critics are mainly interested in peeling away the layers of the present form of the text to get behind it to its

---

5. See the critique in Paddison 40–66. For a basic affirmation of Stendahl's approach, with nuances, clarifications, and a defense of Stendahl against those who have oversimplified, caricatured and misunderstood him, see Barr 1999, esp. 195–205.

sources or to "what actually happened." Numerous scholars, however—including the present one—have recognized that each approach may have something valuable to contribute to the other. Just as numerous hard-line historical critics insist on the theological relevance of their work, so several leading advocates of canonical criticism have emphasized that their approach affirms and incorporates historical criticism.[6]

We modern readers cannot be unaware that 1–2 Thessalonians come to us only as integrated into a firm collection that includes the Jewish Scriptures that became the Christian Old Testament, the Gospels, the stories of Paul in Acts, and the later New Testament Letters. When reading 1 Thessalonians, we already know Paul retrospectively and anachronistically as the martyred missionary hero of Acts and author of major letters in the church's Scripture. The first readers knew him as an itinerant leatherworker (or awning maker, tentmaker) and part-time preacher who worked in a local shop, who still bore bruises from his latest missionary effort in a town some days up the road. His preaching had converted them to a new faith and involved them in a new community, but suddenly he left town when troubles arose, leaving them to bear the brunt of local violence. Now they have a letter from him. The difference between these two starting points for reading the letter cannot be ignored, but accepting the one does not necessarily mean rejecting the other. While the historical critic cannot escape the canonical context of 1 Thessalonians, neither can the canonical critic use the "canonical approach" or "theological interpretation" as a pretext for flight from historical study or for ignoring its results.

The Mediating Context: Church Tradition, Academic Research

All modern readers receive 1–2 Thessalonians from the hands of the church, which included these two documents in the Christian Bible and handed them on through more than nineteen centuries of translation and interpretation. While the modern reader cannot simply ignore this historical context and cultural gap, it need not be seen merely as a barrier that separates original text and modern reader. This history also binds the text to contemporary readers, transmitting it to them along with a rich heritage of interpretation with which it is already bound up. Rather than trying to make exegetical work the means of collapsing the gap between the first and the twenty-first centuries, contemporary interpreters might better explore the resources of this rich heritage. This is more than a borrowing of insightful comments and inspirational paragraphs from great expositors of the past. Reading their—sometimes startling—interpretations of familiar texts may serve to break up the crust of modern readers' percep-

---

6. On the historical criticism side, see, e.g., the preface in Betz 1979, xv; and on the canonical criticism side, see, for example, Childs 1984, 38, 45; cf. 49–50.

tions, cause the text to be seen in a new light, and create space for new insight that transcends both the interpretation offered by an earlier generation and the reader's own previous understanding. One of the biblical scholar's roles is to guard the alterity, the otherness, of the biblical text—in the Bible's own terms, its holiness (Rom 1:2; 2 Tim 3:15). Study of the history of interpretation will both put our own interpretations in proper context and guard against attempts to make the biblical authors sound too much like our own voices. This commentary will occasionally indicate its indebtedness to major interpreters of Paul through the centuries and will seek to help its readers become more aware of the tradition in which we all stand; to do otherwise is inevitably to interpret out of context.[7] "Tradition is not a veneration of the ashes, but a handing on of the fire."[8] This tradition includes not only the ecclesial context, but, overlapping it, the tradition of analytical study of the Bible in the academy.

The Thessalonian Letters in Recent Scholarship

With varying degrees of awareness of the history in which they stand, modern interpreters also do their work in the context of the history of academic research. During the last two centuries, the similarities and differences between 1 and 2 Thessalonians have generated a variety of views of the origins and mutual relations of these two letters.[9] Only two have found substantial support:

1. *Paul wrote 1 Thessalonians, followed in a few months by 2 Thessalonians.* This is the traditional view, generally assumed in the church until the advent of modern historical study of the Bible. The similarities between the two documents are explained by their proximity in time: the structure and wording of 1 Thessalonians were still fresh in Paul's mind when he wrote 2 Thessalonians. The differences are due to Paul's perception of the changed situation of the Thessalonians in the brief interval.

7. A helpful tool is provided by the Blackwell Bible Commentaries, providing summaries of key hermeneutical issues from major interpreters through the centuries, with copious citations from the primary sources. For the Thessalonian Letters, see Thiselton. The same rule applies in utilizing such resources as for the biblical texts themselves: usable excerpts may not be appropriated without regard to their historical context!

8. Attributed to the Austrian Jewish composer and conductor Gustav Mahler, who drew together several different strands of musical tradition into his ten symphonies. See William Faulkner, "The past is never dead. It's not even past," in *Requiem for a Nun* (1951; reprint, New York: Vintage, 2011), 73.

9. The story of NT scholarship, illuminating every aspect of interpretation, is engagingly narrated in Baird 1992–2013. For a detailed history of the variety of proposals regarding 1–2 Thessalonians and their advocates, see R. Collins 1984a and the bibliography he provides.

2. *Paul wrote 1 Thessalonians; 2 Thessalonians was written by a later disciple of Paul.* In the last thirty years, critical scholarship has increasingly moved toward this position, which is now the dominant critical view, and the perspective of this commentary (see intro to 2 Thessalonians, below).

Other proposals include the following:

* *Paul wrote both letters about the same time, to different groups in the same church.* Adolf Harnack argued that 1 Thessalonians was written to the Gentile Christian majority, and 2 Thessalonians was addressed to the Jewish Christian faction of the congregation that met separately. Martin Dibelius suggested that 1 Thessalonians was written to the church leaders, while 2 Thessalonians was intended for liturgical reading in the congregation as a whole. E. Earle Ellis reversed this argument, contending that 1 Thessalonians was written to the whole church, while 2 Thessalonians was only for the leaders and coworkers, who had authority to deal with the problematic "idlers." Abraham Malherbe has recently argued that 1 Thessalonians was written to those whom Paul had converted and knew personally, and that 2 Thessalonians was written a short time later, to those converted in the meantime, who had not known Paul directly and had appropriated a distorted understanding of 1 Thessalonians.[10]
* *Paul wrote both letters at the same time, but to congregations in different towns.* First Thessalonians was written to Thessalonica, but 2 Thessalonians to a church in a different town in Macedonia, perhaps Beroea or Philippi.[11]
* *Paul wrote 2 Thessalonians prior to 1 Thessalonians.* Since the seventeenth century, a number of scholars have resolved the difficulties of the traditional view by arguing that 2 Thessalonians was written first.[12] This hypothesis requires a lost letter, since 2 Thess 2:15; 3:17 could not refer to 1 Thessalonians. A place for the writing of 2 Thessalonians must be found in the history Paul rehearses in 1 Thess 2:17–3:10, which reads as though there had been no

---

10. Harnack; Dibelius 1937, 57–58; Malherbe 2000, 350–53, 364; Ellis.

11. Beroea was suggested by Goguel 4:335–37. Schweizer proposed Philippi. Each nomination died for want of a second.

12. This argument, first made in 1642 by Hugo Grotius (*Annotationes in Novum Testamentum*, 1641–50), is currently represented by Wanamaker. A good summary of the arguments for the priority of 2 Thessalonians, and the reasons most scholars do not find the arguments persuasive, is found in Best 42–45; and Bruce xlii–xliii.

previous letter. It also requires that 1 Thessalonians be read as an interpretation of 2 Thessalonians, and that 2 Thessalonians be regarded as the earliest extant Christian document. These difficulties have proved insuperable to most contemporary interpreters.

• *Paul wrote a number of letters that have been combined into 1 (and 2) Thessalonians.* A few have argued that the two canonical letters are editorial compositions of three or more letters.[13]
• *Paul wrote neither letter.* F. C. Baur and his disciples, the nineteenth-century Tübingen school, regarded only four New Testament Letters as from the hand of Paul: 1–2 Corinthians, Galatians, and Romans (the *Hauptbriefe*). Scholarship of the early twentieth century, conservative and liberal alike, took these challenges seriously and responded with detailed refutations and positive argument.[14] Today, 2 Thessalonians is often considered deuteropauline, but the Pauline authorship of 1 Thessalonians is virtually unchallenged.

The Historical Context of 1 Thessalonians

Each of the contexts discussed above is crucial to understanding. Hearing the text in its ancient historical context is the most difficult task for the modern interpreter, and will require the most attention in this commentary.

In the Context of Paul's Life

First Thessalonians[15] is here understood to be not only the earliest Pauline letter that happens to be preserved, but also the first such letter ever written (see below, on the "Apostolic Letter"). This does not mean it was written early in his missionary career, or that it represents Paul's early, "undeveloped" thought. Paul's theology represented in the extant letters changed over the years, but this is a matter of adapting and rethinking his core convictions under the pressure of new situations, not an evolutionary development from primitive to sophisticated. This first apostolic letter was not the product of a neophyte missionary-theologian, advocating rudimentary ideas that the more mature Paul would abandon. All the extant letters of Paul come from a relatively brief period near the end of his missionary career. In the chronology here followed, the

13. Schmithals argues that elements of four Pauline letters were combined into the canonical two (1972b, 123–218). A view similar to Schmithals's is now defended by Richard, arguing that an earlier letter (2:13–4:2) has been combined with a letter (1:1–2:12; 4:3–5:28) to form our present 1 Thessalonians (1995, 11–19 and passim).

14. See, e.g., Zahn et al. 1:248–50; Moffatt 69–73.

15. For an introduction to 2 Thessalonians, see pp. 209–227 below.

period from Paul's conversion until his final letter spanned twenty-four years, 33–57 C.E. All his extant letters were written in the *final* seven or eight years of that period, beginning with 1 Thessalonians in 50 C.E. and concluding with Romans in 57 C.E. Neither Acts nor Paul's Letters contain much information about the first 70 percent of his missionary career, the years 33–50, from his conversion until the writing of 1 Thessalonians. To be sure, in relative terms, 1 Thessalonians is early in the framework of the 50–57 period of his letters. The pressures that would trigger the responses of 2 Corinthians, Galatians, and Romans, where the legitimacy of Paul's apostleship and "justification by faith apart from the works of the law" become key themes, had not yet occurred.[16] Yet the formative events of Paul's life had already happened long before he first appears on the New Testament scene as the writer of 1 Thessalonians—the work of a seasoned missionary and mature theologian.

Saul of Tarsus, hard-liner Diaspora Pharisee, zealous opponent of what he saw as a deviant group within Judaism, had joined in the efforts to neutralize or destroy this group that was relaxing the Torah and admitting uncircumcised Gentiles to the holy people of God, thus threatening the very foundations of Judaism (1 Cor 15:9; Phil 3:6; Gal 1:13). In or near Damascus around 33 C.E., Saul the zealous opponent of aberrant Jewish believers in Jesus, convinced that he was doing the will of God, was encountered by the risen Christ (1 Cor 9:1; 15:8; Gal 1:15–16; Acts 9:1–8; 22:6–11; 26:9–18). Paul was converted into the Hellenistic church. Even if Paul had previously been in Jerusalem and knew something of the church there, it was in Damascus that his understanding of everything was turned upside down—he would have said "right side up"—and that he became a representative of the Hellenistic church.

Three years after his conversion he made a brief visit to Jerusalem, then worked for some time as a missionary of the Antioch church. The church at Antioch was an innovative, integrating Christian community that began among the Gentile God-fearers in the synagogues, but then formed its own congregations of (mostly) Gentile Christians. Here for the first time the church was recognized as a distinct religious community separate from the synagogue, not a subset within Judaism, and for the first time its members were called "Christians" (Acts 11:26).[17]

---

16. Missing from 1 Thessalonians are not only any specific concern for or defense of his apostleship, but also (what will later become) key theological terms: *sarx* (flesh), *hamartia* (sin), *thanatos* (death), *sōma* (body [yet used incidentally in 5:23]), *eleutheria* (freedom), *zōē* (life), *dikaioō* and the whole "justification" vocabulary, *baptizō* (baptize), *nomos* (law), *stauros* (cross), and *stauroō* (crucify). Exposition of Scripture plays no role, nor does the collection from the Gentile churches to be presented to the Jerusalem church. Thus 1 Thessalonians represents the (relatively) "early Paul" in this important sense, but it is not a document of early Pauline theology in the comprehensive sense. See Schnelle 1986.

17. The term "Christian" is a convenient anachronism in discussing the Pauline Letters and churches. While, according to Acts 11:26, the term *Christianoi* had already been used of believers

Paul's several years as a missionary of the Antioch church was a formative period for what came to be identified as "Pauline" theology: Antioch receives traditions from Jerusalem and elsewhere, both Aramaic and Hellenistic, transmitting and interpreting them with varying degrees of loyalty to traditional understandings of torah and temple, reflecting a spectrum of theological beliefs and practices of the church expanding from Jerusalem. This period was characterized by a dialogue from which Paul received and to which he contributed. Much of what later emerges in 1 Thessalonians and later Pauline writings was hammered out during this dynamic, formative period. With his Jewish Christian colleague Barnabas and uncircumcised Gentile Christian Titus, he represented the Antioch church at the Jerusalem Council (Gal 2:1–10; Acts 15:1–29), where the Gentile mission of welcoming converts without the requirement of circumcision received approval from the Jerusalem leaders.

The Jerusalem Council had preserved the unity of the new movement by recognizing the parallel existence of two forms of Christian mission within the one church. It did not deal with an issue that could have been foreseen—how Jewish and Gentile Christians could live and work together in one congregation, respecting the convictions of both, without violating the conscience of either. This issue soon came to a head in the "Antioch incident," as it has come to be called, in a confrontation between Peter and Paul. Acts is silent about the incident, which Paul reports (from his perspective) in Gal 2:11–21. Visitors to Antioch claiming to represent James and the Jerusalem church insisted that Jewish Christians must continue to maintain the Jewish way of life, including the purity laws related to food: Jews may not eat with Gentiles as a matter of ritual purity (Gal 2:12). This was not a matter of bigotry or religious snobbishness. From their theological perspective, it was inherent in the vocation of Israel, the people of God, to remain faithful to the covenant and its stipulations, a conviction for which Israel's martyrs had died. They did not claim that *Gentile* Christians need live by these laws, but insisted that when *Jews* became Christians, they were not free to violate them. This meant that Jewish Christians could not continue the table fellowship with Gentile Christians, and some withdrew, including Peter and Barnabas. In Paul's version of the incident, he soundly denounced and defeated the compromising Peter and "even Barnabas," his former colleague in the Gentile mission. Since Peter remained in Antioch, and Antiochene Christianity turned away from its previous radical openness in the direction of the more conservative Jacobite Jewish Christianity

---

in Jesus in Antioch while Paul was working in the church there, and could be used as a general term for church members in Rome near the end of the 1st cent. C.E. (see, e.g., 1 Pet 4:16), neither "Christian" nor "disciple" is found in Paul's Letters as a designation for those who believed in Jesus as the Christ. It is difficult to avoid such anachronisms; the proposed substitutes (e.g., using "the Jesus movement," "Jesus' followers," or "Christ community") are themselves not found in Paul's Letters and are burdened with the baggage of later associations.

of Jerusalem, it appears that Paul lost the debate and decided he could no longer participate in the Antiochene mission program. Peter would remain in Antioch, and Paul would leave, never to return.

In studying 1 Thessalonians, it is important to see that the church in Thessalonica was established *after* Paul's break with Antioch. Although the new converts were instructed to understand themselves as a congregation belonging to the same church as their sister congregations in Judea (1 Thess 2:14), they would not have understood themselves as a mission project of the mother church in Antioch or Jerusalem. The Aegean mission was an independent Pauline mission in the sense that Paul was no longer operating as a representative of the Antioch church: he did not consider himself subordinate to the Jerusalem "Pillars" (Gal 2:1–10).

The movement into the Aegean area, within which the church in Thessalonica was founded, was for Paul a fresh beginning. He could even refer to his mission to Philippi, just prior to the church-founding visit to Thessalonica, as the "early days of the gospel" (Phil 4:15). Paul chose Silvanus ("Silas" in Acts) as his new coworker, a Jewish Christian and prophetic leader in the Jerusalem church who was affirmative of the Gentile mission. The two missionaries set out along the land route from Syria through Cilicia, visiting congregations previously established (Acts 15:40–41). According to Acts, Timothy is converted by Paul at Lystra and, at Paul's invitation, joins the mission team (Acts 16:1–3; cf. 1 Cor 4:17). Guided by divine revelation (Acts 16:6–10), they are led through northern Galatia, where Paul's illness requires an extended pause. It was probably during this time that the Galatian churches were founded. Guided by the Spirit and visionary experiences, they cross over to Macedonia and begin their mission work in Philippi.

The Aegean mission represents a new missionary strategy on Paul's part. His plan of action is not to try to visit each town and village separately, but to establish a mission center in major metropolitan areas, especially provincial capitals, from which his missionary team and the new converts can evangelize neighboring regions. From such centers (Philippi, Thessalonica, Corinth, Ephesus), Paul's plan is to evangelize the surrounding region with the distinctively Pauline gospel, establishing a symbolic and functional beachhead for the dissemination of the faith and the gathering of the eschatological community. Previously he has evangelized as the missionary sent out by a major mission center. He made "missionary journeys," accompanied by a senior colleague such as Barnabas, and returned to report to the church that had sent him. So long as Paul understood his own commission and theology to be in harmony with the church that sent him, his consciousness of being personally sent and called by the risen Christ did not constitute any problem for his serving as missionary delegate of a central church. The "Antioch incident" changed this situation. Henceforth Paul would not function as the representative of a mission center, making "missionary journeys" in its behalf, but with his own coworkers he himself would found new mission centers in major cities. First Thessalonians was not written on "the second missionary journey," but at the beginning of his own mission, which would continue uninterrupted until concluded by his final visit to Jerusalem.[18] Henceforth he needed to be clear that as an *apostolos* (apostle, one who is authorized and sent, missionary), he is the authorized representative of the risen Lord, not merely of other human beings (cf. Gal 1:1; 2 Cor 10–13), but this had not yet become problematic when he writes 1 Thessalonians.

The mission team began a new church in Philippi, on the Egnatian Way, which leads to Rome, already on Paul's horizon as the key destination of his mission to the Gentiles (cf. Rom 1:13; 15:22). In Philippi, the missionaries founded a church with which Paul would have an enduring friendship. He and Silvanus are arrested, beaten, and briefly imprisoned by the local authorities (Acts 16:16–40). Upon their release, they and Timothy journey to Thessalonica, where, amid tumult and trouble, they also successfully establish a new congregation. When the missionaries are forced to leave Thessalonica, Paul travels to Athens (with Timothy? see on 3:1). From there he sends Timothy back to Thessalonica to check on the church. Paul then journeys alone to Corinth, where he arrives "in weakness and much fear and trembling" (1 Cor 2:3). There, in cooperation with Priscilla and Aquila (recently arrived from Rome as a result of Claudius's expulsion of the Jews in 49 C.E.), he begins a new Christian congregation. A few months after his departure from Thessalonica,[19] Paul is joined by Silvanus and Timothy, who arrive from Macedonia with the good news that the church in Thessalonica is flourishing despite its persecution. From Corinth in about 50 C.E., Paul (and Silvanus and Timothy) write the encouraging and

---

18. The traditional terminology of "missionary journeys," associated with maps often printed with the Bible, is not found in the NT itself and is problematic for at least two reasons: (1) It is based on the demonstrably inaccurate chronological scheme of Acts, not on Paul's Letters. (2) It is modeled on the modern missionary movement of the 19th cent., in which missionaries from Europe and North America traveled to other countries for a mission trip, then returned home. When applied to Paul, it suggests that Paul's normal state was to be settled in his "home church," Antioch, from which he made three extended mission trips. Rather, after his conversion and particularly after the Antioch incident, his normal state was to be traveling in the Aegean, settling down temporarily in Corinth and Ephesus. At the end of this years-long mission project, he made a trip to Jerusalem to deliver the offering, and there he was arrested and sent to his eventual death in Rome.

19. Malherbe (2000, 72) calculates the travel times involved between Paul's leaving Thessalonica and writing the letter:

Thessalonica to Beroea (Acts 17:10–13), 1 week
Beroea to Athens (Acts 17:14–15), 3 weeks
Return of Paul's companions from Athens to Beroea (Acts 17:15), 3 weeks
Timothy's journey to Athens and return to Thessalonica (1 Thess 3:1–3), 6 weeks
Timothy's journey from Thessalonica to Corinth (1 Thess 3:6–8; Acts 18:5), 4 weeks

Thus the period between leaving Thessalonica and writing 1 Thessalonians was about four months.

clarifying letter that comes into the Christian Bible as 1 Thessalonians, the earliest extant Christian document.[20]

In the Context of Thessalonica

Much modern reading of Paul's Letters tends to identify with the author. The reader stands behind Paul, so to speak, looking over his shoulder, out to the Thessalonians. We have so far done this, treating Paul before the Thessalonians. There is value in this. It is an aspect of the canonical context of 1 Thessalonians and thus the modern reader's context. We approach the text of Thessalonians already knowing quite a bit about Paul from his later letters and Acts, information and perspectives the first readers did not know and could not have known.

The reader who wants to understand the text needs to identify primarily with the *ancient reader*. This means we do not stand with Paul in Corinth looking north to Thessalonica, but with the new converts in Thessalonica looking south to Paul. We Bible readers are accustomed to following the biblical story line and *"going"* to Thessalonica with Paul. The original readers were already in the city, had been there a long time, and they see the newcomer Paul arrive. They knew their city, their social and cultural life that included (what we would call) economics, politics, and religion; they did not know Paul. We need to get acquainted with them, join their circle as much as historical and cultural distance will allow, see Paul with their eyes, and hear his message with their ears. Rather than looking over Paul's shoulder as he writes to Thessalonica, we might better identify with the Gentile residents of the city, who already have their own religion, and ask how they perceive this itinerant leatherworker who sets up shop in their town with a radical new message that somehow wins them over.

The City

If there are visitors to modern Thessaloníki who anticipate finding a quaint "biblical" town, they are in for a shock. According to the 2011 census, the official municipality of Thessaloníki has a population of 322,240, while the Thessaloníki Metropolitan Area extends over an area of 1,455.62 square kilometers (562.02 sq. mi.), with a population of well over a million. The harbor is the largest and busiest port in the north Aegean, near the mouth of long, navigable rivers, including the Axios and the Haliakmon. The city is located on the Via

---

20. For evidence and rationale, see Boring 2012, 182–315, esp. summary of chronological issues, 314–15. For more comprehensive discussions and alternative views on particular points, see Donfried 1992; Schnelle 2005, 47–386; Dunn 322–1166. Donfried dates 1 Thessalonians much earlier than most, ca. 43 C.E., several years before the Jerusalem conference and the "Antioch incident." For his argument for an "early Paul" based on this chronology, see Donfried 1990; 1993a, 9–12, esp. 12: "in the general period of Paul's first visit to Corinth, AD 41–44."

Egnatia, with a constant stream of international traffic; Thessaloníki International Airport *Macedonia* connects the city with the rest of the world. Today's tourist sees occasional evidence of the city's antiquity, but the city has been continuously occupied since ancient times. Ninety-five percent of the city of Paul's day still lies beneath the modern buildings and thus cannot be excavated.

From the ancient perspective as well, Thessalonica was considered a large city. At the beginning of the first century C.E., the geographer and historian Strabo refers to Thessalonica as a *metropolis* (mother city), the largest city of the whole region. Some have calculated the population as about 100,000 in Paul's time, but most consider this too high, with about 40,000 being the typical estimate—still a sizeable city in the Hellenistic world. Thessalonica was among the outstanding provincial capitals; it should not surprise us that Paul chose it as a mission center.

In Paul's time the city already had a proud and illustrious history. For centuries before Paul's time, the strategic location and good harbor had been the site of numerous settlements and towns. Alexander's conquests in the late fourth century B.C.E. left his general Cassander in charge of Macedonia. Cassander (re)founded the city, incorporating neighboring villages into the new city, named after his wife, Thessaloníki, Alexander's half-sister—the last surviving member of ancient Macedonian royalty. As the Roman Empire expanded to the east in the second century B.C.E., the Macedonian kingdom was defeated, and the local leadership was deported to Italy and replaced by Roman administrators and their sympathizers. In Paul's time, the city had been the capital of the Roman province of Macedonia for more than two centuries (since 146 B.C.E.). During the internal power struggles among the imperial leadership, Thessalonica seems to have successfully walked the tightrope of staying with the winning side. At the decisive second battle at nearby Philippi in 42 B.C.E., Thessalonica was the only city in the region to support Octavian (later called Augustus) and Antony against Julius Caesar's assassins Brutus and Cassius. Coins and inscriptions document that the victors were celebrated in Thessalonica, which was rewarded by being declared a "free city"—dependent economically on Rome, but free from tribute, and encouraged to flourish economically. Their "freedom" was relative, dependent on continued loyalty to the Roman regime and support of Roman policy.

The symbiosis was beneficial to both sides and continued into Paul's time. The location on the Via Egnatia meant both that Thessalonica was an important station on the route further east, and that travel from and to Rome was relatively easy. The city was thus frequently chosen as a place of (temporary) exile, since it had a Roman atmosphere and Rome could be reached quickly, even in winter. Residents of Thessalonica would be concerned with developments in Rome, supported a stable government there, and wanted to be seen as ally of Rome. When Vespasian came to power in 70 C.E. after a period of chaos in which the identity of the future emperor was in doubt, he punished the cities that had not rallied to his support by rescinding their freedom from taxes. Again, Thessalonica retained its special status, though they had not supplied Vespasian with "volunteer" troops during the war in Palestine that put down the Jewish rebellion. Local, grassroots support of the Caesar cult became of increasing importance as an index of support for a stable Roman government (see below). Vespasian's propaganda cast him in the role of Augustus; Vespasian too had ended civil war and brought peace and prosperity, and once again Thessalonica had succeeded in appearing to support the winning side all along. Observations about the 70s period are irrelevant for 1 Thessalonians, written twenty years earlier, but would have been important not only for Thessalonica, but also for the Pauline churches generally of the second and third generations, the probable setting for 2 Thessalonians. The Flavian line continued through Titus and Domitian, who would have seen themselves as the legitimate heirs of Vespasian and would have insisted on loyalty in order to forestall any doubts about their legitimacy.[21]

Despite the Roman political dominance, Thessalonica remained a thoroughly Greek city.[22] Alexander's cultural heritage prevailed. The Greek language continued to take precedence over both the ancient pre-Greek languages and the administrative Latin after the Roman takeover. Inscriptions indicate Greek names still prevailed over Roman in the jobs of city administration. The economics had a Roman cast: alongside the local bronze coins, the common currency was the Roman silver denarius. The yearly calendar remained Greek, even Macedonian. The Roman element had not changed the routine life of most of the city's residents. First- and second-century architecture displays a Roman character, but this does not mean a dramatic change in the everyday life of the city. Thessalonica did not become thoroughly Roman until the fourth century. Except for the Caesar cult and the worship of Roma associated with it (see below), there are no large-scale cultural changes in the first century—thus different from the situation in neighboring Philippi.[23] Of the more than 1,000 inscriptions, only 47 are in Latin—again, in contrast to Philippi, where Latin appears prominently in inscriptions. Official documents (imperial decrees and such) relevant to the city are all in Greek, not even bilingual. The Romans who settled there had been integrated into the Greek-speaking population. The Thessalonians of Paul's day thought of themselves as a Macedonian, Greek city, not a Roman city—and Paul, of course, wrote to them in Greek. Nonetheless, in 200 years of Roman domination, the perspectives and mind-set of the superpower had inevitably influenced virtually every aspect of life, including religion.

21. See Roh 114–15.
22. Cf. documentation in Vom Brocke 89–101.
23. "Neighboring" must be thought of in ancient terms. The 2-hour bus trip from Philippi to Thessaloníki of today = 5 days of hard walking in Paul's day.

Religion in the "Empire-Saturated Context" of Thessalonica

Paul did not bring religion to an irreligious city, or persuade secularists and atheists to start believing in God. He proclaimed the Christian gospel in a setting that was already thoroughly religious (cf. 1 Cor 8:5–6; Acts 17:16–23). As elsewhere in the Hellenistic world, "religion" was not a separable element in Thessalonian life and culture: it penetrated every dimension of political, economic, and community life. Paul's "religious" vocabulary adopted, adapted, and sometimes provided an alternative to the socioreligious usage his key words already had in Roman imperial practice and propaganda (e.g., *ekklēsia* [church, assembly], *apostolos* [apostle, messenger, envoy], *ta ethnē* [gentiles, nations], *kyrios* [Lord], *sōtēria* [salvation, security], *eirēnē* [peace], *asphaleia* [security]).[24]

In Thessalonica, religion manifested the usual array of Greco-Roman cults. The standard reference work of Greek inscriptions lists under "Res sacrae" fifty names of gods and heroes in connection with Thessalonica. The two-story series of columns with a variety of images of different gods was designated with the term *eidōla* (images).[25] Among those documented by archaeological evidence are the cults of Serapis, an Egyptian god who had become an international favorite in the syncretistic Hellenistic religious world, and Isis, whose promises of salvation and eternal life found widespread and passionate response. Initiates were received into a cult in solemn and impressive nocturnal rituals, after declarations of humility, confession of sin, and repentance. When Paul and his missionary colleagues arrived, such concepts and vocabulary were already common in the religious life of Thessalonica. From the earliest beginnings, Christian missionaries have never brought the conceptuality and ritual of religious life with them to irreligious people, but always found religious concepts and rituals already there. Their task has never been to introduce such concepts as sin and practices as prayer, but to reinterpret them and fill them with new meaning in the light of the Christian kerygma.

Another popular cult was that of Dionysus. As the god of fertility and the joie de vivre, his domain included not only wine and sex, but also music and the profundities of Greek drama. His worship was related to some of the mysteries and was popular in Thessalonica. The ubiquitous phallus symbol pointed to the life-giving power of the god. The nighttime revelries, providing a foretaste of the promised joys of eternal life, may have evoked a response from Paul, to whose Jewish eyes such "religion" could be reduced to wine, sex, and debauchery (see on 1 Thess 5:5–7).

---

24. See, e.g., Punt, esp. 198 and the bibliography he provides. The phrase "empire-saturated context" is from 199.

25. See Donfried 2002a, 21–48. Vom Brocke (116–18) cites *IG* 10.2.1.

The local variation of the Cabiri cult may have been the most important religious group in the time of Paul. A center of Cabiri worship was located on the nearby island of Samothrace, where the parents of Alexander the Great, Philip of Macedon and Olympias, had been initiated into the cult. The Cabiri (pl.) were twin fertility gods and were believed to protect people in danger, particularly at sea, a protection that extended into the next life. The two brothers were sometimes merged in popular thought with the Dioscuri, Castor and Poly-deuces (or Pollux), the twin sons of Leda and Zeus and the brothers of Helen of Troy. In Thessalonica, however, it appears that only Cabirus (sg.) was honored. Portrayed as a beardless young man, he appears to have been the patron deity of Thessalonica in Paul's time. The Thessalonians not only participated in the variety of international cults, but also had their own favorite, local god who had a special interest in the welfare of the city.

Within this syncretistic variety, the presence and importance of the emperor cult associated with the goddess Roma was clear in first-century Thessalonica, symbolizing the city's loyalty to Rome and undergirding the "peace and security" of the city (see on 5:3). An inscription from the time of Augustus (27 B.C.E.–14 C.E.), KAISAROS NAOS (Temple of Caesar), documents the existence of a Caesar temple. The city's coins were imprinted with the head of Caesar, replacing the figure of Zeus. The Caesar cult involved not only sacrifices to and for the emperor, but also a large number of civic events and festivals (= vacation) days. Hesitancy about participating in such community celebrations could only be interpreted as not having the city's welfare at heart; it could not fail to be noticed. The cult was not imposed by the Romans but initiated and encouraged by local citizens, a grassroots movement rather than an alien, top-down imposition.

Was there a Jewish community in the Thessalonica of Paul's time? The Acts account portrays Paul as preaching in the synagogue and winning numerous converts among God-fearers (Gentiles who attended the synagogue without converting to Judaism). In Acts there is no reference to preaching to Gentiles there. Paul's success in the synagogue evokes a violent reaction, and he is forced to leave the city. This account is the only explicit literary evidence for Jewish residents of Thessalonica in Paul's time.[26] The Acts 17 narrative fits Luke's stereotyped pattern and thus is suspect unless there is corroborating evidence. First Thessalonians makes no reference to Jews, Jewish opposition, or Judaism in Thessalonica; Paul writes to Gentiles who have converted from pagan religion (1:9–10). Nor is there any archaeological evidence for a Jewish

---

26. Philo cites a letter of Agrippa I in which Macedonia is called a home for many Jews (*Legat.* 281). Since Thessalonica was the capital of Macedonia, the statement could reasonably be understood as documenting the presence of Jews there. A tomb inscription (discovered in 1965, not published till 1994) mentions synagogues in the area of Thessalonica, but it is dated almost two centuries after Paul's time (cited in Blumenthal 102).

community in first-century-C.E. Thessalonica. Numerous scholars argue that this absence from the archaeological and extracanonical records is a matter of mere chance—most of the ancient city remains unexcavated—and that there must have been Jews in Thessalonica, as there were in virtually every major city of the Roman world. However, evidence is also lacking for a synagogue in Philippi, where Paul and his colleagues had been immediately before coming to Thessalonica. Even the Acts account only mentions some women Godfearers and a place of prayer beside the river, but no synagogue and nothing about a confrontation with Jews or Judaism in this "leading city of the district of Macedonia," a Roman colony, and on the Egnatian Way (Acts 16:12–13). It is possible that a Jewish community and synagogue existed in the Thessalonica of Paul's time, but if a small number of Jewish Christians were in the new church, there is no reference to them in 1 Thessalonians, which addresses Gentile Christians.

In first-century Thessalonica, paying due respect to the prevailing religious practices was not only a matter of religious conviction, but also important as a manifestation of civic loyalty and allegiance to the Roman Empire. Jewish residents of every urban center had long since learned how to negotiate their precarious way in a pagan city. This was a concern not only for Jews—if there was in fact a Jewish community in Thessalonica—and not only for the authorities charged with maintaining public order and a functioning economy. The local population also fused what modern Westerners would call patriotism, religion, and community loyalty into one all-permeating cultural reality; hence they would be suspicious of any group that might upset the symbiosis and balance of competing powers that made life good for all. Though Paul and his few dozen converts would not seem to pose a threat in this large city, his message of an alternate king and kingdom, and his rejection of local gods and long-established religion, all could be perceived by both Jews and Gentiles as upsetting this fragile stability, and the Christians would be resisted, even with violence.

The Church-Founding Visit

Acts 17:1–10a recounts only briefly the church-founding mission in Thessalonica, focusing on Paul's preaching in the synagogue (three Sabbaths), his rejection by Jews but the acceptance of his message by large numbers of Godfearers, and his abrupt departure. This is a minimal picture of the events surrounding the Thessalonian church's founding, and some elements may reflect Luke's theology more than the historical reality. By Luke's time it was clear that the Christian movement had begun among Jews, had been mostly rejected by them, but was finding acceptance among Gentiles. Luke recounts the story of each new mission church as the history of the whole church writ small. Acts typically represents Paul as beginning his mission by preaching in the synagogue, being rejected, and only then going to the Gentiles (13:13–48; 14:1–7; 18:1–11; 19:8–10). Paul's experience in Thessalonica is portrayed in the same stereotypical pattern.

Though Acts provides minimal hard data about the founding of the church in Thessalonica, statements and inferences from Paul's own letters provide firsthand information. For instance, several times Paul points out what they "already know" or what he had taught them while he was present—though he tells them anyway, informing the modern reader of what transpired during and after the founding visit (1 Thess 1:5; 2:1, 5, 9, 10, 11; 3:3–4; 4:2, 9; 5:1). A critical combination of data from Acts and 1 Thessalonians yields the following outline.

Arrival and reception. Paul and Silvanus arrive in Thessalonica in about 50 C.E., after having been arrested and mistreated in Philippi (1 Thess 2:2; cf. Acts 16:11–40). The presence of Timothy is probable, but disputed (see on 1 Thess 1:1; 3:2). They had followed the well-traveled Egnatian Way from Philippi, about ninety-five miles southwest to Thessalonica. This all-weather superhighway built by the Romans for military and commercial purposes did not go directly through the city (unlike the modern main street called by the ancient name), but skirted Thessalonica on the west. Hence, though coming from the northeast, Paul and Silvanus would have entered Thessalonica by the western gate, after four or five days of hard walking, carrying the tools of Paul's trade, still bearing the marks of their maltreatment in Philippi. They are the first Christian missionaries in the city. The missionaries began at square one.

Lodging, support, and work. There is no indication that either Paul or Silvanus had any previous contact with the city. It is possible that Lydia, the newly converted businesswoman in Philippi who had provided quarters for the missionaries, had contacts in Thessalonica, and recommended them to Jason, who provided hospitality and became Paul's patron (cf. Acts 16:14–15; 17:5–7).[27] The brief account of Acts also emphasizes the conversion of several women of high social status. But both Jason and the wealthy women seem to reflect Luke's interests in painting the new church in respectable colors rather than the actual socioeconomic status of the new converts.[28] The letter itself gives no evidence of such influential citizens in the new congregation. Paul earned his own way, not asking the new converts for support, and not wanting to give the impression that he was sponsored by a local patron (1 Thess 2:9; cf. 1 Cor 4:12; Acts 18:1–3). Presumably Paul rented or leased a small workspace that included sleeping quarters. More than once while in Thessalonica, he received financial support from the new church in Philippi, with which he had established a trusting relationship (Phil 4:16).

27. So Vom Brocke 236–37.
28. So Coulot.

Location of his preaching. Thessalonica was a busy commercial crossroads, accustomed not only to business travelers but also to visiting philosophers, teachers, magicians, and charlatans who found a ready or disdainful audience among the passersby on the docks or in the agora. Paul and his colleagues may have done some of this, but in 2:1–7 he seems to be contrasting himself with the typical itinerant teachers, who tried to attract hearers and their money among the throngs on the street. Some scholars argue persuasively that Paul was not a street-corner preacher like the Cynics, did not harangue people in the marketplace, but that the setting for his preaching was more like an informal schoolroom, attracting a group of curious hearers around him in his workplace or in private homes. After one or more house churches were founded, they would become the focus of Paul's evangelistic work.[29]

Jews? God-fearers? Gentiles? The letter itself is addressed to Gentile Christians (1:9–10). If the congregation contained a small minority of converts from Judaism, there is no indication of this in the letter.[30] Yet Paul himself continued to be a Jew his whole life; even after the Jerusalem Council, he was committed to being "a Jew to the Jews, in order to win Jews," subjecting himself to the discipline of the synagogue (1 Cor 9:20; 2 Cor 11:24). Some interpreters thus judge that there must have been a Jewish community in Thessalonica, that Paul must have preached to them, must have convinced some, and that the church included a minority of Jews, or even that most of his converts had been God-fearers familiar with and appreciative of their synagogue heritage.[31] It is sometimes argued that Paul could presuppose a knowledge of Judaism and its Scripture among most of his converts, and that this is what allowed him to found a new church and move on quickly, leaving it in the hands of the God-fearers-now-become-Christians. Otherwise, the argument goes, the readers of his letters would not have understood the frequent allusions to Scripture and Jewish tradition. Such an understanding does not reckon with the intensity of new converts in learning and adopting the language of their new symbolic universe, and with Paul's rhetoric of sometimes speaking over the heads of his hearers, whom he expects to rise to the level of his discourse. Moreover, if there

29. Cf. Hock 1979; 1980.

30. Todd Still (222) argues that Jews were in Thessalonica at the time of the founding visit and that they persecuted *Paul* as a renegade Jew, but he is not convinced that the *church* included Jewish Christians.

31. So, e.g., Holtz 1986, 112 and passim; Crossan and Reed xi. Most interpreters remain unconvinced by Reiser's argument that the aorist *epestrepsate* of 1:9 should be translated "had (already) turned to God from idols," which would mean that most of the congregation was composed of God-fearers from the synagogue. A few have argued that in any case God-fearers formed "a world of fuzzy boundaries," and that Gentiles who attended the synagogue would not necessarily have given up polytheism; Paul includes such God-fearers in his address (so Lieu; Blumenthal). In any case, it remains clear that 1 Thessalonians is addressed to Gentiles who, whatever their previous history, were first converted to the one true God in their encounter with the Christian gospel.

had been a significant number of Jews in the Thessalonian congregation, one would expect some reflection on the continuing (non)role of the Jewish law in the church, and the relation of Jewish and Gentile Christians to the purity code.

Social level. First Thessalonians provides no direct evidence of the social level of the new converts. Paul's admonition, "Live quietly . . . and work with your own hands" (1 Thess 4:11) seems to presuppose that the congregation was generally composed of working-class people. There is no reference to wealthy and influential members, to slaves or slave owners, or to problems resulting from clashes or misunderstandings among members of differing social levels. Later Paul will refer to the "extreme poverty" of the Macedonian churches in general (2 Cor 8:2)—though the church in Philippi was able to continue to support Paul during his Thessalonian mission (Phil 4:16).

Initial message. According to the pattern advocated by C. H. Dodd, a distinction should be made in the communications of the early church between *kerygma* (*kērygma*), the initial evangelistic message addressed to outsiders, and *didachē*, instruction in the Christian faith given to those already converted.[32] Although the two types of communication overlap, this remains a useful distinction.

The church was founded on the Pauline kerygma, the message proclaimed by Paul and Silvanus that the Thessalonian converts heard as "the word of God" (1 Thess 2:13). What was the content of the Christian preaching and teaching that caused such a change in the lives of the new believers, and caused them to be suspect and harassed by their neighbors? First Thessalonians is our only direct source for answering this question. The new converts only knew what Paul and his coworkers had taught them: no other Christian teachers had been to Thessalonica when Paul writes this letter. Of this, *we* only know what can be inferred from the letter, a procedure that is risky and certainly incomplete. The initial kerygma seems to have focused on the following core items:

- There is one true and living God (in contrast to lifeless idols, 1:9).
- This God sent his Son to die for us (5:10).
- God raised him from the dead and made him the living and reigning Lord (4:14).
- The Son of God will soon come again, for the salvation of believers (5:9).
- By this gospel, God now calls into being the eschatological people of God, the renewed holy people of the last days (1:4; 2:13; 4:7).

The message is focused on the Christ event, yet for those who respond, it includes the act of God's election of the hearers: responding to this message

32. Dodd 1960b.

means that God has chosen them to be included among the eschatological people of God elected not for privilege, but for witness and suffering. God is the actor throughout this drama. The christological proclamation points to God and results in a church: Christology implies an ecclesiology. The Christ event is not yet complete but points ahead to the eschatological consummation. For those who accept it, this kerygma generates a new symbolic universe. The new converts are not only transformed individuals; they also live in a new world, shortly to come into its own as the fulfillment of God's purpose.

This is an extension of apocalyptic Jewish missionary proclamation: One God, the Creator, will be the final judge of the world and save those who are in right relation to God. The crucial difference from Jewish apocalyptic, of course, is that the expected future Messiah, a central figure in some apocalyptic expectation, has already appeared in history, and will *return*, not just *appear*, as Messiah. This bare outline surely does not do justice to the full and powerful message that had transformed the lives of Paul's converts. It is, however, the authentic outline, not random elements of his preaching, and represents the central core and structure of Paul's missionary message. It corresponds to what we know of this message from Paul's other letters and from Acts (cf. 1 Cor 15:3–5; speeches in Acts). Some themes are striking by their absence from this core outline: there is no reference to the Scriptures and to the "life and teaching of Jesus," no reference to sin as the human problem separating human beings from God, no focus on the death of Jesus as providing forgiveness, or on the concept of justification by faith. In all this, we emphatically notice that Paul's kerygma did not begin with the human condition, attempting to convince his hearers that they were in need of forgiveness, but with the act of God in Christ. The human plight was revealed only in the light of God's saving act; the question became clear only when one heard the answer.[33]

The kerygma, in the sense of an abstract constellation of words or statements, did not stand alone as the generating power that called the faith of the new converts into being. The preaching of the gospel was accompanied by manifestations of the presence and power of the Spirit of God, and embodied in the committed lives of the missionaries (1 Thess 1:5). To some, it was overwhelmingly convincing and transforming.

Conversion. Although Paul's life had been completely transformed and reoriented by his encounter with the risen Christ, Paul himself had never been converted in the sense of leaving one religion and adopting another, nor in the sense of adopting an entirely new symbolic universe. He can indeed speak of his "earlier life in Judaism," acknowledging the sea change that had occurred in his relation to the religious world in which he had grown up, but he continued to speak of himself as a Jew, a member of the people of Israel (Gal 2:15; Rom

33. See E. P. Sanders 1977, 442–46.

9:4). His call to be an apostle did not call for a fundamental rearrangement of his worldview and mind-set.[34] Before becoming a Christian, Paul already believed in the one God, the Creator; he already believed that this one God had called into being a covenant people to be God's witnesses before the world; he already had an eschatology and already expected the "day of the Lord." The Thessalonians, on the other hand, were converted to a new symbolic world. Their acceptance of the Christian faith was a true conversion: they were called to leave their old religious world behind (1:9–10). From experience and vivid memory, they knew what this involved; Paul's letter does not rehearse the process, the particular elements or "steps" involved in conversion. From incidental references in 1 Thessalonians and Paul's other letters, we may confidently assume that their conversion involved (from the human side—Paul assumes their conversion was a matter of divine election and action, a response to God's primary act):

- Coming to faith as a response to the missionary preaching. "Believers" is a primary term in Paul's description of their new situation.
- *Repentance*, the standard Jewish term for turn/return to God, is absent from 1 Thessalonians, but *epistrephō* (turn) occurs as the crucial one-word summary (1:9). Thus "believing" and "turning" are not separate diachronic acts, but two sides of the same coin.
- Declaration of one's faith, confession, testimony, taking a public stand that identifies one with the Christian community—all are implicit throughout 1 Thessalonians, but nothing explicit is mentioned. Paul and the Thessalonians know what this involves.
- Baptism is not mentioned, but Paul assumes that all Christians are baptized, always arguing *from* this assumption, never *for* baptism (Rom 6:3–4; 1 Cor 1:14–17; 12:13; Gal 3:27). Baptism would be a public declaration of belonging to the new community of faith; it would also be associated with the presence of the Spirit at work in both individual and church and with incorporation into the Christian community.

Public faith. Modern Western readers will miss the historical and cultural reality if they imagine that, after their baptism, the new converts retired to their private lives, to practice their new faith as a matter of individual internal spirituality, on their own or in association with a small group of Christians out of the public eye. The whole concept of "private lives" was virtually unknown in Hellenistic society; this is one of the cultural differences that impede understanding the New Testament. Life in the Hellenistic city was essentially public. The mild

34. For this helpful terminology and for the distinctions between worldview and mind-set, see now Wright 2013, 23–36, 63–66, 1391–93.

winters and hot summers, combined with the small living quarters of most of the population (used mainly for sleeping and eating), meant that life was lived in the open. Cities were planned with broad plazas and large public areas, often with as much as 25 percent of the civic space devoted to public buildings. "The street was their living room. . . . In that sense, then, everyone spent his day at work or play in his neighbor's house."[35] In such a setting, changes in lifestyle were obvious. The new converts' lack of participating in activities previously enjoyed, especially cultic-patriotic events, would be conspicuous and provocative, with results that would have social and financial dimensions. Disruptions in patron-client relations were not trivial or minor inconveniences: they would not go unnoticed. The new converts would need to learn how to respond.

Duration of the founding visit. Acts portrays the missionaries preaching in the synagogue for "three sabbath days," winning several converts, and being expelled from the city shortly thereafter (Acts 17:1–10). Though older scholarship adopted this scene as historical, the picture from Paul's letter seems to require a longer time. The new congregation at Philippi repeatedly sent Paul financial help while he was in Thessalonica. A typical round trip would require eight or ten days of travel, plus the time between trips. By the time of Paul's departure, the new group of converts seems to have developed a level of congregational life that would require several weeks or months. The founding visit perhaps lasted about three months.

Departure. The missionaries left abruptly and involuntarily (1 Thess 2:8, 17). They seem to have been expelled, but no details are given in this letter; both author and readers know what happened. Paul and his coworker(s) have left behind an energetic and devoted congregation (1:3, 6), but a church still vulnerable to destructive attacks, and with gaps in its grasp of the faith (3:5, 10).

The New Congregation: Faith and Order, Life and Work

When the new converts in Thessalonica were baptized, they became part of a cohesive community of faith. When Paul and Silvanus were forced to leave Thessalonica, they did not merely leave behind a group of individuals who had experienced a life-altering conversion, but also a church feeling its way forward. They had been taught to think of themselves as now belonging to the holy people of God; they were struggling to come to terms with this new identity.[36] What was the life of this church like? Actual data are scarce. Inferences with

---

35. MacMullen 63, cited from Kloppenborg (274–75), whose insights are adopted in this paragraph.

36. Kraus (1996) rightly argues that Paul's ecclesiology can best be pictured as an ellipse with two complementary focal points: christologically, the body of Christ; strictly theologically, the elect people of God. The latter dominates in 1 Thessalonians.

varying degrees of support from the available evidence suggest the following plausible picture.

Regular assembly. The new converts met regularly together. Paul had always been accustomed to weekly worship and study on the Sabbath. The earliest church seems to have adopted the "first day of the week," the day of Jesus' resurrection, as their corresponding holy day. The practice likely began in the earliest days of the Palestinian churches, with Christian groups meeting informally on Saturday evening after the synagogue Sabbath service. In terms of the Jewish calendar, in which the new day begins at sundown, this would have been on Sunday. Paul seems to have instructed his new churches in this practice (cf. 1 Cor 16:1–2; Acts 20:7). While we do not have firm evidence for consistent Sunday worship among Christian congregations until early in the second century, we should probably picture the church in Thessalonica as having already established the practice of meeting regularly in the home(s) of sponsoring members, most likely on Saturday evenings or Sundays.

Worship. In 50 C.E. there was as yet no formal liturgy. Three or four years later in Corinth, worship was still spontaneous, led by the Spirit, but Paul insists that it should be "decently and in order" (1 Cor 14:26–33, 39–40). Assemblies of the new Christian community in Thessalonica were also enlivened by the spontaneity of the Spirit. Differently than in Corinth, some are inclined to *under*value it (1 Thess 5:19–20; cf. 1 Cor 12–14). It is not clear whether the congregation in Thessalonica followed the synagogue in making their worship mainly a service of the word, or whether the Eucharist already had a firm place. The extensive instructions in 1 Cor 11:17–34 seem to presuppose regular celebration of the Eucharist, in conjunction with a fellowship meal. There is every reason to believe that the eucharistic tradition Paul was establishing in Corinth at the same time he was writing 1 Thessalonians had already been established in Thessalonica when the congregation there was begun a few months earlier. The liturgical ending of 1 Cor 16:20–24 indicates that, at least a few years later, the sacramental meal normally followed the instruction of the community; the Revelation of John likewise seems to presuppose that the letter would be read in a worshiping congregation gathered at the eucharistic table. Later still, it could be assumed that the "breaking of bread" was the central act of the worshiping community (Acts 20:7).

Scripture? It is striking to the reader of Paul's other letters that there is no explicit appeal to Scripture in 1 Thessalonians. While there are a few allusions (e.g., 1 Thess 3:13//Zech 14:5; 1 Thess 4:5//Jer 10:25; Ps 79:6), these indicate that, here as elsewhere, Paul's own mind is steeped in biblical imagery and phraseology, not necessarily that he is alluding to Scripture for the benefit of his readers. One could say that, since it is a predominantly Gentile church, newly founded, the readers would not be expected to be familiar with the Jewish Scriptures. Yet the same is true of the churches founded later in the Pauline mission, and from 1 Corinthians onward, Paul regularly cites the Scriptures as though his readers were expected to recognize them. The earliest extant Christian creed, taught to the Corinthians and presumably to all the Pauline churches (1 Cor 15:3–5; cf. below), declares that the Christian message is *kata tas graphas* (according to the Scriptures). In any case, for Paul himself, it would have been inconceivable to have a Jewish or Christian congregation in which the reading (aloud) of Scripture did not play a central role.

It is thus very likely that the Thessalonian congregation had a copy or copies of the Scripture, read them regularly in worship, and that the contrast with Paul's later letters in regard to biblical citation calls for an explanation. First, the letter is not a didactic letter (see below on genre). Had Paul been intent on providing theological instruction, biblical citation would have been more appropriate. Second, and perhaps more important, the letter does not address a polemical situation in which proof from the Bible or evidence that what Paul is teaching is in accord with the Scripture is necessary. Thus he neither claims explicit apostolic authority nor cites the Bible in support of his teaching, which he assumes is unproblematically welcomed. On the chronology of Paul's Letters adopted here, this will also be the case for his next two letters, Philippians and Philemon, neither of which appeal directly to apostolic or biblical authority. This will change in 1 Corinthians and all later letters, after Paul becomes aware that rival Christian missionaries are dogging his tracks, challenging both his apostolic authority and the biblical basis for his mission.

The new Christian congregation in Thessalonica thus probably read the Scriptures in worship and was intensely engaged in their interpretation. It is likely that there was instruction in the Scriptures during Paul's stay of three months or so, and in the intervening months since his departure and the arrival of his letter. Modern secularized church members with a more casual approach to Scripture might ponder how much a serious and intense group, with qualified leadership, can learn in a few months. The question remains of how they obtained a copy of the Scriptures. How available were biblical scrolls in Thessalonica in the mid-first century? If the congregation included converts from the synagogue, would or could they have brought a copy with them? Did Paul and other Christian missionaries carry copies of (parts of?) the Scriptures with them, to be left with the new congregations? How practical would this have been? How expensive?

Leadership, ministry, officers. We have no way of estimating the size of the Thessalonian church; the congregation probably numbered dozens rather than hundreds. It was large enough, however, that some leaders had emerged, and Paul and his colleagues had selected and trained teachers, so that the congregation had some sort of established leadership. Despite its size and lack of institutionalized structure, we should not think of the new church as merely a small group of enthusiasts enjoying their new spirituality. There was enough structure that Paul could note and discourage deviations from the normal "order" (see on 5:12–14). However structured, the life of the congregation seems to have included those responsible for teaching, with some authorization to do so.

Instruction, catechesis. First Thessalonians repeatedly appeals to what the readers "already know" (1:5; 2:1, 2, 5, 11; 3:3, 4; 4:2; 5:2). While some of these are appeals to their memory of events that transpired while Paul was with them, others reflect teaching they had received then and in the interim after Paul's departure from the city (3:3, 4; 4:2; 5:2). The new symbolic universe that was inherent in accepting the gospel could not be communicated and assimilated instantly but required instruction and thoughtful appropriation. This would likely include repeated reading not only of biblical texts, but of Paul's letter (see on 5:27). It is difficult for the modern reader to grasp the radically new world the converts had entered, a world that involved apocalypticism, a telic view of history, a Christology that reversed previous expectations (a Christology the Thessalonians did not earlier have), a new self-understanding of themselves as belonging to the holy people of God, a new ethic, the meaning of faith, hope, and love.

While Paul adapted his instruction to different local situations, it is clear that he did not simply improvise in each new church; instead, he had a solid body of traditional material that he regarded as important for each church, material he had often already rethought in his own terms. Even to a church that he did not found and had not personally visited, Paul can regard as self-evident that a common body of teaching had been developed, that the church knew its content, which had not only been delivered to them, but to which they had been "delivered" (1 Cor 11:2; Rom 6:17; 16:17). Paul never spells out the content of this material he has already taught and presupposes is available in the churches, but only alludes to it as the occasion demands. He can cite a core creedal statement he has himself been taught when he joined the church, and that he continues to transmit in the churches he established (1 Cor 15:3–5), and the liturgical formula for the eucharistic celebration (1 Cor 11:23–26). Paul can cite a body of ethical teaching, "my ways in Christ," and indicate that he communicated this "in every church" (1 Cor 4:17, sent to the church founded immediately after Thessalonica). See also Paul's words to the Philippians, the church founded immediately before Thessalonica: "Keep on doing the things that you have learned and received and heard and seen in me" (Phil 4:9 NRSV). In later letters, Paul will cite firm baptismal traditions such as Gal 3:26–28. It is likely that these had already been developed in the Antioch church while Paul was there, and that he taught them in his new churches in the Aegean mission.

Moreover, a series of texts in the Pauline corpus seem to stand out from their context as discrete units and to manifest unpauline vocabulary, but have points of contact with Jewish wisdom tradition. Such texts were not created ad hoc for their present contexts, but seem to have been preformed units that had been shaped in the discussions of students and teachers around Paul, the products of a Pauline school tradition that began already in Paul's lifetime (e.g., 1 Cor 2:6–13; 13:1–13; Rom 1:18–32).[37] Such samples may represent only the tip of the iceberg. Paul's experience as a Pharisee could well have prepared him to think in terms of developing a core of students who transmitted traditions. His strategy of establishing a mission center in important cities from which trained coworkers could be sent to the new churches in the region presupposes the training of these partners and assistants in the framework of a school-like setting.

Since the work of Malherbe in comparing Paul's statements to those of traveling Cynic teachers, the section 1 Thess 2:1–12 has often been regarded as illumined by regarding Paul's self-understanding in this light: the church founder is also a teacher, who instructs the new community in a particular tradition and prepares others to do so (see on 2:1–12). Further, the unproblematic way Paul uses such terms as "Son of God," "Christ," "church," "kingdom of God," and "saints" indicates that he and his colleagues must have given some instruction during the church-founding visit. This instruction included the learning of some new words, but mostly it involved using the old vocabulary with new meanings.[38] The new symbolic universe brought with it a new language, the idiolect of the in-group, which distinguished them from outsiders. This renewal of language expressed in the new dialect of the church as the elect people of God was inherited from earlier churches, transmitted by tradition, expanded and enriched by their own situation and experience. This new language and grammar of faith was partially absorbed by participation in the Christian community, and partially intentionally transmitted by Paul and the teachers he had trained. This teaching did not cease when the founding missionaries left town. Within the Pauline congregations, the teachers formed an identifiable group (1 Cor 12:28–29; Rom 12:7; cf. the later Eph 4:11). The church had teachers, trained and appointed by Paul and authorized by the Spirit.[39]

---

37. The concept and term "Pauline school" was already used in 1880 in the work of Holtzmann on the Pastorals (117). In more recent research, this view has been widely though not universally accepted, furthered esp. by the work of Conzelmann 1974; 1979. See now Schmeller and Cebulj 16–17; and Vegge.

38. A key example would be the term fundamental to the new faith, *Christos* (Christ), an ordinary secular word that means "smeared" (with oil or other ointment) but now was filled with the Jewish Christian tradition of messianic faith in Jesus as the one anointed by God, the promised eschatological Savior. Many other common words underwent similar transformations: e.g., the common word for getting up in the morning or erecting a statue (*anastasis*, rising) became the word for eschatological resurrection. *Agapē* was a secular word for "love," with a broad spectrum of meanings from erotic love through the love of money to the compassionate care of a mother for her child. In the Christian idiolect, *agapē* became the key word for caring for others and could sum up the Christian ethic as such.

39. See Martyn (552) on Gal 6:6, which explicitly refers to church teachers. So also Hays 2005a, 8–9.

Ecclesial self-understanding. In accord with Paul's preaching, the little congregation had accepted its identity as part of the ongoing people of the God of Israel, the one true God. It was not a local Jesus club, but the group knew that it belonged to the one church, the wider network of Christian congregations that already reached from Judea to Macedonia and Achaia (1 Thess 1:8; 2:14). It established and maintained contact with these sister congregations and was known by them. It saw itself as having a mission to proclaim God's word to the world. It was willing to suffer for its faith (1:6; 2:14) and to share the faith with others. It became a mission center from which other congregations were founded, and became well known among the network of new churches (1:8–9).

Conflicts, troubles, distress, persecution. From the beginning the new converts in Thessalonica knew that their confession of faith, baptism, and formation of a new religious community would place them in fundamental tension with their society and that they would suffer for it. This was part of the initial proclamation (see on 3:3–4). Troubles in Thessalonica forced the missionary team to leave. If there was a Jewish community in Thessalonica, those people might well have opposed Paul's preaching, whether or not Paul attempted Christian missionary preaching in the synagogue, as reported in Acts 17:1–2. Paul's preaching typically generated conflicts with the synagogue, as indicated by Acts and confirmed by his own letters (2 Cor 11:24; Acts 13–14, 17–18). When Paul came to Thessalonica, Claudius had just expelled Jews, including Jewish Christians, from Rome because of rioting within the Jewish community generated by the preaching of Christian missionaries. This unsettling news may have reached Thessalonica while Paul was there. It is even possible that refugees from Rome, including Jewish Christians, had followed the Egnatian Way to Thessalonica, where they would not be pleased to find Paul preaching the message that had just caused so much unrest in Rome. Neither Thessalonian Jews, if there were such, nor local authorities responsible for law and order in the city would be inclined to welcome representatives of the faith that had caused the emperor to expel them from the capital. We do not know the details or who was directly responsible, but the mission in the city seems to have come to an abrupt end. The hostilities that had caused Paul to leave have continued to plague the new converts, who suffered abuse because of their new faith. It was a tumultuous time (Acts 17:6, "These men have turned the world upside down") in which Jews in cities outside Rome opposed the new group not only on the basis of religious convictions but also as a matter of political and social prudence: if others regarded the new Christian group as a party within Judaism, the Jews' own precarious economic and social position was endangered.[40] If there was a Jewish community in Thessalonica, it would look askance at missionaries

---

40. Cf. Acts 19:33–34, where Christian troublemakers are identified by the local populace as Jews. This is what Jews wanted to avoid, and why they joined the Roman side against Christians.

calling attention to Jews precisely when they were trying to maintain a low profile. Likewise, citizens grateful for the order, peace, and prosperity brought by Rome resisted what appeared to be a subversive cult proclaiming that an Easterner who had been executed as dangerously anti-Roman was alive and would inaugurate a new kingdom (Acts 17:7–8; cf. below on 1 Thess 2:14–16; 3:3, 7).

The Letter

Text

The oldest extant manuscript of any part of the Thessalonian correspondence is found in the Chester Beatty Papyrus $\mathfrak{P}^{46}$, copied about 200 C.E. This codex had numbered pages, so we can determine that it originally contained 104 leaves. The 86 leaves presently known to exist show that this collection of Pauline Letters included, in order, Romans, Hebrews, 1–2 Corinthians, Ephesians, Galatians, Philippians, Colossians, and 1 Thessalonians. The leaves have mostly been preserved whole and in good readable condition, though a few exist only in fragments. Unfortunately for our present interests, the Thessalonian Letters are represented by only two small fragments, containing parts of 1 Thess 1:1–2; 1:9–2:3; 5:5–9, 23–28. The physical structure of the codex shows that there was room for 2 Thessalonians (but not the Pastorals), but no fragments have been preserved. Most of the words of 1 Thessalonians are fragmentary, but recognizable; only nineteen words are preserved intact. None are particularly important for textual criticism. So far as 1–2 Thessalonians are concerned, the significance of $\mathfrak{P}^{46}$ is in documenting that, at least by the end of the second century C.E., 1 Thessalonians (and presumably 2 Thessalonians) circulated as part of the Pauline corpus.

From the third century C.E. we have fragments of two other manuscripts (MSS) of 1–2 Thessalonians, $\mathfrak{P}^{30}$ and $\mathfrak{P}^{65}$; and $\mathfrak{P}^{92}$ is from the late third or early fourth century C.E.; but these are of little significance for reconstructing the original text. $\mathfrak{P}^{30}$, with fragments of 1 Thess 4–5 and 2 Thess 1, is our earliest extant MS evidence of 2 Thessalonians. It is not until the great fourth-century MSS Vaticanus (B) and Sinaiticus (ℵ) that we obtain complete texts of 1–2 Thessalonians. These, along with the fifth-century Codices Alexandrinus (A) and Ephraemi rescriptus (C) and the sixth-century Claromontanus (D^P), when critically compared with each other and selected later MSS, provide a solid basis for approximating the original text very closely.

In relatively few instances is there real debate as to the original text. A comparison of the current 28th edition of the standard Nestle-Aland text with the text of the 25th edition in 1963, the last major revision of the text, reveals only thirteen editorial changes in the 2,309 words of Greek text. A standard handbook discussing all the significant variations examined by the Nestle-Aland and

UBS[4] editors discusses only 28 variants in 1–2 Thessalonians.[41] There are thus no dramatic variations in the MSS of 1–2 Thessalonians that compare with the endings of the Gospel of Mark, the conclusion(s) of Romans, or the *Comma Johanneum* (1 John 5:7). Nonetheless, at several points there are textual variations of some significance for the meaning of the text, which will be discussed in the translation and textual notes for each section of the text.

Epistolary Genre and Rhetorical Analysis

1 Thessalonians Is a Letter

First Thessalonians is a letter (*epistolē*, 5:27). It is not an essay or treatise, not a collection of inspirational verses. Nor is it a "book." Yet in the ancient world, the generic label "letter" covered a broad spectrum. Just as today a business letter, a letter to the editor, a letter applying for a job, a letter of condolence, a letter of recommendation, and a personal letter of friendship—all are found under the broad heading of "letter," so also the term *epistolē* was used in antiquity to designate a variety of genres and subgenres. Virtually all readers of this commentary have been instructed in the schoolroom on the proper form for personal letters and the different forms of business letters, memos, open letters, and letters to the editor—and the genre bending involved in combinations such as the blend of a personal and business letter. We would be startled or amused to receive a letter from a friend on a personal subject that was formatted in the style of a "business letter," and we would be unlikely to receive a job interview if our application were in the form of a personal letter. In the ancient world too, the content, function, and effectiveness of a letter were closely related to the category into which writer and readers understood it to fit, and the forms associated with each type.

Does 1 Thessalonians belong to a particular type of Hellenistic letter? Letter writing was a refined art in the Hellenistic world. Already in Paul's day, there were handbooks on letter types, with instructions and brief samples, apparently written for professional scribes in the employ of public officials. A manual attributed to a certain Demetrius, *Epistolary Types* (*Typoi epistolikoi*), lists twenty-one types, including friendly (*philikos*), praising (*epainetikos*), admonishing (*nouthetēkos*), and apologetic (*apologētikos*).[42] When previous generations understood all of Paul's Letters as repositories of Christian doctrine, 1 Thessalonians was understood as a *didactic* letter. However, while 1 Thessalonians has much to teach the modern reader about Paul's preaching, teaching, and theology, and about the life of an early Christian community, it had little

41. Metzger 629–34.
42. An ET is available in Malherbe 1988, 16–20.

new doctrinal content to teach the Thessalonians. It was not a didactic letter, like 1 Corinthians and Romans. It magnifies teaching, refers to teaching that Paul had done while present, but does not present itself as a teaching document. First Thessalonians has sometimes been understood as an *apologetic* letter, but the main purpose of the letter is not to defend either Paul's conduct or his theology. Recent discussion has centered on whether 1 Thessalonians is a *paraenetic* letter, giving directions and exhortations for the Christian life (so Malherbe); or a *paracletic* letter, offering comfort, encouragement, and consolation, a *consolatio* (so Donfried).[43] From the latter perspective, the central question addressed by the letter is whether it is worthwhile to continue as a professed Christian believer when it can endanger one's place in society and even one's life. We shall see that in 1 Thessalonians, Paul adopts and adapts the conventions of Hellenistic writers, without strictly following one particular model.

1 Thessalonians Is a Real Letter

"I am working for later generations, writing down some ideas that may be of assistance to them." So wrote Seneca, Roman philosopher and statesman, a contemporary of Paul (ca. 4 B.C.E.–65 C.E.), who wrote hundreds of letters (*Ep.* 8.2; cf. 21.5). A collection of 931 letters was published after his death. No doubt he too wrote brief personal notes that qualify as real letters, but these are mostly lost. Preserved in Seneca's literary legacy is a collection of 124 letters written to his friend Gaius Lucilius. We know that Lucilius was a real person, but the documents addressed to him in letter form are not real letters in the sense that 1 Thessalonians is a real letter. Even if Seneca's compositions were actually delivered to Gaius Lucilius as letters, it is clear that as Seneca writes he is composing not just for Lucilius, but producing essays and book-like compositions, with the wider world and future generations looking over his shoulder. In Seneca's published letters, the letter form is a literary device, and has a fictive character. A literary letter is like a book in that the author does not know the intended readers personally but is writing for whoever is interested. A real letter is composed for a particular person or limited group sharing a common history, known to the author and addressing the particularities of their concerns. That is the case here.

1 Thessalonians is a real letter. Real letters mediate the presence of the writer to the distant reader. The letter is not only a substitute for the writer's personal presence, but is also the bearer of the writer's living voice. Paul wanted to be present and address his readers face-to-face (cf. 1 Thess 2:17–18; 3:10). When

---

43. Donfried (2002b, 137–38) details his disagreements with Malherbe on the genre of the letter and argues that the *consolatio* includes paraenesis as well as elements of apologia. See Charles Favez, "Consolatio," *OCD* 279.

this was not possible, he composed a letter to be read forth to the assembled house-church congregation. The letter mediates his person and presence; when read aloud to the worshiping congregation, it is Paul's voice that they hear.

Ancient theorists of letter writing considered the letter to be a continuation of, or substitute for, an oral conversation. A letter is half of a conversation, but in contrast to the first readers, it is the only half the modern reader hears. Both the Thessalonians and Paul knew all the events from his first arrival, through the stormy times he was with them, his sudden departure, what had happened in the meantime, Timothy's visit with them—and now they receive this letter. Newcomers to the community needed to be brought up to speed in order to understand the letter. All the more so for the modern reader. This is the role of historical study.

Even though the letter itself was a written text, the oral/aural medium of communication must be kept clearly in mind. The author dictated the letter to a scribe or secretary, speaking as he would speak to the addressees. The "readers" were in fact hearers, as the letter was read forth in the congregation. All reading was truly an oral/aural experience; even private reading was a matter of reading aloud and hearing what one read.[44]

1 Thessalonians Shares the Form of Hellenistic Letters

Early Christianity was born in a letter-writing culture. We have more than 14,000 examples of ancient letters. Most are brief private letters recovered from the dry sands of Egypt, but hundreds are from collections of literary letters that circulated in the ancient world, readily available to all educated people. Hans-Josef Klauck lists 38 such freestanding collections of Greek letters, as well as numerous letters quoted, embedded, or summarized in other literary works, and a comparable number of Latin collections and letters, as well as copious examples of letters from the Old Testament, Jewish, and other ancient litera-ture.[45] This array of ancient letters provides an extensive grid against which to examine and compare New Testament letters.

Paul's Letters manifest an identifiable form and structure that is more or less consistent through all his letters, a form that consists of Paul's own transforma-tions of the conventional Hellenistic letter, with features adopted from Greek rhetoric and Jewish epistolography. Typical letters in the Hellenistic world

---

44. Cf. Acts 8:30, in which Philip hears the Ethiopian official reading to himself; in John 8:8–9, those around Jesus *hear* what he has written on the ground, i.e., it is read aloud. Cicero is purported to have said: "I am sorry I have not responded to your letter sooner, but I have had a sore throat." In the 5th cent. c.e., Augustine still marveled that Ambrose read silently (Augustine, *Confessions* 6.3). Cf. Doty 7.

45. See Klauck 17–42, "Standard Letter Components"; Doty 27–43; Stowers 49–174.

consisted of three parts: introduction, body, and conclusion. Each part might be subdivided as follows:

I. Introduction
  A. Prescript (Greeting), in three stereotypical parts: A to B, greetings
    1. sender: *superscriptio*
    2. addressee: *adscriptio*
    3. greeting: *salutatio* (*chairein*, greetings; lit., "rejoice")
  B. Proem (Thanksgiving), which may consist of one or more of the following:
    1. prayer-wish (*euchomai*, I pray)
    2. thanksgiving (*eucharistō*, I give thanks)
    3. intercession, remembrance (*mneian poioumenos*, making remembrance) before the gods
    4. expression of joy (*chara, echarēn*, joy, I rejoice)
II. Body
  A. Body opening, sometimes with conventional formula such as "I want you to know"
  B. Body middle: information, instruction, request, recommendation, exhortation
  C. Body closing: summary exhortations, travel plans
III. Conclusion
  A. Epilogue: concluding exhortations, future plans
  B. Postscript:
    1. greetings from those with the writer, to those with the reader
    2. farewell (*errōsthe*, lit., be strong)
    3. final words in author's own hand
    4. date

The Form of 1 Thessalonians Is Influenced by Ancient Jewish Letters

The early twentieth-century rediscovery of Paul's Letters as real letters instead of religious treatises, represented especially by the work of Adolf Deissmann, concentrated on the Greco-Roman letter as Paul's point of departure.[46] In Deissmann's wake, Hellenistic epistolography was thoroughly studied, but minimal attention was given to the possible influence of *Jewish* epistolography on Paul's epistolary practice. Yet Paul was familiar with Jewish epistolary forms and functions found in the numerous letters embedded in the Jewish Scriptures, especially in the LXX. One thinks readily of the two letters at the beginning of

46. Deissmann 1957, 7–26.

2 Maccabees (1:1–9; 1:10–2:18), official letters from the leaders of the Jewish community in Jerusalem, with instructions that encourage them to adopt the new Feast of Dedication (Hanukkah). Probably more important to Paul was Jeremiah's letter to the exiles (29:4–28), which deals with the conduct of the covenant people in an alien environment, the roles of officers and people, and the hopes of the covenant community—themes reflected in 1 Thessalonians. Jeremiah was a significant figure for Paul (see on 5:27). Paul would also have known the variety of "regulatory" letters sent by Jewish leaders to synagogues and communities of his own time. This potentially illuminating influence on Paul's letter writing has recently been thoroughly explored and will be considered at relevant points in the commentary.[47]

1 Thessalonians Is Influenced by Rhetorical Practice in the Hellenistic World

When we speak of ancient rhetoric, we are not using the term with the connotations it has sometimes acquired in contemporary culture: insubstantial or deceitful fluff that avoids or conceals one's real intent. In the ancient world rhetoric was simply the art of skilled communication and persuasion, a matter of advanced, graduate-level education, a skill needed by good leaders. Hearers and readers listened with a set of expectations of what constituted a respectable speech, and they could peremptorily dismiss those who did not measure up. There were rhetorical handbooks on effective communication that both exhibited and nurtured such skills and developed the expectations of educated people as to what a good speech or composition should be. The analysis of communication strategies built into a text can facilitate the reader's understanding of not only what it means, but also *how* it means, how it leads the reader to a conclusion.

Paul's opponents and detractors sometimes accused him of lacking rhetorical ability—though they acknowledged that he wrote powerful letters (2 Cor 10–11)—and Paul himself sometimes seems to disavow rhetorical skill, and to contrast it with the real power of God (1 Cor 2:4–5). Today it is widely accepted that Paul, as an educated person deeply embedded in his own culture, knew something of rhetorical practice and put his knowledge to work in composing his letters. This is only natural, since Paul thought of his letters as his own speech, communicated in written form but delivered orally and heard as his own voice by the listening congregation. Thus as he composes his letter, he would be thinking not only of epistolary form, but also of rhetorical structure.[48]

---

47. See now esp. Doering.

48. A helpful chart of overlapping epistolary and rhetorical structures in 1 Thessalonians is provided by Ascough 2009, 570. We must not draw too firm a line between the categories of epistolography and rhetoric. Several of the 21 *epistolary* types cited in the handbook of Pseudo-Demetrius are designated with the technical terminology used in *rhetorical* study. Cf. Hughes 1990.

The extent and intentional explicitness of his use of rhetorical forms continues to be disputed.

The issue of which rhetorical category provides the framework and structure for the composition of 1 Thessalonians continues to be discussed. Aristotle provided the rhetorical categories still used in the Hellenistic world: the *epideictic*, *forensic*, and *deliberative* genres. *Epideictic* rhetoric focuses on the present and uses praise and/or blame in trying to persuade the audience to maintain or reaffirm a particular point of view. *Forensic* rhetoric defends or accuses, attempting to persuade the hearers to make a judgment about some past event. *Deliberative* rhetoric points the hearers to the future, often the near future, as the speaker tries to persuade them to adopt a particular course of action. While it was popular in a past generation to regard 1 Thessalonians as an apologetic letter defending Paul's conduct during the church-founding visit, most now place the letter in the epideictic genre. Its purpose is primarily to praise, encourage, and console, not to defend or persuade. This is in contrast to the rhetoric of 2 Thessalonians, which belongs to the category of deliberative rhetoric.[49]

Most contemporary Pauline scholars see value in rhetorical criticism,[50] but many regard the composition of a Pauline letter as more complex than presupposed by rhetorical handbooks, and so they hesitate to see Paul as rigidly following set rhetorical patterns. Both epistolary and rhetorical forms were known and used by Paul, but Paul's sense of the new, eschatological situation in which he was participating as an apostle of the risen Christ moved him toward the generation of a new form that creatively combined a variety of elements: the "apostolic letter."

1 Thessalonians Is a New Generic Departure, the Apostolic Letter

The Thessalonians had read and heard letters before, but they had never experienced anything quite like what they heard when, at Paul's insistence, his letter was read aloud to the assembled congregation (1 Thess 5:27). The Pauline letter form was not, of course, absolutely new or unique—only God creates ex nihilo—but it is increasingly recognized that with this earliest Pauline letter, Paul intentionally created a distinctively new epistolary genre that may be called the "apostolic letter."[51] Here "apostolic" does not mean merely "written by an apostle," as though the personal claim to authority were paramount, but

49. So, e.g., Donfried 1993a, 3–9; Hughes 1989. For a recent strong argument reasserting the apologetic genre of 1 Thessalonians, see Kim 2005.

50. For an up-to-date, succinct, and nuanced summary, see Lampe.

51. The Pauline letter as a new, distinctive genre was already recognized at least as early as Rengstorf's 1964 article; see Karl H. Rengstorf, *"apostellō ktl.," TDNT* 1:398–447; idem, *"epistellō, epistolē," TDNT* 7:593. This view has been affirmed and elaborated by, e.g., K. Berger 1974; Koester 1979; Olbricht; John White 1983; R. Collins 1984a, 26.

"mediator and norm of the apostolic faith," bound up with Paul's sense of being entrusted with the gospel, which must be shared by the church as a whole (see on 1 Thess 2:4). In the new situation of the Aegean mission, Paul consciously formulates a new means to instruct and direct "his" congregations in the apostolic faith. No longer working under the direction of the Antioch church, he has found himself responsible for the founding, leadership, and pastoral care of scattered congregations struggling to formulate and maintain their new identity and self-understanding. He writes "under daily pressure because of my anxiety for all the churches" (2 Cor 11:28 NRSV). Paul writes as an interpreter. The gospel itself is a given; Paul is not interpreting himself or maneuvering to maintain his own power and control. It is the gospel that must be interpreted in the continuing life of the church. Paul constantly finds himself having to be the interpreter of his own message, applying it to the particular issues that emerge in his congregations.[52] In the letters, we see Paul the interpreter at work, building the road as he goes. He did not choose or utilize the letter form casually, but consciously and intentionally devised it as a means of communication, instruction, warning, and encouragement. He would come to use the letter as an image for the church itself, a letter from Christ to the world (2 Cor 3:1–3).

This is an extraordinary phenomenon, not always appreciated by those who have long been familiar with the shape and contents of the New Testament. Readers not inside the Christian tradition or dulled by familiarity with the Bible may be struck by the domination of the letter form in the New Testament. No other religious community includes letters as a pervasive element in its sacred writings. The Letters of Paul established a tradition followed not only by the Deuteropaulines but also by the Catholic Letters, Revelation, and much patristic literature. While not absolutely unique, the combination of characteristic features that came at the turning point in his mission represented by 1 Thessalonians set the Pauline letter apart as a distinctive new epistolary genre. These include the following features:

- *Length*. Except for Philemon, all the Pauline Letters are much longer than the typical Hellenistic letter.
- *Plural authorship*. Except for Romans, written to a church he had not founded and had never visited, all the Pauline Letters represent themselves as sent not only by Paul but also by one or more coworkers (see commentary on 1:1). This is unique among ancient letters.
- *Addressed to communities*. No extant Pauline letter is a private missive. Even the letter to Philemon is addressed to the church.

---

52. Cf. Keck and Furnish 63–108, ch. 4, "Paul as Interpreter."

Paul expects it to be read aloud to the assembled congregation, in Philemon's presence, and to function accordingly. Paul's Letters functioned within a social network and were quasi-official, like the letters some Jewish leaders sent to their communities.[53]

* *Incorporation of tradition and liturgical forms.* Form criticism shows that 1 Thessalonians was intended to be read in community worship, incorporating liturgical and catechetical forms. Although the Thessalonian Christians have never heard a letter that greets them with "grace and peace," they have probably heard the phrase—in Paul's preaching and in the liturgical greeting and blessing.

* *Prophetic self-understanding.* Paul's own self-understanding as an apostle included a prophetic consciousness: an awareness that he was called and sent by God, that he spoke with the authority and sometimes with the very words of the risen Lord (see on 5:27). The Thessalonian congregation was familiar with charismatic and prophetic speech in its own worship. The authority of the absent Paul is mediated by the apostolic letter. As it is read forth in worship, it carries the overtones of prophetic address.

Outline and Structure

The preceding considerations suggest the following conclusions. First Thessalonians initiates a new epistolary genre. The letter is not a random structure, but Paul's creative adaptation of the standard Hellenistic letter form, influenced by elements from Jewish epistolography and aspects of Greek rhetoric. In Paul's later letters, initial greeting is followed by the thanksgiving (the angry Letter to the Galatians being the only exception; 2 Corinthians has a thanksgiving in the form of a blessing); then as a separate section comes the main body of the letter. The body of the Pauline letter reflects the basic structure of Paul's theology, an ellipse with two inseparable poles. The primary orientation point for all of Paul's thought is the conviction that God has acted in Christ for the salvation of the world. The secondary orientation point is the human response; God's grace calls for human gratitude. The Christian life is not a new law, not a moralism, but is the believer's grateful response to the saving act of God. God's saving acts in the past, present, and future call for the believer's actions in the present.[54] These two poles can be expressed in a series of descriptive complementary pairs, inseparable and dynamically related:

---

53. Cf. Doering 383–93.

54. This pattern is, of course, here outlined more abstractly and schematically than in Paul's actual letters, to facilitate the modern readers' grasp of the basic Pauline pattern.

A	//	B
God's act	//	human response
God the Savior	//	the saved community's life
euangelion (gospel)	//	paraenesis (exhortation)
Grace (*charis*)	//	gratitude-faith, thus
charis-as-God's-grace	//	*charis*-as-human-gratitude
theology	//	ethics
indicative	//	imperative
promise	//	challenge
narrative	//	exhortation
kerygma	//	*didachē*

These two poles must first be clearly seen, but must be seen in such a way that neither element can stand alone. The left column taken by itself results in theological abstraction. The right column in isolation tends toward legalistic moralism. Taken together, the two poles correspond to the shape of covenant commitment in the Old Testament and the Bible as a whole: God's gracious act makes authentic human response both possible and necessary. This pattern is seen most clearly in the Decalogue (Exod 20:2–17), prefatory to the Book of the Covenant, 20:22–23:33, which begins, "I am the LORD your God, who brought you out of the land of Egypt, out of the house of slavery. // [Therefore] you shall have no other gods before me" (NRSV). This pattern had been adopted in some Jewish letters prior to Paul.[55] Doering points out that the letter 4QMMT was very popular at Qumran, where six copies have been found. It manifests the bipartite structure of a halakic section followed by a homiletic section.

For Paul, these two foci are not diachronic, with a "doctrinal stage one" followed by a "hortatory stage two," and by no means a "theoretical part" by "Paul the theologian" followed by a "practical application" provided by "Paul the pastor."[56] The two poles are not fragmentary or sequential, as though Paul's complete view might be obtained by combining them. The dipolarity of Paul's theology is analogous to the force field of a magnet: all magnets are dipolar, with no possibility that either pole could exist alone. It would thus be a total misunderstanding to regard salvation and Christian life for Paul as a matter of parts: God's part and the believer's part. In this juxtaposition of indicative and imperative, each pole of the dynamic force field represents Paul's view in its entirety. Occasionally Paul uses the theologically thick term *paraklēsis* to represent the fusion of these two foci in the apostolic preaching: the announcement of the saving eschatological act of God in the Christ event is fused with (= seen

---

55. Doering 197.

56. This point was already made powerfully and repeatedly in Furnish's 1968 classic work, now revised and reprinted as Furnish 2009b; see esp. 98–111, "The Problem of 'Kerygma' and 'Didache.'" See now also Wright 2013, 1098–99 and often. For a critique of a too-simple and too-rigid understanding of the indicative/imperative scheme, see esp. Zimmermann.

together with) the invitation and encouragement to respond. The act of God calls for human response, and the imperative has the tone of invitation and appeal, not demand in the legal sense (see further trans. note d and comments on 2:3).

The typical structure of the body of Paul's Letters corresponds to the dipolarity of his theology, the interaction of two poles, sometimes separated into two distinct sections.[57] In Paul's Letters, this structure is most visible in Romans, his latest, longest, and most systematic letter, written to a church he did not found and to which he had never been, a letter in which he could express the structure of his own thought most clearly. Broadly speaking, Rom 1–11 represent God's act, and chapters 12–16 the human response. The transition is marked by the "I appeal to you *therefore* [*oun*] . . ." of 12:1. This structure is also seen in Gal 1–4 / 5–6.[58]

An adaptation of this pattern is already apparent in the composition of 1 Thessalonians, where the thanksgiving that begins at 1:2 modulates into the more indicative first part of the letter body, which extends through 3:13, followed by the more hortatory second part of the body beginning at 4:1 (see comments at 1:2 and 4:1). While the division between the two parts is not rigid or mechanical, it can hardly be without significance that the twenty-eight imperatives or hortatory subjunctives all occur in chapters 4–5. Part one, the thanksgiving/body A, concludes with a prayer in the rare optative mood (3:11–13), just as does body B, the second, paraenetic part of the letter body (5:23). These considerations lead to the following outline of 1 Thessalonians:

1:1	Greeting
1:2–3:13	Thanksgiving to the God who calls the church and keeps it holy until the end
1:2–10	The Thessalonians' reception of Paul's gospel
2:1–12	Apostolic missionaries worthy of God
2:13–16	God's word and human opposition
2:17–3:10	Mutuality of the mission: Timothy brings good news
3:11–13	Transitional summary and prayer

57. Unlike a synchronic image—mental or graphic—in which everything is before the viewer simultaneously, a letter is a diachronic text in which one element must necessarily follow another. This necessary discursive separation should not be thought of as a distinct separation of theological and practical sections. In Paul's Letters, theology and practical pastoral concern are interwoven throughout, two sides of the same coin. In particular, it would be utterly unpauline to think of Paul as saying to himself, "Well now, that's it for the theoretical section—on to the practical application."

58. Though the indicative/imperative, dialectical structure of Paul's thought remains evident in 1 and 2 Corinthians as well, the literary pattern is obscured in 1 Corinthians by the serial treatment of particular problems, and in 2 Corinthians by the fact that the present form of the letter is the result of a later editorial process. The deuteropauline Col 1–2 / 3–4 and Eph 1–3 / 4–6, no longer constrained by addressing the situation of one particular church, repristinate the Pauline pattern.

Theological Perspectives on the Letter Form

Why letters? It is not self-evident that Paul should have devised the "apostolic letter" as the written means of communicating with and administering the new churches he had established. He could, for example, have written a creedal document, theological essay, or something like the Qumran *Manual of Discipline* (1QS) outlining his basic principles, and then had this delivered and deposited in the churches he established. But letters have an inherent generic appropriateness as expressions of the Christian faith.

Appropriate to the incarnation. We have seen that Paul writes real letters (as distinct from books and literary letters) that are not general, but written by a particular person to particular people and deal with particular situations. Rather than stating grand general truths, they fully enter into the particular situation of their readers. If Paul had mistakenly taken the Letter to the Galatians and sent it to the Christians in Thessalonica, they and we would understand it entirely differently—even though it would contain exactly the same words.[59] This scandal of particularity is inherent in the Christian faith. The early Christians did not believe that God became incarnate in humanity in general, or in some abstract principle, but in one particular Aramaic-speaking Jew, born in an obscure land under Roman rule, crucified under the local governor Pontius Pilate. Paul's Letters participate in this particularity: they are not directed to humanity in general or to the universal church, but to the nitty-gritty of particular congregations. This particularity is related to the essential character of human life. No one lives in general; every human life is unique. The Letters of the New Testament are appropriate to the incarnation.

Narrative World, Symbolic Universe, and Ethics

Real letters project a narrative world that is important for their interpretation. "Letters have stories."[60] The letter represents a segment of a narrative line shared by author and reader(s). This becomes important in studying the Pauline

---

59. Furnish 2009a, 16, citing Willi Marxsen. Cf. now Nasrallah 2012, 53–74, whose essay well illustrates her thesis that "Paul's letters are occasional and specific. . . . *The places to which they were sent matters*" (54, with original emphasis).

60. Petersen 1985, ix, 2. On the narrative world of epistolary literature, see Boring 2007; B. Longenecker, and the bibliography there provided.

and other New Testament Letters: *to understand a letter, one needs to recognize the narrative in which it is embedded and which it projects, for the letter is a narrative form.*

Human existence has an essentially narrative character. Human beings exist diachronically, in space and time. To be human is to have a story. As a human being, I do not exist as a timeless essence, but as a sequence of events in space and time. I cannot discover my true self by looking within for some nuclear center that defines my being. I become who I am by the decisions I make as I inevitably move through time and space. Under the space-time conditions of human existence and the sovereignty of God, I am the author of the story that I am. As a human being, my story is not something optional or extra that I as a human self "have." I am my story. Just as I am not an immaterial "soul" that exists encased *in* a material body, but exist *as* a body, so I do not only *have* a story, but in my essential being I *am* a story, and I do not exist as a human being apart from the narrative that defines my being.

The little narrative that defines my life is a segment of a larger story. My self-understanding is shaped by how I see this larger symbolic universe that gives meaning to my life. By assuming (not "teaching") a particular narrative world that encompasses my little life, the letter indirectly—softly but powerfully—challenges me to pose the question "In what cosmos do we actually live?"[61]

The New Testament Letters are written to instruct the readers on how to live in the light of Christian faith. These letters include paraenesis that seems to present this instruction directly: "Do this," "Don't do that." Such paraenetic materials are heard differently, however, when read within their epistolary setting, which is a narrative context. The reader does not merely look at the command or exhortation and decide whether or not to do it, not even on the basis of weighing the arguments or authority expressed in the letter's discourse. Rather, readers of letters are addressed as though they actually live within a particular narrative world that undergirds a way of life represented by the commands and exhortations, and they must decide whether or not this strange new world is the real world. This indirect communication of the Pauline apostolic letter functions in a way analogous to the parables of Jesus.[62]

The Community and Its Mission

Related to the particular character of the New Testament Letters is their orientation to community. There are no letters to individuals in the New Testament.[63]

---

61. Martyn 23.

62. Cf. Funk 124–32, "Parable and Letter"; and Barth 1957.

63. Even Paul's Letter to Philemon includes "Apphia our sister, Archippus our fellow soldier, and the church in your house"; and 3 John is not strictly only to Gaius (cf. v. 15). The pseudepigraphical Letters to Timothy and Titus in reality address the wider Christian community, as made clear by the concluding pronouns in the plural.

A letter assumes a common community experience, evoked in Paul's Letters by expressions such as these: "as you yourselves know," "as you remember" (cf., e.g., the concentration of such phrases in 1 Thess 2:1, 2, 5, 9, 11; 3:3, 4). A real letter can say "we" in a meaningful sense, can address the readers in the second-person singular or plural, whether or not the author knows the readers personally, for it assumes a shared history and concerns. In the New Testament, even letters addressed to a particular readership are also projections of the sender's purpose into the wider world. And the author/sender is himself sent, intensely conscious that his message does not originate with himself. The New Testament Letters represent a segment of God's mission into the world: God → Christ → apostle → letter → church → world. Letters are appropriate to apostolicity, for communicating the apostolic faith. There is a connection, theological if not strictly linguistic, between *apostle* and *epistle*.

* * *

For introduction to 2 Thessalonians and cross-references between the two letters, see below, after the commentary on 1 Thessalonians.

COMMENTARY ON
1 THESSALONIANS

Title

To the Thessalonians A' [a]

a. *PROS THESSALONIKEIS* A' (To [the] Thessalonians A'). This brief form is found as title in both ℵ and B and as the concluding subscript in 𝔓³⁰ A B* and other early MSS. Some later MSS add "written from Athens" (A B¹ and most others) or "written from Corinth by Paul, Silvanus, and Timothy" (81 and a few others). This distinctive form, the preposition *pros* + accusative case, is never found in the examples of addresses on Hellenistic letters (outside the NT), which have the simple dative case without the preposition.

Hellenistic letters typically designated the addressee on the outside of the rolled or folded letter, the verso. The address often included extensive directions to guide the bearer of the letter to the addressees. If Paul placed an address on the outside of the letter, it probably was a simple *Thessalonikeusin* [(to the) Thessalonians], but since Paul's Letters were delivered by his own coworkers, an external address would not have been necessary. Such addresses, if they ever existed, have not been preserved in the copies we possess.

Our earliest extant MS of the Pauline letter collection, the second-century 𝔓⁴⁶ Chester Beatty papyrus, already has brief titles as headings for the individual letters. The present titles were not, of course, part of the original Pauline letter. They were added when the Pauline corpus was formulated, perhaps with an overall title *EPISTOLAI PAULOU* (Letters of Paul) or the like, analogous to the later Gospel titles. The individual titles served to separate and distinguish one text from another within the Pauline corpus, thus revealing that our earliest copies of 1–2 Thessalonians already circulated as part of a collection, not individually. The A' and B' indicate that from the time of the earliest known collections, the two letters circulated together: 1 and 2 Thessalonians were read and interpreted in the light of each other and the Pauline corpus as a whole. This is another indication that all later generations receive the biblical texts from the hands of the church.

1:1 Prescript (Greeting)

1:1 Paul, Silvanus,[a] and Timothy, to the church[b] of the Thessalonians[c] in[d] God the Father and the Lord Jesus Christ. Grace to you and peace.[e]

a. Silvanus (*Silouanos*) is a Latinized form of the Greek name Silas (*Silas*). This is analogous to Epaphroditus (*Epaphras*); cf. Phil 2:25; 4:18; Col 1:7; 4:12; Phlm 23.

b. *Ekklēsia* means "assembly" in Hellenistic Greek. To translate the word as "church" is, of course, an anachronism, if the word be thought of in later terms. The word itself can be understood in the cultural sense as referring to the general public assembly (as in Acts 19:32, 39), with political overtones, but it needs to be translated here in such a way as to preserve the theological connotation it had already attained in Paul's instruction. Early Christian usage, including Paul's, was decisively influenced by the LXX, which uses *ekklēsia* more than 100× for the *Qāhal Yahweh* (assembly of Yahweh) and *Qāhal Yiśrā'ēl* (assembly of Israel, as in Deut 31:30; Josh 8:35; 2 Chr 7:8).

c. Elsewhere Paul always designates the church by its location (in Corinth, Galatia, etc.). Only here (and the deuteropauline parallel 2 Thess 1:1) does the prescript designate the congregation by the genitive plural of the people, "of the Thessalonians" (cf. Col 4:16, "church of the Laodiceans," but not in the prescript). Theoretically, the genitive could be *possessive* ("the Thessalonians' church," so CEB), *content* ("the church composed of Thessalonians"; cf. Acts 6:9, "synagogue . . . of Alexandrians"), or *partitive* ("the church of those called out from among the [other] Thessalonians").

d. The common Greek preposition *en* has a broad range of meanings. BDAG lists and illustrates twelve main categories, with numerous subheadings. In this text, the major issue is whether *en* should be understood spatially ("in") or instrumentally ("by"). The phrase *en theō* (in/by God) is rare in both the NT and the LXX, occurring 5× in each. The instrumental usage is rare with persons, usually expressed by *hypo* + gen. *En theō* with instrumental meaning is occasionally found, so that 3× the LXX can properly be translated "by God," with God as the cause of the action (2 Sam 23:4; 1 Chr 14:14; Hos 12:7 [6 ET]). Except for the possible instances in 1 Thess 1:1 and the parallel 2 Thess 1:1, there are no clear instances of this usage in the NT. While there is no doubt that Paul understands the church to have been chosen and called into being by God (1 Thess 1:4–5; 2:12; 4:7; 5:24), *en theō* here is better understood in spatial terms, an extension of Paul's "in Christ" terminology. Contrary to English usage, Greek usage of this preposition does not necessitate a choice between "in" and "by": the church is not alone in the world, but lives its life both *in* the reality of the divine presence, *by* the help and power of God who calls it into being.

e. Most of the earliest MSS, representing both the Alexandrian and Western text types, have only the short reading translated above (e.g., B G Ψ 1739 and representatives of the Old Latin, Vulgate, Syriac, and Coptic versions). The 4th-cent. codex ℵ, 5th-cent. A, and most later MSS have some variant of the expanded form found in all Paul's later letters: "from God our Father and the Lord Jesus Christ." The KJV follows these later MSS; virtually all modern versions follow the short text. Since 2 Thess 1:1, even in the oldest MSS, has exclusively the long text, this is an indication that it was composed later, after Paul's Letters were circulating in an edited form that had made 1 Thess 1:1 consistent with other Pauline Letters.

The Senders

Paul was known to the readers. Most of them knew him directly and personally; his preaching and teaching had effected a disruptive transformation of their lives. In the months since Paul's departure, new believers had been added to the little congregation, converts who did not know Paul directly. They needed to learn something of the fascinating story of this traveling preacher who had founded their church (see intro, "Context of Paul's Life"), and they were instructed by those who already knew the story. From the beginning, Scripture requires a Christian community and tradition in order to be understood.

This is the earliest New Testament reference to *Silvanus*, mentioned elsewhere in the undisputed Pauline Letters only in 2 Cor 1:19 along with Paul and Timothy as the missionary founders of the church in Corinth (cf. 2 Thess 1:1; 1 Pet 5:12). As the Silas of the Acts narrative, he is portrayed as a Christian prophet who played a prominent role in the transition from Jewish to Gentile Christianity (Acts 15:27, 32). After the Antioch conflict, Paul chose him to replace Barnabas. Silvanus worked with Paul in founding the church in Philippi, was beaten and imprisoned with him, continued with him to Thessalonica, and shared in the missionary work there.

The New Testament references to *Timothy* are richer and more complex. In historical (not canonical) chronology, Timothy first appears on the scene as a coworker with Paul and Silvanus in founding the Corinthian church (2 Cor 1:19). He is then sent back to Thessalonica to check on the church and encourage it in its duress (1 Thess 3:1–2). His return to Corinth is reflected in 1 Thess 3:6. Paul will later send him as troubleshooter, teacher, and encourager to other congregations (cf. Phil 2:19; 1 Cor 4:17; 16:10). As in 1 Thessalonians, Timothy's name will be joined with Paul's as cosender in letters to the Philippians, Philemon and the church in his house, and the Corinthians; Timothy is with Paul in Corinth as he composes Romans, his last letter (Rom 16:21). Timothy thus stands alongside Paul in the first words of his first letter, and he is mentioned in almost the last words of Paul's last letter. The Pastorals will remind a later generation that others abandoned Paul in his time of need, but not Timothy (2 Tim 4:9). The image of Timothy as a mature, responsible Christian leader and coworker with Paul, who undertakes lengthy and dangerous trips as Paul's representative to the churches, ordains other ministers, and calls presbyters to account, continues into the deuteropauline tradition (Col 1:1; 2 Thess 1:1, 1 Tim 1:2, 18; 5:1, 19; 6:20; 2 Tim 1:2). In this tradition, Timothy is described as Paul's "true child in the faith," and "my child," meaning Paul's convert (cf. 1 Cor 4:17), and the legitimate heir and authorized representative of Paul to a later generation. This use of "child" language in describing Timothy, coupled with the servile role he is assigned in Acts, has contributed to the misunderstanding of Timothy as young and immature, Paul's "boy assistant preacher."

The reader of Acts would never suppose that Timothy had participated with Paul and Silvanus in founding the church in Thessalonica. In the first scene in which Timothy is mentioned, Paul finds him already belonging to a Christian family in Lystra, wants Timothy to accompany Silas and himself on their mission tour, and circumcises him "because of the Jews who were in those places" (Acts 16:1–3 NRSV). Thus in Acts, Timothy's main narrative function is to represent the theology of the author, becoming the example of Paul's accommodating his gospel to his Jewish critics, giving them no offense for the sake of church unity. In the Acts narrative, Timothy has no role in the evangelization of Philippi, is absent from the scenes in which Paul and Silas are beaten and imprisoned, and is not mentioned in the story of the founding of the church in Thessalonica (17:1–9). He first resurfaces as Paul leaves Beroea, left behind there when Paul must be abruptly hustled out of town (17:10–15). But 1 Thessalonians clearly presupposes that Timothy was one of the founding missionaries, and that he is being sent back to a congregation where he is already known. The readers of the letter in the young congregation that is suffering distress for its new faith are greeted by all three members of the mission team that founded their church, leaders who have suffered with and for them.

Plural authorship? We are accustomed to thinking of this document as the first letter of *Paul* to the Thessalonians. Yet the first verse declares that the letter is from Paul, Silvanus, and Timothy. It was virtually unheard of in the ancient world for letters to be sent in the name of more than one person. Of the hundreds of ancient letters of which we are aware, only one has a coauthor (Cicero, *Att.* 11.5.1). Yet Paul's Letters generally join other names with his as cosenders—the only exception being Romans, his only letter written to a church he has not founded. How should we understand this?

In contrast to Paul's later letters, throughout 1 Thessalonians the first-person plural occurs very often, but the first-person singular only rarely, thus strengthening the impression of joint authorship.[1] Like many writers ancient and modern, Paul sometimes uses the first-person plural when referring only to himself (clear examples: 2 Cor 10:11, 13; Rom 1:5 [cf. 1:1]; Gal 1:8, 9). Yet the plural is to be taken seriously. Paul did not consider himself to be a solo performer. He had numerous coworkers and did not work alone. A list of about forty can be assembled; the brief letter to Philemon alone mentions nine such, six of whom are with him as he writes, three among the addressees. He often uses the term "coworkers," or "fellow workers," in a quasi-technical sense (Rom 16:3, 9, 21; 1 Cor 3:9; 2 Cor 1:24; 8:23; Phil 2:25; 4:3; 1 Thess 3:2; Phlm 1, 24). He sometimes authorizes his coworkers to remind his churches of his teaching, to

---

1. First Thessalonians uses first-person-plural pronouns or verbs 47×, but the first-person singular occurs only 3× (2:18; 3:5; 5:27). The proportion of "I" to "we" verbs in the undisputed letters: 1 Thessalonians, 3/47; Philippians, 66/4; Philemon, 16/0; 1 Corinthians, 192/71; 2 Corinthians, 94/144; Galatians, 68/24; Romans, 112/84.

continue it, and he charges the churches to attend to his teaching given through his colleagues (cf. 1 Cor 4:17; Rom 6:17; 16:17).

There are reasons to believe, however, that Paul is the responsible author of 1 Thessalonians, and that our earliest Christian text is not a product of joint authorship in which Silvanus and Timothy are coauthors with Paul. The "we" is sometimes interchangeable with "I" (2:18; 3:2, 5). Paul sometimes says simply "I." In 1 Thess 5:27 he speaks authoritatively in his own name, with no suggestion that elsewhere he and his coworkers are speaking. When Paul writes 1 Thessalonians, his authority as an apostle has not yet been challenged in the churches of the Aegean mission. He is no individualist, sensitive about placing himself in a special category. Paul can emphasize the corporate mission shared by his coworkers and the congregations they are establishing without detriment to his apostolic status. The repeated we-form is an indication that Paul's Letters, thought direct and personal, are also intended to represent the Pauline mission, the missionary team, and the supporting churches in which the mission is integrated. The letter is not composed by a committee chaired by Paul. He includes his coworkers in the greeting as *cosenders*, not as *coauthors*. Paul writes (= dictates) the letter; he is the responsible author.[2] But Paul's theology was not hammered out in isolation. The greeting is personal and warm, from three persons well known to the new little Christian community in Thessalonica, with whom they share a life-changing faith, and with whom they have suffered.

Form and Meaning

When Paul, with counsel and conversation of his missionary colleagues fresh in mind, began to dictate his first apostolic letter, his own compositional and theological creativity was influenced by three overlapping streams of tradition in which he stood: the Hellenistic letter form, the tradition of Jewish epistolography, and early Christian liturgical forms.

The Hellenistic letter form (see intro, "Hellenistic Letters"). The standard Hellenistic greeting form can be easily observed in the New Testament itself. A clear example is found in Acts 23:26 (cf. also Acts 15:23; Jas 1:1). The Roman tribune in Jerusalem writes to the governor in Caesarea, beginning his letter:

Claudius Lysias to his Excellency the governor Felix, greetings.
(NRSV, from 7 Greek words)

This standard letter prescript has three brief elements: A → B, *chairein*. These elements are not related syntactically into a coherent grammatical

---

2. An anonymous scribe was responsible for physically writing the letter. Throughout the commentary, such expressions as "Paul wrote" are intended as shorthand for "Paul as the responsible author, representing the mission team of which he is the head, dictates to the scribe."

structure, but function as a conventional phrase, like "Dear Colleagues . . . Sincerely yours, John," as the framework of an English letter. The ungrammatical unit is composed of the sender's name in the nominative case, followed directly by the addressee in the dative case (represented by the preposition *to* in English), then the infinitive of the verb *chairō*, which means "to be happy, to rejoice." Such infinitive forms function in letter prescripts as imperatives, "Be happy," but have no more actual content than the "Dear . . ." and "Sincerely . . ." of English letter forms. This phrase has no "meaning," but a function; it is merely the polite and expected way to begin a letter.

Jewish epistolary forms (see intro, "Ancient Jewish Letters"). Some Jews, when writing in Greek, simply used the standard Greek letter form. Thus the Greek items from the Bar Kochba Letters have the usual A → B, *chairein*.[3] There was, however, a typical Jewish variation of the Hellenistic form, which substituted the Hebrew "peace" for Greek "rejoice": A → B, peace. Sometimes there were minor variations (see Dan 3:31 MT [4:1 ET]; 2 Macc 1:10; cf. also 9:19; 11:16).

Paul would have known these letters embedded in his Bible, just as he was presumably familiar with Hebrew and Aramaic letters read in the synagogue and academic settings. The key point here is the insertion of the Jewish "peace" into the typical Hellenistic prescript, sometimes alongside *chairein*, sometimes replacing it.[4]

Pre-Pauline Christian usage. Theoretically, epistolary and liturgical forms prior to Paul could have influenced his own letter form. According to Acts, while Paul was at Antioch the Jerusalem Council sent a letter to the Gentile Christians in Antioch, Syria, and Cilicia, which included the Apostolic Decree (Acts 15:23–29). The letter was in typical Greek form, with the A → B *chairein* greeting and customary "farewell" (*errōsthe*) conclusion. This is the only evidence that Paul might have heard a letter of instruction from Christian leaders in another congregation read to a congregation of which he was a member. It is historically unlikely, however, that the letter was sent at this time, if at all (see the commentaries). Like Acts 23:26–30 (discussed above), it seems to be a Lukan composition, the form reflecting what he deemed appropriate for the occasion. In his formation of the apostolic letter genre, it is unlikely that Paul

---

3. For original texts and documentation of the following points, see esp. Doering 72–73, 406–15. For the *2 Baruch* text, see the intro and trans. by A. F. J. Klijn in *OTP* 1:615–20, 647–48, though the translation "*grace* and peace" for 78.3 is erroneous.

4. The letter embedded in the *Syriac Apocalypse of Baruch* (*2 Bar.* 78.2) is sometimes cited as representing a model that Paul adapted for his opening formula. However, it is problematic to use this text as background data for Pauline Letters. (1) It was probably written a generation after Paul's time. (2) The extant Syriac text is, as the text itself states, a translation from Greek, which translated the original Hebrew. (3) "Mercy and peace be to you" is reminiscent of the Pauline "Grace and peace," but it is different in both vocabulary and syntax.

had early Christian epistolary models he could adopt for his own apostolic letters. It may be that the "grace and peace" form was adopted by Paul from liturgical usage in Antioch, Damascus, or Jerusalem. There is an element of truth in
the suggestion, since Paul intended the letter to be read in the worship service
of the assembled congregation, where it functions as a greeting and blessing.

Pauline theological creativity. The prescript to 1 Thessalonians, like the letter as a whole, represents Paul's creative new beginning of the apostolic letter
tradition (see intro, "Apostolic Letter"; and below on "grace and peace"). He
does not formulate these first words casually, but on the basis of Hellenistic
and Jewish epistolary practice, creates a solemn and joyful greeting. Though
the shortest of all Paul's greetings (19 Greek words), the prescript to this inauguration of a new literary tradition is longer and more elaborate than the conventional form. It will be further developed and elaborated in later letters. In
his latest extant letter, the prescript becomes a substantial theological statement
(Rom 1:1–7, with 93 Greek words).

Unadorned personal names. Only here (and the parallel in the deuteropauline 2 Thess 1:1) does the prescript begin with the bare name(s) of the senders,
without titles or further descriptions. All later Pauline Letters provide a theological elaboration of both sender(s) and addressees. In his first apostolic letter,
Paul is very personal, feeling no need to call attention to his status (see on 2:7).

To the church of the Thessalonians. This is the letter's only reference to the
addressees as a "church"; the word occurs elsewhere in 1 Thessalonians only
in 2:14, in the plural, referring to the Christian congregations in Judea. Prior to
the mission team's arrival in Thessalonica, the first readers would never have
been addressed as an *ekklēsia* (assembly), which they would have understood
only in the sense of the local political assembly. Yet there is no explanation, as
though they are hearing the word in Paul's sense for the first time. They have
become accustomed to thinking of themselves as a church in the Pauline sense,
as incorporated into the holy people of God, in continuity with biblical Israel
(see intro, "New Congregation"). This new self-understanding was among the
basic items of Christian teaching that Paul and his colleagues had imparted during the founding visit, giving them a new symbolic universe. Thus, although
the term does not yet have the connotations of later ecclesiastical tradition, it
already has a distinctive meaning that differentiates it from its prior reference
to the local assembly—though it retains these political overtones as well. Paul
assumes their new self-understanding derived from his previous instruction (cf.
the repeated *oidate*, "[as] you know," 9× in 1 Thessalonians). Under the guidance of those who continued to instruct the new converts after Paul's departure,
they were continuing to learn what it meant to belong to the church.

In God the Father and the Lord Jesus Christ. God, father, and *Lord* were
words already familiar to the Thessalonians in their pre-Christian cultural settings, words that had to be filled with new content in the light of the Christian

gospel. The key term *Christ* (*Christos*, messiah, anointed one) was different in this respect; it would have been familiar to Jews as a title for the eschatological king, but not to Gentiles—except in its secular sense of "smeared, anointed." Paul and his mission team could not assume that the people to whom they preached knew the meaning of the term in the sacred, theological sense of Judaism, as though the only question was whether or not Jesus of Nazareth was in fact the Christ.[5] The missionaries had to find ways to communicate the meaning of this key term of Christian faith and proclamation, and they had done so.[6] It is an oversimplification to claim that *Christos* has become merely a proper name for Paul. Like *kyrios* (Lord), it is always resonant with a theological claim.[7] Paul uses the title ten times in this letter, always without explanation. The letter is not a christological-didactic letter, but assumes that previous Christian instruction has been effective.

Addressing the congregation as "in" God and Christ is most unusual, even startling (see trans. note d above). "In God" is rare in Paul (only here and Rom 2:17 in the undisputed letters [+ twice with the article, apparently with no difference in meaning, in 1 Thess 2:2 and Rom 5:11]). However, "in Christ" is a common phrase, found (including the variations "in the Lord," "in Jesus," "in whom," "in him") 98 times in the undisputed Pauline Letters, and an additional 72 times in later New Testament documents, always in dependence on Pauline tradition. In this earliest letter, the phrase is already found seven times, including one instance within traditional material (4:16, probably a Pauline insertion). This strikingly new phrase that characterizes Christian existence may not be absolutely original with Paul, but it was Paul who injected it into what became the mainstream of early Christian conceptuality and vocabulary.[8] "In Christ" does not designate location in the literal space-time sense, but does point to the reality of the new sphere of existence in which believers live their lives, somewhat analogous to the way modern Americans might speak of being "in debt" or "in love," but with an ontological claim lacking in such modern English phrases. The roots of the concept appear to be in some streams of theology represented in the Jewish Scriptures. In Hebrew thinking, there is no firm line between the individual and the community of which one is a constituent

---

5. There were various anointing rituals throughout the Hellenistic world that designated the person or object as no longer common but sacred, but there was nothing like the Jewish messianic understanding of a unique anointed one as the ultimate savior figure in God's plan for universal history. See Schnelle 2009, 183; Karrer 211.

6. See Reinhold Niebuhr (2:1–34) on preaching Christ where there is no expectation of a Messiah.

7. Cf. du Toit 295; Wright 2013, 816–25 and passim.

8. For elaboration, see Boring 2012, 310–12 and the bibliography given there. The phrase seems to have been a constituent element in some pre-Pauline baptismal traditions (1 Cor 1:30; 2 Cor 5:17, Gal 3:26–28)—but it was Paul who injected it into the mainstream of early Christian conceptuality and vocabulary.

element. A clue to Paul's usage is that Paul himself can speak of human beings as being "in Adam" (1 Cor 15:22), with "Adam" being not only the individual of the Genesis story but also the humanity constituted by him (Rom 5:12–21; cf. also "in you" [i.e., Abraham], Gal 3:8; "in Isaac," Gen 21:12 = Rom 9:7; "in David," 1 Sam 19:1; 2 Sam 19:43; 20:1; 1 Kgs 12:16; 2 Chr 10:16). For Paul, believers are baptized into Christ and are incorporated into the body of Christ (1 Cor 12:13; Gal 3:27; Rom 6:3); "in Christ" expresses this transcendent reality in which they participate as the determining factor of their lives. The life of the new church of the Thessalonians is determined not only by their location in Thessalonica and Macedonia, but also by their location "in God the Father and the Lord Jesus Christ."

The use of such language was not casual or uncontroversial. The new converts had turned away from idolatry to serve the one God (1:9–10), who is here called *Father* (cf. 1:1, 3; 3:11, 13, often elsewhere in Paul). From Homer to Epictetus, this was the title commonly given to Zeus, Father of Gods and humans (Homer, *Il.* 1.544; *Od.* 1.28; et al.; Epictetus, *Diss.* 3.24.16). Acclamation of the God revealed and active in the Christ event as Father was a countercultural claim, replacing the cultural god with the one biblical God,[9] just as acclamation of Jesus as Lord was countercultural, placing the risen Jesus in the religiocultural slot claimed by the Caesar.

Grace to you and peace. It is no triviality when, in place of the infinitive *chairein*, Paul substitutes a brief sentence of pronouncement and blessing. Those who have often heard this phrase in worship or seen it often in Christian literature may have had their senses dulled by familiarity, but it is a striking opening greeting, laden with theological overtones. In contrast to the traditional infinitive *chairein* functioning as a weak imperative ("Be happy"; "I hope this letter finds you OK"), in the Pauline greeting formula "grace" and "peace" are subjects, in the nominative case and beginning a new sentence, with the one-word dative pronoun *hymin* (to you) between, not following, the two nominatives. Like Jesus' Beatitudes, this is performative language: not pious verbiage, but a pronouncement that actualizes what it says, an expression of Paul's prophetic-apostolic self-understanding: "I hereby pronounce God's grace and peace as applying to you."

Grace (*charis*) is the basis of God's call and act, God's free gift, independent of human merit, the expression of unconditional divine love manifest in the life, death, and resurrection of Jesus.

Peace (*eirēnē*) was a significant word in the Hellenistic world, generally meaning merely the absence of war. Yet in Paul's Thessalonica it also evoked

---

9. The imagery of God as Father participates in the patriarchal imagery of the biblical world. In North America for the past thirty years or so, discussion of Father language for God has often been dominated by issues of patriarchy without perceiving its theological overtones and countercultural dynamic. See now the extensive discussion in Feldmeier and Spieckermann 51–92.

the popular phrase "the Pax Romana," the Roman peace with overtones of salvation, the political and economic security that was the gift of Augustus. Paul's use of the word in greetings, strikingly different from the usual letter form, poses an alternative claim as to who it is that grants true peace (cf. on 5:3). Paul uses the word in its Hebrew-Jewish sense (*shalom* = *eirēnē*), denoting the blessed fullness of life as God the Creator intends life to be, the result of God's gracious act. "Peace" thus calls to mind the Jewish greeting, but its resonance is deepened by evoking the saving act of God in Christ and hence becomes virtually a synonym for "salvation" (see, e.g., Rom 5:1; 8:6; 14:17; Phil 4:7 [where it means much more than "peace of mind"]). God is the "God of peace," the God who brings salvation (Rom 15:33; 16:20; Phil 4:9; 1 Thess 5:23).

Paul's combination of grace and peace in a letter greeting is unique. This form, "Grace to you and peace [be given]" (not "grace and peace to you"), with the verb understood, is found in *all* Paul's Letters, and *nowhere* else in all literature except in dependence on Paul. It has often been noted that Paul's *charis* represents a serious wordplay on the conventional Hellenistic *chairein* (though the words are not linguistically related), which Paul combines with the Jewish *shalom*. This once-popular suggestion has fallen out of scholarly favor, often replaced by the view that Paul modifies the Jewish "mercy and peace" into "grace and peace." These are not alternatives. It should not be understood as though Paul begins with the Hellenistic *chairein* and hits upon *charis* as a similar-sounding term from Christian theology. He may well have had the Jewish "mercy and peace" in mind, and then substituted *grace* for *mercy* not only to accentuate the significance of grace in early Christian theology, especially Paul's, but also because *charis* sounded like *chairein*. The result, intentional or not, is a striking new form that echoes both Greek and Jewish terminology, markedly appropriate for the Jewish Christian apostle to the Gentiles. This formula became his trademark, in the first line of each letter calling his hearers-readers to ponder the significance of this new language.

1 Thessalonians 1:2–3:13
Thanksgiving to the God Who Calls the Church and Keeps It Holy until the End

In Hellenistic letters, the greeting was often followed by a brief phrase express-ing the writer's wish for the reader's good health or a stereotyped prayer of thanksgiving to the gods. The form was not as rigid or consistently present as the prescript greeting. Typical would be "Before all else I pray that you are well, for I myself am well."[1]

In virtually all his letters, Paul includes a thanksgiving section immediately after the opening greeting. The only exception is Galatians, written in anger, in which this expected element is conspicuously absent. A recognizable Pauline pattern develops. (1) The thanksgiving is a clearly defined segment of the let-ter, following directly on the prescript and preceding the letter body. (2) The thanksgiving is a substantial paragraph, much longer than the conventional Hellenistic thanksgiving. The example from Apion cited above is eleven Greek words. The Pauline thanksgiving paragraphs average about a hundred words. Paul has transformed the conventional brief thanksgiving into a full-bodied theological composition that anticipates and signals the themes of the body of the letter. (3) The stance of prayer and thanksgiving are taken seriously. The letter is to be read in worship, both reflecting and setting the tone for apostolic address within the context of prayer and praise.

Interpreters are not unanimous on how these considerations affect the inter-pretation of 1 Thessalonians. The data are as follows: The thanksgiving period begins at 1:2, but its end and the transition to letter body are not clearly marked. The initial *eucharistoumen* (we give thanks) of 1:2 is followed by a second, identical thanksgiving form at 2:13, with a third variation at 3:9, *gar eucha-ristian dynametha tō theō antapodounai peri hymōn?* (How can we thank God enough for you?). Structural clarity first emerges at 4:1, where form and content indicate that the reader is now in the *second* part of the letter body, the parae-nesis (see intro, "Outline and Structure").

Where does the thanksgiving end and the first part of the body begin? How should the reader understand the structure of 1:2–3:13? The major proposals are as follows:

---

1. From the *Second Letter of Apion* (BGU 2:632), cited in Klauck 15.

1. Corresponding to the typical pattern of the later Pauline Letters, 1:2–10 is the thanksgiving, 2:1–3:13 is letter body A, and 4:1–5:22 is letter body B. Though the thanksgiving proper ends at 1:10, the body of the letter contains two further thanksgiving notes, 2:13 and 3:9.[2]

2. The repeated thanksgiving formulas mean that the thanksgiving is very lengthy, 2:1–3:13, so that the main body of the letter does not begin until 4:1.[3]

3. The actual thanksgiving is very brief, 1:2–3. Paul then shifts to a narrative report, 1:4–3:13, occasionally picking up the thanksgiving thread with which he began (2:13; 3:11–13).[4]

4. The repeated thanksgiving formulas (with several other features) signify that the letter is composite, combining the thanksgiving sections of two originally independent letters.[5]

5. The three thanksgiving statements, with intervening material, cannot be explained in terms of epistolary structure at all, but rhetorical analysis provides the key. The section 1:2–5 (or 1:2–10) is the typical introductory exordium, intended to gain the attention and favor of the hearers, followed by the *narratio* (1:6–3:10 or 2:1–3:10), which gives the reasons for thanksgiving.[6]

6. The thanksgiving begins at 1:2, modulates into the body of the letter, and continues as a fused thanksgiving/letter body A through 3:13. Letter body B begins at 4:1. The present commentator regards the extended section 1:2–3:13 as the interweaving of the thanksgiving and letter body A, a construal argued by numerous recent commentaries and interpreters.[7]

This analysis is not intended to suggest that Paul at a certain point says to himself, "I am now composing the thanksgiving, and at point *x* will switch over to the body." With his colleagues, Paul thinks through what he wants to say to the new converts in Thessalonica, imagines them present in worship during which the congregation too gives thanks (1 Thess 5:18), and declares what he has to say to them in this context of worshipful thanksgiving. The thanksgiving of the letter becomes, when it is read forth to the assembled congregation, a real prayer; it is an aspect of the Pauline letter as oral-liturgical discourse.

2. So, e.g., Roetzel 2009, 90.
3. So, e.g., Aune 1987, 206.
4. So Fee 18–20.
5. So, e.g., Richard 1995, 7–19.
6. See Jewett 1986, 68–78; Wanamaker 72–73, 90.
7. E.g., in the pioneering classical work of Schubert 26: "The thanksgiving itself constitutes the main body of 1 Thessalonians. It contains all the primary information that Paul wished to convey." More recently see John White 1972, 116–17; Lambrecht, who provides rich insights on the structure of this section; O'Brien.

1:2–10 Thanksgiving for the Thessalonians' Reception
of Paul's Gospel

The section 1:2–10 is a coherent unit in which there is no break in the thought, but the syntactical structure is not clear. How many sentences are there? Ancient manuscripts had no punctuation, no differentiation between capital and small letters, or spaces between words, clauses, or sentences; hence later editors and translators must decide how they are to be divided into sentences and clauses and how they should be punctuated. The Greek text gives syntactical pointers and clues, but editors of printed Greek New Testaments make different judgments on how these are to be interpreted, as do translations into English and other languages. The "rules" of what constitutes a proper sentence are not the same in Greek as in English, just as English varies in some respects from other modern languages such as French and German. Verses 2–5 are clearly one sentence in Greek, but it is not clear whether vv. 6–10 are the continuation of vv. 2–5, constituting a compound sentence; or whether they constitute one or more independent sentences. English translators often divide the long sentences of the Greek New Testament into shorter English sentences, partly because different combinations of Greek and English syntax are brought into play, and partly due to considerations of readability and English style.[8] The TEV divides these verses into ten sentences, the CEV into twelve. The translation in this commentary attempts to follow the Greek structure even when it is unwieldy or inelegant in English, to facilitate a close reading by the modern student. Verses 2–5 are construed as a single sentence, as in the Greek text.

1:2–5 Work, Labor, Steadfastness in the Power of the Spirit

Here begins the conventional thanksgiving section of the letter, unconventionally combined with the first part of the letter body, and extended through 3:13. This reconfiguration transforms both thanksgiving and letter body.

1:2 We always give thanks to God for all of you, continually mentioning you in our prayers, 3 remembering before our God and father your work generated by faith, your labor that grows out of love, and your steadfast endurance empowered by hope[a] in our Lord Jesus Christ,[b] 4 since, brothers and sisters[c] beloved[d] by God, we know your election, 5 namely, that[e] our [proclamation of the][f] gospel did not only come to you in word, but

---

8. The whole paragraph can be seen as "one long untidily constructed sentence" (Best 65). The editors of NA[28] conceive the text as four sentences, with a full stop after vv. 5, 6, 8, and 10. The latter three sentences all begin with coordinating conjunctions, so that vv. 6–10 can be seen as one extensive compound sentence (so, e.g., Furnish 2007, 39). Greek (and esp. Hebrew) style was more amenable to beginning a sentence with a conjunction. English versions have often adjusted to the style of the biblical languages: many sentences in ET begin with "And" or "For"; John 3:16 is the best known of hundreds.

also in power and in the Holy Spirit and with full conviction, just as you know what kind of people we were when we were with[g] you, for your sake.

a. Each of the genitive phrases could be correctly, but not adequately, translated with the simple "of": "work of faith, labor of love, steadfastness of hope." The sense of the genitive can often be grasped by placing the genitive term before the noun it modifies, connected with a hyphen: "your faith-work, your love-labor, your hope-steadfastness," then expressing this meaning with a more precise description. The translation above is not a paraphrase but an attempt to express the nuance of the category, *genitive of source*, in which the second item in each pair is the generative source of the first.

b. The phrase *tou kyriou hēmōn Iēsou Christou* is objective genitive. The content of the hope is the future coming of our Lord Jesus Christ, not the subjective hope that Jesus had, nor hope "in Christ" in the sense that this is the sphere of the believer's life.

c. Although the singular nouns *brother* and *sister* are distinguished in Greek as in English, the masculine plural *adelphoi* was used in Greek generically of brothers and sisters in the same family (see BDAG 18, *adelphos*, for nonbiblical evidence for the masculine plural *adelphoi* in the inclusive generic sense). Of numerous biblical examples, see Deut 15:12, where, in both the MT [*ʾāch*] and LXX [*adelphos*], "brother" is explicated as "man or woman." The translation "brothers and sisters" is thus not merely accommodation to contemporary sensitivities, but actually a proper translation of the contextual meaning.

d. *Ēgapēmenoi* (beloved) is not an adjective, as in English, but a perfect passive participle. This means that it points to an action of God, not a quality of the Thessalonians. The perfect tense designates an action in the past, the effects of which continue in the present. God's love was made known in his act in Christ and in the act of calling the Thessalonians into the church; these acts continue as a present reality that determines their existence (cf. Rom 1:7).

e. The conjunction *hoti* can be understood here either as causal or epexegetical. The decision has a domino effect on how the syntax of the rest of the paragraph is construed. If taken as causal ("We know your election, brothers and sisters beloved of God, because . . ."), this would be the beginning of a list of reasons why Paul knows the Thessalonians belong to the elect community, a list that extends through several clauses to the end of v. 10. Taken as epexegetical, as here, the *hoti* clause gives the content of what is known, functioning in apposition to "election" ("We know your election, . . . namely that . . ."). The construction is common in the NT; Pauline examples include 2 Cor 8:1–2; Gal 1:11; 1 Thess 2:1; cf. Phil 1:12. It thus seems best to construe the sentence construction as translated above, with the *hoti* clause characterizing the election, and beginning a new sentence at v. 6.

f. "Our gospel," lit., but Paul is not using the term here as a possessive genitive. Paul can speak of "my gospel" in the sense of his distinctive understanding of the Christian message (Rom 2:16; cf. Gal 1:11), but the genitive is not possessive. Here, as in 2 Cor 8:18, *gospel* is a *nomen actionis*, a noun derived from a verb, referring to the act of preaching the gospel.

g. The sentence ends with two parallel phrases in Greek, *en hymin di' hymas*, underlining Paul's point: "You know what kind of people we were when we were with you, for your sake [rather than for our own profit]." The preposition *en* (in, among), here translated as *with*, is missing from ℵ A C P 048, several minuscules, some MSS of the Vulgate, but present in B D F G Ψ and the vast majority of later MSS. Without it, the translation would be "what sort of persons we became for you." That the context seems to call for the preposition can be taken as evidence for either its originality or scribal "correction." Since the omission is easily explained by haplography, the strong MSS evidence should be taken as evidence for the reading translated above.

The barebones structure of this sentence is the statement of thanksgiving, followed by three subordinate participial clauses. When these are translated by English participles—often not the best translation in terms of preserving the original meaning—and descriptive phrases are omitted, the structure is clear:

> We thank God for you,
>> mentioning you in our prayers,
>> remembering your work, labor, and steadfastness,
>> knowing your election.

[2] Paul thanks *God* for the Thessalonians' response to the gospel. He does not thank *them* for responding. This is partially a cultural difference between ancient Mediterranean culture and our own. In modern Western social settings, people say "Thank you" many times a day, on the horizontal level, as one person thanks another in ways ranging from conventional trivialities to profound gratitude. Not to do so is considered insensitive or boorish. In the Mediterranean world of the New Testament, people thanked God or the gods for what someone had done, a vertical instead of horizontal communication, "overheard" by the person on the horizontal level. To say a direct "Thank you" *to* someone meant something like "the matter is finished, we are even, we need have no further obligation to each other." Few readers of the Bible have noticed that there is *no* "thank-you" on the horizontal level in the entire Bible, where the numerous expressions of thanks are always directed to God [cf. even Luke 17:18, and 17:9, which regards thanking a slave as not appropriate]. Even Paul's Letter to the Philippians, expressing his gratitude for their financial support, thanks God for them, but has not a word of thanks to them for their gift.[9] Yet the matter cannot be reduced to sociology: it is also theological. That there is a church in Thessalonica is neither Paul's doing nor his readers' action, but the result of God's election, calling through the gospel, and sustaining the new believers in the power of the Holy Spirit. Addressing the Thessalonians, Paul offers grateful praise to God.

[3] Paul's gratitude is for something specific and concrete. He has just learned from Timothy's return (3:1–6) that the small, fragile congregation of

---

9. See Malina xi–xiii; Malina and Pilch 299.

new converts that he had been abruptly compelled to leave was continuing, indeed flourishing, despite the hardships with which they were contending. He characterizes this new life into which the Thessalonian Christians have entered as "faith-work, love-labor, and hope-endurance" (cf. translation and textual notes above). This is the first occurrence in Christian literature of the familiar faith/love/hope triad, which most Bible readers will think of in terms of its later occurrence in 1 Cor 13:13, where "love" is placed at the climactic end point due to contextual considerations. The order here is probably the original. The formula may have been adopted by Paul from previous (Antiochene) tradition, or may be his own formulation, here or earlier. The triad first appears in this Pauline text, and all later occurrences seem to be dependent on Pauline usage (1 Thess 5:8; Gal 5:5–6; Rom 5:1–5; Col 1:4–5; Heb 10:22–24; 1 Pet 1:3–8). Here Paul seems to be adapting prior tradition, since what he wants to express his gratitude for is not their faith, hope, and love per se, but their perseverance as a Christian community. In 5:8 Paul seems to force the triadic schema on the two-membered armor taken from Isa 59:17, which might argue for its traditional character. Traditional or not, the formula, especially in its order here, is an appropriate summary of the experience of the interwoven past-present-future dimensions of Christian faith. Understood as something of a chronology, the triadic formulation expresses the conviction that permeates the whole letter: the lives of the new Christians in Thessalonica have been incorporated into the time line of God's saving program for all history: their *faith* in God's past actions in the Christ event and God's call of the Thessalonians, their present existence as mediators of God's *love*, and their confident *hope* of God's future to be manifest at the Parousia.

Work (*ergon*) is here combined unself-consciously with *faith* (*pistis*). Neither here nor elsewhere does Paul contrast faith with work as such. Paul's later resistance to the idea that justification is by "works of the law" (plural, not singular, as here) deals with the attempt to impose the ritual requirements of the Jewish torah on Gentile Christians, including the identity marks of circumcision, Sabbath keeping, and ritual purity of food. That issue is not in view here. Paul is not allergic to work or nervous about good works that believers are called to do; even in his later writings he always understood faith to be manifest in works, meaning deeds in which God's call to holiness and love are expressed (e.g., 1 Cor 13:2; Gal 5:6; 6:10; Eph 2:8–9 understands this in the Pauline sense).

Labor (*kopos*) is to some extent simply a synonym of *work* and may be added here simply in order to correspond to the triadic formula Paul wants to use. But New Testament usage of *kopos* shows it is often used with a distinctively Christian connotation of spreading the gospel (cf. 2:9; 3:5; 2 Cor 11:27), and the Thessalonians have been active in this way (1:8). Such activity is a matter of *agapē*, loving concern for others. In the paraenetic section, it will become clear that "work of faith" and "labor of love" do not refer exclusively, or even mainly, to "religious works" done "for the church," but to one's daily work (see on 4:9–12).

Steadfastness (*hypomonē*), translated "patience" in the KJV and ASV, is not a passive high threshold of irritation, but—like work and labor—an active manifestation of one's commitments. Nor is it simply a generalized positive character trait; here Paul refers to the tenacity with which the new congregation of believers has held on to their faith despite resistance and persecution, a hanging-in-there against the pressure to keep a low profile or backtrack on their commitment to the Christian faith. Corresponding to this, the *hope* that empowers such steadfastness is not wishful thinking, but confident assurance, not "perhaps" or "maybe" but "surely." Such hope is not subjective, a matter of chirpy optimism, but is already grasped by the reality of a concrete objective event on the horizon, the Parousia of the risen Lord at the near consummation of history. Here hope is identified with the coming of the Lord Jesus Christ; in 2:19, hope is identified with the Thessalonian believers themselves (see comments there). Like Christian faith, Christian hope is not merely an attitude, but has content (1:10; 2:19; 3:13; 4:13–5:11). While such steadfastness need not be frothy cheerfulness, neither is it grim determination: it lives in the glad confidence of the ultimate future triumph of God.[10]

[4] The sentence continues with the third reason for the missionaries' thanksgiving, expressed in the third participial clause, "knowing . . . your election . . . ." (translated above as an adverbial participle "since we know . . ."). Before elaborating this reason in an extended clause, Paul addresses the readers directly as "brothers and sisters beloved by God." "Brothers and sisters" as a designation for believers was common in the early Christian community, found in every New Testament writing except 2 John and Jude. It is especially common in Pauline usage and is intensified in 1 Thessalonians, where it is found nineteen times. Combined with the image of God as Father, "brother and sister" expresses the reality of church as the newly created family of God (see 1:1; 2:7, 11). While Zeus could be called "Father," and "brothers" was occasionally used metaphorically in the Hellenistic world for members of religious associations, there were no pagan communities of God's children called into being by their divine father. Influenced by Jesus' use of family language for the new community gathering around him, the early Christians adopted the practice of Judaism, where members of the community of faith were considered brothers.[11] New proselytes were said to be loved and called by God: they have been

---

10. For a brief, readable summary of the biblical meaning of hope, contrasting it with cultural meanings, see Moule 1963.

11. Doering (32–33, 38) cites numerous Jewish letters designating the addressees as "brother" and "sister," as already used in Elephantine Jewish letters from the Persian period (5th cent. B.C.E.). The famous "Passover Letter" appears to address the whole Jewish colony as "brothers." Simeon bar Kokhba addresses military people at Ein Gedi as "brothers." Pauline usage exceeds

incorporated into the people of God, whom God has loved, called, and chosen.[12] "Beloved by God" is thus not a general characteristic of the loving God, but refers to God's specific act of calling the Thessalonians into the community of faith. The language of "beloved" and "election" is thus "ecclesiological," community language, not designations of individual Thessalonians. The new converts now belong to the beloved, called, chosen community, adopted by God as their Father and joined to each other as brothers and sisters in the family of God. An important part of their new identity is not only horizontal, looking out into their present world where they are now brothers and sisters to each other in the new Christian community in Thessalonica and beyond (2:14, Judea; 1:7–8, Macedonia, Achaia, and beyond). They also receive a new chronological, historical identity, for they are now incorporated into the ongoing history of God's people. Paul relates their identity as "brothers and sisters beloved by God" to their *eklogē* (election), their belonging to the called and chosen people of God, separated from the mass of humanity under the *orgē* (wrath) of the righteous God (1 Thess 1:4, 10; 5:9).

With this one word *election* (*eklogē*), Paul taps into a deep and broad stream of Jewish biblical theology. The term suggests two paths to contemporary readers, either of which leads to misunderstanding: (1) To many readers in the Christian tradition, the word immediately connotes, for good or ill, philosophical-theological systems that explain God's choice of individuals for salvation or damnation. Though it has predecessors and successors, the historical fulcrum for this line of thought is Calvin's *Institutes* 3.21, "Eternal Election, by Which God Has Predestined Some to Salvation, Others to Destruction."[13] (2) Another large group of readers, overlapping but not identical with those of the first group, respond negatively to the biblical and theological vocabulary of election because they hear it within the framework of the modern cluster of ideas of freedom, fairness, equality, impartiality, and individual responsibility.

Neither Paul nor the Thessalonians thought in the later terms of Augustine, Calvin, or of nineteenth-century democratic ideals. Paul's thought is shaped by the biblical narrative of God's salvific, covenant-making acts in history, which revealed and effected God's ultimate plan for the creation, focused on God's *choice of Israel* as witness to and agent of God's redemptive action for all people. Paul wants the new converts in Thessalonica to understand their experience within this symbolic universe, new to them, but absolutely crucial to Paul's understanding of their new identity. Hovering in the background of Paul's thought were such texts as Deut 7:6–8:

---

and intensifies this, and *adelphoi* becomes a fundamental term for the identity of his congregations. See Horrell 2005, 110–15 and the bibliography he provides.

12. Malherbe (2000, 110) cites *Gen. Rab.* 70.5; *Num. Rab.* 8.2; *Midr. Tanḥ.* 6; *Jos. Asen.* 8.9. These Jewish texts are all later than the NT yet reflect earlier practice.

13. Calvin 1960b, 2:920–86.

You are a people holy to the LORD your God; the LORD your God has chosen you out of all the peoples on earth to be his people, his treasured possession. It was not because you were more numerous than any other people that the LORD set his heart on you and chose you—for you were the fewest of all peoples. It was because the LORD loved you and kept the oath that he swore to your ancestors. (NRSV)

Neither here nor elsewhere in 1 Thessalonians does Paul cite or directly allude to such texts, but they form the matrix of his theology and even shape the language of his thought. Paul's thinking was also inevitably shaped by his personal history, which in his view was integrated into the climax of God's eschatological plan. God had chosen him, called him, and made him the apostle to the Gentiles. He had not been seeking or striving for something else: he had been quite satisfied in his own religious situation and had opposed the new faith. God chose him, called him, and gave him a mission within the church, the eschatological people of God that God was calling into being. Through these lenses, Paul saw what had happened in Thessalonica and the other mission churches. A group of people in Thessalonica, previously pagans, had come together to constitute a congregation of God's people; yet this was not the product of Paul, the courageous missionary who dared to step over the religious and cultural barriers erected by traditional Judaism and include Gentiles in the people of God, but the act of God, who chose them and incorporated them into the chosen people.

The language of election, like the biblical language of salvation in general, is insider language, the confessional language of the believing Christian community. It is not the objectifying language of the spectator, who assumes a transcendent perch from which to evaluate the purported acts of God, critically analyzes the coherence of such language, draws out its implications, weighs it in the logical balances, and finds it wanting. Confessional language is the retrospective confession of faith, "God has chosen us," which functions authentically on another plane than the language of logical inference, "therefore, God has rejected them." Such language makes a confessional statement of grateful praise to God about "us," not a doctrinal statement of analytic logic about "them." It is the language of a community, not the individualizing language of personal choice and responsibility (see further on interpreting "the coming wrath" in 1:10 below).

Key words such as *eklogē* (election) are not discrete topics that can be discussed and analyzed separately, but aspects of a single reality that was already dawning, already bringing the ultimate plan of God to reality. *Election* is inseparably bound to words woven into the texture of 1 Thessalonians such as *charis* (grace), *kaleō* (call), *ekklēsia* (church), *pneuma hagion* (Holy Spirit), and *Christos* (Christ), and the whole eschatological vocabulary (*parousia* [coming, presence, advent], *thlipsis* [tribulation, suffering], *egeirō*, raise [from the dead], etc.). The umbrella term for this linguistic cluster is *eschatology*, which cannot be restricted to explicit texts that deal with the Parousia, but permeates the thought of Paul and forms the ground (not merely "background") for understanding every word of 1 Thessalonians. Yet the letter is not the thematic discussion of a topic. It is not "about" eschatology, but about God: the one God who has acted decisively in the death and resurrection of Jesus; the God who calls the eschatological community into being, giving it the Holy Spirit as the power to be and act in response to this call; the God who can be counted on to complete the work he has begun (5:24, which forms a bracket with this text).

[5] When Paul says the gospel came "not only in word," the operative word is "only." The gospel did come in word (singular), but also in words, the human words of the missionaries (2:13). Paul is not indulging in the modern Western disdain for words in contrast to deeds ("empty talk"; "Don't tell me, show me"; "Sticks and stones may break my bones, but words will never hurt me"), a contrast also widespread in the ancient world. Interchangeably or in close association throughout 1 Thessalonians, *word* and *gospel* are used as the vehicle of God's transforming power (see 1:5, 8; 2:2, 4, 5, 8, 9, 13; 3:2; 4:15, 18).

The event that brought the new converts into the church was a word-event, replete with God's power, the Holy Spirit, and full conviction. For Paul, "spirit" is not a soft, dovelike image, but as in the biblical narratives and prophetic oracles, an image of creative power (e.g., Gen 1:1–2; Judg 13:25; 1 Sam 10:6; 1 Kgs 18:12; Ezek 37:1–14; Mic 3:8). As in the later book of Acts, receiving the Spirit is the mark of God's choice and election (Acts 10:34–48; 11:15–18). On the founding visit, the missionaries' preaching in Thessalonica had been accompanied by powerful signs of the presence of God's Spirit, and the church continued to experience charismatic phenomena (see on 5:16–22). Thus "the one who gives his Holy Spirit to you" functions in 1 Thessalonians as a veritable divine name (4:8). A few years later, Paul's detractors in other churches will claim that his mission is not authorized and empowered by God, that he does not exhibit the "signs of an apostle"; then, with reluctance, Paul will refer to the signs of the Holy Spirit present in his ministry (cf. 1 Cor 2:4; chs. 12–14; 2 Cor 12:9–12; 13:3–5; Gal 3:5; Rom 15:19), though he will contrast these with the true power of God at work in the weakness of the crucified Jesus. Although miraculous phenomena accompanied the apostolic preaching, Paul is not contrasting the weakness of word-without-miracles and the power of word-plus-miracles. The contrast is between mere human word and the power of God's word, a contrast also drawn in 2:13.

1:6–10 Imitators of the Lord and of Paul

This account of the *eisodos* (1:9), the founding visit and response, is drawn into the thanksgiving and thus becomes much more than a reminder or report.

1:6 And as for you,[a] when you received the word with joy inspired by the Holy Spirit, even though it involved much suffering,[b] you became imitators[c] of us and the Lord, 7 with the result that you became a model for all the believers in Macedonia and Achaia. 8 For from you the word of the Lord has sounded forth not only in Macedonia and Achaia, but in every place the news of your faith in God has become known, so that we have no need to say anything. 9 For the people themselves report your response to our founding visit,[d] and how you turned to God from idols to serve the living and true God, 10 and to wait for his Son from heaven, whom he raised from the dead, Jesus, who delivers us from the coming wrath.

a. The pronoun *hymeis* (you) is unnecessary grammatically, being included in the verb form, and thus is emphatic. The introductory *kai* (and, but, also, even [etc.]) is here taken as introducing a mild contrast. The previous sentence dealt with the missionaries; the apostle now turns to the Thessalonians, whose experience also testifies to their election.

b. *Thlipsis* has a broad semantic field and cannot be translated consistently by a single English term. The noun is derived from the verb *thlibō*, the basic meaning of which is *press*, the noun for which would be *pressure*. The basic meaning expands to mean crowd, put pressure on someone in a hostile sense, *oppress*. The noun shares this range of meanings; in the NRSV the 20 occurrences in Paul's Letters are translated *anguish* (once), *suffering* (4×), *hardship* (1×), *affliction* (7×), *distress* (2×), *pressure* (1×, 2 Cor 8:13), and *persecution* (4×, all in 1 Thessalonians). *Persecution* is here avoided because it connotes a more systematic and official series of events than was probably the case in the Thessalonians' initial reception of the Christian message, which is in view here. See comments on 2:14; 3:3–7.

c. As in the 15th-cent. devotional classic by Thomas à Kempis, "imitation" is meant in the biblical sense of "following as a disciple," "accepting as a model for one's own life," precisely the opposite of its contemporary overtones of "not authentic, impersonation."

d. More lit., "what sort of entrance [*eisodos*] we had among you." Paul uses *eisodos* only here and 2:1 (elsewhere in the NT only in Acts 13:24; Heb 10:19; 2 Pet 1:11). *Eisodos* means *entrance* and can be used of a gate or road into a city. By extension, *eisodos* can mean *welcome, acceptance*, but that is not Paul's meaning here (or in 2:1, where I have translated it *initial visit*). Paul uses it in a more comprehensive sense for the missionaries' arrival, and the response to it, all that he refers to in 1:5, 9–10; 2:1, 13; 3:6. This is similar to Acts 13:24, which refers to Jesus' coming on the scene, his preaching, and the people's response.

[1:6–7] Just as their whole experience of conversion and church formation can be called "election," so it can be called "receiving the word" (see above on vv. 4–5). What they received was the word, the Christian message. Accepting this message involved much suffering. Every convert in early Christianity suffered a kind of alienation from their culture, an uncomfortable and sometimes hostile marginalization. What Paul here refers to is not only an instance of this general phenomenon. The Thessalonian Christians suffered something specific that was not typical, not the same as in Philippi or Corinth. A particular situation or series of events had troubled the life of the church in Thessalonica. This may have involved incidents in which members of the new congregation suffered violence or were killed.[14]

While Paul does not develop a theology of suffering in 1 Thessalonians, he does place the new converts' distress in a theological framework. The term used (*thlipsis*) is not a technical term, but for Paul it has been colored by its frequent use in the LXX (132×, with 35× in the Psalter), where it is the mark of the true people of God. In the eyes of society, the Thessalonians are getting along worse since their conversion than before, and Paul has told them it would be so (3:3). Furthermore, Paul has instructed the new converts in his apocalyptic view that the suffering of the faithful intensifies just before the end. Such sufferings are not meaningless, not the random violence of a world out of control, but belong to the birth pangs of the cosmos preceding the advent of the Messiah, the "messianic woes." This means that for people of Christian faith, suffering and joy are not alternatives. They can rejoice in sufferings, in the power of the Holy Spirit, and celebrate amid their troubles, counting them as integral to the life of faith in the eschatological community, to which they now belong (Rom 2:9; 5:3; 8:18–39; cf. Mark 13:19, 24; John 16:21, 33). Participation in Christ means sharing his suffering. Such joyful endurance is not a native attitude or aptitude, but a grace.[15] Their joy in the Holy Spirit is an observable reality, to be gratefully acknowledged, not an exhortation to be dutifully obeyed; such joy is an indicative, not an imperative. They are not urged to "be cheerful."

Already the Thessalonians have observed in Paul and his colleagues this reality of joyful suffering they now experience, and behind both the Thessalonians and Paul stands Christ. Paul is grateful that the suffering they have experienced because of their commitment to God has not caused them to abandon the faith. In declaring that the new converts have become imitators of both Paul and the Lord, Paul is not here pointing to particular features of his (or Jesus') personal life that have been copied by the new believers, but to the pattern of his life as a whole, a pattern he received from and shares with Christ: remaining faithful through suffering. The word *typos* (type) does not refer to a pattern to be copied, but to the mold used to form the stamp or seal that leaves its impression. As the stamp has been formed by the mold, so it marks other things with its own impression. In an extended sense, it can then be used to mean "example." The word has a Janus face: as it has been stamped or molded, so it stamps or molds others. Paul uses this word of himself as a *typos*/model for his congregations.

14. See on 2:14 below; and Donfried 2002b, xxi, 43.
15. See Bassler 2007, 4.

By his encounter with the risen Christ, he has been stamped into a certain form; his life has been molded into a certain shape. He in turn, in his interaction with the new converts in the mission churches he establishes, exercises a molding influence on them. They, molded by him, shape the lives of others. Such "imitation" is not primarily ethical but is the authenticating badge that identifies the new congregation as participants in the eschatological saving act of God, which includes the sufferings of the end time.[16] As Paul himself is an apostle molded by Christ, he represents the reality of Christ, a reality the church in Thessalonica now shares. Thus already in 1 Thessalonians, though the cross and crucifixion are not directly mentioned, Jesus as the suffering and crucified one imitated by his apostle and then by his church—this Jesus is already taken seriously. The Thessalonians have become a *typos* to the other churches in Macedonia and Achaia not merely as an admirable example, but also as an encouragement to mission, as Paul and Jesus had become, whom they imitate; knowing all this is encouraging to the Thessalonians and something to be celebrated in the Pauline thanksgiving. Paul's ethic of mimesis is oriented to the Christ myth, the story enacted on the cosmic stage, not on the Galilean hillsides. It is the story of the preexistent Son of God, who gave up heavenly glory, came among human beings to share their lot, was obedient to God, suffered and died, was exalted by God to his present status as heavenly Lord, who will come again to establish the reign of God's justice (cf. Phil 2:5–11; 2 Cor 8:9; Rom 15:3).[17]

[8–9a] Such language as we find here ("... in every place ...") is of course not literally true, but it should not be dismissed as merely frothy hyperbole. While it does function in much the same way as contemporary enthusiastic praise ("Everybody's talking about it"; "you're the talk of the town"), the (repeated!) reference to the Macedonian and Achaean churches is not only bragging on the faith and perseverance of the Thessalonians, but also reminding those who have now been excluded from much of their local society that they belong to a new community that spans the generations and the continents (cf. also 2:14). They have not only gone out of one world, but also into another, the ecumenical church. When Paul writes 1 Thessalonians, we need not think of numerous churches in Macedonia and Achaia. From Paul's Letters we know of Philippi, Thessalonica, Corinth, its neighbor Cenchreae, and perhaps some believers in Athens. Acts would add only Beroea. The incidental reference to Cenchreae (Rom 16:1), whose evangelization is not elsewhere mentioned, suggests that there were other congregations besides these few. The new churches have themselves become informal centers of evangelism.[18] Paul's language indirectly

---

16. Cf. Schnelle 1986, esp. 212–13.

17. See Betz 1967.

18. See Ware. Ascough (2014) points out that this need not be seen on the model of missionaries in Acts or in the 19th-cent. missionary movement of European and North American Christian

reflects both this spread of the new faith to other cities by the new churches and the network that connected them. Aquila and Priscilla coming from Rome, who are with Paul as he writes 1 Thessalonians, may have learned about the new church in Thessalonica from contacts along the Egnatian Way (cf. Acts 18:2, 18). By 50 C.E. there were certainly Christian communities not only in Macedonia and Achaia, but also in Judea, Syria, Cilicia, Asia (the Roman province), and Italy; probably the churches of Galatia, Alexandria, Cyprus, Ethiopia, and Mesopotamia already existed. There was a network over which a lot of information and news flowed.

Paul's strategy was to found a community that itself would be an evangelistic center. This corresponds to the nature of the gospel: those who believe it is true must believe it applies not only to themselves, but also that they have been grasped by something that inherently belongs to all. To evangelize is not merely sharing their spiritual experience or imposing their religion on others, but "one beggar telling another where to find bread."[19] Located on the Via Egnatia, with people passing through and with some of the Thessalonians themselves traveling, they became gospel communicators and not merely consumers. The faith and life of the new Christian communities was not a marginal concern, but the center of their new life. They believed it was true, and if it was indeed true, then it was what mattered most, what they believed in, thought about, talked about. In speaking of the evangelistic mission of the new little congregation in Thessalonica, we need not picture them quitting their day jobs and preaching on street corners and going door-to-door throughout neighboring towns and provinces. But we must picture them as people who knew that in accepting the Christian faith they had accepted the responsibility to share it, and they did so.

[9b–10] These verses that summarize the conversion experience of the Thessalonians are not expressed in the vocabulary that was later to become typical of Paul: the language of faith, justification, reconciliation, the meaning of the cross. On the other hand, they contain several expressions unusual or absent from Paul's writings elsewhere. Thus the verb "turned" (to God) is *epistrephō*, never elsewhere used by Paul for conversion.[20] Outside the Pauline corpus, it is used for conversion from idolatry to the living God, as here (Acts 9:35; 14:15). Likewise, the verb for "waiting" for the Parousia is not Paul's typical *apekdechomai* (live in expectation; cf. 1 Cor 1:7; Phil 3:20; Rom 8:23; Gal

---

churches. Finding similarities between the new congregation in Thessalonica and the voluntary associations and unions of handworkers among whom Paul worked, he argues that reports of the successful founding of the new group in Thessalonica are analogous to the propaganda of such associations, which glorify not only their gods but also their founders and benefactors.

19. The oft-quoted definition of evangelism by D. T. Niles, ecumenical missionary theologian of Sri Lanka.

20. Elsewhere in Paul only 2 Cor 3:16, in a quote from Exod 34:34; and Gal 4:9, of believers who are in danger of turning back to their previous life.

5:5), but *anamenō* (wait). The vocabulary is reminiscent of Hellenistic Jewish missionary propaganda. *Joseph and Aseneth* 11.8–11 has a similar cluster of vocabulary: "I worshiped dead and dumb idols. . . . The God of the Hebrews is a true God and a living God. . . . I will turn to him." So also Tob 14:6 looks forward to the day when "the nations in the whole world will all be converted and worship God in truth. They will all abandon their idols" (NRSV).

Since these verses can be readily construed as a discrete unit with a well-defined structure, this has often been considered an item of pre-Pauline tradition and designated as a creed or hymn. The composition does indeed include pre-Pauline elements, using vocabulary that had become traditional in Hellenistic Jewish mission propaganda. Yet it is difficult to imagine this text as either a creed or hymn in which a believing congregation confesses its faith or addresses God in praise. The content of this summary is not the faith of the worshiping and confessing congregation or a sketch of the mission preaching during the church-founding visit, but focuses on that visit's *results*. The modern scholar cannot infer the outline of early mission preaching from this text.

Neither is the composition an element of Pauline tradition he had taught them after their conversion. Modern interpreters might well remind themselves that as Paul writes 1 Thessalonians, he is in Corinth, in the process of founding the church there, only a few months after leaving Thessalonica. During the church-founding mission in Corinth, in which he is presently engaged, he is teaching them elements of the faith that have already become firm Christian tradition (e.g., 1 Cor 11:23–26; 15:3–5). Not long before, Paul and his colleagues have been instructing the new converts in Thessalonica. He has surely done the same there (cf. 1 Cor 4:17; 11:2). If we ask why Paul does not cite such traditions in 1 Thessalonians, the answer seems to be that they appear in 1 Corinthians only because he is instructing the Corinthians on issues that have become disputed, and 1 Corinthians is mainly a didactic letter, dealing with such problems. The traditional elements cited in 1 Corinthians are postbaptismal instruction on disputed points, not a summary of his missionary kerygma or of their conversion experience. As Paul writes from Corinth to Thessalonica, the situation there is different from the later situation in which he writes to Corinth, and 1 Thessalonians is not a didactic letter. In this letter he is sharing neither his original kerygma nor the elements of traditional Christian doctrine he has taught them after their conversion. Because he is thankful for them, he is summarizing what has happened to them, their experience for which he gives thanks to God.

The summary has a narrative substructure; this is the way Paul thinks, in the categories of the macronarrative of the saving acts of the one God. The manner in which they are expressed, without explanation, indicates they are not new to the readers, but represent basic elements of Christian faith and experience in which he has instructed them and with which they are already familiar. Paul is not here "teaching"; the letter evokes and summarizes previous teaching.

The implied narrative. Paul's summary in 1:9b–10 has a narrative structure, but it is not a chronological program of his evangelistic strategy. It is *not* the case that here he pictures the missionaries as first preaching monotheism over against pagan polytheism; after convincing some Thessalonians that there is only one God, he can move on to his second christological point: this God has acted in the history of Israel and definitively in Christ. Then, to those convinced that Jesus is the Messiah, he can move on to point three, eschatological instruction about the last things. Imagining such a three-step process would be a misunderstanding of the genre of the text. Likewise the question of whether Paul's preaching was theocentric or christocentric is a false alternative. If the question is nevertheless posed in this way, the answer must be that the message of Paul the Jew remains theocentric. The Thessalonians are not said to have been converted to Christ, but to turn from idols to God. The word *God* occurs thirty-six times in 1 Thessalonians, more than *Jesus*, *Christ*, and *Lord* together. From first letter to last, Paul's message of the "gospel of God" proclaims a gospel of which God is both source and content: the phrase is both subjective and objective genitive (1 Thess 2:2, 8–9; Rom 1:1, 16; 15:16). The one God is producer and actor of the whole drama of salvation, not only its first act. While data gleaned from the whole Pauline corpus can be used to fill in the outline of this creation-to-eschaton macronarrative of Paul's theology in more detail, and in more than one way, Paul's summary in 1 Thess 1:9b–10 implies the following proclamation that was effective in the Thessalonians' conversion. It is a drama in seven acts:

1. One God the Creator. Throughout his mission, Paul continues to proclaim his Jewish view that Gentiles "do not know God" (1 Thess 4:5) and that faith in the one God is foundational for everything else (1:9).[21] Neither the verb *ktizō* (create) nor the nouns *ktistēs* (creator) or *ktisis* (creation) occur in 1 Thessalonians. Here Paul is not teaching a doctrine of creation; he is not teaching at all, but gratefully evoking the memory of their conversion from devotion to idols to serving the one God. Polytheism, however, has no deity who transcends the whole universe and is responsible for it all; reality is apportioned to a number of powers who are themselves part of the universe, which has no creator but is a given. To be converted from this understanding of reality and the meaning of one's own life is a radical, life-changing step, not an exchange of one religious theory for another. Though not spelled out here, the one God is the creator God, not a dependent part of reality, but the one on whom everything is dependent. That this one God is the *true* God not only contrasts God's reality with the sham reality of the false gods; "true" (*alēthinos*) is resonant with the attributes of the living God of the Jewish Scriptures, who is faithful (*pistos*; cf. 5:24), the

---

21. Cf. Bultmann (1:66–67, 74, 79), who points out that monotheism is inherently related to both creation and eschatology.

promise-keeping God of the covenant people among whom the Gentile Thessalonians are now numbered.

II. Rebellion, judgment, wrath. The world as Paul knows it is still the world created by God, but it is a world under judgment. Humanity as such, all human beings, are disobedient to God, have exchanged obedience to the true God, which would represent their true humanity, for service to nongods, idols. This represents not merely falling short of an ideal, but especially rebellion against their creator and lord. When asked why, if there is one God who is both righteous and powerful, this God does not establish justice, the answer of mainstream eschatological Judaism, nourished by its biblical faith, was clear: God will. The world is a story, a story that has a beginning and is under the author's control. And the story is not yet over. No matter how the world looks now, in the final chapter the divine author will bring the world to a worthy conclusion and establish justice. Inherent in this imagery is the reward of good and destruction of evil. The coming kingdom of God means both blessing and wrath; it is a way of speaking of the justice of God, which will not remain frustrated forever, but will finally be realized. As in the biblical prophets, the day of judgment and God's justice will be the day of wrath. Depictions of the coming kingdom, the establishment of justice, the day of the Lord, and the wrath of the holy God are interwoven in a kaleidoscope of imagery. The holiness of God cannot tolerate human sin; the wrath of God that will destroy evil at the end of history already sometimes flashes forth in the present.[22] God's wrath occurs twenty-one times in Jeremiah alone, a book that had a profound effect on Paul (see on 5:27). Both John the Baptist and Jesus are represented as proclaiming the wrath to come (Matt 3:7; Mark 3:5; Luke 21:23). Some of Jesus' parables portray, in violent pictures of God's wrath, the God of justice who finally punishes and destroys evil (e.g., Matt 22:1–14; 25:14–46; Luke 12:41–53; 13:24–30). Apocalyptic imagery regularly portrays the coming kingdom of God, in which God's justice will be established, as the day of God's "wrath" (e.g., Rev 6:12–17). The judgment, the wrath, is future, though it casts its shadow into the present.

In the undisputed letters, Paul does not elaborate this violent imagery (as, e.g., in Rev 6), but his depiction of the coming wrath of God on a world already judged to be universally sinful is more than the impersonal, mechanical working out of the moral principle of the universe, as evil receives its due in progressive moral degeneration.[23] But neither is God's wrath "anger" in the sense of emotional rage, an outburst of bad temper. The coming wrath is the personal

---

22. This imagery is found scores of times in Paul's Bible; e.g., Num 11:1; 16:46; Deut 9:8, 19; 29:19; 2 Kgs 22:13; 23:26; 2 Chr 28:18–19; 36:16; Pss 21:9; 59:13; 110:5; Isa 13:9, 13; Jer 7:20; Ezek 7:19; 20:33; Zeph 2:3; Sir 5:7; see especially Mal 3:13–4:4 for the imagery that has shaped Paul's understanding, now rethought in view of the Christ event.

23. Contra, e.g., Dodd 1932, 47–50.

response of the personal God, God's response to injustice and the human arrogance that claims to be in charge of the world, summed up in Paul's own later phrase "the day of wrath, when God's righteous judgment will be revealed" (Rom 2:5 NRSV; cf. Rev 11:18; cf. Calvin on Rom 2:16: "*Wrath,* without any additional term, means the judgment of God").[24] Paul is faithful to his Bible and his Jewish past when, as a nonnegotiable article of his theology, he maintains that the one God is God-the-judge. This is a given, absolutely axiomatic, not something for which he must argue, but an encompassing image from which he could always argue (e.g., see Rom 3:6).[25] Before the one God, all human beings live their lives under judgment, which means under the reality and threat of the coming wrath. This already/not-yet understanding of the wrath of God is preserved and illustrated in such texts as the "Battle Hymn of the Republic" (often cited in the sermons of the nonviolent Martin Luther King Jr.) and John Steinbeck's *Grapes of Wrath.*

Paul does not elaborate any of this in 1 Thessalonians. The matter-of-fact way in which he assumes this reality, in a letter to people who had not thought this way before their conversion, indicates that during his brief time with them Paul has taught them the rudiments of the new symbolic universe that comes with the Christian faith, including an understanding of the nature of human existence founded on a Christian interpretation of Gen 1–3. We know that a relatively short time later, Paul will be elaborating this teaching in the didactic letters of 1 Corinthians and Romans: the old, Adamic humanity, to which they no longer belong, is under the judgment of God (cf. 1 Cor 15:45–57; Rom 5:12–21). He has probably instructed the new congregation in Thessalonica in this tradition, and the teachers he has equipped continued this instruction in the interval since his departure. In any case, Paul himself presupposes all this in his summary of their conversion.

III. Election of a beloved people of God created by grace. Likewise, Paul's summary presupposes, but does not elaborate, the next act in the divine drama that had happened long before Paul's arrival in Thessalonica. The creator God's response to human rebellion was not to abandon humanity to their fate. From within sinful and rebellious humanity, God called into being a particular people to receive his grace and to be his witnesses to the rebellious peoples of the world and God's instrument in their salvation (see on 2:12–13). Conversion, turning to God from idols, was not a matter of individual enlightenment, but of being incorporated into this elect people and its mission, as Paul has already reminded them (see on 1:4).

---

24. Calvin 1960a, ad loc. While neither Paul nor his better interpreters believed in a vindictive God or relished the punishment of God's enemies, Paul's understanding of God's grace and love did not exclude imagery of divine judgment, including "wrath." So John Chrysostom 383, *Homily 2* on 2 Thessalonians: "Let us not be over-soft."

25. Cf. Boring 1986, 277–78.

IV. The Christ event: death, resurrection, exaltation to be Lord. For Paul, the central act of the divine drama is the Christ event, concentrated in the incarnation, death, and resurrection of the Messiah. In turning to God, the Thessalonians turn to *this* God, the true and living God. Paul's life as Christian and apostle began with his encounter with the risen Christ; his preaching in the Gentile world began by announcing God's act in the resurrection. Paul's proclamation of Jesus Christ was theocentric. The resurrection was God's act; Jesus did not "rise," but "was raised" (see on 4:14). It was not an isolated act affecting only the individual Jesus, but the leading edge of the final events, the establishment of God's just reign at the consummation of history. The resurrection of Jesus was absolutely fundamental for Paul, not one event among others in the life of Jesus, not the happy ending of an otherwise tragic story, but the beginning of God's new world of justice and peace. Paul can sum up the consummation of God's purpose for the world in the one image of "life from the dead" (e.g., Rom 11:15). In 1 Thessalonians, only here does Paul refer to Jesus as God's Son. The language of sonship and resurrection here means not just that Jesus was restored to life, but that in the resurrection event God exalted him to his true (preexistent) status.[26] Later Paul will cite a traditional creed from Jewish Christian circles where the title "Son of God" expresses his installation into the heavenly glory as Son of God at the resurrection (Rom 1:3–4).

V. Conversion. Not just Paul's conversion, but also the conversion of his readers, is important in his theology and a reason for thanksgiving. The Thessalonians have actually been *converted.* Their conversion was not from being irreligious to being religious or "spiritual," but from false gods to the one true God. This was different from Paul's own conversion. When he became a Christian, Paul did not need to change the framework of his symbolic world, but found that the story line that unfolds within this framework had been radically reoriented by the death and resurrection of the Messiah. The Thessalonians, on the other hand, were converted to a new symbolic universe. They had to experience a "conversion of the imagination."[27]

The human response to God's act is expressed by three verbs: they turned, they serve, they wait. We may again recognize the tridimensional past/present/future dynamic of faith in Paul's theology. The verbs are active: they turned (1:9), but they also were turned. Paul has already declared that they were chosen by God—not that they chose God. The present summary makes conversion

---

26. See Haufe 29. There is nothing explicit about preexistence and incarnation in 1 Thessalonians, but a little later Paul will cite the hymn of Phil 2:5–11 with no suggestion that this is a new christological insight. It is unlikely that a fundamentally new christological perspective occurred to him only late in his career. In any case, Paul is not "teaching Christology" here and is not analytically thinking through the pool of imagery that forms the matrix of his thought, a pool that already includes preexistence.

27. Hays 2005b.

their own act. Such apparently conflicting statements should not be "harmonized" by parceling them out in such a manner that conversion is "partly" human responsibility and "partly" God's sovereign act. Humans are entirely responsible; God is entirely sovereign (cf. the expression of this paradox in Phil 2:12–13). The focus here is on their own act. The new converts are not passive, not spectators to their own salvation.

Both Paul and the new Thessalonian Christians understood that they had made a radical break with the transitory, evil world soon to be re-created as God's kingdom. They no longer belonged to the old world that was passing away. Such a conversion was felt as a revolutionary step and was so regarded by their associates and neighbors. The Greco-Roman world was generally tolerant and syncretistic on such matters, so long as they did not conflict with the Roman ideology. Exclusive monotheism[28] was known only in Judaism. But now a new congregation has been called to a strict renunciation of the world and its gods. In the first-century Mediterranean world, religion, culture, politics, and everyday life were fused in a close symbiotic union. We can thus readily understand that the new group was looked on with suspicion and hostility. Neither the new converts nor their neighbors regarded their conversion as "just their own business." Even with the adaptability that Paul will later commend in 1 Cor 8–10, the Christians' rejection of traditional religion might represent a danger for community, city, and state. "Citizens of Thessalonica worried whether the gods, whose home on Mount Olympus they could see a mere fifty miles away to the southwest, might punish the whole city for the sacrilegious actions of a few."[29] This does not mean that the new Christians were in principle disloyal to local and empire-wide government. They did not see themselves as having joined a community of political protest. But their new commitments generated tensions that were potentially violent, and they knew this from the beginning.

VI. Life between the times: serving and waiting. Conversion brought an entirely new perspective on the lives of the new converts. The stories of their little individual lives, previously framed by birth and death, are now inserted into the grand narrative of the plan of God for the world, from creation to consummation, and their little congregation has been incorporated into the ongoing story of the people of God, which they are learning about from the Scripture. They live between the times, looking both backward and forward. They look back to the death and resurrection of Jesus, only twenty years earlier, and forward to the Parousia and coming of the kingdom of God in the near future. The little congregations of Christian believers are already fragmentary realizations

---

28. The "inclusive monotheism" of, e.g., Cleanthes in the 3d cent. B.C.E. ("O Zeus of many names . . .") did not affirm worship of only one God in the sense that other gods did not exist, but regarded worship of any god as in fact worship of Zeus.

29. Weima 2014, 108.

of the new reality that dawned in the resurrection, beachheads of the coming triumph of God. Paul sums up this in-betweenness of Christian existence with two active verbs: "serve" and "wait."

The present character of the Christian life is expressed by the active verb "serve" (*douleuō*), the Greek verb for "be a slave." The word was not common or popular in Greek thought and literature as a term for relation to the gods; it had too servile a connotation for the freedom-loving Greeks—who *had* a lot of slaves, but disdained the idea of identifying *themselves* as slaves. By contrast, the Jewish Scriptures and Judaism do not regard human beings as such as free and autonomous individuals, but as creatures of the one God, who owe God obedient service. In the biblical and Jewish tradition that formed Paul's understanding of the world and life, slave/servant of God was a title of honor. Israel's heroes were "servants of God"; doing God's will is service to God. Paul develops this Jewish usage that was already native to him. In his later and more doctrinal Letters to the Galatians and the Romans, being enslaved to sin/law/ world/death is contrasted with being enslaved to God. Salvation is deliverance from slavery to sin and the hostile powers that rob life of its meaning. This salvation, however, is not deliverance to individualistic autonomy. In Judaism and Paul, human life was essentially service to someone or something (Rom 6). Conversion was a change of masters. Idols were sometimes seen by Paul as nonexistent (1 Cor 8:4), sometimes as demons (1 Cor 10:19–20). In either case, human life had previously been enslaved to them and now has a new master, "in whose service is perfect freedom."[30] Already in Judaism, "service" meant more than the liturgical act of worship service, but the total binding of oneself to God as Lord of life. In 1 Thessalonians, service to God is found only here, but the manner in which Paul introduces it, without explanation and in a summary of their conversion, indicates that it was familiar to the Thessalonians, and that Christian life as service to God had been a part of the founding missionary proclamation and later instruction.

Paul sums up future orientation of Christian life in the active verb "wait" (*anamenō*), found only here in the New Testament. Pauline usage elsewhere makes clear that he does not mean a passive waiting, but the confident expectation of that which is vividly real but not yet present. The time between Jesus' resurrection and the Parousia is not a parenthesis, but instead fulfilled time, energized by the presence of the Spirit and the responsibility of witness, mission, and mutual edification in faith, love, and hope (5:4–11). Such waiting also acknowledges that things are not finally in our own hands and lets God be God.

---

30. From the Book of Common Prayer. Cf. Martin Luther's 1520 treatise *On the Freedom of a Christian*, which has in its opening words, "A Christian is a perfectly free lord of all, and subject to none; a Christian is a perfectly dutiful servant of all, and subject to all" (Luther 2).

This between-the-times existence is not a passive waiting for Jesus to come, but is filled with active content. It is the time to serve God, to live in a manner that corresponds to their new faith, living "worthy of God," and "pleasing God" (2:4, 12; 4:1–3; 5:18), in love for their new brothers and sisters in the family of God, as well as those outside the Christian community.

VII. The consummation: deliverance from the coming wrath. The Parousia hope was not an addendum, the last chapter of the Christian story, but was foundational. For members of the first Christian generation, the return of Jesus in the near future was part of the Christ event, part of the resurrection faith, the completion of what had just happened, not an unconnected event to happen in the distant future.

The new life of the believers in Thessalonica is portrayed as waiting for Jesus, who delivers from the wrath to come. Wrath enters the picture only as something from which believers are saved, not as a threat used to terrify them. Here it is important to understand the nature of such confessional language, the language of insiders who confess their faith, not objectifying spectator language that fits into a logical system from which inferences may be drawn (see on 1:4 above). There is nothing vindictive here, no gloating over what will happen to others, not even any statement that God's wrath will be inflicted on others. Such language of worship and prayer is not objectifying description of the fate of outsiders, but the confession of faith of insiders. The avoidance of such language in mainline churches, along with the language of salvation in general, is mostly due to the misunderstanding of the function of such language. Serious, reasonable, and compassionate Christians rightly reject such language when it is used to portray a vengeful God who finally condemns to torment most of the human race, or when it functions as a threat to keep believers in line. But avoiding or eliminating such language eviscerates the substance of the biblical message and reduces it, in Richard Niebuhr's words, to a bland spirituality in which "a God without wrath brought men without sin into a kingdom without judgment through the ministrations of a Christ without a cross."[31] Nor is the issue to find a way of getting around the hard texts in the Bible, as though it were a matter of being too tenderheartedly liberal to just accept the biblical teaching of the wrath of God. The issue is understanding the nature and function of such language. It must be retained, but it must be rightly interpreted. Paul's thanksgiving does not make affirmations about the fate of unbelievers; instead, it is grateful praise that in turning from idols to the God revealed in Jesus, they now look forward to his Parousia as the one who delivers from wrath.[32]

31. H. Richard Niebuhr 193.

32. Although Paul does not infer the fate of outsiders from such confessional language, the author of 2 Thessalonians does do so. This is another reason why it is important to be clear on authorship issues, for interpreters who understand 1 Thessalonians on the basis of 2 Thessalonians

2:1–12 Apostolic Missionaries Worthy of God

This is not a new topic nor an interruption or digression from an old one. Paul sees his apostolic existence as embraced in God's mission that has been effective among the Thessalonians, and he is grateful. Though there are apologetic dimensions of this section, it is not an apology but a continuation of the thanksgiving. Paul has already anticipated this section in 1:5.

2:1 For[a] you yourselves know, brothers and sisters, that our initial visit[b] to you was not without results, 2 but, as you know, even though we had already suffered and been mistreated in Philippi, with God's help[c] we had the courage to proclaim the gospel of God to you, in spite of strong opposition. 3 For when we preached to you, our appeal was not based on delusion,[d] or made with mixed motives or some sort of trickery, 4 but, just as we had been tested and approved by God to be entrusted with the gospel, so we speak not to please human beings, but to please God, who tests our hearts. 5 For as you know and God is our witness, we never appeared among you with flattering words, nor with a pretext for what was actually greed, 6 nor were we seeking honor—not from you, not from anyone else 7 (though we could have insisted on our importance[e] as apostles of Christ), but when we were with you we were [like] little children,[f] like a nursing mother tenderly caring for her own children, 8 caring so much for you that it was our joy to share with you not only the gospel, but also our own selves, so beloved[g] you had become to us. 9 For you remember, brothers and sisters, our labor and hardship; working night and day so as not to burden any of you, we proclaimed to you the gospel of God. 10 You are witnesses, and so is God, how holy, upright, and blameless our conduct was toward you believers, 11 just as you well know, how we dealt with each one of you like a father dealing with his own children, 12 making our appeal, encouraging you, and pleading with you to lead your lives[h] in a way worthy of the God who calls[i] you into his own kingdom and glory.

a. The conjunction *gar* begins a new sentence, but there is no major break in the thought. Chapter and verse divisions appear much later.
b. For *eisodos*, see note on 1:9, the only other occurrence of this word in the Pauline corpus.

---

cannot understand Paul's language in the way interpreted above. For a more extended discussion on the nature of confessional language and the interpretation of symbolic, mythological language, see Boring 1984, 91–114; 1989, 51–59, 116–17; 2012, 107, 299, 448, 653, and the bibliography given there.

c. *En theō*, lit., "in God." As in 1:1 (see note and comments there) this rare phrase in Paul indicates that the missionaries were not operating on their own, but in the presence and power of God, i.e., with God's help.

d. *Planē* can have either an active meaning, *deceit*, or a passive meaning, *being deceived, deluded*. Paul is expressing his thanks to God that they considered him neither deluded nor deceitful.

e. The Greek expression includes the word *baros* (weight) and could be colloquially translated "throwing our weight around." It is echoed in v. 9, "so as not to *burden* any of you" (*epibarēsai*).

f. Here the interpreter faces a problem of both text and translation. The textual problem is that the MS evidence strongly supports the reading *nēpioi* (babes, children; 𝔓⁶⁵ ℵ* B C* D* F G I Ψ* and MSS of the Old Latin, Vulgate, and Coptic versions), while the context seems to favor *ēpioi* (gentle; ℵᶜ A C² D² K L P Ψᶜ 0278 33 81 104ᶜ 326* 365 630 1241 1505 1739 and most later MSS). The earliest extant support for *ēpioi* is the 5th-cent. Alexandrinus; all the oldest and best MSS read *nēpioi*, but most have been "corrected" to *ēpioi*, followed by the majority of later MSS. On the basis of the overwhelming MS evidence, and following the principle that the more difficult reading is likely to be original, both NA²⁸ and UBS⁴ read *nēpioi*. However, many English translations, including the NRSV, assume *ēpioi* to be correct and translate "gentle as a nurse" (major exceptions only TNIV, NIV11, CEV). The problem is perceived to be Paul's violent switch of metaphors, comparing himself both to a little child and to a nurse, and the awkward syntax resulting from reading *nēpioi*. The above translation understands *nēpioi* as the original text, with an understood verb (*to be like*, corresponding to the next clause) that facilitates the double comparison. The meaning "to be like" for the rare combination *hōs [e]an* is found in Judg 7:5 LXX.³³

g. As in 1:4 (see note and comments there), the word connotes God's choice and acceptance as well as being loved by the missionaries.

h. Verbs for "walking" (*peripateō, poreuomai*, often with *hodos*, "way") to refer to leading one's life could sound a bit strange in Greek, but this was standard biblical and Jewish vocabulary (cf. Deut 5:33; 2 Kings 20:3 and often in the LXX, and examples in BDAG 803; *TDNT* 5:942–43). One's life is not thought of as a static essence or interior reality, as in some streams of Greek thought, but a "walk," a progression between beginning and end that must be conducted in a certain way, guided by a particular rule toward a particular goal. Life is actualized by one's deeds, by one's "walk." Thus in Judaism, *hālak, hǎlākâh*, the verb and noun for "walk," are key terms for ethics. See intro, "Theological Perspectives."

i. The present *kalountos* is found in B D F G H K L P and most later MSS. The aorist *kalesantos* is read by ℵ A 104 326 945 1505 2464 and the Latin, Syriac, and Coptic versions, which would make the calling refer to a past act and suggest that believers are presently already in the kingdom of God. This is appropriate in Gal 1:6, from which some scribes presumably took it, and in the series of verbs in Rom 8:30, which refer to salvation as a past event. Here, however, the verb refers to the ongoing call of God to

---

33. For full discussions of the textual and syntactical issues in translating this verse, see Burke 154–56; Fee 65–71; Gaventa 2007, 17–20; Fowl; and their related bibliographies.

persevere in the Christian life, which leads to salvation. See 1 Thess 5:24, where there is no ambiguity and no variation in the MSS.

Recent interpreters have devoted much study to the genre of this section as a key to understanding it.[34] Following are some genres considered.

Apologia? A durable scholarly tradition understands this section to be an apology in which Paul defends himself and his colleagues against actual charges that were being made against them in Thessalonica. Although no charges are cited, this approach employs the technique of mirror reading, assuming that Paul's denials respond to actual accusations, that he represents himself as he does in this section because he is being misrepresented by opponents in Thessalonica. The older variation of this view, accepting the historicity of the details of the Acts 17:1–9 account, supposes that representatives of the Jewish synagogue continue to circulate malicious reports about the missionaries and understands much of 1 Thessalonians as responding to these false charges.[35] A more recent version of this view regards these verses as an "apologia for his own apostolic work, a self-defense against possible suspicions that he acted from self-interested motives—making propaganda for his gospel, flattering his hearers, seeking his own glory, and even wanting to enrich himself at their expense."[36] A large city such as Thessalonica would have been familiar with traveling preachers and teachers who passed through, some of whom were deceptive scoundrels interested only in lining their own pockets before moving on to the next town. Legitimate teachers defended themselves against being perceived as such frauds, as a conventional part of the way they presented themselves.

Paraenesis? The work of Abraham Malherbe has influenced a number of recent scholars, persuading them that this section is not really an apologia against actual charges, but a conventional, expected topos in which a teacher declares his own integrity. The paragraph functions as paraenesis, not apology, and cannot be used to reconstruct actual opponents in Thessalonica.[37] *Paraklēsis* (2:3) is a key element, here as elsewhere, encouraging the Thessalonians to continue in their faith despite the hardships it entails. They are not suspicious of Paul, evoking an apologetic statement from him, but wavering in their commitment to the Pauline message and wondering whether it is worthwhile to continue.

---

34. Only one example: a series of international conferences involving most of the major scholars who had written or were writing commentaries on the Thessalonian correspondence focused on the genre of 1 Thess 2:1–12, resulting in a book-length collection of essays and responses: Donfried and Beutler.

35. This view is classically represented by the studies of Frame; Milligan; and continued among contemporary scholars by, e.g., Holtz 1986, 94, 110–12.

36. Bornkamm 64.

37. Malherbe (2000, 133–63) sums up and explicates his several contributions to the debate.

Narratio/autobiography? Some interpreters who see firm rhetorical patterns as shaping the structure of the letter argue that it corresponds to the *narratio* section of a persuasive speech, giving the basis for Paul's appeal.[38] The "auto-biographical" section Gal 1:12–2:14 is taken to be such a *narratio*. Without adopting the rhetorical categories, some see the section as autobiographical in the sense of some sections of the biblical prophetic books.[39]

Continuation of the thanksgiving? This is the construal pursued in the present exegesis, holding that 1 Thess 2:1–12 should not be interpreted as a discrete section, but as a continuation of the thanksgiving that began in 1:2 and continues to 3:13 (see above at 1:2). There is no break in the thought at 2:1. While elements of apology, paraenesis, *narratio*, and autobiography are included, the whole section is embraced in the ongoing thanksgiving. The overarching point of the thanksgiving is reached in 2:13, where *eucharistoumen* (we give thanks) explicitly appears again. Paul is grateful that they received his word as the Word of God, which has called the church into being in Thessalonica and brought about the dramatic transformation of their lives. That they received this word not as a human word but as God's word is elaborated in advance: the missionaries were not the typical traveling Hellenistic preachers and teachers seeking to exploit their hearers for their own profit. The theocentricity of the whole mission is evident. It is not about Paul, not about the Thessalonians, not even about Jesus and the experience of the Spirit, but about the initiative of God with Paul and the Thessalonians, for which Paul continues to give thanks.

Structure and intention. On the issues involved in sentence division, see above on 1:2–10. The sentence division adopted in the translation above is based on the following considerations. The first three sentences of this paragraph have the same structure (2:1–2, 3–4, 5–8). Each is introduced by the conjunction *gar* (for), followed by a series of negative clauses introduced by a form of *ou* (not), then the contrasting conjunction *alla* (but) introducing the positive point Paul is making.[40] Verse 9 is a single sentence, combining Paul's twin theses: he came to bring the gospel to them for their benefit, not his, and supported himself while he was doing it. The whole is then summarized in one complex sentence, vv. 10–12: Paul worked among them as a father works for his own children, for their sake, as the instrument of God's call. This structure is then compactly repeated in 2:13, where Paul explicitly resumes

38. See Jewett 1986, 68–78; Wanamaker 72–73, 90.

39. E.g., R. Collins (1990, 775) says 1 Thess 2:1–12 is an "autobiographical confession, similar in some respects to the confessions of Jeremiah." Paul's understanding of his own mission is certainly influenced by Jeremiah (see on 5:27), and there are elements of this influence that shine through his confession here, but there is no genre shift, and the paragraph cannot be called a confession in the Jeremianic sense.

40. This structure is very common in the Pauline tradition. Of the 326 verses in the NT exhibiting this pattern, more than half (172) are found in the undisputed Letters of Paul.

his thanksgiving that they received the missionary message *not* as the word of human beings, *but* as God's own word. This is not an apology in which Paul is reacting to someone else's agenda, but a thanksgiving in which he is actively pursuing his own program. The mood of thanksgiving dominates the whole: Paul is giving thanks for what has happened in Thessalonica, and he illustrates it by contrast with illustrations of what did *not* happen.

[2:1–2] The *for* relates this paragraph to the preceding one, as a continuation of the thanksgiving; *yourselves* relates to the same word in 1:9—not only do others report your response to the gospel, you yourselves also know how you responded. With the repeated phrase "you know," Paul evokes the experience of the Thessalonians. Though the phrase is found nine times in this brief letter,[41] Paul never uses it in 1 Thessalonians in a polemical or argumentative sense, nor to defend himself, but as an appeal to remember their own life experience they have shared with him, for which he gives thanks. Paul calls to mind their response to the arrival of the missionaries: although the Thessalonians might well have taken the recent rejection and mishandling of the missionaries in Philippi as a reason for keeping their distance, neither missionaries nor Thessalonians had been discouraged (cf. Acts 17:1–9; intro, "Context of Paul's Life"). Their preaching was not in vain (*kenos* = empty, without results, as in 3:5; 1 Cor 15:10; 2 Cor 6:1; Gal 2:2; Phil 2:16). The message they proclaimed is not only *about* God (1:9–10); it also comes *from* God. The "gospel of God" (2:2, 8, 9) is both genitive of content and genitive of source. God emboldened both preachers and hearers to accept it (cf. 2:13), which they did despite the strong opposition they experienced in Thessalonica, just as had happened in Philippi. To the Philippian congregation, Paul will later write of the suffering and conflict both apostle and congregation endured, using the same word, *agōn* (struggle, conflict; Phil 1:29–30).

[3–4] In the preceding sentence, Paul has described his bold, courageous speech when he first preached to them with a term, *parrēsiazomai* (verb form of *parrēsia*, free, bold speech), frequently used of the freedom of speech considered an essential virtue of the authentic Hellenistic teacher. The paragraph continues with several echoes of the claims made by such traveling philosopher-teachers, who found it necessary to distinguish themselves from uneducated charlatans who roamed about, crowd pleasers who passed themselves off as legitimate teachers, fleecing their audiences and moving on. Paul, too, claims that he speaks fearlessly, with a divine commission (v. 2); that his message is

---

41. The specific form *oidate* (you know) is found 63× in the NT, 25× in the undisputed Pauline Letters, 9 of which are in 1 Thessalonians (1:5; 2:1, 2, 5, 11; 3:3, 4; 4:2; 5:2). Outside 1 Thessalonians, more than half the occurrences are in the construction *ouk oidate*, a challenging question "Do you not know?" = "You do know, don't you?" which never occurs in 1 Thessalonians. In this letter, Paul is reminding and encouraging, not challenging or berating.

not a matter of error, impurity, or trickery (v. 3); that he is not a crowd pleaser (v. 4), a flatterer on the lookout for a quick profit (v. 5), but earned his keep by his own manual labor (v. 9), dealing with the Thessalonians in purity, honesty, and blameless conduct (v. 10), like a father (v. 11). Except for the claim that he supported himself by manual labor, the list is somewhat vague and general, analogous to the conventional vice catalogs found in the Pauline tradition (cf. 1 Cor 5:10–11; 6:9–10; Gal 5:19–21; Eph 4:31; 5:3–5; Col 3:5, 8; 1 Tim 1:9–10; 6:4–5; 2 Tim 3:2–4; Titus 3:3). Just as the vice lists function to warn against evil as such, and need not be read as indicating that the congregation addressed is guilty of the particular sins itemized, so Paul is not to be understood here as defending himself in response to actual charges. He is rejecting standard stereotypical objections so his claim to be an authentic teacher of divine truth can be taken seriously, but all this is more rhetorical than precisely descriptive. Since Paul presents himself as a role model for his converts (see on 1:6–7 above), this portrayal of his character and conduct serves indirectly as paraenesis.

It is striking that Paul can sum up the proclamation of the apostolic missionary message as *paraklēsis* (translated "appeal" above), a multilayered secular word of normal Greek vocabulary, which Jewish and early Christian tradition had filled with new meaning. (1) In prebiblical and parabiblical Greek, the noun *paraklēsis* and the verb from which it is derived (*parakaleō*) have the basic sense of "calling to," often with the nuances of calling for help, inviting, or summoning. (2) A second sense intensifies this basic meaning: "beseech," as when one calls on the gods in prayer, or implores social superiors for a favor. In a polite reversal of this sense, superiors can, in official letters, "invite" or "request" their subjects or inferiors to carry out their orders. (3) In a third sense, the words are used for "exhortation" or "encouragement," the effort to win someone over to one's own point of view. It thus became a philosophical term used by itinerant preachers and teachers of ethics. (4) A fourth, and somewhat rare meaning in secular Greek, is "comfort," giving encouragement in times of trouble and sorrow.

The biblical use of the word is important for Paul. In the framework of Paul's own symbolic universe, he is not representing himself as a legitimate philosopher-teacher over against frauds, but as standing in the line of the biblical prophets, especially Jeremiah (see on 5:27). The translators of the LXX used *paraklēsis* or *parakelō* to render *nḥm*, the term that came to be used for God's eschatological comfort/consolation of Israel, becoming a synonym for eschatological salvation, the fulfillment of God's plan for history, the coming of the kingdom of God (e.g., Isa 40:1 KJV, familiar to many as the opening words of Handel's *Messiah*: "Comfort ye, comfort ye my people"). In some later Jewish thought, the Comforter (*Menaḥem*) even became the name of the Messiah. Jesus probably, and early Christianity certainly, drew from this stream of tradition in which the language of "comfort" and "consolation" expresses eschatological salvation. Those who mourn, who lament the unjust state of the world and long for the coming kingdom of God, are promised that they will be *comforted* (Matt 5:4; the future passive represents the fulfillment of God's promise of eschatological salvation). The coming of the Messiah fulfills Israel's hope for the "*consolation* of Israel" (Luke 2:25). The eschatological gift of the Holy Spirit, and even the Messiah himself, is called the *paraklētos* (Paraclete): comforter, encourager, advocate (John 14:16, 26; 15:26; 16:7; 1 John 2:1). All this,[42] of course, makes clear that, when heard with the associations of modern English words, translating the terms as "comfort," "consolation," or "encouragement" is not only inadequate but also misleading. There are no connotations of feel-good subjectivity in "comfort," no associations with "prize for losers" in "consolation," and "encouragement" has nothing to do with pep talks or cheerleading (contra, e.g., *The Message*'s paraphrase of *parakalesai* in 3:2 as "cheering you on"). The words are resonant with the final realization of God's promise of a new creation of justice and peace.

When Paul adopts and uses this vocabulary[43] he fuses it with his evangelistic appeal, God's call/invitation to respond to this message. The appeal to respond in faith is grounded in the prior act of God: the invitation and call is inseparably woven into the announcement of the good news of what God has already done. Paul's use of *paraklēsis* terminology to sum up his whole message is beautifully captured in 2 Cor 5:19–21; the opening paragraphs of 2 Corinthians are saturated with this vocabulary (ten times in 2 Cor 1:3–7!). The "exhorter" (*parakalōn*) in the Pauline churches is the preacher who in one speech act both announces the saving act of God in Christ and invites/encourages/exhorts/appeals for response. Like the term *gospel* by which it is here bracketed (2:2, 4), *paraklēsis* has the double sense of gift and demand, communicated in an encouraging tone of voice. In Phlm 7–8, *paraklēsis* is contrasted with "command."[44] This sort of *grounded appeal* is the quintessence of the Pauline *paraklēsis*, to which he refers in this letter (see intro, "Religion in Thessalonica").

Paul sums up his self-understanding, which has been accepted by the Thessalonians, that he is one who "had been tested and approved by God to be entrusted with the gospel." All this talk about himself is not a matter of ego. Throughout his missionary career, Paul continues to be stunned that God has

42. This is only a brief sketch, of course. For further details and nuancing, see Thomas and the bibliography he gives.

43. Paul uses this language more than any other canonical author. Of the 139× *paraklēsis* and the related verb form *parakaleō* occur in the NT, 59 are in the undisputed Pauline Letters, with an additional 16 in the Deuteropaulines.

44. See Malherbe 1983; Merk 104.

entrusted him with the Christian message, a message that belongs to the world. It is not Paul's message that he generously shares with the world, but the world's message, which God has entrusted to Paul to be delivered to its rightful owners. He insists that this has actually happened. God has acted in Christ for the salvation of the world, and God has acted in his own life to entrust him with the gospel. Paul has been called, tested, approved, and entrusted with the gospel: thus he is an *apostle* (cf. 2:7). The passive verbs used in this terminology are divine passives, pointing to God as the actor who calls, tests, approves, and entrusts. The Thessalonians are not merely responding to Paul; it is the gospel of *God* with which both Paul and the Thessalonians have to do. He gives thanks that the Thessalonians have accepted him as such a messenger, as an authentic apostle.

[5–8] Not only did Paul and his colleagues not attempt to impress the Thessalonians with flattery, or attempt to manipulate them for their own illegitimate purposes; they also did not appeal to their legitimate apostolic authority, though they *could* have done so. The text before us represents the earliest extant appearance in literature of the Christian technical term *apostle*. Its specific Pauline meaning was not new to the original readers, however; otherwise it could not have been introduced so casually. The word itself was not new. Like all technical religious vocabulary, such words had a secular meaning before being adopted and adapted into the Christian community.

The English word *apostle* is the transliteration (not translation) of the Greek word *apostolos*, a noun form derived from the common verb *apostellō*, used 783 times in the LXX and the New Testament, which means simply "send." The word itself has no religious significance. It can be used of God's sending people on a special mission, as when Moses is sent to Pharaoh (Exod 3:10), and is thus used of God's sending the prophets to Israel (Isa 6:8; 61:1; Jer 51:4 LXX), but there is no sense of special mission in the word itself. As used in secular Greek, the noun *apostolos* likewise had a common secular meaning, anything *sent*; it was often used, for example, of the invoice, or bill of lading, accompanying exported goods, or of a ship or expedition sent from one port to another. *Apostolos* was, however, occasionally used for persons sent for a specific purpose, with the context determining the purpose and status of the person sent. Although the Jewish Scriptures were familiar with the concept of divine commissioning and sending, the term *apostolos* is found at most once in the LXX (1 Kgs 14:6, only in Codex Alexandrinus, in reference to the prophet Ahijah). The word is thus virtually absent from Paul's Bible, and it is almost completely missing from the voluminous literature of Hellenistic Judaism; for example, it is entirely missing from Philo, and occurs only once in Josephus (*Ant.* 17.300).

There were no *apostoloi* in first-century Judaism. In Palestinian Judaism, however, there was a particular usage of a word derived from the Hebrew verb "send" (*šlḥ*), the noun *šlyḥ*, vocalized as the *šālîaḥ*, which came to mean a messenger authorized to act in behalf of the one who sent him.[45] Already in earliest Palestinian Christianity, the word seems to have been adopted with the meaning "authorized representative" and translated into Greek as *apostolos*, one commissioned and sent as the representative of some other person or group. It thus can be translated as *delegate, deputy, messenger, ambassador, representative*, or any other commissioned person. Thus Jesus can be called God's apostle (Heb 3:1), and those commissioned to particular tasks by the churches are called apostles. In Phil 2:25, Epaphroditus is called *apostolos* (NRSV *messenger*; cf. marginal note). In 2 Cor 8:23 the duly elected representatives of the churches of Asia, Macedonia, and Achaia who would accompany Paul on his trip to Jerusalem are called *apostoloi* (NRSV *messengers*). In Acts 14:4, 14, Barnabas and Paul are called *apostoloi*, authorized missionaries of the Antioch church (cf. Acts 13:1–3). In the first generation of Christianity, the term *apostoloi* quickly developed a more narrow, technical meaning: those who had been directly chosen by Jesus Christ, either during his earthly life or by a special appearance after the resurrection, to be the authorized interpreters of what became the "apostolic faith." The adjective *apostolikos* (apostolic) used in this sense is found in second-century patristic writings, but not in the New Testament. Alongside this, the other, broader usage continued to be applied to authorized representatives of the churches commissioned for particular temporary tasks. Still later, in some circles the term began to be restricted to the Twelve. Originally the apostles were a larger group, of which the Twelve were only a part; this was still the situation in Paul's time (cf., e.g., 1 Cor 15:5–8). The later situation is represented in the "twelve apostles" of Matt 10:2; Luke 6:13; Rev 21:14, and the usage of Acts throughout (where Paul is not considered an apostle in the same sense as the Twelve).

From the time of his conversion onward, Paul understood himself to be an apostle. The risen Lord, who had appeared to him, called him not only to be a Christian believer, but also to be an apostle, an authorized representative of the risen Christ. Under the auspices of the church at Antioch, for some time Paul worked as a missionary, as one of its authorized representatives (probably also the case with his relationship to the church at Damascus). There was no conflict between his identity as an authorized representative of a particular church and an apostle directly authorized by Christ: Paul was both until the "Antioch incident" of Gal 2:11–21 (see intro, "Context of Paul's Life"). Thereafter Paul launched his independent mission in the Aegean cities, with Philippi

45. K. H. Rengstorf ("*apostellō ktl.*," *TDNT* 1:414–20) argues for an institutionalized office, and more recently J.-A. Bühner ("*apostolos*," *EDNT* 1:142–46) has argued for a special legal usage, but no *šālîaḥ* office. Becker (79–81) helpfully summarizes the Pauline understanding of apostleship in this context.

and Thessalonica as the first outposts of the new work in which he no longer saw himself as an apostle of the Antioch church, but as one directly commissioned by the risen Christ. Paul understood himself to be an apostle, witness, accredited messenger, fully authorized representative, example, *the* apostle to the Gentiles (Rom 11:13 NIV). He thought of himself as standing in the line of the prophets and of Jesus (see on 5:27). When he writes 1 Thessalonians, he has had this understanding of himself for at least fifteen years: in this letter we do not have an "early," still embryonic self-understanding.

The legitimacy of the Aegean mission and of Paul's apostleship were soon to be challenged. When Paul writes 1 Thessalonians, this development, painful in the extreme for Paul, had not yet begun, or Paul had not yet become aware of it. Here he can assume his apostolic status and introduce his letter, as from himself, Silvanus, and Timothy, with no reference to his apostolic office (1:1). In 2:7 he can refer to all three of the founding missionaries as *apostoloi* without feeling any necessity to clarify that he is an apostle in a different sense from his colleagues. He has seen the risen Lord and has been commissioned directly by him; this was not the case with Silvanus or Timothy. They, to be sure, are Christ's missionaries in the general sense but not apostles of Christ in the special sense Paul claims for himself and the limited group of representatives directly authorized by the risen Christ.

Paul has no need here to go into an explanation or defense of his apostleship. Within the comprehensive thanksgiving/body of the letter 2:1–3:13, he is declaring reasons for his gratitude to God for the new congregation in Thessalonica. Among these is the manner in which they have received him, as he preached to them without flattery, guile, or greed, and without throwing his weight around by insisting on his apostolic authority—which he *could* have done but did not. Instead, Paul reminds them that they now belong to a community in which the love and mutual care of a family prevails (see on 1:4). From time immemorial, the language of home and hearth, family and clan, has been a wellspring of religious imagery. From the *Odyssey* and the Prodigal Son through Thomas Wolfe's *You Can't Go Home Again* (1940) and Eric Knight's *Lassie Come-Home* (1940); from the Steven Spielberg film *E. T.* (1982) to Bernhard Schlink's *Homecoming* (2008)—images of home and family have captured the human spirit. This was true in both pagan and Jewish imagery, as it was in the message of Jesus, the early church, and Paul.[46]

The intensification of family imagery in this paragraph of 1 Thessalonians is no accident. Conversion to the Christian faith had sometimes caused strained relationships within families, or even uprooted the new converts from their family life, and they needed the reassurance that they belonged to a new and

46. For a detailed treatment of both social context of the imagery and exegesis of the relevant texts in 1 Thessalonians, see Burke.

greater family. This kind of language is not merely descriptive or hortatory but also performative: it brings into being the reality it describes.[47] The general picture is clear: the church is bound together not by institutional authority but by the tender bond of family relations, as manifested in Paul's own relation to them. The imagery is that of brothers and sisters in the family of God (see on 1:4 above), of mothers and wet nurses and fathers, infants and little children, of fathers and orphaned children. Even though the images clash and the nuances and details of Paul's collage are not clear, the main point of the pastiche of metaphors is the self-giving love, even the sharing of one's own body for the good of the other, that is the reality of a loving family. Paul is grateful—he is still speaking within the framework of the epistolary thanksgiving—that the new community has come into being in which, as he will later express it, the love of God has been poured into human hearts (Rom 5:5; cf. 1 Thess 1:3–4; 2:8; 3:6, 12; 4:9; 5:8, 13), and that he himself belongs to this community as a member of the family, not merely as church founder.

Shockingly, Paul's initial picture of himself within this collection of ecclesial icons is not that of the paterfamilias, but that of a *nēpios*, a term that can be used for children from infancy (1 Cor 3:1–2; Heb 5:13) to puberty (1 Cor 13:11; Gal 4:1). So far from slyly attempting to take advantage of them, Paul here represents himself and his colleagues as conducting the church-founding mission among them, not with duplicity, but being as vulnerable and innocent as little children (cf. 1 Cor 14:20, where the related verb form is used). This leads directly to the next image, the *trophos*, which usually refers to the nurse charged with taking care of children. This is not the nanny of modern British and American culture, but the *'āmâ*, the wet nurse who breast-fed infants when the mother could or would not. In the centuries before formula and baby bottles, the *trophos* was a common and beloved family figure. While Paul's metaphor possibly pictures the mother herself, the image of the tenderness with which the *trophos* nurse cares for *her own* children most likely points to a nurse who also has her own children, one who not only is competent and responsible in her job, but also manifests authentic mother love to her biological children—and cares for them without being paid.[48] Paul does not hesitate to apply such maternal imagery to himself and his fellow missionaries (see also Gal 4:19). The verb "share" has a double object, "the gospel" and "our own selves"—inseparable in Paul's understanding. When Paul affirms that it was the missionaries' joy not only to share the gospel with the new converts, but to share their own selves,

---

47. Cf. Meeks 1983, 86–88; and Gaventa 2007, 27.

48. Donfried (1985) argues that Paul adapts the image of nurse from the cult of Dionysus, popular in Thessalonica, where the women who play a key role in the cult are called "nurses." Even so, the cult would have borrowed the terminology from the role of nurses in family life. See Gerber 418.

men may need to be reminded that such care has a bodily component, but mothers who have breast-fed their children understand, as did the Thessalonians.

[9] The reference to Paul's (and his colleagues'?) manual labor does not begin a new topic. Connecting to the preceding with the conjunction *gar* (for), Paul continues the thought that the missionaries have given not only the gospel, but also themselves, to the new converts. His metaphor has conjured up the image of the nursing mother, who nourishes from her own body. He now mentions the reality of physical labor. The expression "night and day" is conventional, but no less real (cf. "worked my fingers to the bone"). It does not necessarily picture Paul as "moonlighting" in order to support his daytime preaching ministry, but portrays the normal workday of the manual laborer, sunup to sundown. Paul's evangelism was probably not street-corner preaching, but located in his leased workshop space, where he spoke to his coworkers, customers, and passersby, and in the homes of interested inquirers and new converts (see intro, "Context of Paul's Life"). This does not mean it was casual workaday chitchat. He speaks of "preaching the gospel" with the muscular verb *kēryssō* (16× in the undisputed Pauline Letters, only here in 1 Thessalonians), used in the Hellenistic world of official declarations and public announcements, and in the LXX of the preaching of the prophets. In New Testament usage, the word is often used for public preaching, but the focus is not on the action or location, but on the content—the announcement of an event, not the discussion of ideas. Paul communicated the gospel, announced the good news of God's saving act in Christ and the call to respond, while supporting himself by manual labor.

Such labor, generally disdained by the sophisticated Greco-Roman world, located Paul among the lower social class. In Paul's Jewish background, such work was typically evaluated more highly, but not always. The later rabbinic tradition will insist that even scholars, scribes, and rabbis must learn a trade and not be dependent on their teaching for their livelihood (*ʾAbot* 2:2; 4:5). In the second century B.C.E. the worldly-wise Ben Sirach is already leaning in the Hellenistic direction, arguing that only the man of leisure can be a teacher, not—almost using Paul's exact words—"the artisan, who labors by night as well as by day" (Sir 38:24–39:11, esp. 38:27). Here Paul speaks within the Hellenistic framework, considers his work a hardship that must be endured for the sake of the gospel, and reminds his readers that he has done this as part of his self-giving for the beloved community.

Paul worked so as not to burden his new converts by asking them for support, though he could legitimately have done so; "burden" (*epibareō*) echoes *baros* in v. 7. Paul did not ask his converts for money, though while he was in Thessalonica he did, more than once, receive money from the new congregation in Philippi (Phil 4:16).

In 1 Thessalonians there is no hint that Paul's working to support himself was a problem for the church. Later, in Corinth, the church was embarrassed that their founder was a common worker, a situation exacerbated by their awareness of opposing missionaries who claimed that Paul was no real apostle or he would insist on being supported by the church. In the Corinthian church, where there were a few wealthy members who would have liked to be Paul's patrons, Paul had to defend himself for refusing payment for his services and earning his own keep (1 Cor 9; 2 Cor 11:7–11). The membership of the Thessalonian church seems to have been working-class people like Paul, and he presents himself as one of them, as brother, who has shared their life for their sake. He thus presents himself as a model (see 1:6–7), and may also already be thinking of the appeal he will make in 4:10–12 for the Thessalonians to work with their own hands and be dependent on no one. Paul's later disciple and interpreter will certainly understand the instruction in 1 Thessalonians in this manner (2 Thess 3:9).

[10–12] Paul recapitulates the preceding in one lengthy and complex sentence, broken up in English translations for the sake of readability. Only one verb holds the somewhat convoluted structure together, the versatile *egenēthēmen* (lit., *we became*), already used twice in the paragraph (vv. 5, 7), and here translated "our conduct was." Calling God and the Thessalonians themselves as his witnesses, he characterizes the conduct of the missionaries during the founding visit with a series of three adverbs—pure(ly), upright(ly), and blameless(ly). It would have been grammatically crisper to have used adjectives, but the adverbial form points to the actions of the missionaries, what they actually did, not to a static quality of their character. The first two form a familiar pair in both pagan and biblical Greek, usually translated "devout and just," in other words, doing what is right in the eyes of both divine and human beings. This is another instance of familiar vocabulary filled with new content. In the pagan context "devout" meant "showing proper respect for the gods by doing what is required to maintain the balance between the world of the gods and the human world," thus offering prayers and sacrifices; "just" referred to proper conduct according to prevailing human standards. Even in the pagan sense, during the founding visit the missionaries conducted themselves with piety and propriety: they did not attack pagan religion or its gods, could not be accused of being irreligious, did not violate either the law of the land or common decency. In the LXX, the same phrase is applied to God and God's people (e.g., Deut 32:4; Ps 144:17 LXX [145:17 ET]; Prov 21:15; see also *Pss. Sol.* 15.3), usually translated "holy and just." Paul is thinking ahead to the specifically paraenetic section of the letter, beginning in 4:1, where he will give more instructions on the meaning of a life lived in accord with such a God. In claiming that the missionaries were blameless in all their relationships with the new converts, Paul does not intend to imply that the validity of the readers' new faith depends on the integrity of the missionaries, but on God, who called the church into being through the gospel. He is concerned that (false perceptions of) the character of the preachers must not become a hindrance to receiving the gospel, but even more is at stake: the new little congregation has become personally dear to Paul and his colleagues, and it would be painful to be misunderstood.

Changing the imagery once again, Paul claims that the missionaries' conduct during the founding visit was like that of a father with his own children. Contrary to the popular impression, Paul seldom uses fatherly imagery to portray his relation to his churches: only here in 1 Thessalonians, then in Phil 2:22 Timothy serves with him like a son with a father, in Phlm 10 Paul became Onesimus's father by converting him to the Christian faith, and in 1 Cor 4:15 Paul claims to have become the father of the Corinthian congregation through the gospel. The paternal image need not be understood paternalistically or even in terms of first-century patriarchy. Neither should it be reduced to a generic parental attitude. Paul has already used the tender, nourishing image of the nursing mother for himself and his fellow missionaries (v. 7). Here the image of fatherly responsibility within the family is surely recognized by his readers as conveying the responsibility of the father for the socialization and moral instruction of the children, especially the boys. This is Paul's meaning here. Within the collage of family imagery (see above), he introduces the role of the father to instruct his children—perhaps the "each one of you" is meant to emphasize that women are included—in the ethos of the new world into which they have been born. The missionaries' preaching and their response to it has torn them out of their old world and given them a new symbolic universe as the reality within which they are to shape their lives. They needed instruction in order to do this. The father is responsible for *re*educating them.

This reeducation is expressed with three participles, translated "making our appeal, encouraging you, and pleading with you." Though Paul is capable of speaking as an apostle who commands, here his fatherly instruction is not a matter of blind obedience but of response to explicit, substantial teaching. The first term includes the others. "Making our appeal" (*parakalountes*) forms a bracket with the *paraklēsis* of v. 3 (see above, trans. note d and comments on v. 3). The appeal is to "lead lives worthy of the God who calls you." "Lead your lives" is, literally, "walk" (see trans. note h). As a father, Paul and his colleagues teach the new converts how to walk in the responsibilities of their new life.

Their walk is to be "worthy of the God who calls you." "The One who calls you" is virtually a title for God, as in 5:24. The biblical God is the one who calls the worlds into being (Rom 4:17), who calls Israel into being (Isa 48:12), who continues to call the people of God into being (2 Cor 4:6). God's call is not an invitation in the RSVP sense; instead, it is performative language, which accomplishes what it states. Without minimizing human responsibility and decision, Paul regards the new Christian congregation not as volunteers, but as draftees (see above on 1:4). The church called into being by the word of God (2:13) cannot be grouped with the other good "volunteer organizations" that make the community a nicer place in which to live. Paul, his fellow missionaries, and the teachers they have commissioned in Thessalonica have begun to fill in the content of a life appropriate to those who are surprised to find themselves in a community called into being by God. In the paraenesis that begins at 4:1 of this letter, that process will continue.

The ultimate goal of this call is the kingdom of God. This is the only occurrence of this phrase in 1 Thessalonians, but the eschatological reality it points to is not dependent on vocabulary. That the phrase is introduced without explanation presupposes some instruction during the founding visit. Though the "kingdom of God" had been central to the message of Jesus, for early Christianity and for Paul the proclaimer had become the proclaimed, and Jesus' message had been taken up into the larger framework of the good news of God's act in Christ. Yet the kerygma of the earliest church and of Paul was not discontinuous with that of Jesus. Paul continues to use the language of the kingdom, but it is no longer the encompassing image. The phrase is found only eight times in the undisputed Letters of Paul, only once (Rom 14:17) in his longest and most explicitly theological letter. As was true for Jesus, the coming of God's reign is the eschatological hope, the reality of the ultimate victory of God already dawning, its reality already making itself known and shaping the present. Some specific aspects of this "daybreak ethos" will be spelled out in chapters 4–5.[49]

2:13–16 God's Word and Human Opposition

Excursus 1: Interpolation?

Already in the nineteenth century a few scholars such as F. C. Baur understood 1 Thess 2:16c to refer to the fall of Jerusalem and thus as evidence for regarding all of 1 Thessalonians as deuteropauline. More recently, some scholars have argued that the passage is an interpolation into a letter otherwise regarded as from Paul himself. This tendency is in part due to the increased post-Holocaust sensitivity to actual or perceived anti-Judaism, though it cannot be reduced to that. Substantial arguments for an interpolation have been presented, beginning with the 1971 essay of Birger Pearson that has become something of a classic.[50] Although there is no manuscript evidence for an interpolation, and no statement from an ancient author suggesting unpauline authorship of this paragraph, five lines of argument have led several scholars to accept the interpolation hypothesis: (1) The paragraph interrupts the context and is out of place, comparing the Thessalonians' problems in their Macedonian context to earlier problems of the church in its Judean context. The warm flow of family language is interrupted by a hateful tirade against "the Jews." (2) Only here does Paul claim that the Jews killed Jesus. (3) The

---

49. This phrase for NT ethics is from Keck (2005, 289) and is more precise than Wright's "For them the sun is already up, . . . the new day, which had already dawned in Jesus," which blurs the already/not yet distinction. See Wright 2013, 1291; better is 1367: "The night was already nearly over."

50. See Pearson.

charge that the Jews "displease God and oppose everyone" sounds like the common Gentile charge against Jews for their clannishness and standoffishness, taking care of each other but otherwise "haters of the human race," a charge that fits later Gentile Christian anti-Judaism but that Paul, himself a Jew, would not likely repeat. (4) The announcement that God's wrath has come on the Jews "at last" or "to the full" is a retrospective anti-Jewish interpretation of the 70 C.E. destruction of Jerusalem, and in any case is hard to reconcile with Paul's more positive perspective on God's final acceptance of the Jews in Rom 11. (5) The paragraph contains unpauline items of vocabulary, syntax, and style.

These arguments have been analyzed, evaluated, and challenged by competent and detailed counterarguments.[51] Most scholars continue to regard the passage as from Paul. In my own opinion, as the Pauline Letters were collected and edited into what became their present canonical form, some passages were added to the original texts (e.g., 1 Cor 14:34–35). In the course of my exegetical work on this paragraph, I have become convinced that this passage is best understood as from Paul himself. The following exegesis thus does not make defending its authenticity a major concern—this would require much more space than a commentary affords—but in the course of the exegesis I have incidentally offered some reasons for interpreting the text as part of Paul's original letter to Thessalonica.

Paul sums up his gratitude to God that the new converts received his message not as his own word, but as God's word, which continues to be effective in them. They need this assurance, for they have suffered for their faith at the hands of their Macedonian neighbors. They are not alone in this suffering. Not only are they imitators of Christ and of Paul and the other missionaries in this regard (1:6); they also are imitators of the parent church in Judea that has suffered at the hands of their Judean neighbors. While Paul's statements in 2:14–16 have tragically been read as an expression of and encouragement to anti-Judaism and anti-Semitism, in their context they are intended to encourage the new Thessalonian Christians by exhibiting their continuity with the original church in Judea and their place in the ongoing history of God's saving acts. God's people suffer as inherent in their calling, as manifest in the prophets, Jesus, the original church, and Paul himself.

2:13 And[a] this is in fact why we constantly give thanks to God, namely, that[b] when you received the word of God that you heard from us, you accepted it not as a merely[c] human word but as what it truly is, the word of God, which continues to work[d] among you believers. 14 For you, brothers and sisters, became imitators of the churches of God in Judea in Christ

51. In addition to virtually all recent commentaries in English, French, and German, see esp. Schlueter; Simpson, with a thorough form-critical analysis and argument; Weatherly, with detailed argument based on form and style; Johanson 1987, 94–98, 169–72, with linguistic arguments favoring Pauline authorship, exactly opposite of Schmidt; Holtz 1990, arguing that these two texts are both from Paul and complementary, not contradictory.

Jesus, in that[e] you suffered the same things from your fellow Macedonians[f] as they did from the Judean Jews[g] 15 who killed both[h] the Lord Jesus and the[i] prophets and who drove us out,[j] who are displeasing to God and are opposed to the wholeness of the human race,[k] 16 by trying to prevent us from speaking to the Gentiles that they might be saved, so as to be constantly filling up the measure of their sins. But they have already begun to experience the ultimate wrath to come.[l]

a. The conjunction *kai* is here used twice: *kai dia touto kai*. This construction seemed strange to some scribes, resulting in the omission of the first *kai* in D F G H K L 0278 33 104 365 630 1241 1505 2464 𝔐 lat sy[p]. The first *kai* reflects the overuse of the "and" conjunction in biblical Greek to begin sentences and clauses, under the influence of the Hebrew *wāw*, with which sentences typically begin. It is difficult to imagine this "extra" *kai* having been added. It should thus be retained, as in ℵ A B P Ψ 6 81 1739 1881 m sy[h]; Ambst.

b. The second *kai* has often been understood as "also" and taken with "we," giving the meaning "we too give thanks . . . ," as though Paul is adding the names of missionaries to the list of those who give thanks (so NABRE, NAS95). Alternatively, it has been construed with "this," to mean "for this reason also," as though he is adding another reason to give thanks (so NJB, "Another reason why we continually thank God"; and CEB, "We also thank God constantly for this"). Several translations such as the NRSV are ambiguous, retaining the *kai* with "we" and translating "we also . . . ," so that it could go with either "we" or "this" reason for giving thanks. The ubiquitous conjunction *kai*, however, also has the function of summarizing what has previously been said and can be translated "namely that," as understood here.[52] The *dia touto* is then retrospective, referring back to the previous discussion, which is here summarized (cf. Matt 6:25; 12:27; Mark 6:14; Luke 11:19; Rom 1:26; Heb 1:9), not forward to a new, additional reason for thanksgiving.

c. The word "merely" does not appear in the Greek text. It is appropriate here because Paul has made a point of stating that the word the Thessalonians heard was the human word of the missionaries, which he contrasts with the word of God they accepted; cf. also 1:5, where the contrast with mere human word and the power of God's word is explicit.

d. The form *energeitai*, here taken as middle, could theoretically be passive, "it is made to be effective [i.e., by God]," but this is not Pauline usage. The subject here is *logos* (word), thought of as sent by God, but working powerfully and effectively. Paul is thinking along the lines of Isa 55:11.

e. The *hoti* is not causal and should not be translated "for" or "because," as in the KJV tradition through the ASV, RSV, NRSV, ESV, and others (CEB, "this was because"). It was not "because" the new converts in Thessalonica were suffering that they became imitators of the Judean Christians. The *hoti* is epexegetical, as in 1:5, giving the content of what precedes (so, e.g., NJB).

___

52. See BDAG 495.1.c; Ellingworth and Nida, par. 46026 of Accordance module; Moule (1960, 167) translates this text "That is in fact why we give thanks."

f. "Macedonians" does not occur in the Greek text, which has the plural of *symphyletēs*, one who belongs to the same tribe, clan, or national group, a compatriot. The provincial name is added here to correspond to "Judeans," with which it is paired, and because it is part of the traditional folk identity of the Thessalonians, just as "Jews" and "Judeans" are overlapping terms with religious, political, and geographical connotations.

g. *Ioudaioi* here clearly means "Jews" in the ethnic and religious sense, but also seems to have a geographical, provincial sense, "Judeans," in contrast to the Macedonians addressed in the letter. "Judeans" alone is too broad, for Paul does not blame the residents of Judea as such for the death of Jesus. "Jews," on the other hand, is too broad in a different sense, for readers ancient and modern can hardly hear the word without thinking too generally of ethnic-religious Jews. I have tried to capture something of this nuance with the doubled "Judean Jews." On the punctuation (without a comma after "Judeans"), see comments below.

h. The conjunction *kai* (and) occurs 3× in the first ten words of this clause, the first two of which represent the Greek both-and construction, binding together "Jesus and the prophets" in one phrase. The third *kai* then continues with what happened to "us," Paul and his fellow missionaries to the Gentiles.

i. All the oldest Greek MSS, including ℵ A B D* F G, and the Latin and Coptic traditions in their entirety read as above. However, the vast majority of later MSS add *idious* (their own), specifying that it was the Jewish, i.e., the biblical, prophets who were killed. The antiquity of the shorter reading, the inclination of scribes to add rather than omit, the tendency to make this clause parallel to the preceding one, where it is "your own" compatriots who have persecuted the Thessalonians—all together make it virtually certain that the original text is translated above. No significant translation since the KJV has translated "their own prophets."

j. *Ekdiōkō* can be the intensification of *diōkō* (persecute, harass), or the prefixed *ek* can be taken locally, to mean "drive out," as in Ps 36:28 LXX (cf. 37:28 ET). Either fits the context, but Paul is probably thinking both of his recent expulsion from Thessalonica and how it parallels the rejection of Hellenistic Jewish missionaries by the Jewish community in Palestine-Syria because of their advocacy of admitting uncircumcised Gentiles to God's people. Paul identifies himself with this group, hence "us."

k. *Pasin anthrōpois* is often used in the LXX for the human race as a whole. The singular is used as the translation of *kl bśr*, "all flesh," as in the flood story (cf., e.g., Gen 6:13). The plural, as here, is sometimes used with explicit overtones of God as the creator of all people (not just Israel), who will be both judge and savior to the whole human race, and/or echoing the Gen 12:3 promise of blessing and salvation to come to all people through Abraham (cf. LXX: Num 16:29; Add Esth 13:2; 2 Macc 7:34; 4 Macc 4:12; Prov 30:2; Wis 13:1; Sir 17:32; 33:10 [parallel to "Adam"!]; 44:22 [related to Gen 12:3!]; Ezek 38:20; Dan 4:22; 6:25).

l. More lit., "But the wrath has come upon them to the end." The phrase *eis telos* literally means "to the end," in the temporal sense, which can fade into the adverbial sense of degree, "completely." Both meanings are seen in, e.g., Deut 31:24; to read a book to the end is to read it completely. Thus some translations render the phrase "to the uttermost" (ASV) or "completely" (TNIV mg.). The context here points to the temporal, eschatological sense, already beginning to be realized, expressed by the ingressive aorist *ephthasen* (thus the NABRE, "has finally begun to come upon them"). Some scribes (represented by

B D* Ψ 0278 104) have tried to "clarify" Paul's already/not yet dialectic by changing the aorist to the perfect *ephthaken* (has come), which eliminates the future dimension.

The thanksgiving motif that had been subterranean for several sentences reemerges explicitly and summarizes the preceding in the contrast of human words and divine Word. The location of the paragraph 2:13–16 corresponds to the triadic structure A-B-A', which Paul often uses in 1 Thessalonians and his later letters. He begins a topic, expands on a point, then returns to the main topic.[53] Paul has already used several such triadic compositions in 1 Thessalonians: 1:3, 5, 9–10; 2:3, 5, 11–12. Thus all of 1:2–2:16 is structured on this pattern: A = 1:2–10, B = 2:1–12; A' = 2:13–16. This accounts for the parallels between A and A'. In 2:13–16 Paul is not returning after a "digression," but completing the thought begun in 1:2–10, illustrated by 2:1–12.

[2:13] This verse is a single complex sentence. It is not a new beginning, not a "second thanksgiving," not an interruption or interpolation, not a return after a digression, or evidence that two letters have been editorially joined together. The *dia touto* (lit., because of this, for this reason) connects the sentence causally with the preceding; the double *kai* indicates that the sentence is a summary of what has just been said (see trans. note above). In this extensive section Paul thanks God for the kind of *eisodos* (founding visit and response) the missionaries have experienced in Thessalonica, for how *you* perceived *us*. The preceding paragraph has focused on the missionaries. The focus now shifts to the Thessalonians. This is not a new topic, but the other side of the same coin.

Paul is grateful that they responded to the missionaries' message not as a merely human word, but as the word of God. Though this text has often played a role in discussions of biblical inspiration, the subject here is not the Scripture— the Bible is neither mentioned nor specifically quoted in 1 Thessalonians—but the missionary kerygma of Paul and his colleagues. He has not been concerned that the Thessalonians might regard the Bible as only a human book; but he has been worried that under the pressure of conflict and persecution, their faith generated by the apostle's preaching might have wavered, and that they might have decided that, after all, the missionaries' preaching was merely a human message, like those of the other traveling preachers who had visited their city. The reference is to the way the Thessalonians responded to Paul's message despite the persecution it brought, as 2:14–16 goes on to develop: it was God's word, not a human word, that called them to such a life. They validated it as word of God by responding with obedience, not merely by giving it a proper theological evaluation.[54] This continues the thought of 1:6, where the new converts endure suffering as imitators of Jesus and Paul. Rejection and persecution proceeds

53. Cf. the argument and examples in Hurd.
54. So Calvin 1960a, ad loc; see on 5:20–22 below.

from Jesus to the prophets, to the churches in Judea, to Paul, and now to the Thessalonians: persecution follows the track of faithfulness to God's word.

Paul's complex sentence expresses four important points:

1. The word proclaimed by the missionaries is the message of Christian faith. Paul uses the singular *logos* (word, message), a synonym for *euangelion* (gospel, good news), as in 1:5–6; 2:2, 9. He is not referring to the words, but to the word, the message.

2. This message is expressed in human language, the words of the missionaries that were heard by the Thessalonians. It is not simply a vertical message directly from heaven to individuals, but delivered horizontally, on the plane of human relationships. Paul speaks of the reception of the Christian message by the Thessalonians by using the word *paralambanō*, which had become a semitechnical term for the receiving of tradition (cf. 1 Cor 15:3–5; 11:23). This word of God mediated by the tradition did not begin with Paul, and it did not end with the Thessalonians. Paul had himself received this gospel from the Christian community. He communicated it to the Thessalonians, and they shared it with others (1:8).

3. In and through the preaching by Paul and his colleagues, some (apparently not many) residents of Thessalonica heard the message not only as a human message, but also as the word of God. This was not merely their subjective opinion ("for me it is the word of God, though it may not be for you"), but objective, ontological reality. This is the same kind of simultaneous paradox as in New Testament Christology. The truly human Jesus of Nazareth is the truly divine Son of God.[55] The apostles' preaching manifested not only the horizontal human dimension, but also and simultaneously the transcendent divine dimension. The believers in Thessalonica had heard the Christian message not only as the *report* of an event in the past that had its source in God, communicating what had happened in the Christ event of the past, but also as *address* in the present, as God spoke to them, generating faith and transforming their lives.

4. The word of God that called the church into being continues to be at work effectively in the Christian community. The power of the divine word continues to have its effect as the church constantly calls to mind the original message in which it was expressed, as it is transmitted and interpreted by Christian teachers and preachers who have continued to communicate it after Paul's departure, and by prophetic figures in the congregation who continue to speak the word of the Lord by charismatic revelation (see on 5:19–21). Speaking the word that

---

55. Cf., e.g., Mark 15:39, where the same adverb is used, *alēthōs* (truly, in reality). The paradox of God speaking his own word in the words of human communication of the gospel is analogous to the christological paradox, indeed is based on and results from it. As in Christology, the human and divine, human word and word of God, cannot be parceled out; it is not partly human and partly divine. The Christian message is entirely in human words, but as such is the word of God that generates faith.

generates faith is not simply a two-party transaction, the missionaries and the Thessalonians. "God is the 'third party' in the proclamation of the Gospel."[56] God is active in the event of preaching as an imminent power, not the mere transcendent observer of human preaching or as the divine initiator of the first link in Jerusalem, in a chain that now extends to Thessalonica (cf. Rom 10:8, 17; 2 Cor 5:20; rightly understood, Eph 2:17).[57] Throughout this passage, Paul is thinking of the word of God at work in the community, not merely in individuals who ponder it in their hearts. The phrase *en hymin tois pisteuousin* here means "in you as a body of believers," not only "in each one of you." In the next verse Paul compares them to the churches in Judea, not to individual believers (2:14).

[2:14–16] To grasp this difficult paragraph in terms of Paul's intention, it may be helpful to sketch the moves of his train of thought:

> Paul is grateful for their receiving the word of God,
> which means entering into a community called to suffer.
> It was so from the very beginning,
> when the churches in Judea suffered at the hands of the Jewish
> leaders there.
> This is typical of the response of the people of God to the prophets God
> has sent them,
> climaxed in the killing of Jesus,
> continued in the persecution of the prophetic leaders of the church.
> God's wrath has come upon those who have rejected his messengers,
> which Paul expresses in the mode of rhetorical excess and prophetic
> denunciation,
> using the words of a popular sneer
> that Jews are "godless" and "haters of humanity."

The paragraph 2:14–16 is one lengthy and complex Greek sentence. In the interest of readability and liturgical use, English translations typically divide it into shorter sentences. Closely related to the preceding by the conjunction *gar*, it does not begin a new section or topic. The paragraph is integrated into the preceding context by the theme of the persecuted prophets: the word of God proclaimed by the prophets had always been effective, had always generated both faith and opposition. Paul continues his gratitude to God that the new converts have accepted the missionary message as God's word, despite opposition

---

56. So R. Collins 1993, 46.

57. In such texts, the risen Christ is the preacher, speaking through the proclamation of Christian missionaries. See Keck 2005, 249; Bornkamm 164; the view had already been developed by Bultmann 1:305–6.

and suffering. He has been brought up to date on these by Timothy's report (3:1–6). The word of God inevitably evokes opposition. The hostility they have experienced from their fellow Macedonians, though it separates the new converts from their previous compatriots and neighbors, joins them to the ongoing people of God. Their suffering corresponds to that of the earliest Christian believers in Judea, who suffered at the hands of their Judean neighbors. This triggers a vehement denunciation, in the style of the biblical prophets, of those who oppose the work of God that now comes to its eschatological climax.

[14] Mimesis is a major feature of Paul's ethic, the new life to which believers are called (see on 4:1). Christ is the supreme model. As always in Paul, the focus is not on particular deeds of the earthly Jesus, but on his self-emptying obedience to God, which led to suffering and death (see on 1:6–7). This *imitatio Christi* has been and is being realized in the lives of the Christian missionaries, including the mission team that brought the gospel to Thessalonica. Suffering incurred by responding to the call of God is not, however, confined to a special group of ministers, but is inherent in the life of the people of God. Paul wants to show that it is of the essence of Christian faith to experience persecution (so 1 Thess 3:3–4), that it is not incidental, some random occurrence that was happening only to them. Persecution is not unexpected, not "something strange" (1 Pet 4:12 rightly understands Paul, as does 2 Tim 3:12). The Thessalonians belong to a faith community that spans the world, a community that began in Judea and that began in persecution. So what has happened to them is par for the course; the new converts in Thessalonica are joining a noble company.

They are imitators not only of Christ and the apostles, but also of their fellow Christians from the very beginning, the "churches of God in Judea in Christ Jesus." Paul portrays the present experience of the new converts in Thessalonica as parallel to that of the earliest converts in Judea. To clarify the meaning of the present text, three issues need to be addressed: (1) Who were the *Ioudaioi* who persecuted the earlier Christians in Judea? (2) Who were the *symphyletai* who were persecuting the new Thessalonian Christians? (3) What were these persecutions endured by both the Judean and Thessalonian Christians?

1. According to this text, those who persecuted the earliest congregations in Judea were *Ioudaioi,* "Jews," a designation that may be thought of in terms of three concentric circles: (a) Geographically, it means "Judeans," residents of Judea, which could be understood narrowly as the southern part of Palestine, or more broadly as including Galilee, Samaria, and southern Syria. "Judea" is used in its broad sense, restricted neither to the Roman province nor to the biblical territory of the tribe of Judah (cf. Luke 1:5; 4:44; Acts 10:37; 21:10; 26:20; Josephus, *Antiquities* 1.160; Tacitus, *Histories* 5.9; BDAG 477–78). Geographically, Judea would include numerous Gentiles and the whole spectrum of ethnic and religious Judaism. (b) Within this geographic region, the

ethnic and religious[58] community of Judaism are called "Jews" in distinction from Gentiles, whether in Judea or elsewhere. (c) The Jewish leaders, those who embodied and enacted the program of Judaism as centered in Jerusalem, can be called "Jews" in distinction from the Jewish people as a whole. This usage is prominent in the Gospel of John. Paul typically uses "Jew" in the sense of category b, but in 2 Cor 11:24 he reflects the third sense. His use here, in conjunction with "Judea," may indicate that he is using polemical expressions developed in the theological reaction to Jewish pressures in Antioch, where conflicts with Judean Jews may have become violent. During Paul's service as a missionary of the Antioch church, he may have adopted such vocabulary, along with other Antioch traditions.[59]

Here Paul seems to refer to people like himself before his conversion, people who not only shared and affirmed the ethnic history of Judaism as their own, but also took its religious convictions with utmost seriousness. These were the "zealous" Jews (Acts 21:20; 22:3; Gal 1:14) who would insist on the discipline and punishment of other Jews perceived to be renegades and threats to the Jewish people. At this point punctuation of v. 14 becomes important for meaning, and verse division has compounded the problem. The original text, as we know, had neither punctuation nor verse divisions. In English translations, placing a comma after "Jews" makes the following "who" clause nonrestrictive: "the Jews, who . . . ," as though all Jews were meant. Beginning a new verse with a new number reinforces this impression. Without the comma, however, "the Jews who" is restrictive, applying only to those Jews involved in the death of Jesus and the prophets, and it is no longer a universal statement embracing "the Jews" generally.[60] Paul is not speaking about Jews as Jews, as a racial, ethnic, or religious community as such, but primarily about the opposition of some Jewish leaders to the spread of the law-free Christian gospel.

2. The new converts in Thessalonica were suffering at the hands of their *symphyletai*. This rare word is found only here in the New Testament, not at all in the LXX. Etymologically, it refers to people who belong to the same *phylē* (phylum, class). Though originally referring to those related by blood, by New Testament times it had long since been used for subcategories of people, thus having somewhat the same flexibility as in the English "one's people,"

---

58. The reader is again reminded that this way of discussing the issue is inevitably modern, and that 1st-cent. Jews and Gentiles would not distinguish "religion" from their cultural and political life in general, into which it was inseparably integrated.

59. So, e.g., Becker 460–61.

60. This argument is extensively developed by Gilliard and has been welcomed by some scholars since it seems to relieve Paul of anti-Judaism. Yet Furnish's cautionary note (2007, 72) should be heeded: the language of invective is hardly amenable to such considered judgments. Even if initially used in a restrictive sense, this seems to be forgotten as the long sentence continues.

"my kind of people," which may have familial, racial, ethnic, social, religious, or other connotations. Attempts to narrow the focus have proceeded in two directions.

a. It has traditionally been argued that the sharp anti-Jewish polemic of this passage can only be explained if Jews were somehow involved in the troubles experienced by the Thessalonian church, and that *symphyletai* includes Jews.[61] We have already seen the difficulty of positing a significant Jewish factor in the church situation in Thessalonica, either in or outside the church (see intro, "Religion in Thessalonica"). Moreover, the parallel Paul draws is not between Jewish persecutors in Judea and Jewish persecutors in Thessalonica, but between persecutors in Judea (Judeans/Jews) and persecutors in Macedonia (Macedonians/*symphyletai*). The latter group is certainly not limited to Jews. It is not clear whether they could include Jews, but it seems that if it were a matter of Jews or Jewish Christians who were troubling the new church, Paul would certainly have said so, as he does elsewhere (2 Cor 11:24!).

b. Other interpreters have argued for a narrower meaning for *symphyletai*. Thus Vom Brocke fills in the lack of literary sources with inscriptional evidence, arguing that *phylē* and related words had a particular meaning in 50 C.E. Thessalonica.[62] A *phylē* was a social-religious subgroup (cf. "phylum," the Latin form used in biology and linguistics); most of the residents of Thessalonica would have considered themselves members of such a group. Vom Brocke pictures the Thessalonian church as composed of ex-members of a social-religious phylum, a workers' guild with religious associations. They are now suffering harassment from their previous associates, so such translations as "fellow countrymen," "fellow citizens," and "compatriots" would be too broad. This would also mean that the Christians who belonged to the phyla (guilds) were not slaves or freedmen, but citizens, mostly or entirely male. But full citizens were a small percentage of the population, and it is difficult to read 1 Thessalonians as directed to a narrow group, a church composed mainly of males belonging to the same workers' guild, mostly (ex-)members of pagan cultic associations.

---

61. So most older commentaries. More recently, cf., e.g., Schnelle 2005, 163, 173. See Still 1999, 20 et passim: Jews persecuted Paul during the founding visit, and Gentiles persecuted the church in Thessalonica after Paul's departure. In any case, in this context "those who drove us out" refers to his Jewish opponents in Judea, an experience Paul shares with the Hellenistic Jewish Christian missionaries, and only secondarily, and by way of analogy, to his recent expulsion from Thessalonica. He shares the experience of rejection with Thessalonian Christians, which was by their fellow Macedonians, for he knows what it is like to be rejected by one's own people. In 1 Thessalonians, Paul gives no indication that he was opposed by Jews in Thessalonica, and this text cannot be used as evidence for a Jewish community in Thessalonica in Paul's time (contra, e.g., Weima 2014, 20, 25, and often, who subordinates 1 Thessalonians to Acts).

62. Vom Brocke 155–65.

Paul's intended point seems to be directed to a broader readership than either ex-members of Gentile cultic *phylē* or those facing organized Jewish resistance: just as the original church was persecuted by its Jewish compatriots in Judea, so the new church in Thessalonica is persecuted by its Gentile compatriots in Macedonia. If there were Jews in Thessalonica, they may have opposed the initial preaching of the Christian message in Thessalonica, they may have continued to play a role in instigating the church's troubles, and they may have fanned the flames, but the persecuting actions were carried out by Gentiles.

3. Paul addresses the new converts in Thessalonica as people who are enduring the same sufferings as their sister congregations in Judea. What were these sufferings? This question has two interrelated dimensions, historical and exegetical-rhetorical. The historian of early Christianity rightly wants to know what happened in the interchanges between Palestinian Jews and the emerging church in the first decades after the death of Jesus. The exegetical-rhetorical issue is concerned with the meaning and function of this text addressed to the new converts in Thessalonica. The modern reader pursuing historical questions cannot know just which sufferings of earlier Palestinian Christians Paul is referring to, for he gives no details of the earlier troubles in the churches of Judea. Presumably the mission team had related the story of Christian beginnings to the Thessalonians during the founding visit. Silvanus (= the Silas of Acts) had been a prophetic leader of the Jerusalem church (Acts 15:22, 32), one who risked his life "for the sake of the Lord" (Acts 15:26). Paul had then been on the other side, a persecutor of the church (1 Cor 15:9; Gal 1:13; Acts 8–9; 22:4–15). Paul the Jewish Christian indicates that after his conversion he continued to be subject to the severe disciplinary punishment "by the Jews" (2 Cor 11:24–25). Acts relates several incidents of persecution in the earliest days of the church (Acts 4–9), and other New Testament references point to "persecution" of Jewish Christians by other Jews (Mark 13:9–13; Matt 10:17, 21; 23:34–36; Luke 11:49; John 16:2). From the insider's point of view, such judicial action was an internal Jewish matter for the protection of the Jewish way of life. Jews had no interest in "persecuting" Gentile Christians and did not have the political power to do so. It does appear to be the case, however, that there is sound historical evidence that some Jews inflicted violence on some Jewish Christians perceived as deviant Jews. They may occasionally have initiated action against Jewish Christians and collaborated with Gentile authorities in having them punished, perhaps including the death penalty. Something analogous to whatever had happened in Judea was now happening in Thessalonica.[63]

---

63. According to E. A. Judge, followed by Karl P. Donfried and others, the background to such persecution is to be found in the provincial loyalty oaths sworn by local leadership to the Caesars. Administrators swore that they would pursue any enemies of Caesar. The oath included the words

[15] The verse division is unfortunate and does not indicate a new sentence. The reference to "the Jews" is elaborated in a series of charges and a final condemnation. To be sure, they are expressed with passion, but not as an emotional outpouring against Jews or Judaism as such. The Greek sentence formulates the charge and denunciation as a series of five subordinate clauses, four of which begin with participles, the other with an adjective functioning as a participle, all having the same sonorous long ending *–ōn*; these are represented below by italics.[64] When diagrammed or read aloud, the series of clauses are seen or heard as a powerful rhetorical structure:

> the *Judeans/Jews*
> > *who killed* both the Lord Jesus and the prophets and
> > *who drove* us out,
> > *who are displeasing* to God and
> > *who are opposed* to the wholeness of the human race by
> > *trying to prevent* us
> > > from speaking to the Gentiles that they might be saved,
> > > so as to be constantly filling up the full measure of their sins.

The series of charges is framed by the killing of Jesus and the attempt to prevent Christian missionaries from preaching the message of salvation to Gentiles, which Paul sees as one consistent act of resistance to the eschatological purpose of God. Only here does Paul blame the Judean Jews for the death of Jesus. His typical perspective is theological, attributing Jesus' death to the salvific purpose of God, expressed as Jesus' own self-giving love for the sake of others. On the only other occasion when Paul does speak of the human agents involved in Jesus' condemnation and crucifixion, he lays the responsibility on the "rulers of this age/world," the demonic spiritual powers and/or their agents, the Roman government (1 Cor 2:6–8). The vocabulary and formulation of 1 Thess 2:14–16 are not characteristically Pauline. Paul is here likely using elements of tradition forged in the Antioch church, which had formulated such charges and denunciations in the heat of conflict, while it struggled with strict Jewish Christian interpretations of the faith as it began the Gentile mission.[65] Such traditional phraseology might explain the elements of unpauline vocabulary and syntax. Thus the virulent content of the passage is not necessarily evidence that it is a later interpolation, but neither does the probability

---

"I shall not cease to hunt him down by land and sea, until he pays the penalty to Caesar in full." For discussion and further bibliography, see Harrison 53–55.

64. Cf. Schlueter 115, who documents from Quintilian that such a list, building to a climax with each item "ending with a similar sound," is a studied rhetorical device.

65. As argued, e.g., in Becker 460; Haufe 48, 50; Donfried 1993a, 31.

that Paul is here using traditional material get him off the hook of his alleged anti-Jewishness. Though he does not originate it, Paul repeats and affirms the tradition. In any case, Paul is not charging the whole Jewish people with responsibility for Jesus' death, but the same group of Palestinian Jewish leaders who violently resisted both Jesus and the earliest church. Nor is it his last word on the matter. In another context, he will insist on the reliability of God's mercy for "all Israel" (Rom 11:26).

In the tradition Paul cites and affirms, the guilt for Jesus' death is combined with responsibility for the death of the prophets. There was a firm tradition in both Judaism and early Christianity that charged previous generations with killing the prophets.[66] This tradition is reflected elsewhere in the New Testament (Mark 12:1–12; Matt 5:12; 22:1–14 [cf. v. 6]; 23:29–33, 37; Luke 13:34; Acts 7:52; Rom 11:3; Rev 11:3–12; 16:6; 18:24). Interpreters typically understand Paul as here referring to Israel's rejection of its own prophets. This tradition does indeed hover in the background of Paul's charge. It is part of the history of Israel, part of the sinful, rebellious character of the chosen people of God. For Paul, the specific actions of a relatively few synagogue leaders of his own time reveal an enduring characteristic of God's people: their resistance to the messengers God sends to them.

In this context, the reference to the murder of the prophets probably refers specifically to church figures of Paul's time. Elsewhere in the New Testament, the chronology begins with the rejection of the series of biblical prophets and is climaxed with the rejection of the Messiah, as in Mark 12:1–12. In 1 Thessalonians, Paul combines the death of Jesus with that of the prophets, but the order Jesus → prophets → Paul suggests that (Jewish) Christian prophets are in view. Paul frequently refers to the renewed gift of prophecy among the charismata of the Holy Spirit active in the church (Rom 12:6; 1 Cor 11:4–5; 12:10, 28–29; 13:2; 14:3–6, 22, 24, 29, 32, 37; 1 Thess 5:20); his citation in Rom 11:3, which alludes to 1 Kgs 19:10, 14, "I have been very zealous for the LORD, . . . for the people of Israel have forsaken your covenant . . . and slain your prophets," may have been triggered in part by events in his own experience.

The biblical prophets are not elsewhere mentioned in 1 Thessalonians (though Paul surely instructed the new converts about them: cf. intro, "Church-Founding Visit" and "New Congregation"), but the congregation is familiar with prophets in its own midst (1:6; 4:8–9, 15–18; 5:11, 19–20). Two of the missionary founders of the Thessalonian church were themselves prophetic figures. Silvanus was a Christian prophet from the earliest church who had played a role in the launching of Gentile mission, who had "risked his life for the Lord" (Acts 15:25–32), and Paul presented himself as such a prophetic leader

---

66. Already beginning in the OT (Neh 9:26; 2 Chr 36:15–16), this tradition was elaborated and solidified in early Judaism. Cf. Fischel; Schoeps; Steck.

(e.g., 1 Cor 14; see esp. 14:37).[67] It was not the historical Jesus, but the risen Lord of the church's faith, speaking through Christian prophets, that led the earliest Christian community to begin the mission that included uncircumcised Gentiles within the people of God without the condition of keeping the law (Matt 10:5; 28:16–20; Acts 2–15; Eph 2:11–22, esp. vv. 19–20). Such prophets were resisted by the Jewish leadership, who denied that the spirit by which they claimed to be inspired was the Holy Spirit, claiming that such a spirit must be demonic, attempting to mislead the people of God. This leadership resisted such prophets, sometimes with violence, perhaps with lethal violence, as portrayed in the Stephen story (Acts 7:1–60). The Torah prescribed the death penalty for false prophets who misled Israel (Deut 13:5). It may well be that some Christian prophets had been killed in the early struggles in Palestine-Judea-Syria. Whatever the historical reality, Paul here sees the sufferings of the new congregation in Thessalonica not as random violence, but as fitting within the apocalyptic framework in which God's final prophetic messengers are rejected by God's own people. Rhetorically, Paul is not speaking about what "the Jews" did, but about what the faithful suffered. So also, when the "Judean Jews" are charged with opposing the apostles' preaching to the Gentiles, the point is not what they did wrong, but what the apostles were doing right. And the wrath that comes upon them is what the believers are saved *from*, which is the main point. This is confessional language, or something analogous to it, as well as rhetorical exaggeration, "polemical hyperbole."[68] The reference to what the Jews have done is only illustrative material for Paul's point that has to do with Christian faithfulness, not with Jewish opposition to the faith. "The Jews" are actors in the historical drama, yet the drama is not about them, but about people suffering for their faith. As literally in Revelation and apocalyptic generally, Jewish and Christian, a theological framework is provided that makes suffering meaningful and bearable. When Paul's confessional language (see on 1:4, 9–10) has been misunderstood as objectifying language, and his rhetoric has been misunderstood as reporting, tragic consequences have resulted, to which church history bears horrific witness.

When Paul declares that "the Jews" are "displeasing to God and opposed to the wholeness of the human race," it is helpful to realize that such language is not original with him. Paul adopts and reinterprets a popular sneer of pagan anti-Judaism. Two common themes of pagan anti-Judaism were the Jews' atheism (displeasing the gods) and out-group misanthropy. Jewish rejection of the Greco-Roman gods was seen as "godless." Their keeping themselves separate from Gentiles and their resistance to integration into Hellenistic society at large

---

67. To be sure, Paul never explicitly designates himself a prophet, but the role of prophet is included in his apostolic self-understanding. See Boring 1982, 30–36.
68. Schlueter 75.

were interpreted as clannishness and "hatred for humanity."[69] Paul, and all Jews, had heard these libels their whole lives, recognized them for what they were, and accepted such defamation as part of the price of faithfulness to God. Paul knows, of course, that failure to participate in the worship of Hellenistic gods does not mean that Jews are godless, and he knows that Jews do not hate all non-Jews. Here Paul is thus making an ironic reversal of this familiar charge. Like the biblical prophets, Paul uses the language of the Gentiles to address the failure of God's own people.

As a Jew, Paul affirmed the Jewish faith in the one God who is creator of all peoples, and he knew of the Jewish hope of the ultimate reunification of humanity. Several streams of Jewish theology, rightly appealing to the Scripture as the basis of their hope, regarded the present fragmented human scene as only penultimate, to be overcome at the eschaton by God's reuniting of all peoples under the divine rule (cf., e.g., Isa 2:1–4). Until then, it was Israel's responsibility to maintain their distinctive separateness as a witness to the one God. Those Jews who believed that the Messiah had come thus believed that now is the time of the final reunification, that the barrier between Jew and Gentile was not needed and in fact no longer existed, and that one human race uniting Jews and Gentiles was God's eschatological purpose, now being realized. This is what Paul's Jewish opponents opposed, an opposition shared by some Jewish Christians. Paul regarded those Jewish and Jewish Christian leaders who opposed the church's proclamation of salvation to Gentiles without requiring them to become Jews first as actually opposing the divine plan for history: to unite all human beings under the rule of their one Creator. It is not that Jews hate all Gentiles as individuals—Paul knows this is untrue. What Paul's Jewish opponents hate, he believes, and what makes them displeasing to God when they intend to please God, is the human race in the messianic age as one united whole, a humanity without distinctions (see trans. note k). They hate the idea of "all human beings" in a sense analogous to modern conservative nationalism's hatred and suspicion of the idea of "one world." Paul himself, in his later most comprehensive development of this theme, will use "all human beings" (*pantes*

---

69. Diodorus (mid-1st cent. B.C.E.) states that the Jews "made the hatred of humanity [*to misos to pros tous anthrōpous*] into a tradition" (*Hist.* 34.1.2). Similarly, Tacitus comments that the Jews are "godless" and "are extremely loyal toward one another, and always ready to show compassion, but toward every other people they feel only hate and enmity [*apud ipsos fides obstinate, misericordia in prompt, sed adversus omnis alios hostile odium*]" (*Hist.* 5.5); cf. also Philostratus, *Vit. Apoll.* 5.33; Juvenal, *Sat.* 14.103.4. For further documentation, see Still 239; Dibelius 1937, 11, 29–31. As in Paul's case, eschatological sectarian Jews who had been rejected by emerging mainstream Judaism could make such a charge against other Jews. The Qumran community charged nonmembers of their sect with displeasing God and hating all other people (CD 2, 8). Cf. Schlueter 108–9. Haacker argues that Paul took over two important themes of pagan anti-Judaism: opposition to other people (out-group misanthropy) and failure to please God (atheism).

anthrōpoi) in this comprehensive sense of "the wholeness of the human race" (Rom 5:12, 18), and the later Pauline tradition will continue to use the phrase in that sense (1 Tim 2:4; Titus 2:11; cf. Acts 17:30; 22:15; also Ephesians [2:15; 3:5–6; 4:8], which rightly understands Paul on this point).

[16] Paul knows whereof he speaks. Before his conversion, he had shared the convictions of his present Jewish opponents. In his view, they are indeed intent on doing God's will (= "please God") by their torah observance and exclusion of Gentiles, but in fact they are opposing God's will in these eschatological days, in which God's purpose of uniting Jew and Gentile in one saved community is coming to fulfillment. Their persistent and continuing opposition to the Gentile mission means they are actually "filling up the measure of their sins." What they see as preserving the integrity and mission of the covenant people, Paul, who once had passionately shared that view, now sees as opposing the salvation of the Gentiles and the fulfillment of the Creator's ultimate plan for humanity. Their well-intentioned attempts to prevent Paul and his fellow missionaries from preaching to Gentiles are not just another transgression in the long history of Israel's failures; also, as part of the end-time events that include the Gentile mission, their obstruction is the crowning act of a sinful history and takes on an eschatological character. This is not mere Pauline petulance, but prophetic pronouncement of judgment in the tradition of Israel's prophets. Though the material may have been adopted from the recent conflicts at Antioch, Paul affirms its logic: those leaders of Israel who hinder the Gentile mission oppose God's will and stand under divine judgment.

The ultimate coming of the kingdom of God and establishment of God's justice, expressed here as "the wrath" (see on 1:4, 10), is not only a matter of the future, even though Paul believed it would be realized in the near future. Just as for Jesus the coming kingdom of God was not yet fully realized but already dawning, and could occasionally be spoken of as already present (Matt 12:28// Luke 11:20 uses exactly the same word as here, *ephthasen*, "has come"), so Paul could speak of the coming wrath as already in a sense present, already beginning to be experienced. The earliest church, including Paul, shares something of the perspective of the Qumran community, which saw itself as the eschatological remnant and pronounced the wrath of God on "outsiders," meaning fellow Jews. This coming wrath has already come "completely," or "to the uttermost," in other words, eschatologically.[70] It is not necessary to see here a retrospective reference to the 70 C.E. destruction of Jerusalem, or to see such a presumed reference as evidence that the sentence is a post-Pauline interpolation. Paul could have in mind events that have just happened or are happening in 50 C.E. as the present manifestation of the coming judgment of God: the death

---

70. See 1QM 3.9; 4.1–2; 1QS 2.15–17; 4.13–14; 5.12–13. Cf. also *T. Lev.* 6.11; *1 En.* 91.9. For elaboration see Kuhn 344–46.

of Agrippa in 44 (Acts 12:20–23), the insurrection of Theudas in 44–46 (Acts 5:36), the famine in Judea in 46–47 (Acts 11:27–28), a massacre of 20,000 Jews in Jerusalem during the administration of Cumanus, 48–52 (Josephus, *Ant.* 20.5.3; *War* 2.224–227), the expulsion of the Jews from Rome in 49 (Acts 18:2). It is not necessary, however, to try to identify some catastrophic event in particular. In the apocalyptic perspective, the quite "normal" tragedies of history take on an ultimate, foreshadowing-the-end perspective, as all the modern apocalyptic movements make clear.[71]

The extreme language of apocalyptic employed by Paul is illuminated by two further considerations: (1) the rhetoric of excess, and (2) the style of prophetic denunciation:

1. *Paul often expresses his convictions in terms of rhetorical hyperbole.*[72] The vice lists, for example, do not catalog the particular faults of the church Paul addresses or of society in general, but function rhetorically to warn his readers against evil as such (e.g., 1 Cor 5:10–11; 6:9–10; Gal 5:19–21). Jesus, the early Christian preachers, the Gospel writers, and especially the author of Revelation all used such powerful, nonliteral, nonreporter language to communicate their message (e.g., Matt 8:18–20; 19:23–26; the whole of the Sermon on the Mount, Matt 5–7; the whole of Revelation). The paragraph 1 Thess 2:14–16 represents the rhetorical style of the apocalyptic theologian. Paul's later interpreters, for whom this style may represent an alien symbolic universe, must work at trying to understand him on his own terms.

2. *Paul is steeped in the imagery and language of his Bible.* In particular, he understands his apostolic mission in continuity with that of the biblical prophets, especially Jeremiah, appointed by God as "prophet to the nations" (Jer 1:5), which corresponds to "apostle to the Gentiles" (Rom 11:13; see on 1 Thess 5:27). The prophets of Israel, as passionately concerned spokespersons to their own people, address Israel's failures with bombastic threats of divine judgment. Their threats, directed principally at the leaders and teachers of Israel, expand to include the people as a whole. Much of the prophetic literature is comprised

71. One need only think of the dozens of political events, natural disasters, and social movements that have been confidently identified by modern dispensationalists of the last two generations as the beginning of the end-time events (e.g., Hal Lindsey's 1970 *The Late Great Planet Earth*; the 16 vols. of Tim Lahaye and Jerry B. Jenkins's Left Behind series, 1995–2007). This particular brand of dispensationalism is modern, the extended shadow of John Nelson Darby (1800–1882) and Cyrus Ingerson Scofield (1843–1921) of *Scofield Reference Bible* fame; yet in every generation of Christian history those who believed they were living in the last times have easily found contemporary events to validate their predictions. On the interpretation of biblical apocalyptic imagery, see comments on 4:13–18 and on 2 Thess 2:1–12.

72. This feature of Pauline rhetoric is thoroughly explored, documented, and fruitfully applied to this text by Schlueter. On the rhetoric of apocalyptic, see Wilder 1971; 1973. The rhetoric of excess was expected and conventional in polemic. For an extensive discussion with numerous illustrations, see A. Collins 1983; Freyne; Johnson.

of oracles of prophetic denunciation by a Jewish prophet against his fellow Jews. For Jeremiah, one need note only such texts as 2:29–30 (which also charges Israel with killing its own prophets); 2:35 (one of numerous texts that identify God's judgment as the coming wrath); 5:1, 11, the whole people (i.e., the people as a whole) are delivered over to the coming wrath (6:13, no exceptions); 6:17–18, Judeans refuse to hear, but the Gentile nations hear; 18:19–23, Jeremiah invokes the wrath of God against his own people who have rejected his message. This prophet denounces the whole people of Judah, in extreme and comprehensive terms. Jeremiah loves his people, weeps for them, and believes God has a blessed future in store for them. In Jeremiah, the two elements of prophetic denunciation and prophetic promise lie side by side and may not be parceled out between a core original text and later expansions.[73] Nor is it necessary or helpful to see the "early" Paul making extreme and absolute statements, which he then "moderates" in his final letter. "Wrath" is found in Paul's earliest letter three times (1 Thess 1:10; 2:16; 5:9) and then does not recur until his latest letter, which has twelve instances (Rom 1:18; 2:5 [2×], 8; 3:5; 4:15; 5:9; 9:22 [2×]; 12:19; 13:4, 5). Both 1 Thess 2:16 and Rom 11:26 represent the real Paul, who knew that both God's judgment and God's grace are beyond the grasp of finite minds (Rom 11:32–36). Paul learned to preach both judgment and hope from his Bible. The modern interpreter can learn this from both Jeremiah and Paul; 1 Thess 2:13–16 sounds more Pauline after reading Jeremiah (and Romans!).

2:17–3:13 Mutuality of the Mission: Timothy Brings Good News

The preceding discussion has been necessarily long, to help bring the contemporary interpreter within hearing distance of a difficult text. Its length may have caused the modern reader to lose the thread. Paul, however, has not lost his grip on his line of thought. Every paragraph of the thanksgiving/body of the letter, 1:2–3:13, is permeated with Paul's thanksgiving to God for the Thessalonians, who have become dear to him. Christian faith creates deep interpersonal relationships, as illustrated by the tender family language throughout. Paul writes not only as pastor-teacher and theologian, but also as a human being whose life has been interwoven with the lives of the new converts in Thessalonica. He intends the letter to be read in the context of community worship (5:27)

---

73. Though the category of "interpolation" is not appropriate for how the text of Jeremiah developed, there is a certain analogy to the issue of interpolations in the Pauline corpus. The MT of Jeremiah is approximately 12 percent longer than the LXX form of this book. The Qumran MSS document the fluidity of the text of Jeremiah in Paul's time, so we cannot know what form of the text was available to him. But on no analysis do the prophetic denunciations of Jeremiah's own people belong only to the early core or to later expansions. They were in Paul's Bible.

and writes in the mood of worship, praise, and pastoral encouragement, but not devoid of theological instruction. This section will remind the congregation of Paul's forced absence and longing to see them (2:17–20), his sending Timothy (3:1–5), Timothy's return with good news (3:6–10), and conclude with a prayer that leads into the paraenesis (3:11–13).

2:17–20 Separation: Frustration, Hope, and Joy

Though this brief paragraph explains Paul's continuing absence from Thessalonica, it is not a defense or apology but continues the thanksgiving.

2:17 As for us,[a] brothers and sisters, when we were involuntarily separated[b] from you for a little while—physically absent, though present with you in our hearts—we desperately made every effort[c] to see you face-to-face. 18 For time and again[d] we tried to come to you—I myself, Paul—but Satan blocked every road.[e] 19 For what is our hope, or joy, or victor's wreath that we can celebrate[f] in the presence of our Lord Jesus at his Parousia,[g] if it is not you? 20 For you are our glory and our joy.

a. The presence of the pronoun *hēmeis* is in itself emphatic since the subject is built into the verb form and is not necessary. As the first word of the sentence, followed by the particle *de*, it is doubly emphatic.

b. The rare form *aporphanisthentes*, passive participle of *aporphanizō* (only here in the NT), lit. means "orphaned." The Greek word, in contrast to the English, can refer either to children deprived of their parents, or to parents deprived of their children.

c. Paul brackets this clause with a comparative adjective *perissoterōs*, "more/most abundantly," and an almost slangy *en pollē epithymia*. The latter term is used by Paul almost exclusively of passion in the evil sense (10× in the undisputed letters; elsewhere in the positive sense only: Phil 1:23). Paul "has a deep craving" to see them again, "lusts after" a return visit.

d. *Kai hapax kai dis*, lit., "both once and twice," is an idiom that, like the English "time and again," means "more than once," "time after time."

e. *Enkoptō*, lit., "cut into," pictures the military destruction of roads in order to block the progress of the enemy. It came to mean simply "to hinder."

f. *Stephanos kauchēseōs* is, lit., "crown of boasting." The "crown" does not refer to royalty, but to the laurel wreath given to the victor in a race. "Boasting" is not bragging, but the celebration at the end of the race.

g. For *parousia* (presence, arrival, advent), see on 4:15. In its apocalyptic/eschatological sense, Paul introduces the term into Christian discourse in this letter; 1 Thess 2:17–20 is its earliest occurrence in extant Christian literature. Like *baptism, Eucharist*, and *presbyter*, which are transliterated rather than translated, in theological discourse *parousia* has become a semitechnical term, often left untranslated as Parousia, as in this commentary's translation.

[17] The emphatic use of the pronoun is parallel to the "you" of v. 14. Paul has been picturing the endurance of hardship by the Thessalonians; now he shifts the focus to himself and his fellow missionaries. "Orphaned" would be a proper translation to express Paul's feeling of forcible separation from the new converts in Thessalonica, for it preserves the anguished feeling of loss experienced by a child suddenly bereft by the death of the parents. While "we were orphaned" captures Paul's poignant use of family imagery, it makes explicit in English what is left ambiguous in Greek (see trans. note b). His metaphor, however it is taken, makes clear that his separation from the young church was involuntary (*passive* participle!), painful, and the loss of family members. This fits Paul's earlier use of the wide range of family imagery. Just as Paul has previously presented himself as father, mother, nurse, and brother, so here he can well describe himself as a suddenly orphaned child, for he is not concerned about clashing metaphors: "orphaned" is the next word after "brothers and sisters." Since he has no difficulty being both sibling and parent in relation to the Thessalonians, so he can be both parent and child to them. Neither is he concerned to make sure the Thessalonians understand that he is in the parental role and they are his children, for he could make this explicit, as he will later to the Corinthians, in a different situation (cf. 1 Cor 4:15; Phlm 10). Perhaps Timothy has reported that the new converts in Thessalonica feel they were left as orphans by the sudden departure of the founding missionaries, and Paul may be responding, "I know what you mean: we too felt that *we* had been orphaned." The depth of his emotion—there is no professional or apostolic distance here—is seen in both syntax and vocabulary.

[18] For the first time in this letter, Paul shifts (in midsentence) to the first-person singular: "I myself, Paul" (elsewhere in this letter, "I" only in 3:5; 5:27; see on 1:1). Instead of sending Timothy, Paul wanted to return to see the Thessalonians personally, and this despite his being intensely engaged in new mission work in Athens and then in Corinth. Paul did not want the new congregation in Thessalonica to suppose that, once he founded a new church, he moved on, and his interest shifted to his new project. He repeatedly made every effort to return to Thessalonica, but his efforts were frustrated. Paul's reference to Satan is not the-devil-made-me-do-it avoidance of his own responsibility. We do not know whether Paul was attacked by a persistent health problem (also in 2 Cor 12:7–10 his "thorn in the flesh" is from Satan) or was obstructed by some other cause beyond his control. Timothy would have explained the details of his absence.

Whatever the reason why Paul has not returned to Thessalonica, he considers it a roadblock that Satan has placed in his way. Paul sees his mission, and the life of the church generally, as taking place within competing transcendent force fields. "God and Satan cannot sign a pact of non-aggression. . . . Paul divides the world into persecutors and persecuted":[74] there is no neutral middle ground.

---

74. Rigaux 29, 472.

God elects (1:4), calls (2:12; 4:7; 5:24), works within the Christian community (2:13), directs the mission of the church (3:11), teaches believers (4:9), and sanctifies (5:23). But Satan blocks the way (2:18); every departure from the faith is not mere human foible but rather is succumbing to "the tempter/tester" (3:5). Within this context of struggling transcendent powers, Paul believes that all Christians, including himself, must make their own decisions and accept responsibility for them. Such decisions are not made in neutral territory, but always under the pressures of a struggle in which the power of God and the demonic powers of Satan are operative. Sometimes the decision or inability of a missionary to return to help strengthen a new congregation is understood as the will of God (1 Cor 16:12 NRSV mg.). Sometimes, as here, it is seen as the work of Satan. Such discernment is often seen in retrospect.

The *śāṭān*, the prosecuting attorney in the heavenly court (Job 1) who, in later Jewish apocalyptic thought, became the prince of the demonic world, is a figure of the Jewish Scripture and tradition and thus unknown to the Gentiles of Thessalonica. Paul's intent here is not to teach the new converts something about the workings of Satan. The self-evident way in which the work of Satan is spoken of indicates that such aspects of the apocalyptic worldview have been a part of the initial mission preaching and have been communicated in the instruction the congregation has received since, as they have appropriated the new symbolic universe (see intro, "Religion in Thessalonica" and "Church-Founding Visit"). Satan does not play an essential role in Paul's theology; in Rom 1–8 he can develop his understanding of sin, the human predicament, and salvation with no reference to Satan. For the modern reader, the main point is assumed rather than stated—that Paul saw his life and mission as something not his own, in which he was not in control. The challenge to the modern secularized reader, including those who belong to the church and participate in its mission, is the unself-conscious way in which Paul understands the "ordinary" things of life (such as whether or not to return to Thessalonica) in a theological framework. The assumption of the writer of this letter is that if the gospel is actually true, then everything is different. If it is true that there is one God, that this God has acted definitively in Jesus Christ, then everything must be seen in this framework, and the "religious" or "spiritual" life cannot be an appendage to "ordinary" life. For Paul, one's faith is not so much a matter of explicit statements about religious things, but the assumptions on which one habitually acts, the world assumed to be real within which "ordinary" life takes place. Paul's incidental comment about Satan is not "instruction," but for both ancient and modern readers of this letter, it does open up a way of seeing the world.

[19–20] Paul would have returned to see the Thessalonians himself if Satan had not hindered him, for the new little group of believers in Thessalonica are Paul's hope, joy, and laurel wreath of victory. Paul's whole life was oriented to one central purpose. But Paul's dedication was not just to God, a dedication to which his friends, colleagues, and converts fall victim. His dedication to

God includes all these, without which he could not even think of dedication to God. Paul could never have gone into the desert to get away from people so that he could concentrate on God. His new friends, his new brothers and sisters in Thessalonica, have become very dear to him, so that it is painful even to contemplate that they might think he was avoiding them, moving on to more important things.

Verse 19 is one sentence, with a somewhat convoluted structure and a rhetorical question that includes its own answer, which is then repeated in v. 20 more directly: you are our glory and our joy. At the risk of unweaving the rainbow, some analysis might facilitate more clarity for the modern reader. The five praiseworthy items are actually three, with two of the three items in the rhetorical question repeated in the straightforward conclusion:

1. hope	=	Parousia
2. joy	=	4. joy
3. crown of boasting	=	5. glory

"You are our hope" is the overarching category that includes the others, for this is not a list of discrete items about which Paul wants to gush, but dimensions of the eschatological hope in which the new Thessalonian congregation plays an important role. As in 1:3, the Christian hope is identified with the coming of the Lord, so here Paul designates the new converts in Thessalonica as his hope. These are two sides of the same coin: Christian hope focuses on the coming of the Lord, but this is not a separate reality from meeting the Lord and being with him forever (4:17). Likewise, Paul's close relationship to the new Christian community is inseparable from the reality of the gospel itself (see on 3:6): gospel, Christology, and ecclesiology are inseparably fused. Again, in all this Paul is not "teaching eschatology," but his assumed eschatological framework provides the imagery for expressing his love for the Thessalonians and the significant role they play for him. All is related to the impending *parousia* of the Lord Jesus. Although, of course, such words were already familiar to the Thessalonian converts, they are now filled with new meaning. "Hope" is the confident expectation of the future reality that already transforms the present (see on 1:2–3, 10). "Joy" is not subjective feeling alone, but the objective future reality. To understand the image of the "crown of boasting" (NRSV), one must think of the filled stadium and the laurel wreath given to the victor at the end of the race, and the pride and thrill of the winner ("We're number one!" Here is the thrill of victory alongside the agony of defeat). For Paul, this is what the Thessalonians are to him. The image is transformed as it is appropriated. "Winner" no longer implies "loser," and "boasting" is not a matter of pride in one's achievement, but of celebration at having finished the course.[75] This was

---

75. The background of Paul's "boasting" terminology includes Jer 9:23–24.

Paul's concern—whether the young church is still hanging in there despite opposition or has dropped out of the race. Paul will complete the course, will remain faithful until the Parousia, which is soon to come, and he is confident that the little group of Christians will be there to celebrate with him. Implicit in all this is Paul's view that, as apostle to the Gentiles and for the churches he has established, he will present those believers to the returning Christ as the fruit and confirmation of his work. In accord with the dialectical already/not yet of Paul's eschatology, the implied future of v. 19 (which actually lacks a verb) becomes the present of v. 20; the already/not yet of Christian hope is not a doctrinal construct but a lived reality, with eschatological existence in the present. To be given a future is to be given a present.

3:1–5 Timothy Sent to Encourage the Thessalonians

The chapter division is unfortunate; the preceding line of thought continues without a break. The paragraph revolves around the sending of Timothy. It is a unit, composed of three sentences, bracketed by the repeated words of vv. 1 and 5, "no longer" "endure," "sent."

> 3:1 So, when we could stand it no longer, we thought it best to be left alone in Athens, 2 and we sent Timothy, our brother and coworker in God's service[a] in the work[b] of the gospel of Christ, to strengthen and encourage you in your faithfulness, 3 so that no one will waver[c] in these persecutions. For you yourselves know that it is for this that we have been called and chosen.[d] 4 In fact, when we were with you, we repeatedly told you that we would be persecuted, and you now know that it has happened just as we said it would. 5 This is why, when I could stand it no longer, I sent to find out about your faithfulness, wondering whether the Tester[e] had put you to such a test that our labors among you might have come to nothing.

a. The phrase *kai synergon tou theou*, here translated "and coworker in God's service," is almost certainly what Paul originally wrote, though found in only two Greek MSS (D* 33), in two Old Latin MSS (b, d), and thrice in citations in the church fathers (Ambst, Pelagius, Ps–Jerome). These words could be lit. understood as describing Timothy as "our brother and God's coworker." To protect Paul from the heresy of synergism, many later scribes "restored" what they presumed to be the original reading by either changing "coworker" to minister (*diakonos*; so ℵ A P Ψ 0278 6 81 1241 1739 1881 2464 and Latin and Coptic versions), by omitting "God's" (so B and some MSS of the Vulgate), or by some combination of these two. This possibility later generated eight types of variations in the MSS traditions. However, both the principles of preferring the *lectio difficilior* and that of choosing the reading that best explains the others make it virtually certain that the reading here translated is the original. This is an instance where the great majority of modern versions rightly follow a text with weak MSS attestation.

b. "In the gospel of Christ," lit. The gospel is here seen as a sphere of activity, like "law" or "medicine," within which one can work. Thus some translations render "proclaiming," "spreading," or "service." "Work" is here chosen to correspond to "coworker," as in Phil 4:3.

c. *Sainō*, rare in both classical and Hellenistic Greek, is found only here in the NT. The word has two senses: (1) "fawn, be fawned upon." It is used of a dog wagging its tail. The meaning here would be "do not be beguiled by the kindness of those who encourage you to abandon the faith in order to avoid persecution." (2) The ancient versions and patristic interpreters understand it to mean "be upset, cause to be disturbed" (though etymologically unrelated to *seiō*, "shake"). The translation chosen above tries to combine these two meanings.

d. "We have been placed for this," lit. *Keimai* is a flexible word that (lit.) means to lie down or lay something down, and then is used in a variety of senses for placing or being placed in a particular location. Here, as in Luke 2:34 and Phil 1:16, it refers to the divine placing or appointment to a particular task. Paul is referring to their call and election (see on 1:4, 9b–10; 2:12; 4:7; 5:24).

e. *Peirazō* is a neutral word that means "to try, to make an attempt." A derived meaning is "to test" something, to determine whether or not the tested article is the real thing. It then sometimes comes to mean "tempt," in the moral sense. Paul uses the participle, "the testing one, the Tester," as a synonym for Satan.

[1] Timothy's return with good news is the occasion of this letter and the extended thanksgiving that forms the first part of its body. Paul has been desperately worried that the faith of the Thessalonians might have withered under the duress they are experiencing; he has sent Timothy back to Thessalonica to encourage them and to return with a report on their status. The continuing existence of the new church in Thessalonica is a matter of his very life (v. 10). Paul speaks out of his anguish from having been out of touch. In our recently arrived era of instant worldwide communication, it is already difficult to imagine the situation of even fifty years ago, not to speak of Paul's situation. This is yet another instance in which understanding the Bible requires historical imagination in order to get within understanding distance.

The way in which Paul refers to Athens indicates that he is no longer there, and the letter is not written from Athens (otherwise he would have said, "Left alone *here*," not "left alone in Athens"). He is presumably writing from Corinth, where Timothy and Silvanus are again with him, and he is describing the Athens situation in retrospect (see intro, "Context of Paul's Life"). Otherwise the chronology and historical circumstances are not entirely clear. From Paul's letter, the modern reader would assume that both Timothy and Silvanus had been involved with Paul in the initial evangelizing of Thessalonica, that Silvanus had then gone or been sent elsewhere (no reference is made to him in the 2:17–3:6 period between Thessalonica and Corinth), that Timothy had continued with Paul to Athens, and from there was sent back to Thessalonica, leaving

Paul alone in Athens. The alternation between "we" and "I" contributes to the ambiguity, for "we" may be rhetorical/editorial, referring only to Paul, or it may include Silvanus. The emphasis on being alone, however, and the twice-used singular "I," suggests that Silvanus had not accompanied Paul to Athens. In Acts, there is no reference to Timothy in Philippi or Thessalonica. He resurfaces briefly in Beroea, and it is explicitly said that neither he nor Silas/Silvanus was with Paul in Athens (Acts 17:14–15; see above on 1:1). The statement in 1 Thess 3:1–2 can be read in such a way that Timothy was not in Athens, that it was in Athens that Paul was *left alone*, but the *decision* was made elsewhere; Paul decided in Beroea or someplace else in Macedonia to send Timothy back to Thessalonica, and went on alone to Athens, as portrayed in Acts.[76] The issue is not particularly important in the exegesis of 1 Thessalonians, except that it impinges on the question of how much confidence can be placed in Acts as an accurate historical source for illuminating the meaning of 1 Thessalonians.

[2] Paul's travel plans and visits to various cities were not always with the goal of evangelism in the sense of establishing new churches.[77] Timothy is described as "brother" and "coworker in God's service in the work of the gospel of Christ." All believers can be described as brothers and sisters in Christ (see on 1:2, 4), but in the present context "brother" seems to have a special sense, used of ministers or those with a special vocation, as in some Christian congregations in the southern USA and in some religious orders. This is even more true of "coworker" (see note a above; intro, "New Congregation"; comments on 1:1). The basic meaning of *synergos* (*syn*, with + *ergos*, worker) is simply one who works with another; the word can be used of a helper, assistant, colleague, or accomplice in a variety of settings. Like the English and German "assistant," however, the word can be used in a semiofficial sense (dental assistant, academic assistant), to refer to one who has a specialized responsibility. Paul uses the designation *synergos* for a number of people who do not merely offer him some kind of help on occasion, but who also work with him in a particular way, under his direction. Such people did not yet constitute an "order of ministry," but they were more than casual assistants.[78] As such a coworker, Timothy is not only Paul's, but God's—a minister in the service of God. Thus "God's coworker" here does not mean "coworker with God," but "coworker with Paul,

76. So Dobschütz and Bornemann 131; Rigaux 467; and esp. Donfried 2002c.
77. Verheyden, esp. 113.
78. See intro, "Church-Founding Visit" and "New Congregation." Though Paul can occasionally use the term to refer in general to believers who are participants in the Christian mission (2 Cor 8:23), in some instances Paul does seem to distinguish those who are *synergoi* from those who are rank and file (Rom 16:9, 21; Phil 4:2–3). The term occurs in the Deuteropaulines only in Col 4:11; i.e., it was not taken up in the nomenclature of the later, more institutionalized understanding of ministry, not occurring in the Pastorals at all, and not in 2 Thessalonians. For an argument that in Paul's Letters the word is used as a technical term for a special group of ministers, see esp. Ellis.

in God's service." A little later, Paul can use the same phrase to refer to himself and Apollos, who are coworkers who belong to God, not partners with God, as though the mission team was composed of God and the human missionaries (cf. 1 Cor 3:9). That the phrase could be understood in this sense, later considered the heresy of synergism, is seen in the fact that ancient scribes so understood it and "corrected" the manuscripts to save Paul from this heresy. Some modern translations and scholars continue to argue for this understanding.[79]

Why this focus on Timothy, and why the elaborated description of him? He has just returned from the Thessalonians, who know him well and do not need such an introduction. Two overlapping explanations have been given: (1) Timothy is the bearer of the letter, having been sent back to the Thessalonians for a second time, this time carrying Paul's response to what he has learned from Timothy's visit. It was standard procedure to mention and thus authorize the bearer of the letter. Although we know nothing about who actually delivered the letter to Thessalonica, it may be that Timothy was sent back with the letter and that these words both authorize him and validate his previous work among them. The words are not *introducing* Timothy, but *validating* both the present letter and the mission he has performed in Paul's absence. (2) The written text of the letter also documents an important step in the developing scriptural status and role of Paul's Letters. Paul had been in Thessalonica himself for some time, and had taught the new converts personally. He had appointed and trained teachers who continued instruction in the traditions Paul had delivered to them. He had sent Timothy, who had brought a positive report. So why send the letter? It is a written text to be read repeatedly, to all, as the point of orientation for the church's continued teaching, preaching, and life. Early in the Aegean mission, the new genre of the apostolic letter begins to assume a status alongside the Scripture adopted from Judaism, a first step toward the canonization of such texts themselves (see further on 5:27).

When Paul says that Timothy had been sent to *encourage* them and strengthen their *faith*, he once again uses familiar terms in a new, deepened sense illumined by the new faith of the young church. Faith occurs five times in this brief paragraph. *Encourage* (*parakalesai*) is not mere cheerleading or back-patting, but is redolent with the *paraklēsis* of the whole Christian message (see on 2:3). The term for their faith (*pistis*, five times in 3:1–10) is likewise multilayered. (1) Faith can mean the obedience-in-personal-trust of one's relationship with God, trust in the one God, *fides qua creditur*, the faith by which

---

79. Thus the ESV: "our brother and God's co-worker." Cf., e.g., Furnish 2007, 78: "Synergism is a false issue, however. If not in 1 Cor 3:9, which is also ambiguous, at least in 2 Cor 6:1 ('As we work together with him [i.e., God]') Paul does not hesitate to speak of the work of the ministry as jointly divine and human in the sense that God works through the apostles to effect reconciliation (2 Cor 5:18–20)." See also Haufe 57. Paul writes unself-consciously, unconcerned about later distinctions between orthodoxy and heresy.

one believes. Timothy's *paraklēsis* was intended to strengthen this and has done so. (2) Without excluding the former meaning or as an alternative to it, *pistis* can refer to the content of faith, what is believed, *fides quae creditur*, the faith that one believes. Faith has a content: the believer doesn't just believe, but believes *something*, and the content of faith shapes and is shaped by the nature of one's personal trust. Paul immediately refers to this aspect of faith in 3:10; he wants to fill in some lacunae in their faith, to give them further instruction in the contents of Christian faith.[80] (3) However, a third dimension of *pistis* is the focus of Paul's statement here: faith as *faithfulness*, not denying one's commitments, faith as keeping one's promise. In this sense God can be described as having faith, keeping faith, being faithful (Rom 3:3). When used of Christian believers, it also means faithfulness, endurance, hanging in there. While personal trust in God, the content of what is believed, and the holding on to one's commitment to God are all interrelated aspects of faith, here the focus is on faithfulness. Timothy had not been sent to determine whether the new converts were orthodox, but whether the cultural pressures, which had probably already taken a violent turn, have caused them to withdraw from the church or at least keep a low profile. For Paul, withdrawing into oneself, developing a private spirituality, is no longer faith.

[3] The new Christians in Thessalonica have been enduring persecution (see intro, "New Congregation"; and on *thlipsis* in 1 Thess 1:6). Paul wants them to understand that persecution and suffering are inherent in God's call and election, that what they are enduring is nothing strange or arbitrary, not just being at the wrong place at the wrong time, but that the troubles they are experiencing are part of the apocalyptic woes of the end time (see on 4:13–18). Their necessity is not impersonal fate, not the prewritten script for the final act of the divine drama, but neither are they meaningless. They are part of the unfolding plan of God for the consummation of the divine purpose. They thus correspond to the divine *dei* of the Synoptic Gospels ("it is necessary"; cf. Mark 8:31; 9:11; 13:7, 10, 14; and parallels; Luke 24:7, 44), which signals the suffering of both the Messiah and his followers as incorporated into the saving plan of God. Participation in these troubles, being persecuted by the powers of this world that already lash out destructively in their defeat, is inherent in the Christian life as such. As Best pointed out, "Paul is not thinking of a period of persecution which will pass and the church return to normality; normality is persecution."[81]

---

80. Rigaux 185, 485. Faith has a *content*. At first this faith is belief in some facts—i.e., actions, the saving acts of God declared in the kerygma, the gospel (cf. 4:14). It is a believing-that such-and-such happened. This distinguishes the believers in Thessalonica from pagans, as it distinguishes them from their own previous selves. But this faith is active, is itself expressed in actions (1:3), and cannot be separated from faithfulness, since being faithful cannot be separated from the contents of what is believed.

81. Best 135.

[4] Paul announced in advance that the new converts would face persecution, but that does not mean he claimed a special power to predict the future, even though understanding himself in prophetic terms is part and parcel of Paul's self-identity (see on 5:27). Paul understands Christian faith to be eschatological existence, that suffering for the faith is inherent in the divine *kaleō* (call, 2:12; 4:7; 5:24) and *eklogē* (election, 1:4) as such, not only for the apostles who display it before the world. Just as suffering and rejection is the mark of authentic apostleship, so it is the signature of authentic discipleship (1 Cor 4:8–13). This was not news to the young church in Thessalonica. The imperfect tense *proelegomen* indicates that Paul has repeatedly made it a part of his instruction while he was with them. His reminder is not the smug "I told you so," but he calls to their memory the extensive instruction he has given them while present. From the beginning, he has not presented the way of discipleship as easy, in order to attract converts. He has preached the Christian message and believed that those who responded have been called and chosen by God—though they may need to be reminded that this is so.

[5] According to the apocalyptic view that forms the framework of Paul's thought, in the last days before the end the powers of evil are concentrated and intensified, because they know their days are numbered (cf. Matt 8:29; Rev 12:12). Thus Satan tries to hinder Paul from carrying out his mission (2:18) and puts believers to the test, trying to get them to fall away from the faith. Paul may see the political opposition instigated by the local Roman authorities and their supporters as agents of Satan, both prohibiting Paul's return to Thessalonica and testing the faith of the new converts (see intro, "New Congregation"). Although *peirazō* sometimes develops a moral sense, with the meaning "attempt to get someone to do something immoral," it mostly retains the meaning of "put to the test" and should be so translated in such contexts as the "temptation" of Jesus (Matt 4:1–11, where the devil is called *ho peirazōn*, "the Tester"), as here. In the Matthean story, the devil is not tempting Jesus to do something immoral, but is testing him. So also in the familiar words in the Lord's Prayer, puzzling to many who take them seriously, the traditional translation "Lead us not into temptation, but deliver us from evil" is misunderstood if it is supposed that God might otherwise lead the one who prays to do something immoral; and "evil" is rightly understood not as an abstraction but the personal power of evil, the devil. Thus the NRSV rightly renders the familiar words as "Do not bring us to the time of trial, but rescue us from the evil one" (Matt 6:13; cf. REB, "Do not put us to the test, but save us from the evil one"; NABRE, "Do not subject us to the final test, but deliver us from the evil one"; NJB, "Do not put us to the test, but save us from the Evil One"). In the Lord's Prayer, Jesus teaches his disciples to pray that they will not have to face this terrible test of the last days, for the pressure might be too much for them. This is the context of Paul's thought. He knows that the new converts in Thessalonica have not been delivered from the test, but are in the midst of it, and he is afraid they might not have endured. When he learns from Timothy that despite the Tester's efforts to dislodge them, they are holding fast to the faith, he is thankful indeed.

3:6–10 Timothy Brings Good News

In this glowing paragraph, the focus shuttles back and forth between "you" and "we." Though presupposing that church life is lived in the reality of "God the Father and the Lord Jesus Christ" (1:1), the discourse here is altogether on the horizontal dimension of personal relations. In the following, first-person "we" words (verbs, nouns, pronouns, and modifiers) are in **bold**, second-person "you" words in *italics*:

> 3:6 But now,[a] *brothers and sisters*, **we have experienced** the encouragement and comfort[b] of the good news—from *you* to **us**—just now brought by Timothy, telling **us** *your* faithfulness and love, and that *you* always have good memories of **us**, longing to see **us** just as **we** long to see *you*. 7 This good news of *your* faithfulness brings **us** encouragement in the midst of **our** own distress and persecution, 8 because **we now really live**,[c] since[d] *you* are standing fast in the Lord. 9 For what thanksgiving can **we** possibly **render** to God for *you* for all the joy with which **we celebrate** before **our**[e] God on *your* account, 10 night and day **praying** with supergreat intensity[f] to see *your* face, and to **equip** *you* more completely for a faithful life?

a. In contrast to most English translations, *arti de* (but now) is here taken to relate directly to the main verb of this complex sentence (see note b). It corresponds to the frequent Pauline *nyni de* that signals the transition from the old age to the new enacted by the Christ event and the transformation of believers from the old life to the new. It is not merely a matter of chronological time, but esp. of introducing a fundamentally new situation (cf. Rom 3:21; 6:22; 7:6, 17; 11:30; 15:23; 1 Cor 7:14; 15:20; Gal 4:9; Phlm 9, 11).

b. On the difficulty of translating the *parakaleō* word group into English, see above on 2:3. The above translation attempts to preserve something of Paul's sense that the ultimate consolation/comfort/coming of the kingdom of God is already manifest in "ordinary" historical events.

c. The Greek text has no adverb "really," which is here supplied to indicate the life of the age to come, eternal life, the eschatological existence already fragmentarily experienced by believers. See trans. note j on 2 Thess 1:9.

d. Virtually all MSS read the present tense *stēkete*. The subjunctive *stēkēte* is found only in ℵ* D, and a few other MSS not considered worth mentioning by UBS[4]. When followed by the subjunctive, the conjunction *ean* means "if." Here, with the following verb in the indicative, the construction means "since" (though some English versions, esp. in the tradition of the KJV, translate "if," making the clause conditional). Paul is not placing leverage on the Thessalonians by making his own attaining of eternal life dependent on whether or not they remain faithful. He is declaring his gratitude that they have remained faithful and that this does in fact give him new life in the here and now.

e. While the other uses of the first-person plural pronoun are exclusive, meaning "us" in distinction from "you," this final use of the pronoun is inclusive, a "we" regarding missionaries and new converts to be united with each other as believers in the one God (hence the bold italics; cf. 1:9–10).

f. The word *hyperekperissou* occurs only here and in 5:13 in the undisputed Letters of Paul, and very rarely elsewhere in all Greek literature. The genitive of the adjective *perissos* is used adverbially, which is quite regular, but the addition of a double prefix to make *hyper-ek-perissou* is a bit slangy. Paul bends language to express his extreme devotion to the Thessalonians in prayer. The word impressed the author of the deutero-pauline Ephesians, who incorporates a variation of it in Paul's prayer that concludes the body of that letter, its only other occurrence in the NT (Eph 3:20).

[6–8] These verses are a single, complex sentence, as Paul's deep emotion is expressed by piling up phrases and clauses. Yet Paul is not confused about what he wants to say, and the barebones structure is clear. The main clause is thus:

a. *We are encouraged* [since through Timothy's good news we already experience the eschatological encouragement and consolation of the coming of God's kingdom]
   because
b. we really live
   since
c. you are standing fast in the Lord.

Virtually the whole paragraph has to do with the deep personal relations that have been generated by the conversion of the Thessalonians. The firm we-you connections are embodied in grammar and syntax (see translation and notes). Here is a remarkable understanding of Christian faith and mission as recipro-cal and mutual, especially to be noticed since Paul's mission perspective has often been regarded as monodirectional, as though he were the apostle and his churches only recipients of his apostolic message. But here, without dimin-ishing the apostolic character of the faith,[82] both Paul and the Thessalonians endure *thlipsis*, both receive *paraklēsis*, both have *pistis*, both are embraced in the same *agapē*; not only does Paul evangelize them, they also evangelize him.

---

82. Paul's glowing response to the good news Timothy brings is not *only* an expression of the close personal relation he has developed with the Thessalonians. Their holding fast to him, their love for him, is an affirmation of the apostolic office he has. He (and his colleagues) are their link to Christ and God. To hold fast to him is to hold on to Christ and God, to remain a true church. An understanding of apostleship emerges here, not only where the word "apostle" is found. This is assumed and does not yet need to be explicated or defended.

Paul had wanted to encourage them with the eschatological *paraklēsis* of the Christian message, and had done so by sending Timothy, but in sending Timothy back to him with good news, they have also communicated to him the same deep encouragement. The ultimate *paraklēsis* of the Parousia already casts its shadow proleptically over the relations between Paul and the Thessalonians. Not an individualistic piety, Paul's experience of salvation is bound up with the faith and love of the mission churches, and theirs with him.

The modern reader might ponder the amazing fact that in such a short time Paul and his fellow missionaries should develop such a warm, loving, personal relationship with people who were total strangers, in a town they had never before visited. Yet this horizontal we-you is embraced by and transparent to the new world created by God's act in Christ; all person-to-person relations are transfigured as vehicles of the deeper reality in which they participate. This does not diminish them, as though personal friendships were really only a means of being "spiritual" in relation to God. It is not that Paul has no real interest in loving personal relationships, only using them as mediators of religious experience, as though he loves God but not people, or only loves people because they give him access to the spiritual, transcendent world. Placing newfound friendships in the church within the transcendent framework of God's act in Christ—which includes the calling of the church into being—enhances personal relationships by placing them in an ultimate context. Although Paul does not use the word, he affirms the gospel of the *incarnation*, in which God's reality is made known in the reality of human relationships.

This incarnational perspective of the Christian faith transfigures the language in which it is expressed. "Ordinary" encouragement participates in, mediates, is made real by the eschatological *paraklēsis*; "ordinary" good news on the human level that his friends are getting along okay participates in and mediates the good news of the gospel. The use of *euangelizomai* for Timothy's report is usually understood as an exception, a reverting to the "secular" use of the word as generic "good news." This would make 3:6 the only verse in the New Testament to use *euangelizomai* without a direct reference to preaching the gospel, the good news of Jesus Christ. It is more likely that even this is not an exception but instead is consistent with Pauline usage elsewhere: news of the love and concern of Christian brothers and sisters, that they are standing firm in the faith despite opposition, is incorporated into the good news of the Christian faith and is itself a part of the gospel. God's act in Christ is made real in the actions of human beings to each other; these human acts are sanctified because they are embraced and made possible by God's act in Christ. Encouragement, saying thank-you, the joy of human contact—all these are radioactive with the ultimate energy of the universe. To tell of the good things that are happening among God's people in the Christian community is not an appendage to the gospel, but included in it, just as God's act in Christ includes calling the church into being.

This is also the case with the central term "love": love toward Christ and love toward the missionaries are not alternatives. The believer cannot say "I love Jesus" without loving the church's mission; nor can believers just "love people" on the horizontal level with no reference to God's love they have experienced and are called to share. This love is an aspect of love for God. For Paul, too, the first and second commandments cannot be separated: more than once he appeals to the command to love the neighbor in Lev 19:18 (Rom 12:19; Gal 5:14), yet he does not think in terms of the Synoptic combination of the two biblical commands to love God and love neighbor (Mark 12:29–31 par.). "Faith," "love," "good news," "encouragement"—these are not general religious ideals that are here affirmed, as though Paul were indulging in generalizing spiritual-sounding talk, but concrete acts and relationships between the Thessalonians and the missionaries. This is an incarnational view of language. Not only does the Word become flesh (John 1:14), it also becomes fleshly *words*: the words of our ordinary human life are incarnate with the eternal Word and are its vehicles. One does not need to speak of the eternal Word or of the incarnate Word-made-flesh as Jesus Christ in order to speak (of) this word; the "ordinary" human words are charged with the energy of the primal/eschatological event. Paul writes of his longing to see the new converts in Thessalonica. This is not particularly religious, but simply being human, wanting to see one's family. And now this humanness participates in the new humanity of the Christ event; this-worldly events are now radiant and resonant with the new world. Paul does not spell this out, as he will in his later letters—1 Thessalonians is not a didactic letter—yet the conviction is already here.

[7] The good news of the Thessalonians' faithfulness comes as encourage-ment to Paul amid the troubles he himself is suffering in Corinth. We know nothing about these in detail. Yet he and the Thessalonians are bound together both in tribulation and in encouragement. The last time Paul saw them, *he* was escaping danger, but leaving *them* to face the problems his visit had caused. He wanted them to understand that he did not escape persecution by leaving Thessalonica: he and they continue to share the same lot, though they are in different cities.

[8] The "now we live" of v. 8 has the overtones of a resurrection to new life. Though Paul resisted interpretations of the resurrection that reduced it to the present experience of the believer, he did not confine the meaning of resurrection to the future eschatological event. Not only has Jesus already been raised, but also already in the present the beginning and foretaste of the eschatological drama soon to be consummated and the power of the resurrection are made known in the life of the Christian community (cf. Rom 6:1–11, esp. vv. 4, 11; Phil 3:7–21, esp. v. 10). The anxious missionaries, wondering about the steadfastness of the new little congregation in Thessalonica, receive Timothy's report as a new lease on life. Just as the coming kingdom of God, though not

yet fully present but already dawning, allows the believer to live in the light of its reality, so also the resurrection of Jesus, which has already happened, is the beginning and guarantee of the grand resurrection to come. The "ordinary" events in which "minor" victories prevail against the powers of death can already be celebrated and spoken of in terms of the ultimate event. There can be little resurrections because the big one has already happened and will happen; thus Paul can celebrate authentic and eternal life because of the news from the new little church in Thessalonica.

[9] The thanksgiving theme that embraces all of 1:2–3:13 again becomes explicit (see intro, "Outline and Structure"; comments at 1 Thess 1:2). The thanksgiving is to God. Paul does not thank the Thessalonians that they have been faithful (see on 1:2). The "our" of v. 9 is inclusive. The we/you interchange is not ultimate, but both writers and addressees are embraced in their life before the one God.

[10] Paul assures the new converts that he constantly prays for them. "Night and day" is a common rhetorical exaggeration that was meant and heard as "regularly." The word order is not particularly Jewish (as though reflecting Gen 1:5 and the frequent occurrence of "evening and morning" in the OT), but common in the Hellenistic world. Though physically separated, they are always gently on his mind (2:17–20). He has been reassured by Timothy's report, but this is not enough. It was a commonplace in the Hellenistic understanding of friendship that true friends want to be together. He wants to see them personally, because this is the nature of true friendship. But as he brings the first part of the body of the letter to a close, Paul also casts a look ahead: he wants to fill in some deficiencies in their faith. This is not a deprecating reminder that he is apostle and they need to learn from him, but simply states the reality of the situation. They are new converts; they are enduring well under the pressures that beset them. But they, like all believers, continue to need further instruction and encouragement as they mature in the faith, and Paul wants to provide that personally.

3:11–13 Transitional Summary and Prayer

Paul brings this section to a close with a prayer that both sums up the whole section 1:2–3:13 and, by its eschatological perspective, forms the transition to the subject matter of the paraenesis beginning at 4:1. This arrangement corresponds to the prayer in Phil 1:9–11 that directly follows the thanksgiving, with the difference that in 1 Thessalonians the thanksgiving has been greatly extended and combined with the letter body.

The construction of 3:11–13 can be taken as one long sentence, as here (so also ASV, RSV, ESV, NABRE, NAS95); as two sentences (vv. 11, 12–13 in KJV, NKJV; vv. 11–12, 13 in REB); or, for the sake of readability, broken into three or more sentences (so NRSV, NIV11, TNIV, NJB, CEB).

3:11 Now may our God and Father himself and our Lord Jesus clear the way[a] for us to come to you, 12 and as for you, may the Lord[b] make you increase and overflow in love for one another and for all, just as we do for you, 13 so that your hearts may be strong, blameless in holiness, before our God and Father at the Parousia of our Lord Jesus with all his saints. [Amen.][c]

a. *Kateuthynai* means basically "make or keep straight," and thus "lead, direct" (cf. Luke 1:79, direct one's "feet in the way of peace"; Ps 39:3 LXX (40:2 ET), direct one's steps). Paul here has in mind the barrier Satan has erected to keep him from returning to Thessalonica (2:18), so "clear the way" is an appropriate translation.

b. A few later scribes, apparently wanting to clarify the "ambiguity" of whether God or the Lord Jesus is intended, added "Jesus," as in v. 11 (D*, G, and the Syriac tradition). The original text had only "the Lord," as in virtually all MSS; the "ambiguity" is Pauline and is not to be "clarified." The unusual syntax in v. 11 (*ho . . . kai ho* = the . . . and the), with a singular verb for the combination, maintains the distinction between *God* and *Lord* while joining them as one acting subject.[83]

c. Paul can include an *amēn* at the conclusion of a prayer or benediction within the text of a letter, as in Rom 1:25; 9:5; 15:33; Gal 1:5. In Romans, too, Paul includes a prayer that closes the body of the letter and forms the transition to the paraenetic section, as here (Rom 11:36). The two oldest and best witnesses of the text of 1 Thessalonians are split, with ℵ* including the *amen* and B omitting it. Though included in A D* 81 629, the Latin and one branch of the Coptic traditions, most later MSS and versions omit it. Good arguments can be made for both later addition and later omission. Both standard editions of the Greek NT consider it a tossup, including it in the text, but in brackets.

Three things are important for hearing this text:

1. Paul has been talking about praying for the readers. Now he actually prays. As the letter is read in the worship of the little congregation in Thessalonica, separated by several days' journey, Paul joins them in prayer, his voice is heard in prayer; the letter brings author and readers, apostle and congregation, before God in prayer, together. People who have not known Paul personally hear Paul lead them in prayer. This still happens when the letter is read in church.

2. This long sentence sums up the preceding thanksgiving/body of the letter, pointing back to what he has said in 1:2–3:10. It closes the first main part of the letter, speaking of the one God to whom the new converts have turned, the one Lord Jesus Christ, the crucified and risen one who now leads and directs the life of the church, and that not just in general: he can guide particular people to join or rejoin others in the ongoing mission of the church, allowing them to celebrate their newfound friendship and joint task of ministry that has become the meaning of their lives.

83. See Hewett.

3. This paragraph points ahead to the paraenetic section of the letter, chapters 4–5, affirming God's call to live a holy life, the new converts' love for each other, for the whole community of Christian believers, and for all people as God's beloved creatures, in the hope of the near Parousia that will reunite the readers/hearers with their lost loved ones and with all the saints, the holy community to which they now belong and within which they have found their place in the family of God.

[11] Paul's prayer is concrete—that he will soon be able to return to the new congregation. The congregation overhears this prayer made before God, a prayer that already functions indirectly as paraenesis.

Paul does not formulate the language ad hoc, but neither does he adopt and repeat a traditional prayer. Influenced by the liturgical language of the emerging church, the modern reader gets to listen in on the way early Christians prayed, and even to join them. Though Paul is not here teaching Trinitarian (or Binitarian) christological conceptuality, the plural subject—God the Father and the Lord Jesus—are thought of as a unity, and the third-person singular verb is used (invisible in English, which uses the same form for sg. and pl., but unusual in Greek).[84] God and Jesus here function grammatically as a unity. The subject of the next clause is "the Lord," and it would be futile to ask whether Paul means "God" or "Christ," for these often modulate into a functional unity for Paul (in v. 11 "Lord" clearly refers to Jesus; in 4:6, to God). Paul thinks in terms of functional identity, not ontological analysis. Paul the Jewish monotheist cannot now think of the one God apart from the definitive revelation in his Son Jesus Christ; but neither can Paul the Christian who has personally encountered the risen Christ think of Jesus apart from the God who raised him from the dead. These two "persons" modulate into each other in his thought.[85] Neither can be thought of alone.

[12] Paul has just spoken of his prayer for himself, that he will be able to return to them. With "and as for you," his prayer focuses on the Thessalonians and their needs.

For Paul as for Jesus, responsibility to God is summed up in the love command, a love directed not only to the insiders of one's own congregation, but also outward to the whole church and to all people as God's creatures (cf. 5:15).[86] Love is first of all directed to the insiders of the new community. Yet, in

84. In Matt 24:35 "heaven and earth" have a sg. verb; in Matt 16:17 and 1 Cor 15:50 "flesh and blood" take a sg. verb. In each case, as here, the dual subject functions as a unity.

85. This is not unique to Paul, but common in NT theology. Note, e.g., Rev 11:15, "The kingdom of the world has become the kingdom of our Lord and of his Messiah, and he will reign forever and ever" (NRSV). It is offtrack to ask whether the verb in the singular refers to God "or" the Messiah; just as, in John 3:16, "whoever believes in him" points to God-and-the-only-Son as a unity, and to ask whether one is to believe in God or Christ misses the point.

86. Cf. Pregeant 234.

sociological terms, this is not to be reduced to the sectarian self-understanding of a group that reinforces its own sense of belonging by demonizing outsiders and loving insiders. The new community, presumably from different backgrounds and mostly unacquainted with each other before their conversion, must first of all learn the meaning of belonging to the new family of God, where all are loved because they are loved by God. Though the meaning of such care— *agapē* is often best translated by "caring," whose opposite is not "hate" but "not caring"—must begin within the experience of the community itself, it is not restricted to insiders. Such love, whether to the community or beyond it, is not the carrying out of a command, but the overflowing of the love experienced in the community to include all (cf. Gal 6:10). Love "for one another and for all" is not a command, though included in the prayer, but the prayer as a whole, though directed to God, has an "implicitly imperatival aspect";[87] whoever prays like this cannot continue in the old life in which love is restricted to one's own kind of people. They must resist the temptation to allow harassment from outsiders to solidify them into an introverted group. Those who have come to believe in the one God must learn to love all, who are also beloved creatures of the same God. Nor is this just an abstract love for humanity in general, but love for their neighbors and fellow citizens in Thessalonica, including those who are rejecting, harassing, and persecuting them. This is one of the radical implications of a monotheistic faith.

[13] Paul wants to be with the new converts in Thessalonica and guide them from the present to the Parousia, soon to manifest the fulfillment of God's purposes and vindicate the faith, life, and suffering of the new converts. The reference to the Parousia is not mere speculation about the end times, but impinges on the way the Thessalonians lead their lives. Paul wants to be with them and to be their guide toward that great and final day.

The matter-of-fact way Paul uses such language addressed to God and Christ, in which prayer, not christological "speculation," is the point, shows that he had long come to think and speak in this way. He is not tentatively feeling his way forward theologically in this "early" letter, but his preaching and teaching have presupposed such conceptuality and language for several years. When, a few years later as he writes to the Corinthians, he elaborates on the one God and one Lord Jesus Christ, this is not a new development in his theology, but is cited as something that can be assumed as the basis of Christian practice (1 Cor 8:5–6). While we should not imagine Paul giving lectures on Christology to the new converts in Thessalonica, during his time with them they had become accustomed to including the language of Jesus as Lord within the conceptual and linguistic field of the one "living and true God" (1:9–10). At

87. Furnish 2007, 84.

Nicaea and Chalcedon, when the later church struggles to express such faith in more philosophical categories, it does not lose the narrative and functional orientation of Paul's language, which focus on act more than on being.

The new converts perceive their new identity, its rewards and responsibilities, as they hear the apostle pray *for* and *with* them, in a letter addressed *to* them. It is only the Lord who can strengthen their hearts and make them blameless when they stand before him at the Parousia. The combination of address to God and address to the community means they cannot merely wait for God to make them more loving and holy; they also are called to active responsibility.

The most difficult exegetical issue of this text is the intended identity of the *hagioi* (holy ones) who will be "with" the returning Lord at the Parousia. The choice is between the *angels*, thought of as coming from heaven with the returning Lord, or the *saints*, the Thessalonian Christians who have died and other departed members of the community of faith, yet who will be revealed at the Parousia as living. Most English versions take the word as referring to the saints, God's people; several commentators have made a strong case for understanding *hagioi* to refer to angels. This is a more important point than may be immediately obvious (see below and on 4:13–18) and thus deserves thorough investigation.

The arguments for *hagioi* = angels are as follows: (1) Paul is clearly alluding to Zech 14:5, "Then the LORD my God will come, and all the holy ones with him" (NRSV), which seems to refer to angels. (2) The parallels to 1 Thessalonians in 2 Thess 1:7, 10 clearly refer to angels. (3) There is no other reference in 1 Thessalonians where *hagioi* refers to Christian believers. (4) If 1 Thess 3:13 refers to saints, the collision with 4:16 is difficult or impossible to reconcile.

These arguments are not compelling, and some are misleading:

1. Paul is indeed using the language of Zech 14:5, in which the *hagioi* are probably the holy angels (but cf. Dan 7:18, 22). But Paul's hermeneutic is christocentric, not oriented to the historical meaning of the text. He does not ask what Zechariah meant in his situation, but how the text should be heard by those who believe the Christ has come, will soon return in glory, and are concerned about the status of their loved ones who have died (see on 4:13–18). By *kyrios* (LXX: Lord), Zechariah had meant Yahweh (LORD), as the Hebrew clearly states. As often elsewhere, here Paul finds a reference to the Lord Jesus, so that the eschatological coming of God to his people becomes the coming of the Lord Jesus. So also, for Paul, *hagioi* always elsewhere refers to the saints, the holy people of God, into which Gentile Christians have now been incorporated. He reads Zech 14:5 as picturing the coming of the Lord Jesus with his saints. "With his saints" is included not merely incidentally, with no contextual meaning, as though Paul includes the phrase only because it happens to be included in the traditional imagery of Zechariah, but because it is important for Paul's own context.

2. The interpretation in 2 Thess 1:7 does clearly refer to angels accompanying the Lord at the Parousia. If, as argued in this commentary, 2 Thessalonians is deuteropauline, this illustrates how an aspect of Pauline eschatology was understood in one branch of the Pauline school a generation or so after Paul, but has little bearing on how 1 Thessalonians was intended and understood in its own context. In 2 Thess 1:10 the reference to *hagioi* could be taken as referring to the accompanying angels, but more likely is parallel to "those who believe," earthly members of the Christian community (so virtually all English translations). Only a little later, *Didache* 16.7 understands the holy ones who accompany the returning Lord to be Christian saints. Thus the earliest interpretations of this text already exhibit both possibilities, but incline toward "saints" rather than angels.

3. While it is true that elsewhere in 1 Thessalonians, Christians are never designated *hagioi*, there is nothing probative about this for the meaning of the term in 3:13. The word *hagioi* is also missing from Galatians; in each case this is only incidental. Paul uses the *hagi-* word group ten times in this short letter: *hagiazō*, sanctify (1 Thess 5:23); *hagiasmos*, holiness (4:3, 4, 7); *hagios*, holy (1:5, 6; 3:13; 4:8; 5:26); and *hagiōsynē*, holiness (3:13). The Thessalonians understand this vocabulary, take it in the Christian sense in which they have been instructed, and hence would understand *hagioi* to refer to Christian believers.[88] If Paul had intended angels, he would have said so more clearly.

4. If 3:13 is to be understood as meaning that departed Christians accompany the Lord Jesus as he returns from heaven, then there is indeed a clash of imagery with that of 4:16, in which departed saints first return from the dead by being raised immediately upon the Lord's return. This is, in fact, the most natural reading. There is no verb in the clause, however, and nothing specifically indicates that the saints will accompany the returning Lord on his descent from heaven, but only that when he returns, the dead saints will be "with" him, which could mean that they will not be deprived of the glories of the end, but will be raised to share the eschatological glory with those who are still alive at the Parousia. So also in 4:14 NRSV, "God will bring with him those who have died," and they will also be "with" the Lord (4:17). On this understanding, it would thus not be a matter of picturing the dead saints returning with Jesus from heaven, but a tableau of the Parousia en bloc. It is thus quite possible to understand 3:13 as representing the same picture of the eschatological events as 4:16.

---

88. Fee (135) objects that "it is difficult to understand how the Thessalonians could have understood it in that way" (i.e., as referring to Christian believers). This is based on its absence in this sense in the rest of the letter—as though the readers were entirely dependent on this letter to provide them with their Christian vocabulary (see intro, "New Congregation"). One can hardly believe that Paul had not yet begun to use the term *hagioi* of Christians when he writes 1 Thessalonians, more than fifteen years into his mission.

The more natural reading, however, is that Paul does here picture the departed saints as not actually dead, but as alive in heaven with the Lord, who will rejoin their earthly brothers and sisters when they return with him at the Parousia, and that this is indeed a different image from that of 4:13–18. The essential question, then, is whether Paul has a consistent set of eschatological images, each of which can be fitted into one superpicture of "how it really will be" at the eschaton. If Paul has such a consistent eschatological system into which each of his images can be fitted to make up the total picture—like putting together the pieces of a jigsaw puzzle—there are two ways to deal with the *hagioi* of 3:13. (a) The *hagioi* are angels and do not disrupt the picture of 4:13–18. (b) Paul has a clear concept of individual eschatology, in which at death the soul departs to be with the Lord in heaven, while the body is buried in the earth. At the eschaton, the body will be raised and reunited with the soul. In this view, it is the souls of departed Christians that return with Christ from heaven in 3:13, their bodies are raised at 4:16, they are reunited not only with their earthly families and fellow saints but with their own bodies, and there is no conflict between 3:13 and 4:16. This view depends both on the presupposition that Paul has one consistent superpicture of the eschatological events and the skill of the modern interpreter in fitting together the pieces of the jigsaw puzzle scattered through Paul's Letters into the one comprehensive tableau.[89]

The alternative understanding, here advocated, is that Paul, like ancient apocalyptists in general, did not have a single comprehensive picture of the eschatological events. The central affirmation to which all the eschatological imagery pointed was clear—the faithfulness of the one God who will bring history to a worthy conclusion—but various aspects of this conviction could be represented with a variety of imagery, using images that cannot be combined into one consistent picture.[90] As in the Letter to the Philippians, Paul can express this confident hope via imagery in which the believer goes at death to be with the Lord (Phil 1:21–26) *and*, in the same letter, look forward to the future resurrection (3:8–11, 20–21). In the Corinthian Letters the same theological mode is seen in the clashing imagery for the same eschatological hope: future resurrection in 1 Cor 15:1–58, going directly to heaven in 2 Cor 5:1–10. Each image has a certain completeness in itself and does not function only as a fragment of a larger, consistent scheme. Each image is not a discrete statement from which logical inferences can be made, but all this is the language of

89. The most readable argument for this view is Wright (2003), who finds it not only in Paul but also throughout the NT.

90. With British understatement and without condescension, D. S. Russell (9) wrote, "It has to be remembered that apocalyptic writers were not systematic theologians; they were not interested in exact definitions of faith, and logic was perhaps one of their lesser virtues!" Likewise on 375: "Logic and consistency are the least of the apocalyptists' virtues!" See Caird 271–73.

confession.[91] In this view, Paul may intend to portray departed Christians as returning from heaven with Jesus, but the clash of imagery with 4:13–18 is not crucial to its understanding. What is crucial is the insight that all efforts to portray the ultimate victory of God are inadequate to do justice to the subject matter they strive to signify. Eschatological images function as pointers to something beyond their power to express. They function as pastoral care, to comfort (in the full sense discussed at 2:3) grieving Christians in Thessalonica. Paul is not teaching eschatology, but presupposing the eschatological triumph of God; within this framework of Christian faith, he is offering pastoral encouragement by holding before them one image of this final realization of the faithfulness of God. In 4:13–18, he will use a different image for the same function.

The objections to understanding "holy ones" to mean Christian believers are thus by no means compelling. Three positive considerations tend to confirm that Paul is speaking of saints rather than angels. The first has to do with Paul's word usage. The undisputed Letters of Paul contain twenty-four instances of the generic masculine plural of the word *hagios* (holy). In every other case, the reference is to the saints, the holy ones, the members of the Christian community. If 1 Thess 3:13 does not refer to Christians, it is the only such instance in the whole Pauline corpus.

The second reason is not particularly focused on the concerns of the new converts in Thessalonica for their departed loved ones, but with the people of God, the saints of Israel with whom the Thessalonian Christians have now been united. At the eschaton, new members of God's people will join with the saints of all the ages in celebrating the final arrival of God's kingdom on this earth. The departed saints will come with the returning Lord to join the celebration.[92]

The third reason has to do with Paul's stance toward angels, which is consistently negative. The word *angelos* (messenger, angel) occurs ten times in the undisputed Letters of Paul. In these letters, angels are never called holy and are consistently cast in a negative light. Thus in Rom 8:38 they are among the powers that potentially separate human beings from God. In 1 Cor 6:3 the angels are among the evil transcendent powers that will be judged at the last day. In 2 Cor 11:14, what appears to be an angel may be an agent of Satan, who has his own angels (12:7). In Gal 3:19, angels (not God) are the mediators of the law, which enslaves human beings. Paul never has a good word to say about angels,[93] but

---

91. On the interpretation of disparate apocalyptic imagery, see Boring 1989, 51–59; 1994, 57–77; on confessional, referential but nonobjectifying language, see on 1:4 above.

92. So, e.g., Calvin 1960a, 16–17; Cerfaux 1965, 96.

93. The *archangelos* (archangel) of 1 Thess 4:16 is not Paul's own word, but part of the prophetic oracle he quotes. The seemingly positive reference to "receiving me as an angel of God" (Gal 4:14) may be the sole exception, in which Paul adopts the conceptuality of his readers, or it may be ironic (Galatians is permeated with irony): the Galatian Christians are infatuated with (second-rate) angels, and they once received Paul as fitting their expectations.

already manifests the negative judgment that will come to full flower in the proto-Gnosticism of the next generation and the full-blown Gnosticism of the second century: angels are not the benevolent beings sent by God as guides and helpers, but belong to the transcendent world of evil powers that must be over-come for humans to be saved. Other, later New Testament authors do, of course, affirm the biblical and Jewish view of angels as kindly heavenly servants of God (e.g., Mark 1:13; Matt 1–2; and throughout Luke–Acts [not John!]). Some post-Pauline images of the Parousia do portray the returning Messiah or Son of Man as accompanied by a heavenly host of angels (e.g., Matt 25:31; Mark 8:38), and one late text refers to them as the "holy ones" (Jude 14). The Pauline school did not follow Paul consistently in his view of angels and tended to adopt the more positive view of early Christianity in general. But this has not happened in Paul, and 1 Thess 3:13 is probably best seen as anticipating the hope for Christian believers that he will elaborate in the next section.

1 Thessalonians 4:1–5:22
The Life to Which Christians Are Called

We now come to the second major part of the letter. It is critically important to see the dipolar structure of Paul's thought and the corresponding deep structure of his letters (see intro, "Outline and Structure"). But having seen this, the interpreter must not rigidly schematize it (Paul did not). Just as the preceding thanksgiving/body of the letter (1:2–3:13), already permeated by eschatology, is not speculation, which he now puts behind him to talk about practical matters of church life, neither are the following exhortations independent of his grand vision of living at a particular point in the history of God's dealing with the world. The two poles are related more like the poles of a magnet than the halves of a football field. The preceding thanksgiving/body is not only profoundly theological; it also has interwoven into it numerous ethical aspects, not just how to think rightly about the faith, but likewise how to live. And though the paraenesis that follows in chapters 4–5 will surely continue to be permeated with Paul's theology, there is a significant shift in the center of gravity.

The lifestyle to which God calls the new converts is a life oriented by the love of God expressed in care for others, within and beyond the church (4:1–12), a life lived in the confident hope of the coming victory of God and eschatological realization of God's kingdom and justice (4:13–5:11), a life within and responsible to the new community of faith, the local outpost of God's people into which God has called them (5:12–22).

4:1–12 Life Pleasing to God

Paul has formulated 4:1–12 as a unit with three sections: a transitional introduction (vv. 1–2) followed by two complementary sections analogous to the double command of love to God and to neighbor: loving God expressed as doing God's will (vv. 3–8), and loving the neighbor within and beyond the family of God (vv. 9–12). The whole section is framed by the repetition of *parakaleō* (appeal, exhort, encourage) in vv. 1, 10; *parangelia* (command, instruction) in v. 2, cf. the related verb *parangellō* in v. 11; *peripateō* (walk, live) in vv. 1, 12. The theme is set by the repeated *hagiosmos* and related forms (holiness, sanctification; vv. 3, 4, 7, 8) and its opposite, *akatharsia* (impurity), in v. 7.

4:1–2 Introduction to Paraenetic Section

As Paul makes the transition to the second and final major section of the letter, he interweaves three concerns into one long and complex sentence: (1) The following paraenetic instructions about the Christian way of life are not moralistic advice, but result from the theology of the preceding section. (2) As a fellow member of the church "in Christ," he expresses his solidarity with the community that, guided by the Spirit, is called to discern authentic ethical decisions for itself, and is already doing this quite well, so that he is reluctant to issue dogmatic commands. (3) He is doing more, however, than offering either congratulations or advice; he is also reminding them of their responsibility to obey the apostolic instruction he has given them with the authority of the Lord Jesus. The somewhat convoluted structure represents the syntactical tightrope Paul walks as he tries to do justice to all three of these interacting concerns at once.

4:1 As for what remains to be said,[a] then, dear brothers and sisters,[b] we therefore[a] request and appeal[c] to you in the Lord Jesus—just as you received from us the tradition[d] of how we must live[e] in order to please God—that you continue even more in the way you are already living, 2 for you know the commands[f] we gave you through the Lord Jesus.

a. The section begins with the unusual phrase *loipon oun*. The basic meaning of the adjective *loipos* is "the rest of, the remainder" (e.g., Luke 12:26; Acts 2:37; 1 Cor 9:5; 11:34). The accusative *loipon* is used adverbially, "for the rest," and thus can mean "finally" in the sense of "we now enter the last part" (but not necessarily "in conclusion"). In Hellenistic and later Greek, *loipon* also developed an inferential meaning of "therefore," not only leading into the next section but also indicating that it is based on the preceding.[1]

In Paul's later Letters, the inferential particle *oun* (therefore) becomes the characteristic transitional particle from the "indicative" to the "imperative" sections of the typical Pauline letter (see, e.g., Rom 12:1; 1 Cor 4:16; 2 Cor 3:12; 7:1; Gal 5:1; and in the later Pauline tradition, Col 3:1; Eph 4:1; cf. intro, "Outline and Structure"). Most English translations have left it untranslated due to the awkwardness (in English) of combining it with *loipon*, but its importance in signaling the shift to the paraenetic section of the letter should not be overlooked.

The combination *loipon oun* is very rare, found only here in the NT and not at all in the LXX. It does occur in Josephus, *J.W.* 2.390; and in Eusebius, *Hist. eccl.* 4.15.18, in each case meaning "so then," "therefore," "and so, next." In neither case does it mean "finally." The combination is a soft transition that means this second, final section is

1. BDF 235, at §451 (6): "Out of the *loipon* used with asyndeton to begin a sentence 'further, as far as the rest is concerned, now' (cf. §160) there developed an inferential 'therefore.'" They cite Polybius and the papyri; Ignatius (*Eph.* 11.1) offers a clear example: "These are the last times. Therefore [*loipon*] let us be reverent."

based on the first, but states this in a somewhat informal, nondeductive, nondidactic manner.

b. On *adelphoi*, see trans. note c on 1:4. "Dear," not in the Greek text here, is my effort to render the intimate family tone of the address, which Paul intends to balance the commanding tone of the final clause.

c. *Parakaloumen.* On the overtones of the *parakaleō* word group, see on 2:3. In settings such as the present context, the term also functions as a diplomatic, courteous way of making a firm request. Not only can it be used by subjects asking for favors from a ruler; rulers also may use it in addressing their subjects: it is really a royal command, but in the form of a polite request[2]—as when the dean says, "I'm asking you to chair this committee." Paul here uses the term with the connotations of both the eschatological plan of God as the framework of the encouraging appeal and, with warmhearted softness, his apostolic authority.

d. The noun "tradition" is not explicit in this text, but the verb *paralabete* is a semi-technical term for handing on tradition, as in 1 Cor 11:23; 15:3. Thus the NEB appropriately translates "passed on to you the tradition." Paul refers to the firm body of tradition in which they had been instructed during the founding visit (cf. intro, "Church-Founding Visit" and "New Congregation"). This is the horizontal dimension, which is not an alternative to the vertical dimension referred to in the next verse.[3]

e. *Peripatein*, lit., "walk (around)," but used figuratively for the way one lives. Especially in Judaism, one's "walk" was one's "way of life." The Hebrew verb *hlk* and noun *hlkh*, the halakah, expressed the Jewish "ethic," the Jewish "way of life." This walk was based on the torah, the teaching, often translated as "law," which represented the revealed will of God. It was not a matter of general principles, but of concrete commands and practices. Paul's usage carries this substantial meaning of Jewish tradition, which would have been new to the Thessalonians.

f. *Parangelia* is sometimes translated "instructions," but if so, it represents authoritative instruction (again, like the torah), what must be done, not how something is to be done if one should choose to do it. This is the only occurrence in the undisputed Pauline Letters. The other four New Testament occurrences all represent commanding authority (Acts 5:28; 16:24; 1 Tim 1:5, 18).

[1] With more than a suggestion, less than a command (see trans. note c), Paul eases into his appeal to the new converts to (continue to) live their lives in a way appropriate to their new faith. He first makes his appeal from common ground: both he and the Thessalonians now live in the new reality "in Christ," "in the Lord" (see on 1:1). Friendship letters addressed to peers can also contain paraenesis that does not admonish or profess to contain anything new, only to remind the readers of what they already know, expressed gently with the *parakaleō* formula.[4]

---

2. Bjerkelund.
3. On "the Lord" as present and effective in "the tradition," see Cullmann.
4. See Malherbe 1987, 70.

It would have been a stunningly new idea to most, if not all, of the new converts in Thessalonica that there is an essential connection between religion and ethics. They had been religious before they ever encountered Paul and the new faith he proclaimed. And they had been ethical—they had reflected on, and practiced, what the good life was and how it was to be implemented. Jews and Christians were by no means the only people in the Hellenistic world who took seriously the ethical responsibility involved in living an authentic human life. But there had been no essential connection between religion and ethics. If some few in the congregation had been previously associated with the synagogue, they knew the connection within the Jewish Scriptures and Judaism between the will of the one God, revealed in Scripture and tradition, and the ethical responsibilities of those who worshiped this God. Before their conversion, the new Gentile believers in Thessalonica—all or virtually all the congregation—had heard various ethical teachers speak of "pleasing God/the gods," but this was a far cry from how the Christian missionaries had used this phrase. Stoic teachers, for instance, used such language to mean living in harmony with universal reason immanent in the natural world, but had no concept of a personal God who had a purpose for the world and individual human lives. Household codes in the tradition of Aristotle called for a structured family life. Greek drama (especially Euripides and Menander) kept moral issues (honor, duty, responsibility to community standards) before the people. For some, the "will of God/the gods" would mean attending to proper sacrifices and rituals unrelated to personal or social ethics. The gods themselves were often immoral, judging by decent human standards. Ethics would have been understood by most of Paul's readers in terms of the ethos of their own group: "ethic" is derived from *ethos, custom,* conventional standards of the community, commonsense awareness of "what is done." Some would have agreed with Aristotle that ethics is the practical knowledge of how to live well for the sake of one's group, discerned by reason rather than passion. Others would think in terms of honor and loyalty to one's city-state or ethnic group as the content of ethics. For virtually all Paul's readers in Thessalonica, the ethical seriousness of their new faith was a challenge both to them and to Paul their teacher.

As an apostle, Paul gives instructions on how those "in Christ" are to live their lives. In this sense, he has an ethic, but Paul has no ethic in the sense of an ethical system that provides the rationale and content for living a morally good life.[5] Paul's ethic is conceived as the way of life appropriate to people who live as members of God's people in the narrative world between God's raising Jesus from the dead and the Parousia. Both the content and motive of the "Christian way of life" are set forth not systematically, with individual precepts derived

5. See Furnish 2009b; Hays 1996, 60–72; Pregeant 216–62; Wright 2013, 1095–1128, 1371–83; Schnelle 1990.

from a central set of general principles, but as a loose collection of concrete traditions directed to particular situations. The basis and framework for this way of life is likewise not developed systematically, but incidentally (yet not casually). Here, *pleasing God*, doing the *will of God*, is the basis and substance of the new life to which the Thessalonians are called (4:1, 3; 5:18; cf. 2:4, 15).

[2] The new converts have received both the content and rationale for this new ethic from Paul and his coworkers during the founding visit. When Paul was with them, he gave instructions about their having-been-elected-and-called, thus incorporated into the people of God. This means he also gave instructions about how they should live. The letter does not rehearse the content of these instructions. Some of this would be radically new, and much of it would overlap what they had always considered to be common human decency; all of it would receive new depth and seriousness in the light of their new faith.

The instructions were not suggestions or advice, but commands given "through the Lord Jesus." Did they also include sayings of Jesus from his pre-Easter ministry and/or stories about him?

Excursus 2: Paul and the Sayings of Jesus

A commentary is not the place for a full discussion of this important issue,[6] but the following summary points may be made regarding the undisputed Letters of Paul:

1. There are no stories about the pre-Easter Jesus (the only exception is the eucharistic tradition in 1 Cor 11:23–25, a special case). There are no scenes in which Jesus of Nazareth is held up as an example for Christian conduct.

2. There are no explicit quotations from Jesus' teaching. The only possible exceptions are 1 Cor 7:10; 9:14; and 1 Thess 4:13–15. The citation in 1 Thess 4 has no parallel to the teaching of Jesus in the Gospels, and it is cited not as a traditional saying of the pre-Easter Jesus, but as a "word of the Lord," as an oracle of the risen Jesus, speaking through a Christian prophet (see comments below). The two cited references in 1 Corinthians have some similarity to Jesus' teaching in the Synoptic Gospels (7:10 = Mark 10:11 par.; 9:14 = Luke 10:7 par.), but in neither case is there verbal identity. In each case, Paul cites the sayings as "command of the Lord," not as traditional sayings of Jesus.[7] Even if (elements of) each saying originated in the teaching of the historical

6. The literature on the subject is extensive. For the view that Paul cites (what he believed to be) sayings of the historical Jesus in 1 Thessalonians, see representatively Kim (2002), who argues that Paul had instructed the new converts in Jesus' eschatological sayings, and his extensive article on the whole issue (Kim 1993). Allison (28) argues Paul knew collections of Jesus' sayings that are reflected in his letters. However, Tuckett examines all the alleged parallels and finds only 5:2 as an instance where Paul "perhaps" alludes to a saying of Jesus.

7. See also such items as Paul's use of the Aramaic word *abba* as a distinctively Christian address to God, assumed and encouraged by Paul even in the Gentile churches (Gal 4:6; Rom 8:15; cf. Mark 14:36). Although this form of prayer very likely originated with the historical Jesus, Paul does not base this practice on a saying of Jesus, the Lord's Prayer, or the practice of the historical Jesus, but on the presence of the Holy Spirit in the life of the church.

Jesus, Paul cites them as command of the risen and present Lord. In 1 Cor 14:37, without alluding to any saying of Jesus, pre- or post-Easter, Paul insists that his own apostolic letter be acknowledged as "a command of the Lord."

3. There are in fact some similarities between some sayings of Christian paraenesis and some sayings of Jesus in the Synoptics, such as "Bless those who persecute you; bless and do not curse them" (Rom 12:14 NRSV; cf. Matt 5:44). The wording is not identical, there is no indication that Paul is quoting Jesus, and the similarities that exist may sometimes be better explained as later Christian paraenetic tradition affecting the developing Gospel tradition rather than as echoes of Jesus' teaching being incorporated in the letters. In any case, there are vast differences in the estimates of how many "echoes" and "allusions" to Jesus' teaching might be found in Paul's Letters.[8]

4. It is a misguided effort to defend the view that Paul knew, valued, used, and taught the traditions about the pre-Easter Jesus, but does not refer to them in his letters because Paul "presupposes" his readers know the Jesus tradition he had taught them, and does not cite it because such a reference is "not appropriate to the epistolary genre." Such claims rest on a priori judgments about what Paul "must have" done rather than on data in the Letters themselves, by interpreters who find it difficult to imagine a reading of the Pauline Letters and the life of the churches to which they are addressed that does not *presuppose* a knowledge of the kind of narratives and teaching found in four Gospels. But this is because modern readers all know the bipartite canon of Gospels and Epistles, tend to think of the New Testament in the canonical order in which Matthew to John are read as preliminary to the Letters, forgetting that when Paul wrote there were no Gospels, and that it was not until twenty years after 1 Thessalonians that Mark first brought together the kerygma of the earliest churches represented by Paul and the traditions that flowed into the Gospels.[9]

5. Paul was converted after the death and resurrection of Jesus, and in contrast to Peter, James, and others, he did not see or hear Jesus personally. During his first visit to Jerusalem after his conversion (Gal 1:15–18), Paul had ample opportunity to learn the "life and teaching of Jesus" from one of the original disciples and from Jesus' own brother. Yet the issue is not whether or not he had the *opportunity* to be instructed in Jesus' life and teachings by those who had heard him. Paul certainly had this opportunity, though he did not avail himself of it until he had been a Christian missionary for three years. Paul's point is that such knowledge was not necessary to his apostleship (Gal 1:15–18). And while Paul did belatedly spend fifteen days with the eyewitness Peter and Jesus' own brother James, there is no indication that he spent his time learning what Jesus had said on the hillsides and in the synagogues of Galilee. Furthermore,

---

8. The most generous estimate known to me is that of Resch, who found 925 such allusions in the nine Pauline Letters he considered authentic (the undisputed seven plus Colossians and 2 Thessalonians), an average of 7 or 8 "echoes" of Jesus' teaching on each of the 123 pages of Greek text. Hardly any scholar has taken such imaginative enthusiasm seriously. Most would be more inclined to support the detailed argument of Neirynck, who discusses the explicit "commands of the Lord" in 1 Cor 7:10–11 and 9:14, then concludes: "Elsewhere in the Pauline letters there is no certain trace of a conscious use of the sayings of Jesus" (566).

9. For an elaboration of this argument, with further bibliography, see Boring 2012, 5–7, 465–66, 507.

Paul then spent several years in the context of the Antioch church, where he served as an authorized teacher and missionary during the time that the tradition of Jesus' words and deeds was being cultivated among some churches in the Antioch area (Gal 1:21–2:1; 2:11; Acts 9:28–30; 11:19–30; 12:24–25).

6. Paul had the opportunity. Did he have the motive? Paul's understanding of the faith did not require knowledge of sayings from the earthly Jesus and stories about his life. Paul had begun his missionary work, and continued it for three years, without consultation with the eyewitnesses of Jesus' ministry. He felt no need to receive, at this late date, a crash course in the "life and teaching of Jesus" to validate him as a Christian missionary. He preached the same gospel after meeting with Peter as before, a gospel oriented to God's act in Christ, focused on Jesus' death and resurrection. In Paul's view his message did not need to be supplemented by stories and sayings from the life of Jesus.

7. The main point, often missed by interpreters too eager to get the life and teachings of Jesus into the Pauline Letters and churches, is that Paul has a different paradigm for understanding the gospel and the Christian faith than that represented by the (later!) Gospels and the traditions they include and interpret. Paul's faith and theology is profoundly oriented to Jesus Christ, but it is *theo*centric, focused on God's act in the Christ event, not on what the earthly Jesus said and did. Even where we, who have the teaching of Jesus in the Gospels, might expect Paul to make good use of supportive sayings of Jesus, he does not do so. The modern reader, with New Testament in hand, thinks readily, for example, of the absence of Mark 12:17 in Rom 13:1–10, and notices that the new Thessalonian converts are specifically "Godtaught," not instructed in the "teachings of Jesus" (1 Thess 4:9; cf. comments there). It was essential to Paul's theology that Jesus had actually lived, that as the "second Adam" he had embodied the meaning of true humanity (Rom 5:12–21), that he had represented the reality of authentic human existence by being truly obedient to God (Phil 2:5–11), that he had died a truly human death, and that God had raised him from the dead and made him Lord of all. When Paul thought about Christ as example of genuine humility, he thought of the cosmic Christ who laid aside his heavenly glory and became human for our sakes, not of scenes from the life of the earthly Jesus who laid aside his garments and washed the disciples' feet (Phil 2:5–11 rather than John 13:1–17). When he thinks of Jesus' renunciation of wealth for the sake of others, he does not think of the poverty of the earthly Jesus or his teaching about the use of money, but of the heavenly Lord who "though he was rich, yet for your sakes he became poor, so that by his poverty you might become rich" (2 Cor 8:9 NRSV). In the Letter to the Romans—Paul's longest and most systematic letter, which also turned out to be his last, summing up his gospel to a church he had never visited and where he could not presuppose any hypothetical instruction from himself about the "teachings of Jesus"—there is no reference whatever to Jesus' sayings or to stories about him. When he cites Christ as example, he places words from the Scripture in his mouth, not sayings of the pre-Easter Jesus (Rom 15:3 = Ps 69:9). Paul never calls Jesus "Teacher," never refers to the "way of Jesus," but he reminds his churches of "my ways in Christ Jesus, as I teach them everywhere in every church" (1 Cor 4:17 NRSV). In 1 Thessalonians, he never refers to the teaching of Jesus, but he reminds the new converts of the "commands we gave you through the Lord Jesus" (4:2).

8. The later church rightly included the Gospel tradition with the Epistle tradition in the formation of the New Testament canon, without which the Christian community

would be immeasurably the poorer, and placed the Gospels before the Epistles as having priority in the unfolding story of the saving history to which the canon bears authentic witness. This is a different matter, however, from understanding the Pauline Letters in their own historical context.

4:3–12 Holiness and Love in Practice

In vv. 3–8 Paul speaks of holiness as doing God's will, with sexual morality as the focal instance. Verses 9–12 show that love expresses itself in care for one's neighbor, within and beyond the Christian community.

4:3–8 Life according to the Will of God

In terms of syntax, there is more than one legitimate way to regard the words of vv. 3–8 as separate sentences (see on 1:2–10). For the sake of readability, editors of the Greek New Testament and English translations tend to divide them into shorter units. Diagramming the Greek text in terms of both syntax and sense units suggests that 4:3–6a is one sentence focusing on the believers' responsibility to do the will of God. A new sentence begins at v. 6b,[10] grounding human responsibility in God's act: God's call, God's gift of the Holy Spirit, and the Last Judgment, in which believers will stand before God.

The main point and thrust of the compact section 4:3–8 is crystal clear. Numerous details of how this is expressed and illustrated are not at all clear and continue to be researched and disputed. A commentary can discuss the pros and cons of each exegetical decision; the translation must come down on one side or the other of each disputed point. The following translation is necessarily tentative and, with the accompanying notes, provides a particularly vivid illustration of the interrelationship between interpretation and translation. No interpreter can first make a clear translation, and then, on the basis of this, decide exegetical points; every translation is necessarily already an interpretation, the result of exegesis, not its basis.

4:3 For this is the will of God, your sanctification:[a] that you keep yourself from sexual immorality,[b] 4 by which I mean that each of you know (how) to keep your body[c] under control[c] in holiness and honor— 5 not in passionate lust like the Gentiles who do not know God— 6 so that no one wrong or exploit a brother or sister[d] in this matter.

10. According to my own diagram. Cf. Ramey 26–27, who construes all of 4:3–8 as one complex sentence. Baxter, LoVullo, and Koivisto construe 4:3–6, 4:7, and 4:8 as three separate sentences. Syntactically it could go either way, but in terms of content vv. 3–6a deal with human responsibility, vv. 6b–8 with God the sovereign judge.

For the Lord is judge who establishes justice in all these things, just as we have already informed and solemnly warned you. 7 For God has not called us to impurity, but to holiness. 8 Therefore, whoever rejects this is not rejecting a human being, but God, the one who gives the Holy Spirit to you.

a. *Hagiosmos* can be translated "holiness," as in the next verse, but is here rendered "sanctification" as a semitechnical term that would have needed explaining to the original readers, as it still does to their modern counterparts. "Sanctification" also preserves the dynamic of active and passive: believers are *made* holy (by God) and called to *be* holy by their own responsible decisions and actions.

b. *Porneia* is a generic term for various kinds of unsanctioned sexual activity, the specifics being culturally defined. In the LXX it is used both for unlawful sexual practices and figuratively of unfaithfulness to God, thus becoming practically a synonym for idolatry and the unethical life assumed always to be associated with the worship of false gods (Wis 14:12; illustrated in the stories of Jezebel [1 Kgs 16–18; cf. Rev 2:20] and Balaam [Num 22–24; cf. 31:8; Rev 2:14]).

c. *Skeuos* (lit., "vessel"). The meanings of both *skeuos* (vessel) and *ktaomai* (obtain, possess, master) in this context are disputed. The variety of possible combinations of these two key terms has generated a large number of specific interpretations. Ancient interpreters were already divided between "take a wife" (so Theodore of Mopsuestia, Augustine) and "control your body" (so Tertullian, Chrysostom). The current options are represented by the RSV and NRSV: "that each one of you know how to take a wife for himself in holiness and honor" (RSV; so also NABRE, TEV, CEV); "that each one of you know how to control your own body in holiness and honor" (NRSV; so also REB, NJB, TNIV, NIV11, ESV, CEB). The ambiguity of the Greek is followed by KJV, ASV, NAS95. For the translation "keep your body under control," see the detailed comments below.

d. On the translation of *adelphos* as "brother or sister," see trans. note c on 1:4. In the present context, it is important to decide whether or not Paul is addressing only the males in the church.

[3–4] The *will of God* is the content, norm, and basis of Paul's ethics, and of biblical ethics generally (e.g., Mark 3:35; Rom 12:2; Eph 6:6; Col 1:9).[11] The phrase corresponds to the biblical and synagogue usage of *'āśâ rāṣôn 'ĕlōhîm*, to do the will of God, often identified with the revelation of God's will in the Torah (cf., e.g., Pss 40:8; 103:21; 143:10; Ezra 10:11). For Paul, "the good" is self-evidently God's will. He can even use "the will" (*to thelēma*, Rom 2:18) as a shorthand term for the moral life, living as one should. Paul's readers in Thessalonica already knew about ethics, moral seriousness, and doing "the

11. In such contexts as the present one, the *will of God* does not refer to God's will as exercised in the natural world (e.g., Sir 42:15; 43:16), to God's intention in carrying out the divine purpose (e.g., Isa 53:10; Acts 21:14; Eph 1:1; Heb 10:10), or to the issues involved in predestination and free will (e.g., Tob 12:18; Rom 9:19), though it is not unrelated to them.

good." They also were familiar with "the will of the gods" before they had heard the Christian message. But that "the good" is identified with "the will of [the one true] God" (cf. 1:9–10) was a new idea to them—radically new (see above on 4:1). The basis of ethics is not an abstract ideal of "the good," or that which is reasonable, or that which corresponds to the harmony of the universe, or some principle such as the greatest good for the greatest number; instead, it is the personal will of the one God who is the Creator and Ruler of the universe. Paul's mental universe could have no place for such questions as "Does God will it because it is good, or is it good because God wills it?" But if Paul could have posed such a question, he would unhesitatingly have chosen the latter: it is good because God wills it. There is no ideal standard of the good to which God can or should measure up. Packaged with the monotheistic faith comes the view that there is no higher court beyond God to which one can appeal or by which God can be measured. God wills the good; it is good because God wills it.

The will of God is identified as *your sanctification,* which is then explicated with a series of five infinitives:

> *to keep* yourself from sexual immorality,
>> *to know* (how)
>>> *to keep* your body under control, so as not
>>>> *to wrong* or
>>>>> *to exploit* a brother or sister.

Sanctification (*hagiosmos,* holiness) may sound quaintly sanctimonious to modern secularized readers, if they recognize the term at all. It was a new word to the Thessalonians as well. They were already acquainted with a pagan understanding of the "holy" (*hagios*) in the sense of the separation between the world of the gods and the human world, and the cultic concept of holiness as the qualities one needs in order to approach the gods. But holiness in the comprehensive sense of the way one orders one's life had been introduced by Paul and his missionary colleagues. Thus in v. 7 holiness is defined over against its opposite, *akatharsia* (uncleanness). "Sanctification excludes impurity,"[12] both terms understood in the ethical sense. This corresponds to Paul's later usage in Rom 6:19, where both holiness and its opposite are quite general terms referring to the whole of the believer's life, not just sexual or cultic aspects (cf. Rom 12:1). So also in 1 Cor 7:14, Paul can use "holiness" and "uncleanness" to represent the two realms in which life can be lived, even for small children in a family in which only one parent is a believer. Paul does not develop the idea in 1 Thessalonians, but he may have already thought through the idea that the church is the temple of the Lord, in which God dwells as the Holy Spirit (1 Cor

12. Masson 46.

3:16–17). The Qumran texts show that the development of such ideas did not need to await the destruction of the Jerusalem temple in 70 C.E. As the temple is holy, so Christians, as God's temple, must be holy.[13]

For Paul, holiness does not refer to a human achievement of being especially good, nor does it refer to a second level of Christian faith after initial conversion. Sanctification is God's act, is inherent in God's call. It is not as though the Thessalonians are just now being told that, in addition to being converted and having the sure hope of eternal life, they need to move to the next level and start living a holy life. They have already been instructed in this (4:2). The call into the Christian community included the call to holiness, which means being set apart for service to God. Holiness is a matter of separation, of boundaries. The holy God is the God who as the Creator is absolutely distinct from the creation. The holiness to which God calls is to belong to the holy people, the people called to be distinct from the world. "Sanctification consists not in a particular *moral quality* which has been *attained*, but in a particular *relationship* to God which has been *given*."[14] Sanctification thus does not mean physical separation from the world, but it does mean a distinctive life within the world. As the holy people of God, the church knows it is called to live a distinctive lifestyle, no longer oriented to conventional cultural values. It is for the sake of the world that the church is called to manifest its own holiness. If the church loses itself, allows itself to be dissolved back into the world from which it has been called out, it then loses the capacity, even the possibility, of making any difference in the world.[15]

The will of God is sanctification, holiness, which here is focused on the one issue of sexual ethics. However, it is not quite correct to say that Paul then "defines" sanctification as avoiding sexual immorality. Paul is not obsessed with sex, nor does he reduce ethics to this one issue. He does illustrate the meaning of living a holy life according to God's will by focusing on the intimate,

---

13. Cf. Wright 2013, 356–57.

14. Furnish 2007, 155, with added emphasis.

15. The concluding remarks of Holtz (1986, 284) on this section affirm the relevance of the ethic of 1 Thessalonians for the contemporary church. They were written in 1985 in what was then the East German Deutsche Demokratische Republik (DDR), when one could hardly imagine the fall of the iron curtain and the wall that separated East Germany from the West. The church in the DDR existed as small cells of Christians, sometimes painfully distinct from their officially atheist communist context. East German Christians were also distinct from their more numerous and more complacent fellow Christians of the West (including North America). Holtz does not find Paul's instructions to the new little church in Thessalonica to be off-putting and irrelevant because they are concerned with the holiness of the community rather than with changing the social and political structures of the city. Such instructions, heard not as human words but as words of God (2:13), strengthen the church in every age to be what God has called it to be. First of all, this means nourishing its own inner life, without self-centeredness, but as the necessary means of facilitating its participation in God's mission in the world.

fundamentally human aspect of sexuality.[16] The two reasons for this are inter-laced in his instruction: (1) in the Hellenistic world, sexual morality was gener-ally unrelated to religious faith; and (2) in Paul's Bible and Jewish tradition, sexual immorality was directly related to unfaithfulness to God.

All this is quite clear in general: conversion to the one true God means liv-ing a holy life, which means rejection of immorality as defined and illustrated by *porneia,* all types of sexual sins. The details of this instruction, however, are much disputed. The difficulty involves the translation of two key words:

1. The literal meaning of *skeuos,* usually translated "vessel," is any object used for some purpose or other. In the plural, it thus refers to one's "things," one's property (e.g., Mark 3:27; Luke 17:31; in Acts 27:17, part of the ship's gear; in Rom 9:21, of the vessels made by a potter). In a cultic context, *skeuos* can be used for the vessels and equipment used in temple service, as in Heb 9:21. Only rarely does the Hebrew Bible use "vessel" (*kly*) as a metaphor for the human body (1 Sam 21:6 LXX [5 ET], with sexual overtones; Jer 18:4; 19:11). The Jeremiah texts influenced Paul (Rom 9:21–23) and were understood to refer to individual persons. Likewise, the word is common in the LXX for both ordinary and sacred objects, but is rarely used metaphorically.[17] In one late rabbinic text, "vessel" is used as a metaphor for a woman's body, and "to use one's vessel" is a euphemism for sexual intercourse. Some have seen this as of "decisive importance" for Paul's usage here.[18] This metaphorical use of *skeuos* in classical and Hellenistic Greek is extremely rare, and limited to the demean-ing sense of "tool, instrument" for a slave, a nonperson.[19] In 1 Thess 4:4, Paul's metaphorical use thus cannot be explained as his adopting a common metaphor from either his Bible or the surrounding culture. Elsewhere Paul can use the word to refer to a person as an instrument to fulfill God's purpose, and thus for one's body (2 Cor 4:7; Rom 9:21–23; cf. Acts 9:15; 2 Tim 2:20–21; 1 Pet 3:7). Jeremiah was a powerful influence on Paul (see on 5:27); the Jeremiah texts

16. Cf. Gaventa 1998, 51.

17. Of 316 occurrences, only two use the term metaphorically: Jer 22:28, "Is this man Coniah a despised broken pot, a vessel no one wants?" (NRSV); 28:34 LXX (51:34 ET), "King Nebuchadnez-zar of Babylon has devoured me; he has apportioned me; he has seized me, a slim vessel" (NETS). Three further uses, with "as" or "like," are not metaphors, but analogies (Ps 30:13 [31:12 ET]; *Pss. Sol.* 17.23; Hos 8:8).

18. So the influential article of Christian Maurer, "*skeuos,*" *TDNT* 7:358–67. For a strong and nuanced argument that *skeuos* means "wife," see Burke 185–202. It may be that a wife is called a "vessel" in 4Q416 2.2.21: "Do not despise your life nor belittle the body [*kly,* lit. 'vessel'] of your statute" (i.e., the body that belongs to you by law, your wife). Even so, in our view the evidence that Paul adopted a common metaphor is slim indeed. Unless he had specifically instructed the Thessalonians in this rare usage, which is difficult to imagine, they would not have understood *skeuos* to mean "wife."

19. So LSJM 1607. Maurer finds one instance where *skeuos* clearly is a metaphor for the penis (Antistios, 1st cent. C.E.); cf. Aelian, *De natura animalium* 17.11 (*TDNT* 7:359; BDAG 928).

are to be taken seriously here. Unless 1 Thess 4:4 is the sole exception, Paul never uses *skeuos* to mean "woman" or "wife." In similar contexts, when Paul means woman or wife, he clearly says so (*gynē* 43× in the undisputed letters: Rom 7:2; 1 Cor 5:1; 7:1–4, 10–16, 29, 33–34, 39; 9:5; 11:1–3, 5–15; Gal 4:4). In the present context, it thus seems the more likely meaning is "person, self," especially in its bodily aspect, perhaps with sexual overtones.[20]

2. The basic meaning of *ktaomai* is "get, acquire" (so, e.g., Luke 18:12; Acts 1:18). In a later letter, when Paul is charging believers to avoid *porneia*, he does recommend that each man have his own wife, and each woman her own husband, but there he uses neither *ktaomai* nor *skeuos* (1 Cor 7:2). *Ktaomai* is found only here in Paul, so his usage elsewhere cannot be documented, but in the perfect tense it comes to mean "gain possession of, get control over." It is thus possible that Paul is using the word in that sense here, but it is difficult to find clear instances of this meaning. Even the standard Greek lexicon, which lists "gain control of" among the meanings of *ktaomai*, is only able to argue on the basis that if *skeuos* here means "body" or "penis," then "in such cases [*ktaomai*] must mean something like 'gain control of'"—which sounds like special pleading or begging the question (BDAG 572, 927). In support of rendering *ktaomai* as "(get and) maintain control of," however, is the close connection between "buy, acquire" and "have control of," especially in the Hebrew Bible, where *bāʿal* is used for getting, owning, and mastering. In that culture, the husband is assumed to be master, the controlling partner, so that *bāʿal* can mean "possess" in the sense of "maintain control of." Though it is something of a stretch, and not otherwise documented, Paul could have used *ktaomai* in this related meaning. The meaning and translation cannot be decisively settled, but the most probable meaning seems to be "keep your body under control," as translated above.[21]

When Paul introduces sexual morality as the focal instance of ethics, two worlds collide. It is not merely, or primarily, the specific "rules" that are at stake, but their presuppositions, the assumptions on which they are based, the symbolic universe in which they participate. The *assumptions of the Hellenistic world regarding sexual ethics*, shared by the Thessalonians before their conversion, embraced a broad spectrum. These included not only a double standard for men and women, and the typical lack of connection between religion and ethics, but also considerable variety as to what constituted sexual morality in particular. Some were deeply influenced by various forms of the prevailing mind-body dualism that disdained the flesh and its desires as such: to engage

20. Elgvin has now presented a strong case for this interpretation, with support from the Qumran text 1Q26 that this was contemporary Jewish usage.

21. So NRSV, REB, NJB, NIV11, TNIV, ESV, CEB. Cf. Donfried 1993a, 50: "gaining control over the body with regard to sexual matters."

in sexual pleasure was to surrender to one's lower nature. Within this same worldview, others took the opposite option: what the body does has no influence on the soul, so bodily actions are indifferent to the real self, and the body can do as it wills. Many would have shared the assumptions of the prevalent fertility cults, in which sex, the driving force that generates new life, was unrelated to personal or social ethics (see above on the Cabiri and Dionysiac cults).

Others (relatively few) were attracted to the philosophical views of such Stoics as Musonius Rufus, who argued for strict monogamy, that even within marriage sex was only for procreation, not for "lust" (Discourse 12, "On Sexual Indulgence"). Life was to be ordered by innate reason. The wife was to be "honored," not "used" to satisfy "unreasonable" appetites. That casual sex was widely accepted as the norm is indicated by Augustus's laws encouraging marriage and family, which show that even for socially concerned pagans, it was considered a virtue to avoid promiscuity and establish stable homes (*Julian Marriage Laws* 120–123). Many, probably the majority, would have been represented by the citation attributed to Demosthenes, defended by Cicero: "We have courtesans [*hetairai*] for pleasure, handmaidens for the day-to-day care of the body [a euphemism for sex], wives to bear legitimate children and to be a trusted guardian of things in the house."[22] *Porneia* hardly raised an eyebrow; there was no ethos of public or peer pressure to discourage casual sex for men. The easy availability of prostitutes and slaves tended to encourage it. Those who overdid it or seemed to be addicted to sex might be counseled or made fun of, as were those who drank too much or became gluttonous.[23]

Paul's instruction represents a different world. He does not here spell out the ethical directives he has already given the Thessalonians, but reminds them of the radically different understanding they received when they were converted. This understanding represents the biblical and Jewish tradition, which continued to be the assumed framework of his ethics. Right and wrong is not a matter of community standards, reason versus passion, or the like, but the revealed will of God. Holiness does not exclude the sexual dimension of human relationships, but determines their character. Sex is the good gift of God, but it is intended as God's blessing within marriage. All sexual activity outside marriage is prohibited. Adultery is a violation against both one's marriage partner and God. As in 1 Cor 7:1–4, which also deals with *porneia,* Paul's instruction is directed to men and women alike (cf. also 1 Cor 6:12–20). Marriage is considered the norm for Christians, though those with a special calling could choose not to marry.[24] So understood, *skeuos* cannot mean wife-as-"vessel," nor can

22. Pseudo-Demosthenes 59.122, cited from Boring, Berger, and Colpe §809.
23. See, e.g., Langlands and the bibliography she provides.
24. In 1 Cor 7, Paul is much more explicit while dealing with specific issues of sexual ethics in the Corinthian congregation. There he is also more egalitarian, emphasizing the mutual right and

the word be a euphemism for penis, but must mean "body," the self understood in its sexual aspect. Already Calvin argued that "as he addresses husbands and wives indiscriminately, there can be no doubt that he employs the term vessel to mean body."[25] Paul has instructed the new converts in Thessalonica as converts to Judaism would have been instructed in the Hellenistic synagogue in which Paul had grown up and with which he was still associated. Paul's biblical and Jewish mind-set, steeped in the imagery of God-as-husband and Israel-as-wife, moves easily from faithfulness to one's marriage partner to faithfulness to the one God, and vice versa.

With these assumptions, it should not surprise us that Paul speaks of ethics as such in terms of holiness versus *porneia*. Sexual immorality is not merely one sin among others, but the inevitable by-product of idolatry. Paul's biblical and Jewish tradition assumed a fundamental connection between idolatry and sexual sins (cf. Rom 1:18–32). Idolatry was "the mother of all evil" (*T. Sim.* 5.3), and "the devising of idols was the beginning of fornication, and the invention of them the corruption of life" (Wis 14:12, 27). In Israel's Bible and tradition, participation in pagan cults almost always has the overtones of sexual immorality, not only because sex rituals were sometimes involved in fertility cults, but also because worship of other gods was *unfaithfulness* to God-the-husband. To turn from Yahweh to other gods was adultery, the unfaithfulness of Israel the wife to her one legitimate husband, and it inevitably involved sexual sins. Holiness is fundamentally separation, distinctiveness. God is the model. Holiness not only means the "infinite qualitative distinction" between the one creator God and all else, but also includes an essentially moral element.[26] It is not merely that God the Lawgiver gives laws that must be kept; holiness is also a matter of God's being, God's character. The people of God must be holy as God is holy (see above on 3:13; cf. the Holiness Code of Lev 17–26; Rom 12:1; 1 Cor 3:17; 7:14, 34; 1 Pet 1:15).

Responsible sexual ethics is inherent in sanctification (a new concept to the Thessalonians), but is also a matter of honor. In the Hellenistic world, honor and shame played a key role, analogous to the role money plays in modern capitalist society. The new converts were already committed to the crucial role of honor in an authentic ethical life: that this included the rejection of *porneia* called them to radically rethink the meaning of morality.

---

responsibilities of husband and wife, and, though considering marriage the typical pattern, also makes a place for the unmarried and divorced (1 Cor 7:7–9, 25–40). Such specific issues seem not to be involved in the situation in Thessalonica, so that he uses *porneia* more generally to represent a life not conformed to the will of God.

25. Calvin 1960a, ad loc.

26. The phrase is from Søren Kierkegaard, adopted by Barth (1933, 10 and passim) and made a cornerstone of his theology.

[5] Based on the view that idolatry inevitably leads to base sexual sins, the biblical and Jewish tradition in which Paul had been reared sometimes accepted and uncritically assumed stereotypes of Gentile behavior (see, e.g., *Jub.* 25.1; Wis 14:22–26; Rom 1:18–32). We know that there were tender, loving, and responsible relationships within Gentile families, and that such stereotypes should not continue to be assumed and circulated. The prior appeal to honor, and the concern with how those outside the church view Christian morality (4:12; cf. Phil 2:15; 1 Cor 5:1), both presuppose elements of a common moral standard. Nonetheless, the substance of Paul's instruction remains theologically grounded: one's sex ethic is not just one's own business, for it is a matter of one's relation to God, and it affects other people. It thus calls for a break with specific customs and standards set by the culture, for what is socially acceptable is no longer the norm for those who confess Jesus as Lord.

[6–7] There is no change of subject with v. 6. Though *pragma* can refer to an undertaking or occupation, when used of commercial dealings it is generally in the plural, *pragmata*. Context is decisive. "The matter" (*pragma*) at hand continues to be sexual ethics, the rejection of *porneia*. The contrast between impurity and holiness continues to be illustrated and focused on sexual behavior appropriate to those who confess Jesus as Lord. Violating Christian ethical norms wrongs or exploits other people; the brother or sister is both one's marriage partner and the brother and sister in the new family of God, to which the new converts now belong, but Paul's concern is not limited to intrachurch affairs.[27] Here the *adelphos* is identical with the neighbor, the fellow human being, as in Matt 5:23; Rom 9:3; 1 John 2:9. The heavenly judge who is soon to appear will right such wrongs. This is the meaning of *ekdikos kyrios*, sometimes translated "the Lord is an avenger" in all such matters. The only other New Testament instance of *ekdikos* is in Rom 13:4, used of the secular judge (cf. also the use of the cognate verb in Rom 12:19 and its context). The phrase thus does not picture a vengeful God, nursing grudges, who will get even at the Last Judgment. Rather, God is the just judge who takes the wronged person's side, vindicating the one who has been wronged. In Paul's view, irresponsible sexual activity hurts other people and is a sin against God. The Judge will right such wrongs (see further on 2 Thess 1:8).

Again we see that, while Christian and Gentile morality are not altogether different, there is a radically new motivation. Sexual ethics, as a focal instance of ethics as such, is not a matter of enlightened self-interest, is not individualistic, is not flesh versus spirit or reason versus passion, is not a matter of "my real self" versus the fleshly body in which it is encased. The responsible ethical life is not "my own business," but is oriented to God and the new community

27. Yarbrough (73–76) argues that Paul here refers to interfering with the marriage of a fellow member of the church.

to which I belong. Sexual conduct is no light matter to be shrugged off. Paul expresses the seriousness of the matter with a form of *diamartyromai* (solemnly warned), only here in the undisputed Letters of Paul, but the same verb stresses the solemnity of Christian teaching in Luke 16:28; Acts 2:40; 8:25; 10:42; 18:5; 20:21, 23; 23:11; 28:23.

[8] The point is not the source of the authority of the command, as though the meaning were "It is not merely Paul, but God, who gives this command." Paul does not say, as one might expect, "Do this, because I am speaking with the authority of the Holy Spirit, whom God has given *me*." Instead, he speaks of the holy God who gives *you* the Holy Spirit, who calls and empowers you to a holy life. The new converts accepted Paul's authority as God's representative; the focus is on God, not Paul (2:13). Rather, the difficult and crucial point is that sexual misconduct, formerly considered rather trivial by cultural standards, is a rejection of God, a relapse into the idolatry from which they have been delivered (1:9–10). The "living and true God" who has called them is the God who—Paul appeals to their experience—has given them the Holy Spirit. The ethic throughout is theocentric, focused on the character and act of the God in whom they now believe.

Paul concludes this dense section 4:3–8 with the strong reminder that he is not introducing any new instructions: the way of life here described, for which the new converts will be held accountable by the Lord and Judge, who is soon to appear, is the same as Paul has taught them during the founding mission. Paul has told them all this before; the letter does not impose additional requirements on the new converts. But the Thessalonians must continue to be instructed in this new view of what life is about and how it is to be lived.

4:9–12 Life as Care for the Neighbor

To be called into the church gives one a new symbolic universe. In this new world, one's life is no longer curved in upon itself[28] in individualistic self-centeredness and self-assertion, considered to be common sense and socially accepted (even admired!) as simply the way people are. Believers have been called into a new world in which one has been turned outward to the new caring community to which one now belongs, and beyond that to the world for which God cares.

4:9 Now as for love[a] for the brothers and sisters,[b] you[c] have no need for anyone to write to you, for you yourselves are Godtaught[d] to love[a] one another, 10 for you are indeed already putting into practice this love for

---

28. Augustine's apt phrase characterizing sin as *incurvatus in se* is often found in works on Pauline theology, esp. in Luther's commentary on Romans and the works of Karl Barth.

all the brothers and sisters throughout Macedonia. So we can only appeal to[e] you, brothers and sisters, to do so more and more, 11 and to aspire to live unobtrusively, to mind your own business, and to work with your own hands, just as we instructed you, 12 so that you will be thought well of by outsiders, and not be dependent on anyone.[f]

a. Here two different words are translated "love": *philadelphia* and *agapaō*, the verb form of *agapē*. Paul uses them as synonyms.

b. On the inclusive use of *adelphos* (3× in 4:9–10) and Paul's use of family language, see on 1:4; 2:7, 11, 17; 3:11–12. The sibling language contrasts with the "outsiders" of v. 12.

c. The first-person verb *echomen,* "we have [no need]," or *eichomen,* "we had [no need]," is found in a few MSS; yet the second-person *echete* is not only better attested (ℵ* A D[1] and most MSS) but also more appropriate to this letter, in which Paul emphasizes what they already know, not his own role as instructor. The present grammar is awkward (lit., "you have no need to write to you") and was "corrected" by changing "you" to "we" or, in the case of a few MSS, by changing the verb to the passive *graphesthai,* as in 5:1 ("You have no need to have anything written to you").

d. *Theodidaktos* is found nowhere in ancient literature prior to Paul, and only later in dependence on him. He apparently devised it for this occasion. The corresponding English neologism would be *Godtaught*, without the hyphen. An adjective ending in -*tos* is the equivalent of a past participle (e.g., *agapētos* = belove*d*; *eklektos* = elect[*ed*]; esp. *christos* = anointe*d*). With the present tense of *eimi,* the to-be verb, the meaning is like that of the Greek perfect participle, expressing a past act whose results continue into the present (cf., e.g., 1 Cor 10:28, *hierothyton estin,* "This is food that has been sacrificed to an idol"). Thus *theodidaktos* here refers to the present reality as the result of past acts.

e. *Parakaloumen.* See notes and comments on 2:3 for the rich overtones of Paul's use of the *parakaleō* vocabulary.

f. *Mēdenos* may be either masculine or neuter, thus in English either personal or impersonal, "no one" or "nothing." Hence the phrase could be translated "have need of nothing" (so KJV, ASV, REB, NAS95, CEB). Yet in this context Paul's point seems to be doing one's own work so as not to be dependent on others.

[9] *Philadelphia* (brotherly love) is always used outside the New Testament of love for blood brothers (the cognate adjective in 2 Macc 15:14 is the only possible exception). Early Christian teachers and preachers were the first to use it in a metaphorical, but real, sense for the family of believers (on Paul's use of family imagery, see comments on 2:5–8). Such language is in continuity with Jesus' own call to abandon family if it conflicts with service to God (cf. Matt 8:21–22; 10:37–39; Mark 3:31–35 [which relates family imagery to the language of *doing the will of God*, as here]; Luke 14:25–27). Such ideas were not mere theory to the new converts in Thessalonica; their turning away from conventional cultural religion has in some cases meant turning away from their own family, but also being included in a new family. In the ancient Mediterranean

world, family ties were often stronger than in modern society; it was the context for one's whole existence and the center of loyalty.

Why bring up specifically *philadelphia* at this point in the letter? Some interpreters have thought that the transitional phrase *peri de*, translated "now as for" above, indicates that Paul is responding to questions in a letter from the Thessalonians. This phrase is in fact used repeatedly in 1 Corinthians to signal his response to their written questions (1 Cor 7:1, 25; 8:1; 12:1; 16:1, 12), but there Paul makes it clear he is responding to their letter (7:1). There is no evidence in 1 Thessalonians of a letter from Thessalonica to Paul. Elsewhere in the New Testament the phrase is used simply to introduce a new subject or turn in the argument (Matt 22:31; 24:36; Acts 21:25). It is found fourteen times in the LXX, including five times in the Wisdom of Solomon, a book particularly influential on Paul. Thus there is no reason to imagine that Paul now turns to a supposed letter from the Thessalonians, to respond to a specific question about *philadelphia*. Paul is not addressing any particular problem or conflict; it is the nature of Christian love to extend beyond the local congregation to other members of the Christian community, and beyond that to the world, and Paul does not need an inquiry from them in order to make this clear.

Here Paul uses two different words for "love": (1) the abstract noun *philadelphia*, which combines *philia* and *adelphos/adelphē* (brother/sister), normally used only for the love of members of the same biological family for each other; and (2) *agapaō*, the verb form of *agapē*. Like the New Testament in general, Paul uses the two different Greek words as synonyms; *philadelphia* is functionally equivalent to *agapē*. Both terms refer to the loving care of brothers and sisters for each other within the new Christian family (see on 3:12 above). A pop exegetical tradition has developed to the effect that the Greek words *agapē* (noun) and *agapaō* (verb) represent a special kind of unconditional love distinct from the other Greek words for love, *eros* and *philia*. In reality, however, *agapē* and its cognates were used in the ancient world, as in modern Greek, for all kinds of love, selfish and unselfish, sensuous and unsensuous, just as is the case with the English word "love" (cf. *agapē* in, e.g., Jer 2:25; Eccl 5:9 LXX [10 ET]; Luke 6:32; 2 Tim 4:10; 2 Pet 2:15). The special quality of Christian love is not a matter of Greek vocabulary but of christological content: the caring, self-giving, unconditional love revealed in the life and death of Jesus. Love so understood is not a feeling, but an action. Here Paul is concerned with more than warm feelings; in the stressful situation the Thessalonians face, he has in mind practical help for each other, including financial support.

It would be a shabby critique of Paul to point out that he claims it is not necessary to write, but writes anyway—and extensively. This is an example of civil discourse, an instance of paraleipsis, the familiar device of diplomatic communication by which one mentions something in the process of claiming not to mention it (cf. 5:1; 2 Cor 9:1; esp. Phlm 19). It is more than that, however.

Throughout 1 Thessalonians, Paul has emphasized that he is not writing a didactic letter, that they already know (*oidate*, [as] you know, 9× in 1 Thessalonians), that he is only reminding them of what he taught them during the founding visit (4:11b; yet cf. comments on 4:13). This is additional evidence that Paul is not addressing some particular problem that has emerged in the meantime, but is continuing the instruction with which they were already familiar.

They already know the command to love one another because they have been taught by God. Paul does not assume that "we all know what love is" on the basis of general human experience. What he is talking about does not, of course, deny the real depth of human love between family members and friends. But Paul does insist that God's love made known in Christ, now experienced in the Christian community and lived out before others for their sake, is a new reality in which they have been taught by God (on *Godtaught*, see trans. note d). The contrast is not between Paul and God, as in 2:13, but between divine and human origin per se. Being taught by God is a dimension of the eschatological reality promised by the prophets (Isa 54:13; Jer 31:34; cf. John 6:45), now in the process of realization. Such divine instruction is not merely a matter of information, but of relationship to God, the work of the Holy Spirit, who teaches and mediates the love of God (Gal 5:22; Rom 5:5). Paul does not speak of "having been taught by *Jesus*," as though he has instructed the new converts in the love commandment as taught by the pre-Easter Jesus (see on 4:2 above), but as being *God*taught. Paul thinks of the revelation of God's love in the Christ event, of the missionaries' preaching and teaching among them during the founding visit (including the biblical commands to love God and neighbor), of the gift of the Spirit that made God's love real to them, including, but not limited to, charismatic prophets in the congregation who speak encouraging words of love for God and neighbor (see on 5:19–21), and the continuing instruction of congregational teachers (cf. intro, "New Congregation"). The teaching came from human missionaries, but in Paul's view, that the new converts grasped it (= were grasped by it) is the work of God, the effect of the Holy Spirit, God's own work among them (cf. 2:13).

[10] The new converts have already learned that such love extends not only to their local congregation, but also to all the churches in Macedonia (as in 1:7–8). Love is here identified with concrete acts essential for the Christian mission: upholding the work of other congregations and missionary preachers with prayer, financial support, and opening one's home to traveling missionaries such as Paul, Silvanus, and Timothy.

Paul is interested in both community boundaries and extending love beyond these boundaries. The new church in Thessalonica is indeed a new community with firm boundaries; Paul uses insider/outsider language unself-consciously and nonsmugly. Baptism has made a separation, and the whole holiness vocabulary reconfirms it. But the one holy God is the creator and lover of all. The love they have experienced is not to be limited to the congregation or to the church, but extends to the whole world, to the human neighbor as well as to the Christian brother and sister.

[11–12] The charge to "live unobtrusively, mind your own business, and work with your own hands" is not concerned to emphasize the dignity of manual labor as such. Paul's point is not to contrast labor and management, blue-collar and white-collar jobs, but to do one's own work and not be unduly dependent on others. The instruction has both the outsider and the community itself in view. This instruction has been explained in four different but overlapping ways, each of which has something to contribute:

1. In modern times, *eschatology* has been a popular explanation.[29] On the analogy of some later millenarian groups, it has been supposed that some of the new converts, in view of the near Parousia, had quit their jobs and had become dependent on other members of the congregation who were still working. These have then been identified with the *ataktoi* of 5:14 (mistranslated as "idlers"; see comments there). The interpretation of *ataktoi* as "idlers" has been imported from 2 Thess 3:6–13, but there is no basis for this meaning in the word itself, which means "disorderly." Nor is there any suggestion in 1 Thessalonians that some Thessalonian Christians have stopped working for a living because of their belief in the near end. The new congregation was indeed deeply influenced by the expectation of the near Parousia, as were Paul's theology and 1 Thessalonians throughout, but the command to live unobtrusively and do one's own work cannot be reduced to "eschatological excitement."

2. "Living unobtrusively" and "doing one's own work" was a topos of *pop-philosophical discussions* of the first-century Hellenistic world. In general, self-sufficiency and leading a quiet life was considered a virtue in Hellenistic moral instruction. A variety of philosophical views advocated a "conversion" from conventional lifestyles and a retirement to the contemplative life.[30] While Paul's instruction reflects some of this vocabulary, the new converts in Thessalonica did not belong to the social class that could idealize the life of country retirement with a few friends, far from the clamor of the marketplace; for the most part, they had no choice but to earn their living by the work of their own hands.

3. There was a *political* dimension to the situation Paul addresses. Kingdom (*basileia*), Lord (*kyrios*), and assembly (*ekklēsia*) had unmistakable political

---

29. E.g., Frame 159; Rigaux 519–21; Best 175–77; Bruce 91; Marshall 1983, 117; Jewett 1986, 176–78. A variation on this view is Barclay (512–30), who argues that the new converts have quit their regular jobs in order to engage in aggressive evangelistic activity and are thus provoking their non-Christian neighbors. A further variation of Barclay's argument: these "full-time evangelists" now expect support from the congregation, a violation of *philadelphia*. Paul "calls upon these brothers to curtail their evangelistic endeavors and get back to work" (Burke 203–24).

30. See details and quotations in Malherbe 2000, 246–52; Hock 1980, 44–47.

connotations. Talk of the Parousia and the coming kingdom of God could cause the new congregation to be misunderstood as a subversive group plotting or awaiting the overthrow of the empire.[31] They had already attracted enough public attention to generate harassment and persecution. While they were not to withdraw into a sectarian commune, Paul instructs them to maintain a low profile and seek to be respected by society at large. Christians can no longer live by the norms of the pagan culture, for the new life to which they have been called has its own orientation. But they cannot be indifferent to what their neighbors think about the new group, both for the sake of the church and for the sake of the outsiders themselves. "Pleasing the outsider" was not a goal in itself. The new converts had found a new center and point of orientation for their lives: pleasing God, doing the will of God (4:1). Striving "to be thought well of by outsiders" is the furthest thing from flattery, insecure other-directedness; it is the life of those whose security is in the one true and living God, who is also the God of the "outsiders," whether they know it yet or not. Thus Paul calls church members to continue their usual work as a sign that the Christian community belongs in the world and continues its business in the ordered life of the world.

4. The context suggests that *philadelphia*, mutual care for members of the new community of faith, is the main thrust of Paul's injunction. The self-sufficiency for which Paul calls is ecclesial, not individual. The point is that the church is to make a good impression on outsiders by not needing help, not that each individual is to ignore others and look after their own interests. A community concerned for mutual support of its members, including economic support for those who may have lost their jobs or be unable to find work due to their new commitments, is always vulnerable to abuse by those immature members who take undue advantage of the compassionate hospitality the congregation offers to those in need. Paul warns against this, but there is no indication of a specific problem, such as a group of "idlers" that have become disruptive. The instructions are to all, not to a small group of supposed troublemakers.

"Mind your own business" does not mean that either the community as a whole or the individual should withdraw from the world, or retire from public life, turning society and its this-worldly concerns over to nonbelievers. Agape can never mean being unmindful of the needs and problems of others, counting such as "not my problem," nor can the church ignore what outsiders think of them. Within the community of faith, individual believers cannot simply look after themselves: they are called to live in solidarity with their fellow believers, sharing their celebrations and sufferings, and also sharing material goods with each other. This solidarity extends beyond the community, for believers now know that the God who has called them is the creator of all, that outsiders

---

31. Cf. the response to Christian missionaries pictured in Acts 17:6, Paul's own later specific instruction in Rom 13:1–7, and, e.g., Hock 1980, 46–47; Jewett 2003, 1419; Wanamaker 162–63.

are also beloved of the one true God. They must live their lives in a way that does not generate or reinforce misunderstanding, that does not create a false stumbling block to the outsiders' acceptance of the evangelistic message of the church. Thus all this is not mere social conservatism or enlightened self-interest, but indeed strategy for mission.

Paul has been encouraging the new Thessalonian Christians to continue in their "work generated by faith" and "labor that grows out of love" (1:3). Now he turns to their "steadfast endurance empowered by hope" (1:3).

4:13–5:11 Life in Hope of the Lord's Coming

The section 4:13–5:11 is not *the* "eschatological section" of the letter, as though Paul says, "I would now like to turn to a new topic and explain a few things about the return of Jesus." The letter and Paul's theology are permeated with eschatology throughout; it is the horizon of all his thinking. Yet we need to notice the location of these two paragraphs that deal explicitly with what will occur before and at the time of the Parousia: these instructions are in the "practical" part two, not doctrinal speculations on "what happens when we die" or "teaching about the end" (see intro, "Outline and Structure"). This section offers pastoral care for a grieving community.

The section is thus an integral part of the paraenesis of 4:1–5:22. It has two units, 4:13–18, dealing with the status of Christians who die before the Parousia; and 5:1–11, devoted to those who live in the light of the Christian hope. A clear division is marked by the *peri de* (now as for) of 5:1. The first section informs the Thessalonians of what they do not yet know (the only unit in the letter that claims to do this). The second section reminds them of what they already know. Each section concludes with the assurance that believers will be with the Lord, and with the exhortation "therefore encourage one another" (4:18; 5:11). The end of the second unit harks back to the theme of the first, binding the two paragraphs together with "whether we are among those who are awake or asleep" (5:10).

4:13–18 The Dead in Christ

4:13 Brothers and sisters, we do not want you to misunderstand[a] the situation of those who sleep,[b] so that you will not grieve as the others who do not have hope. 14 For since[c] "we believe that Jesus died and rose,"[d] we thus believe that God, acting through Jesus,[e] will bring[f] those who have fallen asleep to be together[f] with him. 15 For this we declare to you by the word of the Lord: we who are included in the surviving remnant,[g] that is, those who are still living at the Parousia of the Lord, will by no means[h] be ahead of[i] those who have fallen asleep. 16 For "the Lord himself, with a commanding signal, the voice of an archangel, and the sounding of God's trumpet, will descend from heaven, and the dead in Christ[j] will rise first; 17 then we who are still living, the surviving remnant,[g] will be caught up together with them in clouds[k] to meet the Lord in the sky,[l] and so we will be with the Lord forever." 18 So then, encourage[m] one another with these words.

a. *Ou thelomen hymas agnoein* (lit., "we do not want you not to know") is a Pauline idiom, found 6× in the undisputed Pauline Letters (Rom 1:13; 11:25; 1 Cor 10:1, 12:1; 2 Cor 1:8; 1 Thess 4:13), and nowhere else in the NT or the LXX. *Agnoeō* is often translated as "to be ignorant," but Paul's term does not have the pejorative overtones of the English word. The negative *ou* plus the alpha-privative (*a-gnoeō*, *un*-knowing) can imply that the readers already have information, but are in danger of misunderstanding (as 1 Cor 12:1), yet can also mean simply "I want you to understand," as in Rom 11:25. The idiom is a synonym of *thelō de hymas eidenai* (1 Cor 11:3), and *ginōskein de hymas boulomai* (Phil 1:12), both of which mean "I want you to know." In Paul's usage, it is a matter not only of information but also of insight.

b. *Koimaō* normally means "sleep" (as, e.g., in Matt 28:13; Luke 22:45), but is a common metaphor for death, in classical Greek (e.g., Sophocles, *Elektra* 509), the LXX (e.g., Gen 47:30), and elsewhere in the NT (e.g., 1 Cor 15:20, 22; esp. John 11:11–14). It is not the case that Paul used the metaphor euphemistically to avoid speaking of the harsh reality of death, or positively because it implies "waking up" at the resurrection. The term is simply a common expression, which Paul drops in v. 16, where he speaks plainly of "those who have died."

c. Here the particle *ei* introduces a particular grammatical structure, the first-class conditional sentence, which does not imply uncertainty or doubt, or only a hypothetical possibility, but assumes the condition to be fulfilled. It is thus rightly translated "since" (so, e.g., NRSV, ESV, CEB). This is the meaning even when translated by "if" (as in Matt 6:30 NRSV: "If God so clothes the grass of the field . . .") and here could be appropriately translated "For if we believe, as we do . . ."[32]

d. The aorist active verbs *apethanen* ([Jesus] died) and *anestē* ([he] rose) present Jesus as the acting subject. In both cases, the usage is conventional and traditional, not Paul's own, and places no emphasis on the actual subject. Paul typically speaks of Jesus' "dying" rather than "being killed" (1 Thess 2:15 is the only exception), but of "being raised" (by God, as in 1 Thess 1:10). The meaning here is simply "Since 'we believe in the death and resurrection of Jesus' . . ." The quotation marks are to signal that the *hoti*, which can be taken as marking either direct or indirect quotation, is here taken as signaling a traditional creedal statement, reproduced verbatim.

e. Syntactically, the prepositional phrase *dia Iēsou* (through Jesus) could modify either "bring" or "fallen asleep." The latter option seems to balance the sentence better, but to "fall asleep through Jesus" is a peculiar though possible idiom (presumably meaning the same as "the dead in Christ"; cf. v. 16, and the ET of v. 14 in KJV, ASV, NJB, NIV, TEV, CEV, CEB). The translation above takes the first option, understanding the

32. So Best 180.

meaning to be that God is the ultimate director of the eschatological scenario, who acts through Jesus to raise the dead believers. The second option has been ably defended by some modern interpreters.[33]

f. The combination *agō* (bring) and *syn* (with) does not here mean that dead believers are pictured as accompanying the Lord on his descent from heaven (in contrast to 3:13; see comments there), but that at the Parousia, God will bring the returning Jesus and dead believers together. *Agō* refers to the eschatological event as a whole, of which God is director and producer. Forms of *agō* are used with reference to the resurrection and/or Parousia in Rom 10:7; Heb 2:10; 13:20. What Paul envisioned by *axei syn autō* (will bring with him) is made explicit in vv. 16–17.

g. *Hoi perileipomenoi* (more lit., "those who are left"). The vocabulary reflects the eschatological ingathering of all the people of God, the "remnant" that has faithfully endured through all the eschatological suffering.

h. Emphatic double negative *ou mē*, as in Matt 16:22; Luke 21:33; 1 Cor 8:13; 1 Thess 5:3.

i. This somewhat slangy translation tries to represent both the temporal (precede) and qualitative (have an advantage over) meanings of *phthanō*.

j. On purely syntactical grounds, the phrase *hoi nekroi en Christō anastēsontai prōton* might be translated "first, the dead will rise in Christ."[34]

k. The usual translation "in *the* clouds" implies location, but there is no article in Greek, and the *en nephelais* is used instrumentally, "by means of clouds," the vehicles of transportation to and from the heavenly world (grammatically analogous to "in balloons" or "in rocket ships"). "With clouds as their vehicle" is too much of a paraphrase. "In clouds" expresses means, not location. So also REB.

l. *Aēr*, often translated "air," has several meanings. "Sky" tries to render the ancient cosmology in contemporary terms without supposing the ancient writer had a modern worldview.

m. See notes and commentary on 2:3 for Paul's use of the *parakaleō* vocabulary.

As in 4:3–8, Paul's central point is clear. The new converts in Thessalonica are upset by the death of one or more of their members and wonder whether those who have died will miss out on the celebration of God's ultimate victory, to come in the near future with the return of Jesus. Paul assures them

---

33. Dobschütz and Bornemann (191) argued for this interpretation and translation already in 1909, recently supported by, e.g., Marshall 1983, 124.

34. A strong case for this translation has been made by Konstan and Ramelli, who argue that *en Christō* goes better with the verb than with the noun. So construed, the statement would mean "the dead will rise in Christ," meaning that it refers to all the dead, and Christ is the means and sphere of their resurrection. The parallel construction in 1 Cor 15:18, that if Christ has not been raised, "then those also who have died in Christ have perished" (NRSV), shows that the translation above is syntactically possible. Context must be decisive. Paul's whole point has to do with the relative status of Christians who have died, i.e., those "in Christ," and believers who are still alive at the Parousia. The translation proposed by Konstan and Ramelli would have Paul abandon his argument and introduce an extraneous statement.

that this is not the case, basing his assurance on the Christian confession of God's act in Jesus' death and resurrection, and on a saying of the Lord associated with detailed apocalyptic imagery. His point is reassuring: all believers, both the dead and the living, will ultimately rejoice together in the presence of the Lord.

The details of this assurance are not so clear, and several matters continue to be disputed among equally competent and careful scholars. This does not mean the interpreter should be satisfied with reducing the imagery to a few general principles or points. The richness of what apocalyptic imagery has to say cannot be captured in conventional propositional language. Exploring the hermeneutical possibilities of such richly textured texts unleashes their vigor, even when their precise meaning cannot be pinned down.

[4:13] *The situation Paul addresses.* In this paragraph Paul responds to an existential concern of the new congregation about the fate of one or more of its members who have died. He has presumably learned of their concern from Timothy (3:1–7). The exact nature of their anxiety is no longer clear to us, but there is no indication that the issue is the reality of life after death as such, or the actuality of Jesus' resurrection. Nor is Paul opposing false eschatological teaching (as in 2 Thessalonians).

Why should the new converts be shocked that some of their members have died? It is too much to believe that the early church, including Paul, expected all believers to live until the Parousia, and that Paul has communicated this expectation to the new converts in Thessalonica. In the twenty years since the beginning of the church, Paul would certainly have known of the deaths of some Christian believers (cf. 1 Cor 15:6, 18). Before his conversion, he may even have participated in the execution of some believers in Jesus who were regarded as dangerous "heretics" or apostates from Judaism (cf. 1 Cor 15:9; Gal 1:13; Acts 7:58; 8:1; 22:4, 20; 26:10; see intro, "Context of Paul's Life"). It is difficult to imagine that he would have assured the Thessalonians that all of them would live to see the Parousia.

Nonetheless it could be that they had understood from Paul's preaching that the Parousia was so near that they all expected to experience it, and then were shocked at the deaths of some of their group, which called into question their whole new symbolic universe. This expectation would have been strengthened by their experience of the Holy Spirit, which gave believers a unity with Christ, a unity that they never expected to be broken by death. The intensity of charismatic manifestations made the participation of some Thessalonian Christians in the divine reality so real that they might have understood that they would not die before the Parousia. Moreover, the election theology of Paul has emphasized that their being called through the gospel has constituted them as the eschatological people of God. They represent the chosen remnant that will endure to the end and celebrate together the advent of the coming kingdom of God (1:3;

2:12, 19; 5:8). The deaths of some church members would then call the validity of their whole experience into question.[35] The belief that believers would not die before the Parousia would have been a misunderstanding of Paul but, in his absence, an understandable (mis)interpretation of his teaching.

Was the new converts' shock and disappointment intensified because some of them had died in a persecution of Christians in Thessalonica? This is quite possible and is plausibly argued by several interpreters.[36] Paul's previous reminders that he had warned the Thessalonians to expect persecution might support this view. It seems strange, however, that if the discussion is triggered by the death of Christians in anti-Christian violence in Thessalonica, Paul says nothing explicit about it here (contrast, e.g., Rev 2:13; 6:9–11).

Paul addresses this situation with new revelatory instruction. The series of *oidate* ("you know"; see on 2:1) reminders stops here and does not resume until 5:2. He has not given this instruction during the founding visit (contrast the perspective of 2 Thess 2:5; see comments there). The new thing Paul has to say to the Thessalonians is not that some Christians might die before the Parousia, but it concerns the resurrection of dead believers. This suggests that the concern of the Thessalonians was not the death of their fellow believers as such, but that those who had died would be absent from the glorious celebration at the Parousia. After some 1,965 years, it is difficult for modern readers to appreciate how closely conversion to the new faith, the experience of the Holy Spirit and life together in the new Christian community, and the hope of salvation were all bound up with the expectation of the Parousia, which had played a major role in Paul's initial preaching that had led to the Thessalonians' conversion (see on 1:9–10 and 4:15 below). This need not be pictured as fanaticism or "feverish eschatological excitement," as though it were borderline pathological, but simply means they took their new faith seriously—though their theological understanding of the faith needed adjustment.

Faith that God had raised Jesus means that the end-time events have already begun to happen. Paul's Jewish framework, in which he preached the

35. So, e.g., Jewett 2003, 1419–20: "It appears that death was thought to have been abolished by the dawning of the new age. . . . In effect, the congregation thinks it has already been raptured by means of its charismatic ecstasy, placing them beyond death. This would explain both the shock at the death of loved ones and the fear that they had 'believed in vain.'" This seems to be a too-enthusiastic exaggeration of a valid point.

36. On "persecution," see the intro, "New Congregation"; notes and comments on 1:6; 2:14; 3:3–7. Donfried (2002b, 41–43) argues that after Paul's departure, Christians in Thessalonica were persecuted, even to death; cf. Donfried 1993a, 21–23, 34, and elsewhere in the same volume. Pobee (113–14) argues that (in 4:14) *dia tou Iēsous*—usually translated "through Jesus" and related to "bring . . . with," as in the above translation—is better understood as related to *tous koimēthentas* ("those who have fallen asleep" = "have died"), so that the meaning is "those who have died on account of their faith in Jesus." The majority view is probably represented by Barclay (514 n. 6), who recognizes the intensity of such conflicts but is moderately skeptical that they became lethal.

resurrection, included and assumed the joys of being part of the final generation (Dan 12:12–13; *4 Ezra* 6.18–28; 7.27–28; 13.16–24; *Pss. Sol.* 17.44; *Sib. Or.* 3.367–80; *2 Bar.* 30.1–3). Faith in the resurrection of Jesus included anticipation of sharing in this eschatological jubilation. Paul's preaching held together the reality of the resurrection of Jesus in the recent past and the celebration of the soon-to-come Parousia, which would bring to completion the new world that had begun in Jesus' resurrection. It is not the case that he had presented a timetable that was now troublesome to the new converts in Thessalonica since some had died. The chronology of the eschatological events had not become an abstract theological problem separate from faith in the resurrection of Jesus, for the expectation of the Parousia was part and parcel of their experienced faith in Jesus' resurrection. Although the Thessalonians seem not to be raising questions about either the resurrection of Jesus or the future resurrection of believers, they were no longer clear about how to think about these two aspects of their faith that were inseparably joined together. Paul wants to reassure them that those who have already died will be present with them to celebrate God's eschatological victory at the near Parousia.

The near Parousia. By 50 C.E. Paul was well aware of the death of believers; there is no indication that this was ever a theological problem for him. He expected to be alive himself, but by the time he writes to the Corinthians a few years later, he already considered this something of an exception (1 Cor 15:18, 51). He would later reckon with the possibility that he too would die before the Parousia. By the time he writes 2 Corinthians, he still thinks of the same two groups, believers still alive and those who have died, but no longer places himself among the living (1 Cor 6:14; 2 Cor 4:14). But in 50 C.E., as he writes 1 Thessalonians, he still assumes he will be among that number, "when the saints go marching in."[37]

---

37. Those who have difficulty believing that Paul could have been mistaken about the nearness of the Parousia have found it difficult to reconcile such alleged mistakes with an authoritative Bible. From ancient times, Paul's language in this text (and others in which the NT "appears" to affirm the near Parousia) has been understood as Paul's "identification" with the last generation, without claiming that he was literally a part of it (e.g., John Chrysostom, PG 62:436). In 1915, the Pontifical Biblical Commission made it official Roman Catholic teaching that Paul did not teach either that the Parousia would occur soon or that he would be among those living at the Parousia (Denziger-Schönmetzer, *Enchiridion symbolorum, definitionum ac declarationum de rebus fidei et morum*, 33d ed. [Freiburg: Herder, 1963], §3630). More recent rulings have rescinded such hermeneutical approaches and conclusions, encouraging Roman Catholic scholars to accept the historical-conditionedness of biblical truth. For a convenient summary, see Brown and Collins, "Church Pronouncements." All fundamentalists and some Protestant evangelical scholars continue to defend the traditional view of 1 Thess 4:13–18 in ways that preserve Paul's and the Bible's inerrancy. See, e.g., Morris 141–42; Witherington 1992, 20–35; Marshall 1983, ad loc. Wright (2005, 56) argues that what Paul expects to come soon is "the impending military crisis in Judea, . . . the destruction of Jerusalem. . . . This is the event that had to happen within a generation" (cf. 142).

This does not mean that Paul later gave up the view that the Parousia would come soon. First Thessalonians is not merely Paul's earlier thought, abandoned when he became more "mature." This view is sometimes supported by pointing to the relaxing of the eschatological hope in the later letters (Colossians, Ephesians, the Pastorals),[38] but, though these letters do represent a modification of the eschatology found in Paul's own letters, they were probably not written by Paul himself. Moreover, the expectation of the near Parousia is not merely Paul's early, provisional view, but also an integral element in his theological thought still found in his last letter, whether Romans or Philippians is considered latest (Rom 13:11–14; Phil 3:20; 4:5). Yet in the years after writing 1 Thessalonians, opposition to Paul increased, and he began to wonder whether he would survive the dangers, beatings, and imprisonments to which he was subjected, even though the Lord was coming soon (see, e.g., Phil 1:20–24 [versus 3:20–21]; 3:8–11; 2 Cor 1:8–9; 11:23–29).

"No hope." Paul does not tell the grieving congregation they should not grieve for the death of their new brothers and sisters in the faith, but he wants to deepen their understanding of the faith so that they do not grieve as do "the others" who "have no hope."[39] They had once been in this situation themselves, before they became believers. Hope is a fundamental reality of the new life. The contrast with "the others" must be guarded from three misunderstandings:

1. Christian hope is not a matter of wishful thinking for something that may in fact turn out to be real, but is instead confidence that it is real, though future (see on 1:3).

2. That "the others" have no hope is not said as a statement of objective reality, as though Paul were declaring "there is no hope *for* them," but he means that "they do not have the Christian hope *in* them" by which they can live.[40] Paul is making pastoral care statements to Christians, not discursive theological dogmas about others.

3. Nor is this an observation about the psychology or personal beliefs of the "others," as though none of the pagans believed in a life beyond death. That was not the case. The Hellenistic world included a broad range of beliefs on the subject.[41] Various philosophers, especially in the tradition of Plato, had a

---

Respected evangelical scholar F. F. Bruce (99), however, does not hesitate to say "the writers [of 1 Thessalonians] rank themselves with those who will live to see the parousia."

38. See., e.g., Dodd (1928, 218), who refers to the time of Paul's later letters, among which he places Colossians and Ephesians, as the time of the mature Paul, "when Paul had outgrown his early eschatological fanaticism" (= rev. ed., 1960a, 206). A more helpful and nuanced approach, with key bibliography, is found with Baird (1971), who neither harmonizes nor appeals to "development" to explain the data, but affirms the variety of Paul's eschatological language.

39. Cf. Nicholl 23–26.

40. Cf. Barth 1962, 908–9.

41. For sample texts, see entries under "death" and "immortality" in Boring, Berger, and Colpe.

firm conviction on the immortality of the soul (cf. Socrates's calm courage and cheerfulness in Plato, *Apology of Socrates* 28D–29; and the whole of the *Phaedo*: Socrates died willingly, courageously, full of hope, "moving to a better home," anticipating a happy arrival in the heavenly world, pleased with his life and sure he had done the right thing, in the presence of his friends who did not abandon him). We do not know how widely these views were shared. Some of the inscriptions on gravestones and burial monuments express assurance in life beyond death, while others, with or without lamentation, indicate that death is the absolute end. For Paul, Christian hope was not limited to some theory of immortality or speculation about what happens to us when we die; instead, this hope means that the believer's life is enfolded in God's plan for universal history from creation to consummation, the defining climax of which is the resurrection of Jesus, the ultimate goal of which is the triumph of God at the end of history, which includes the resurrection of believers (see on 1:9–10).[42]

[14] The modern reader might be surprised that Paul does not respond to the grief of his beloved fellow believers in Thessalonica (2:8; 3:6) in a more personal sense—"I'm so sorry to hear about the death of so-and-so"—especially since it is a small congregation, recently founded. While the church had grown since his departure and now included members he did not know personally, he had surely baptized some of them and knew their names. In a manner that by no means ignores or minimizes his personal affection for them, his response is theological, which indeed is an expression of personal love and care, not an alternative to it (Rom 14:7–9!). He does not formulate his response ad hoc, but reminds them of the basic Christian creed common to all believers, which they already know, and communicates a "word of the Lord" that is new to them, addressing their present situation. Both creed and oracle are affirmations from the life of the church, tradition rather than expressions of Paul's individual concern or merely his personal theology.

The crisp "We believe that Jesus died and rose" is probably (an extract from?) a creedal statement familiar to the Thessalonians, taught to them while Paul and his colleagues were with them on the founding visit. This seems clear from the following data: (1) It begins with "We believe" (cf. Latin *credo*, "I believe"), reflecting the common faith of the church. (2) It is tersely restricted to foundational essentials. (3) Referring simply to "Jesus" without christological titles (Christ, Lord) is not Paul's own style (in 1 Thessalonians only here and 1:10, also a pre-Pauline creedal tradition). (4) Likewise the use of an active form of *anistēmi* (rose) for the resurrection is unusual for Paul (only here and v. 16 in the undisputed Pauline Letters, plus his biblical citations in Rom 15:12 and 1 Cor 10:7). When not citing traditional material, Paul consistently uses the

---

42. Expressed memorably by Gaventa 1998, 68: Paul does not urge them to *refrain* from grief but to *reframe* it. "Those who are bound together in this community remain so, even after death."

passive of another verb, *egeirō* (37× in the undisputed letters), portraying the resurrection as the act of God.[43] (5) The *lack* of a soteriological interpretation of Jesus' death is untypical for Paul.

With the *houtōs* (thus) of v. 14b begins Paul's theological elaboration of the creed.[44] The two creedal summaries Paul cites make clear that the Thessalonians believed in the resurrection of Jesus and in the near Parousia of the resurrected Lord (1:9–10; 4:14; cf. 5:9–10). What they did not understand—whether due to Paul's lack of making it explicit or their own lack of perception—was the combination of these two ideas, their fusion into one encompassing image.

Paul did not invent the kind of apocalyptic thought first documented in his letters, but he is a creative interpreter who stands within the apocalyptic tradition inherited from Judaism and the earliest church and uses that tradition as the framework for his own theology.[45] Neither did this way of thinking originate with the earliest Christians. Earliest Christianity was born in the milieu of a thoroughly apocalyptic Judaism, and it interpreted the Christ event in apocalyptic categories, yet it did not merely take over the conceptuality of Jewish apocalypticism en bloc. Based on their conviction that the expected Messiah had already come, early Christian teachers fundamentally rethought three dimensions of the ideas of Parousia and resurrection:[46]

1. *The resurrection of the Messiah is the beginning of the general resurrection.* At a distance of nearly twenty centuries, modern readers tend to think of Jesus' resurrection as an individual event in the distant past, something special that happened to him alone, and the Parousia as an event in the unknown future. But Paul, and early Christians in general, thought of the coming of the Messiah as the eschatological event, the redeemer who comes at the end of history to bring in the kingdom of God and establish God's justice. The image of the end of history also included the resurrection of faithful believers, not primarily as the guarantee of life after death, but as the vindication of God's faithfulness (see Dan 12). The implicit logic was that if the Messiah has come, then the end of history has come. The end of history means the resurrection of the dead (pl.). The resurrection of Jesus was therefore thought of as the firstfruits of the general resurrection, the first sheaf of the eschatological harvest that is already beginning (1 Cor 15:20–23; cf. Rom 8:29). Affirming that God has raised up

---

43. This is not denied, of course, by the active forms in the traditional creed Paul cites. Both "died" and "rose" are active but simply point to the events as having happened. In the creedal statement, Jesus no more raised himself than he killed himself: he is passive throughout, killed by others, raised by God. Paul's own formulation (following another pre-Pauline tradition; cf. 1 Cor 15:3–5) more explicitly characterizes the Christ event as the act of God.

44. So, e.g., Harnisch 33, with additional bibliography.

45. Cf., e.g., Käsemann 1969a, 82–107; 1969b, 108–37.

46. Cf. A. Brown 59.

the crucified Jesus amounts to claiming that the end-time scenario has been launched, and that those who believe the gospel stand amid a resurrection event that is already and is still underway. Paul does not look back to a discrete Christ event in 30 C.E.; he lives and does his theologizing during the Christ event that is already/not yet, but soon to be consummated.

2. *The general resurrection is still future, but it is seen as inseparably related to the resurrection of the Messiah.* Resurrection of the Messiah and the general resurrection are aspects of a single eschatological event. (This meaning is expressed in the strange story of Matt 27:51–53.) The general resurrection had not occurred at the *advent* of the Messiah, but will happen at the Parousia, the *return* of the Messiah. This is the meaning of Paul's declaration that at the Parousia God will "bring" the dead believers with the returning Jesus (see trans. note f): God will bring them back to life at that time, the resurrection event that began with Jesus will be completed, and the full harvest will fulfill the pledge signified by the firstfruits (1 Cor 15:20–23). For Paul, neither resurrection nor Parousia is an independent theme; each can be spoken of only in relation to the other.

3. *The resurrection of believers is therefore participation in Jesus' resurrection* (cf. 1 Cor 6:14; 15:1–22; 2 Cor 4:14; Rom 6:4–11; 8:11). As is the case with the coming kingdom of God, believers already live by its power. Since Christ's resurrection is the firstfruits of the general resurrection, the believer's present participation in the life of the Spirit is the down payment on full participation in God's future victory and glory. Christian hope does not mean a desperate "We hope so," but a confident "It is real, though still future." For Paul and the Thessalonians, this future was very near.

This is why Paul can cite the fundamental confession of faith in the death and resurrection of Jesus as the basis of Christian hope. Jesus too entered the realm of death, completely dependent on God. That Jesus died affirms his solidarity with Christians who have already died: they are not merely dead; they have indeed died *in Christ* (v. 16).[47] Both Jesus and the dead Thessalonian believers can be counted among the *nekroi* (dead). God's raising and vindication of Jesus is the pledge that God will raise and vindicate the Thessalonian believers who have died. It is not merely a comparison—"As Jesus died and was raised, so it is with believers." Jesus' death and resurrection is the ground of believers' future life. This grand, universal declaration of Christian faith now receives a particular application through the voice of a "word of the Lord."

47. Paddison (177–78) rightly argues that "those who died in Christ" is not just a synonym for "dead Christians." "Just as the dead 'in Adam' means more than 'dead humans,' so the dead 'in Christ' means more than 'dead Christians.'" "The paralleling of the phrase *en tō Adam* [in Adam] and *en tō Christō* [in Christ] in 1 Cor. 15:22 would suggest a juxtaposing of two different spheres of power and dominion." The dead are (not "were") in Christ.

[15] The creed Paul has cited was traditional material, already known and accepted by the new Christians in Thessalonica. Paul now, in his continuing exposition of the meaning of the creed, for the first and only time in 1 Thessalonians, communicates entirely new information he has not taught them during the founding visit. Before discussing the *meaning* of this word of the Lord, its *origin* and *extent* must be considered.

Origin. Where does Paul get this "word of the Lord"? Exegetes have argued for four different possibilities.

1. Paul is not appealing to a particular saying, but to the kind of teaching that circulated in the tradition and was later included in the Synoptic Gospels (Mark 13//Matt 24//Luke 21), which he cites as "word of the Lord."[48]

2. Some have thought that Paul appeals to a particular saying he draws from the oral tradition and regards it as having come from the pre-Easter Jesus.[49] There is nothing like this in the Gospels, however, so it has been argued that the saying is an agraphon, a saying of Jesus that circulated in early Christianity but was not finally included in the Gospels (e.g., Acts 20:35).[50] But the saying addresses a post-Easter situation of early Christianity that did not occur during the lifetime of Jesus. Moreover, Paul rarely if ever cites a saying of the historical Jesus in support of his theological point (see above on 4:2).

3. The words are from Paul himself, delivered by the authority of the risen Lord, but without claiming that he is communicating a saying of Jesus, either pre- or post-Easter. In this view, Paul could simply be using "word of the Lord" as a synonym for the Christian message as a whole (as in 1:8).[51]

4. The most likely view is that Paul is citing, with minimal editorial interpretations of his own, the oracle of an early Christian prophet. This understanding, currently the majority opinion among exegetes,[52] including the present author, was already advocated in the ancient church. Some evidence for this view will appear in the exegesis below, but here we may already note that "word of the Lord" (*logos kyriou*) is a very common phrase for prophetic revelation in the LXX (123×), with Paul's exact wording, *en logō kyriou*, found seven times. The Thessalonian congregation was well acquainted with charismatic Christian prophets (see on 5:19–21) and would have recognized the genre and authority of prophetic oracles. It is unlikely, however, that this "word of the Lord" was revealed to Paul or Silvanus (who was also a charismatic prophet; see on 1:1; 2:15; cf. Acts 15:22, 32) in response to the grief of the new converts in Thes-

---

48. So Rigaux 539.

49. E.g., E. P. Sanders 1995, 39–41; Lohse 68–69; Kim 225–42, esp. 237; Nicholl 38–41.

50. So, e.g., Jeremias 80–83.

51. So Cerfaux 1959, 37–38; cf. Gaventa 1998, 65. This view is now argued in the recent dissertation of Michael W. Pahl; see his summary on 167.

52. See Harnisch (41–44) and Luz (328–29).

salonica. The problem could hardly have first emerged in 50 C.E., twenty years after the beginning of the church (see above). But a plausible case can be made that some years earlier, in Antioch, in the new congregation in which Christian prophets (including Paul and Silvanus) made a lively contribution, the unexpected situation arose that believers were dying and the expected Parousia had not come. Speaking in the name of the risen Lord, the prophet addressed the current need by reinterpreting the apocalyptic tradition, bringing the meaning of Jesus' resurrection to bear on the specific situation.[53] As the creed represents the distillation of Christian tradition formulated and passed on by the church's teachers, new prophetic revelation continues to make the tradition relevant to new situations in the ongoing life of the church.

Extent and wording of the "word of the Lord." With no quotation marks or other punctuation in ancient manuscripts, all such decisions must be made by later interpreters (see on 1:2–10). The issue is complicated by the double occurrence of the conjunction *hoti* (one beginning v. 15b, the other beginning v. 16a). Either of these could mark the beginning of a direct or an indirect quotation, or could indicate inference or cause. Some English translations identify presumed sayings of Jesus by quotation marks or red font, not only in the Gospels but also in post-Easter "sayings of the Lord" in such texts as Rev 2–3; 4:1b; 16:15; 22:7. No English translation, however, ventures to identify any part of 1 Thess 4:15–17 as a direct quotation. Likewise, none of the editions of the Greek New Testament that identify supposed quotations of hymnic and liturgical fragments by different font or formatting give any such indications here. These difficulties have resulted in a variety of identifications of the "word of the Lord" in this text. The major contenders:

1. A few interpreters have argued that the *touto* (this) that begins v. 15 does not refer to the following words but points back to Paul's own statement in v. 14b that God will raise dead believers to rejoin living Christians at the Parousia, a prophetic revelation that came to Paul himself.[54]

2. It is grammatically possible to regard all of vv. 15b–17a as the oracle, introduced as direct quotation by the initial *hoti*, and continued into v. 17 by the second *hoti*, which would be understood as a causal "for." If this construal of the text is accepted, the citation still cannot be understood as verbatim, for the risen Lord would not say "we" in vv. 15 and 17, and would not use the phrase

53. There seem to be other NT instances of prophetic responses addressing the crisis caused by the deaths of believers prior to the Parousia. See 1 Cor 15:51–52 (quite similar in form and content to 1 Thess 4:16–17a) and Mark 9:1, both probably post-Easter prophetic oracles; see Boring 1982, 34, 186, 258. The oracles assure believers that though *some* have "fallen asleep," not *all* the first generation will die before the end comes.

54. So Richard 1995, 226. Though several scholars regard Paul himself as a prophet who received such revelations, few have been convinced that Paul here claims 4:14b as such an oracle.

"in Christ." The duplication and overlap found in vv. 15 and 16–17 constitute a major objection to regarding vv. 15b–17a as one unified oracle. Every word of v. 15b corresponds verbally or thematically to the wording of vv. 16–17a (translated somewhat literally to make this more clear):

v. 15b	vv. 16c–17a
hēmeis hoi zōntes hoi perileipomenoi	*hēmeis hoi zōntes hoi perileipomenoi*
we who are alive, who remain	we who are alive, who remain
eis tēn parousian tou kyriou	*eis apantēsin tou kyriou*
for the Parousia of the Lord	for a meeting with the Lord
ou mē phthasōmen	*anastēsontai prōton*
shall by no means precede	shall rise first
tous koimēthentas	*hoi nekroi [en Christō]*
those who have fallen asleep	the dead [in Christ]

One of these seems to be a summary of the other, or a commentary on it. Which is the oracle, and which is the summary or commentary? There are two options:

a. It might seem reasonable that Paul first cited the oracle, then expanded it in the commentary that follows. Since the supposed commentary contains considerable non-Pauline vocabulary, it is regarded as Paul's adaptation of traditional apocalyptic material, not mainly his own composition.[55]

b. The majority of scholars,[56] including the present author, are more convinced that Paul first summarizes the oracle in his own words (v. 15b), then cites the traditional prophetic "word of the Lord" in vv. 16–17a, with only a few editorial modifications. On this view, the second *hoti* at the beginning of v. 16 both introduces the quotation and provides the basis for the preceding statement. Paul then frames the whole construction with *syn autō* (with him, v. 14b) and *syn kyriō* (with the Lord, v. 17c).

14b	*syn autō* (with him)
15b	anticipatory summary
16–17a	slightly annotated oracular "word of the Lord"
17b	*syn kyriō* (with the Lord)

---

55. As argued by Holtz 1986, 183–86.

56. See, e.g., Nicholl (32–33), Harnisch (40–43), and the bibliography they provide, as well as numerous recent studies and commentaries.

The traditional oracle in vv. 16–17a, with Pauline additions and adjustments removed, probably was like this:

Ho kyrios	The Lord
en keleusmati,	with a commanding signal,
en phōnē archangelou kai	with the voice of an archangel and
en salpingi theou,	with the sounding of God's trumpet,
katabēsetai ap' ouranou	will descend from heaven,
kai hoi nekroi (en kyriō) anastēsontai	and the dead (in the Lord) shall rise,
hoi perileipomenoi	the surviving remnant
hama syn autois harpagēsontai	will be caught up with them
en nephelais	in clouds
eis apantēsin tou kyriou eis aēra.	for a meeting of the Lord in the sky.

Paul the prophetic interpreter. Paul was not merely a passive transmitter of this tradition, but also its active interpreter, re-presenting it with his own prophetic-apostolic authority. Thus his own anticipatory summary in v. 15 is also a constituent element of the "word of the Lord." The summary also reduces the quantity of apocalyptic detail; while Paul thinks within the apocalyptic worldview in general, he exhibits no fascination with the details of the end-time scenario except as they contribute to his pastoral purpose. To focus the oracle on the present situation in Thessalonica, he amplifies the oracle proper by adding "in Christ" (or changes an original "in the Lord" to his typical "in Christ") and "first" in v. 16, and "we, the living" in v. 17. Those who have been baptized into Christ (1 Cor 12:13) have their being "in Christ," which cannot be changed by their death.[57]

In addition, the key change Paul makes in the summary of v. 15 is the replacement of the prophetic oracle's *apantēsis* (meeting; in v. 17) with his own key term *parousia*. In ordinary Hellenistic Greek, *parousia* is an everyday secular word that means simply "coming," "arrival," "presence" (etymologically: *para*, "beside, with" + *ousia*, participle of *einai/eimi*, "to be" = "being with, being present"). *Parousia* has no equivalent in the Hebrew Bible and is found only four times in late books of the LXX, always in this ordinary secular sense, never for the coming of God (Jdt 10:18; 2 Macc 8:12; 15:21; 3 Macc 3:17). Neither in Paul's Bible nor in the Judaism of his day did the word have religious or theological overtones. In Paul's later letters, he too will mostly use *parousia* to refer simply to the arrival or presence of himself or his colleagues (1 Cor 16:17; 2 Cor 7:6, 7; 10:10; Phil 1:26; 2:12), and then will abandon the word altogether. In the period reflected in 1 Thessalonians, however, Paul has made *parousia* a

57. Elaborated in Schnelle 1983, 112–17; 1986, 212–13.

key term in his theology. He may have seen the *parousia* of the Lord Jesus as an alternative to the triumphant ceremonial entry of a Roman ruler into a provincial city, and later backed off from this too-provocative image, which could too easily lead to a misunderstanding of the nature of the Christian community.

In the Hellenistic world, alongside its everyday use, *parousia* had developed a semitechnical usage, somewhat like the word "advent" in English. In addition to its ordinary usage, the word was prominent in two particular settings: (1) *Parousia* served as a sacred expression for the advent of a god or goddess, made known by a revelation of divine power, or whose presence was celebrated in the cult. (2) *Parousia* was also used specifically of the visit of a ruler or person of high rank, especially of the arrival of the emperor or Roman governor in a province.[58] Thus when Paul here speaks of the *parousia* of the Lord Jesus, the expression has two sets of overtones already familiar in the provincial capital Thessalonica. For Paul and the new converts, the Lord (*kyrios*) is neither a cultic deity like those honored in the local religious centers, nor the emperor or his representative (see intro, "Religion in Thessalonica"). Paul is familiar with this imagery, and it has influenced his manner of expression, but his theology on this point is basically shaped by the biblical idea of the "day of the Lord," when God will come to redeem his people and establish the justice of his kingdom (see on 2:16; 5:2). The Lord Jesus will soon appear to bring to fulfillment the kingdom of God already launched in his life, death, and resurrection. The "hope," "joy," "crown of boasting," and "glory" that Paul attributes to the new congregation are all aspects of this Parousia and are seen in its light (see on 2:19).

Summary of analysis: Paul responds to the grieving Thessalonian congregation by citing (v. 14a) and interpreting (v. 14b) the common Christian confession of Jesus' death and resurrection he has taught them, an interpretation made the more sure by a "word of the Lord" (v. 15a). Paul provides an anticipatory summary giving the gist of the oracle as it applies to the pastoral need in Thessalonica (v. 15b), then cites the traditional oracle directly, with minimal modifications (vv. 16–17a), rounding off the unit by completing the framework that makes the point of the whole: eschatological salvation is not an abstract, individualistic "living forever," but the personal "being with the Lord" (v. 17b).

[16] Paul cites the prophetic "word of the Lord" almost verbatim. It may be that he has adjusted some of the language from an original third person to first person, but this shift of subject would also be appropriate to the original oracle. Since Paul is not here concerned with the fate of the living but with the status of the dead, there is no need to argue that he is responsible for the first-person form, so the "we" may be original. The other main possibility of Pauline editorializing is the occurrence of "in Christ," which probably is added by Paul.

---

58. E.g., Polybius, *Hist.* 18.48.4; Josephus, *J.W.* 7.100–103; examples of papyrus usage in Deissmann 1927, List 6; see BDAG 780–81 for further examples of both usages.

For Paul, only the dead in Christ are raised, those who are united with Christ's death and resurrection in baptism (Rom 6:1–11), those whose resurrection is assured by the Spirit they already possess (8:9–11). In contrast to some other New Testament texts, Paul has nothing to say about the postmortem destiny of unbelievers (cf. Acts 24:15; Rev 20:4–5, 11–15; John 5:28–29).

The imagery of this oracle is drawn from traditional Jewish apocalyptic, reinterpreted in the light of Christian faith in the resurrection of Jesus. The image of the *resurrection* of the dead is, of course, itself drawn from this tradition ([Isa 26:19?]; Dan 12:2; 4Q521; *1 En.* 62.15; Josephus, *J.W.* 3.362; *4 Ezra* 7.31–44; Acts 23:6; John 11:24). The *coming of the Lord* at the end of history is also biblical and Jewish eschatology (e.g., Isa 26:21; 31:4; 40:10; 66:15; Hos 10:12; Zech 14:5), as are the numerous texts proclaiming the coming day of the Lord (e.g., Isa 13:6, 9; Ezek 30:3; Joel 2:1, 11, 31; Amos 5:18, 20; Zeph 1:7, 14; Mal 4:5). This imagery was adopted by early Christian prophets (and others), who now understood "the Lord" to be the Lord Jesus.[59] Paul himself, though a thoroughgoing apocalyptic thinker, has no particular interest in the details of the apocalyptic scenario as such. Though angels, for instance, play a large role in apocalyptic thought, Paul himself has little use for angels (see on 3:13) and never elsewhere refers to archangels (elsewhere in the NT only in Jude 9). The Old Testament has no reference to archangels, but does name Gabriel and Michael as presumably leading angels (only Dan 8:16; 9:21; 10:13, 21; 12:1), and the ubiquitous "angel of the LORD" seems to be a special angelic figure who can represent Yahweh himself (56× in MT, as in Gen 16:7; 22:11; Exod 3:2; Num 22:22; Judg 2:1; 2 Sam 24:16; 1 Kgs 19:7; 2 Kgs 1:15; Ps 34:7; Isa 37:36; Zech 1:11; 12:8). Archangels multiply in postbiblical Jewish tradition, especially in apocalyptic (e.g., *1 En.* 9.1; 10.1, 4, 9, 11; 40.9; 54.6; 71.8; *Apoc. Mos.* 40.2; *4 Ezra* 4.36; 1QM 9.14–16; *Num. Rab.* 2.10). Together with the *voice of the archangel,* the *commanding signal* and the *sounding of God's trumpet* represent a collage of biblical and postbiblical apocalyptic images drawn on by the early Christian prophet to express his revelation (cf. Exod 19:16; Ps 47:5; Isa 27:13; Joel 2:1, 15; Zech 9:14; 1QM 2.16–3.12; 7.13; *4 Ezra* 6:23).

When Paul cites this oracle, his purpose is not to give *information* on such topics as "where are the dead," but to give *assurance* on the one point on which he is focused—that all believers will be included in the final triumph of God.

---

59. Such statements are not intended to suggest that biblical prophets gathered their materials in a cut-and-paste manner from earlier apocalyptic traditions and documents. They spoke in the conviction that God or the risen Christ was speaking through them. But the vocabulary and imagery in which they communicated such charismatic experiences necessarily represents their adoption and adaptation of prior tradition. See Lindblom 1962, 108, 125, 134, 158; 1968, 164 and passim; Boring 1982, 71–80. The NT book of Revelation is "exhibit A" in this regard. Though never citing the Bible or apocalyptic texts directly, the author's mind is saturated with such imagery, which he artfully uses in every paragraph to communicate his revelation.

This is typical of Paul's theological and pastoral method. In 1 Cor 6:1–11, for example, he draws on an apocalyptic tradition dealing with the eschatological judgment of the evil angels and pictures Christian believers as playing a role in their judgment. This is not because he wants to share some interesting data about the apocalyptic program, but because the Corinthian Christians are taking each other to court over issues they should be able to settle among themselves. Paul discourages this activity by explaining that if they are capable of judging angels at the Last Judgment, they can surely handle disputes within the congregation. Paul has a firm conviction that the kingdom of God is coming soon, at the Parousia of the Lord Jesus, but he does not have a comprehensive scheme of the apocalyptic events, sometimes introducing this feature and sometimes that. It is unlikely that he could or would have responded to the question "Will the saints judge the angels before or after they themselves stand before God's judgment?" (cf. Rom 14:10; 2 Cor 5:10), or that he would have considered it a valid question. There is no information here about an "intermediate state" of the dead in Christ or a separation of body and soul that will be reunited at the Parousia, nothing about a transformation of the living, no place for a Last Judgment, no last battle or establishing an earthly messianic kingdom.[60] For Paul, life in the power of the already/not yet kingdom and resurrection is real, but not the kind of this-worldly reality that can be parceled out and charted in a diagram. Rather, he seems to have a repertoire of apocalyptic images, which do not fit together into one grand program; from these images he draws as pastoral occasions call for it (on the use of conflicting eschatological imagery, see on 3:13). Here he draws on a Christian prophetic oracle assuring the believing community that—at the return of Christ, which they would soon experience—those who have died in Christ will be raised to join in the celebration of God's eschatological triumph.

[17] The surviving remnant, "those who are left," refers to believers who are alive at the Parousia.[61] Beyond this, it is no longer clear what *hoi perileipomenoi* meant in the original oracle. The Greek expression occurs in the New

---

60. Among Paul's later interpreters, Augustine, Thomas Aquinas, and Calvin may be recognized as concerned to have a more systematic understanding of such things. They were particularly bothered by the possibility that those alive at the Parousia would *not* die, but be assumed without death into the transcendent world without paying the penalty of original sin. In varying ways, they explained that the living would experience something like death and resurrection as they are flying through the air. Thus all will experience the consequences of original sin, all will participate in the death and resurrection of Christ (Augustine, *Civ.* 20.20; 1965, 427–26; Aquinas, *Lectures on Thessalonians*, ad loc; *Summa theologiae* 1a2ae q.81 a.3 ad 1; Calvin 1960a, ad loc.). Such a way of framing the issue is far removed from Paul's own perspective.

61. In the form of modern dispensationalism initiated by John Nelson Darby and popularized in the *Scofield Reference Bible* and various novels and movies, "those left behind" are the unbelievers who remain in this world at the "rapture," when Jesus comes to take true believers to heaven. Such theologies assume that each biblical text provides part of a complex series of eschatological events, which can be reconstructed by combining a variety of biblical texts.

Testament only here and in Paul's anticipatory summary in v. 15, and not at all in the LXX. A plausible case can be made that the Christian prophet was thinking in terms of the eschatological restoration of God's people, which would include those who have remained faithful despite exile and persecution, those who have survived the eschatological revelation of God's wrath, those who are still alive to participate in the final coming of God's reign. Thus "those who are left" are not "left behind" in the sense that they wanted to go but were unable or not permitted. Rather, the phrase has an entirely positive connotation. "Those who are left" are the blessed remnant, not the leftovers or those who are left out, but those who have endured and belong to the final generation that will experience the divine victory at the end of history, when the scattered people of God will be restored.

The Jewish Scriptures include a variety of representations of this hope, in the long history of which "the remnant" became a semitechnical term (see, e.g., Gen 45:7; Isa 7:3 NRSV mg.; 10:22; 11:11; 37:31–33; 46:3–4; Mic 4:7; 5:5–8; 7:18; Zeph 2:7, 9; 3:11–13; Jer 23:3; 31:7; Hag 1:12–14; 2:2; Zech 8:6, 11–12). The "remnant" vocabulary was focused in a cluster of four Hebrew terms (*yeter, pĕlêṭâ, śārîd, šĕʾār/šĕʾērît*), represented in the LXX by forms of the Greek verb *leipō* and its cognate noun *leimma* (*hypoleipō, kataleipō, kataleimma, kataleipsis, kataloipos*). Paul thinks of himself as belonging to this faithful remnant (Rom 11:5–6); those brought into the people of God by his missionary labors, who remain faithful to the end, are likewise included. The hypothesis that *hoi perileipomenoi* reflects this remnant theology would be strengthened if forms of *perileipō* were found in the LXX, but this is not the case (though the remnant theology is represented in Zech 8:6, 11–12 and Hag 1:12, 14 by the related *kataloipoi*). We know that the issue of the relative status of those who have died and "those who are left" was a concern of Jewish apocalyptic. On the basis of divine revelation, *4 Ezra* 13.24 declares, "Those who are left are more blessed than those who have died," but we do not have the original Hebrew (or Aramaic), and the scanty fragments of a Greek translation that have survived do not contain this text. In any case, the "word of the Lord" Paul cites here takes the other option than that of *4 Ezra*: "Those who are left" are *not* more blessed than believers who have died, who will be raised to join the living before the grand reunion takes place when the Lord returns. Paul here envisions the final events in the same manner as a few years later when, writing to the Corinthians (1 Cor 15:51–52), he expects as a matter of course that some will have died before the Parousia:

"Listen, I will tell you a mystery! We will not all die, but we will all be changed, in a moment, in the twinkling of an eye, at the last trumpet. For the trumpet will sound, and the dead will be raised imperishable, and we will be changed" (1 Cor 15:51–52 NRSV). Here too, some have died and some remain, but all will be transformed. Here too, the last trumpet sounds, and the whole is a matter of revelation ("I will tell you a mystery"), as in the revelation Paul cites in 1 Thess 4:16–17.

As Paul pictures it, the believers who have been raised from the dead, together with the surviving remnant, will be caught up in clouds to meet the descending Lord in the *aēr*, the "sky" (see trans. note l). *Nephelai* (clouds) are not merely a meteorological phenomenon but indeed belong to the heavenly world and are the vehicles of transportation between the transcendent world and the earth (see Exod 19:9; Pss 68:4; 104:3; Dan 7:13; Matt 17:5; Mark 13:26; 14:62; Acts 1:9–11; Rev 1:7; 10:1). In ancient cosmology, *aēr* can refer to the air surrounding us (e.g., 1 Cor 9:26; Acts 22:23), to the air directly above the earth where birds fly (e.g., Wis 5:11), or to the vast space between heaven and earth, the locale of stars and of spiritual beings (e.g., Eph 2:2; Rev 9:2; 16:17; *Apoc. Pet.* 3.10). It is what one sees when one stands outside and looks up, the Beyond. Modern readers who take for granted the view of the world through the window of an airliner, looking *down* on mountaintops, may need to remind themselves that no biblical author had ever seen the world from this perspective. What the ancients meant by such words as *nephelai* and *aēr* is better expressed in modern terms by "sky." Though they did not have our modern cosmology, what they intended we might express by "outer space," the regions between our world and the transcendent world. At the Parousia, Paul affirms, the faithful community of Christians, the remnant that has endured, will be caught up into this space to welcome the returning Lord.

Paul knows whereof he speaks. Although Paul is citing an anonymous prophetic oracle from some years earlier and handed on in church tradition, he has himself had an experience of being caught up into the transcendent world (2 Cor 12:1–5). Fourteen years before writing 2 Corinthians, around 42 C.E. and therefore about eight years before founding the church in Thessalonica and writing this letter to them, Paul was caught up (*harpazō*, 2 Cor 12:2, 4, the same verb as in 1 Thess 4:17) into the transcendent world of God, the "third heaven."[62] He has presumably not told the new converts in Thessalonica of this event, just as he did not tell the Corinthians during his time with them. Indeed, he is reluctant even to mention the experience, not to speak of parading it. Paul had numerous such "ecstatic" visionary experiences. When he speaks of *hyberbolē tōn apokalypseōn* ("the abundance of revelations," 2 Cor 12:7) it is not clear whether they extended over several years or were concentrated in the experience he reports in 2 Cor 12 (cf. 1 Cor 9:1; 15:8; Gal 1:12, 2:1–2; Acts 16:9; 18:9; 22:17–21; 27:23). However this may be, he considered them (like glossolalia,

---

62. There was considerable variety in the way apocalyptic writers understood celestial geography. Various authors think in terms of 3, 7, 10, or 72 strata of the transcendent world. See the documentation in Furnish 1984, 525. All such portrayals of heavenly journeys show that Paul is not thinking merely of meeting the returning Lord in the "air" in the way one might take a ride in a hot-air balloon.

1 Cor 14) personal and private, not the substance of the gospel, which is the common possession of the Christian community. It is striking that in responding to the Thessalonians' concern about the status of believers who have died, he does not appeal to his personal revelatory experience, but to tradition that belongs to the whole church.

All believers—the surviving remnant and those resurrected at the Parousia —are taken into the *aēr* to meet the returning Lord. The noun *apantēsis* and its synonym *hypantēsis* simply mean "meeting," but they are consistently used in the New Testament to portray going out to meet someone with the intention of welcoming and accompanying them the rest of their journey, never of going to meet someone who then turns around and returns to the point of origin without completing the initial journey (Matt 8:34 [cf. Mark 5:14–17!]; 25:1, 6; John 12:13; Acts 28:15). The word is also used in this sense in the LXX (e.g., Judg 4:18; 11:34; 19:3; 1 Sam 9:14; 16:4) and in Josephus (e.g., *Ant.* 5.264; 11.327, 329; 13.101; *J.W.* 7.100, 119). In Hellenistic times, the word was often used with the overtones of the celebratory procession that goes out to welcome the emperor or his representative and usher him into the city. The oracle portrays the descending Jesus in the imagery of a Roman ruler's triumphal entry into a provincial city.[63] The returning Lord is met not outside the city gates, but "in the *aēr*" transcending all earthly territories, of which he is already lord de jure, and now will be so de facto.

Neither Paul nor the oracle he cites makes explicit where the believers go after the meeting in the *aēr*. Does Paul think of Jesus as arresting his descent to earth, meeting the company of believers, and taking them to heaven? The word *apantēsis* itself evokes the image of the welcoming procession returning to earth with the triumphant Lord. Thus does Paul think of the Parousia as the ultimate Triumphal Entry, with the saints going out to meet the returning Lord and accompanying him back to earth? This has often become the accepted interpretation in academic circles, but several scholars now regard this as over-interpretation of the word, perhaps partially motivated by the desire to deprive dispensationalists of a key text. The text, however, is dealing with images, not eschatological schedules. This is not objectifying language of which one can ask chronological "Now what?" questions. In this text interpreters can find legitimate support neither for constructing a scenario that includes a rapture to heaven, nor for a return to earth for a millennial reign before the ultimate wrap-up of universal history. It is better to let the cosmic-consoling image have its effect: Christ descends; the dead in Christ are raised and together with

---

63. Since the study of Erik Peterson, *apantēsis* has often been understood as a semitechnical term for welcoming a Hellenistic ruler into a city. Recent study of the text is conveniently and thoroughly surveyed in Plevnik 1999. For further details and relevant bibliography, see Fee 178–82. On the political overtones of *parousia, apantēsis,* and *kyrios*, see on 5:3.

living Christians welcome Christ to the earth. They (in confessional language = "we"!) are forever with the Lord. The image is that of welcoming the triumphant Christ at the Parousia, which has its own function and integrity, even though it cannot be a cog in a larger machine, a piece of a larger jigsaw puzzle. The key words are "together with them": Christian hope is not for individualistic survival but for belonging to the communion of saints—and "with the Lord," which completes the frame of "with him" of v. 14b. Paul finds any other specification of details of eschatological salvation to be gilding the lily (Rom 6:5–8; 8:17, 32; 14:8–9; 2 Cor 5:8; Phil 1:23; 1 Thess 5:10).

[18] Paul delivers these words providing comfort and consolation to the grieving community for their encouragement, words assuring them that their lives are embraced in the divine plan shortly to be consummated. The words of the letter, if received by the community as authentic testimony to the apostolic faith, now belong to the community. These words, which include a reminder of the common confession of faith and prophetic "words of the Lord" handed on in the church's tradition, are no longer merely Paul's words spoken to them, but are also words that they may speak to each other (see on 5:27).

5:1–11 Living in the Light of the Christian Hope

In the preceding paragraph, Paul has been communicating new information. He now reverts to his typical mode in this letter, reminding the congregation of what they already know, interpreting it in a fresh light, and drawing out its implications. Though the composition is his own, it is replete with traditional elements. The structure is clear, comprising three paragraphs and a conclusion.

Verses 1–3 speak of the near end as inevitable (image of labor pains), but its date is unpredictable (image of the thief in the night). The day of the Lord will be the day of judgment, with sudden destruction coming on unbelieving outsiders.

Verses 4–8 portray the present situation of believers in the binary[64] terms of darkness and light, night and day. Believers belong to the day and should live accordingly.

Verses 9–10 picture the end as wrath or salvation. Believers receive salvation. All such language is the confessional language of insiders, not objectifying language about outsiders (see on 1:4, 9–10; 2:15).

Verse 11 concludes the section that began in 4:13, with words similar to 4:18, the conclusion of the first subsection.

---

64. I use *binary* where "dualistic" frequently appears in such discussions, as a reminder that Paul's theology is apocalyptic, but his "dualism" is penultimate. Ultimately, all reality belongs to the sovereignty of the one God, the creator of all, and will be seen to be so. But Paul does not hesitate to portray the present cosmos as divided into these contrary pairs. See Wright 2013, 370 and often.

In the following translation, the NIGHT/DAY contrast introduced in v. 4 and continued in the contrasting pairs *light/darkness*, sleeping/awake, drunk/sober, and **wrath/salvation** is indicated by different font formats.

5:1 Now as for the dates and times,[a] brothers and sisters, you do not need to have anything written to you,[b] 2 for you know very well[c] that the DAY of the Lord will come like a thief in the NIGHT. 3 While people are talking about[d] "peace" and "security," destruction will suddenly come upon them, like labor pains on a pregnant woman, and there is no way[e] they can escape.

4 But you, brothers and sisters, are not in the *dark*, as though that DAY would[f] take you by surprise like a thief; 5 for you are all "sons[g] of *light*," that is, "sons[g] of the DAY." We[h] do not belong to the NIGHT or the *darkness*. 6 So then, let us not sleep, as the others do, but let us stay awake and keep sober. 7 For those who sleep sleep at NIGHT, and those who are drunk get drunk at NIGHT; 8 but since we belong to the DAY, let us be sober, armor-clad[i] with the breastplate of faith and love, and for our helmet, the hope of **salvation**, 9 for God has not destined us for **wrath**, but for attaining[j] **salvation** through our Lord Jesus Christ, 10 who died for us, so that—whether we are among those who are awake or asleep—together we may live with him. 11 So continue encouraging and building one another up—each one the other[k]—just as you are already doing.

a. *Tōn chronōn kai tōn kairōn*, lit., "the times and the seasons," combines two Greek words for time in a hendiadys, i.e., using two synonymous or related words to represent a single idea ("nice and warm," "sick and tired"). Biblical examples: "stranger and alien" (Gen 23:4), "ruler and judge" (Exod 2:14). Though the close association of *chronos* and *kairos* is found 7× in the LXX (Neh 10:35 [34 ET]; 13:31; Eccl 3:1; Wis 8:8; Dan 2:21; 4:37 [text added in LXX]; 7:12) and once elsewhere in the NT (Acts 1:7), the exact phrase appears only here in Jewish and Christian Scriptures. The phrase used in 1 Thess 5:1 is neither a technical expression for eschatological schedules nor a stock phrase and thus is best rendered in contemporary English by the likewise nontechnical "dates and times" (so REB; cf. "times and dates" in NJB, NIV, TNIV, NIV11).

b. The clause is identical to that in 4:9, except there the verb is active, here passive.

c. On the repeated *oidate* (you know), see on 2:1. *Akribōs*, only here in Paul, found 9× elsewhere in the NT, can be translated "accurately" (as in Acts 18:25), but can also mean simply "to be well informed" (as Acts 24:22). Here the word does not imply detailed calendrical knowledge, as though Paul has taught them a precise chronology of the eschatological events.

d. Paul's *legōsin* ([people] are saying) can introduce direct quotations, as in, e.g., Exod 12:26; Ezek 37:18; Matt 24:26; 27:64. Thus several English translations place "peace and security" in a single set of quotation marks, as though Paul were citing a well-known slogan. *Legōsin* can also point to what people are talking about, without indicating direct quotation, as in Matt 5:11 and Luke 6:26. Thus "peace" and "security" are topics of conversation, but not necessarily a fixed phrase.

e. Emphatic double negative *ou mē*, as also in Matt 16:22; Luke 21:33; 1 Cor 8:13.

f. The very flexible conjunction *hina* here means result, "so that," but the negative indicates the purpose is frustrated (see BDAG 477). The day of the Lord *would* surprise them like a thief if they were in darkness, but they are not.

g. The use of *huios* (son) in the sense of belonging to a category, though intelligible to Gentile readers, is mainly a Hebraism. *Ben* ("son," etc.) in the Hebrew Bible is often used without reference to biology or gender. While the phrase might well be translated "You all belong to the light, that is, you belong to the day," or "You are all light-people, that is, day-people," I have rendered the phrase more lit. since Paul apparently intended to call the Thessalonians' attention to this distinctive usage.

h. A few ancient witnesses (D* F G, the Old Latin, some Vulgate MSS, and parts of the Syriac and Coptic traditions) continue with the second-person plural *este* (you are), but here Paul shifts to the confessional language of the first-person plural, which unites him and his readers.

i. The aorist participle *endysamenoi* could be taken as continuing the hortatory "Let us be sober" (so, e.g., NRSV); but for reasons of both grammar and Paul's theology, it is better taken as referring to something that has already happened. The readers are not urged to put on armor but to recognize that they are already armor-clad (so, e.g., REB, ESV).

j. The unusual *peripoiēsis* (only here in the undisputed Letters of Paul) may continue the thought of the preceding clause and thus be translated "receiving" (salvation as God's gift for the elect), or as here, "attaining," reflecting human response. In this case, the two clauses express the same dialectic that salvation is God's gift, actualized by human action, as in Phil 2:12–13.

k. The phrase *heis ton hena* ("each one the other," lit., "one the one") is found only here in the NT, is entirely absent from the LXX, and is rare in secular Greek. While it may be simply a stylistic variation for *allēlous* ("each other"; so BDAG 292), it seems to emphasize the responsibility of each and every individual in the community.

[5:1–3] Though the *peri de* (now as for . . .) introduces a new subsection (cf. 4:9, 13), the issue begun at 4:13 continues: how to understand the present in the light of the near Parousia, even though some members of the congregation have died. Paul has not divided his letter into chapters, and the new chapter at 5:1 in our Bibles did not yet bother either Paul or his readers. The conclusion of this section in 5:10–11 makes clear that the status of living and dead at the Parousia continues to drive the discussion. Paul is not indulging in giving general eschatological instruction—1 Thessalonians is not a didactic letter in this sense—but continues to respond to a specific concern of the new congregation, probably reported by Timothy (3:1–10). The issue now concerns "dates and times" (*chronōn kai kairōn*). From the time of Augustine, some interpreters have distinguished the two words, as though *chronos* refers to chronological, clock time, and *kairos* to special, fulfilled time, but here the phrase is a hendiadys in which the two words are used as synonyms. The usage in Daniel (Dan 2:21; 4:37 LXX; 7:12), with the connotation of calculating where the present generation was on the apocalyptic schedule, was especially influential in Paul's time (cf. Acts 1:7).[65]

The death of members of the community has not only raised the question of the status of Christians who die before the Parousia, dealt with in 4:13–18, but also made the new converts unsure about the time of the Parousia and the chronology of the eschatological events as such. If, contrary to the expected chronology of the eschatological events, some believers have died, does this mean that the Parousia is not so near after all? This earliest extant Christian document already deals with something like the "delay of the Parousia." The theological problem of the "delay" is, in fact, inherent in the basic Christian confession. Christians confessed that the expected Messiah is Jesus of Nazareth, who has already come. But the Messiah was to come at the end and bring the ultimate kingdom of God; if the Messiah has come, but the world continues as usual, including the death of believers, does this call for a basic rethinking of the time of the Parousia? So long as the generation that had experienced Jesus' life, death, and resurrection was still alive, this was not a critical issue. But the death of some members of the congregation in Thessalonica has made it more urgent. When that generation is gone, eschatology will have to be rethought, and with it the meaning of the church and Christian life (see on 2 Thess 2).

Paul has no further new information to share; the Christian tradition they have already received is entirely adequate (cf. on 2:1). But the tradition needs to be further interpreted. As Paul writes the words of 5:1–11, he is not improvising, inventing the material as he goes, but mostly using traditional material with which his readers are already familiar. His response continues to presuppose the nearness of the Parousia but virtually brushes aside the question of "times and periods," replacing the issue of "When?" with "How?" What counts is the manner of Christ's coming and the character of Christian existence in the meantime. Paul makes his point with three vivid metaphorical images, all derived from Jewish and Christian tradition.

1. *The day of the Lord.* This phrase represents a central feature of the eschatological message of the biblical prophets. "The day of Yahweh" and similar expressions (e.g., "Yahweh has a day," "that day," and "the day when") occur almost 200 times in the prophets, Psalms, and Lamentation. It is explicitly described by such expressions as "the day of Yahweh's wrath" (Job 20:28;

---

65. On the influence of Daniel's imagery and apocalyptic timetable in 1st-cent. Judaism, see Wright 2013, 116–17, 170–71, 282–83, 345–46. The distinction between *chronos* and *kairos* often appears in theological discussion but should not be projected back into biblical usage, nor should it be claimed that the Greek language consistently makes this distinction. This overinterpretation has long since been demolished by Barr (1962).

21:30; Ps 110:5; Isa 13:13; Lam 2:1; Zeph 1:18; 2:2, 3), which means the day when God establishes his justice. The phrase evokes the image of the court-room; the day of the Lord is the day of judgment. Pre-Pauline Christianity adopted the image, and the day of Yahweh became the day of the Lord Jesus.[66] The image became common and could be referred to as the "day of Christ" (Phil 1:10; 2:16) or simply "that day" (e.g., Matt 7:22; 24:36; Luke 10:12; 17:31; 21:34; 2 Tim 1:12, 18; 4:8).

The image of the coming of God's kingdom portrays reuniting. When Paul thinks of the coming of the kingdom of God, he thinks of God reestablishing the divine rule over a rebellious humanity, bringing unity to a divided creation. God-as-king is the one who restores unity, either by purging evil from creation or reconciling evil powers under the rule of the one God (Rom 5:14–21; 14:17; 1 Cor 15:24–25). The image of God-as-judge, on the other hand, is an image of separating, of dividing the good from the bad.[67] The present evil world is a complex mixture of good and evil; human judges are not always able to sort it out. But on the day of the Lord, God-the-judge (or God's representative the Lord Jesus) will make the great division (sheep and goats, wheat and chaff, saved and lost, justified and condemned). In 1 Thessalonians, Paul has earlier used the image of the coming kingdom (2:12), and in the preceding paragraph (4:13–18) the coming of the Lord to establish God's kingdom is portrayed as unifying God's people. The emphasis is on all believers, dead and living, being together with the Lord. In that image, *nothing* is said about unbelievers. But when Paul switches to the image of the day of the Lord, the focus shifts to judgment, separation, the difference between believers and unbelievers, insiders and outsiders. Such binary imagery is inherent in the image of judgment. In the courtroom, there are only two categories. This binary imagery will be continued in the next paragraph, in 5:4–8.

2. *Like a thief in the night.* This image is not found in the Old Testament or later Jewish apocalyptic texts. Christian tradition elsewhere in the New Testament connects the metaphor with sayings of Jesus, whether as an element of the teaching of the historical Jesus, or as a saying of the risen Lord (cf. Luke 12:39//Matt 24:43 [Q]; 2 Pet 3:10; Rev 3:3; 16:15). Paul does not here cite a saying of Jesus, pre- or post-Easter, but reminds the Thessalonians of tradition he has transmitted to them (see on 4:2). Without relaxing his conviction that

---

66. This shift was facilitated by the standard practice of translating the Tetragrammaton YHWH as *kyrios* (Lord), a practice expressed in many English translations by rendering the last three letters of Lord in small capital letters. Early Christian preachers and teachers found many places in their Bible where "the Lord" could be understood as the Lord Jesus.

67. In NT theology in general and in Paul in particular, the imagery of ultimate unity and ultimate division are found side by side, without being mediated. Biblical eschatology requires such conflicting imagery. See above on 3:13; 4:13–18; further in Boring 1986.

the Parousia will come soon, he renounces any attempt to calendarize it. In this regard, two types of apocalyptic views circulated in the early church. Some, represented by Mark 13, expected particular signs to occur just before the end, so that perceptive disciples could locate their own time on the eschatological calendar. Others, represented by the Q apocalypse adopted and adapted in Matt 24 and Luke 17:20–37,[68] expected the end to come suddenly and unexpectedly, with no advance signs. There is no indication that Paul had heard or appropriated the first type, with signs of the impending end. The type of apocalyptic teaching represented by Q—perhaps even Q itself—had circulated in the area of Antioch, and it is quite possible that Paul had heard such teaching and incorporated it into his own eschatology, in which the end would come suddenly and without warning.

3. *Labor pains.* As the thief metaphor underscores the unpredictability of the Parousia, the metaphor of birth pangs emphasizes its inevitability. Both the Old Testament and later apocalyptic tradition use this image for the period of suffering that precedes the messianic age, as the world, or God, writhe in labor in order to bring forth the new creation (cf., in various senses, Isa 26:17–19; 45:10; 54:1–6; 66:7; Jer 22:23; 1QH 11 [olim 3].7–12; 13 [5].30–32; *1 En.* 62.4; *4 Ezra* 4.42; for later rabbinic interpretations, see *b. Ketub.* 111a; *b. Šabb.* 118a; *Exod. Midr.* 4.4).[69] The early church, perhaps on the basis of Jesus' own teaching, adopted the metaphor to portray the time of suffering that precedes the Parousia (Mark 13:8 par.; Rev 12:2). Later Paul himself will apply the image to the cosmic suffering that precedes the eschatological redemption of the whole creation (Rom 8:22). While the image can be used to interpret positively the sufferings of the community by locating them in the eschatological plan of God—they are the labor pains before the birth, and thus the present sufferings are a sign of hope to be endured courageously and joyfully—Paul here focuses on only one point: unbelievers who trust in the powers and values of this world can only look forward to the coming judgment that will come when they least expect it, and it cannot be avoided.

"Peace and security." There was a biblical tradition, especially strong in Jeremiah, that associated the deceptively reassuring proclamation of "'peace, peace' when there is no peace" with false prophets within the Israelite community (Jer 6:14; 8:11; cf. 5:31; 23:14–32, esp. 23:17; also Ezek 13:10; Mic 3:5). Paul was certainly aware of this tradition and particularly influenced by Jeremiah (see on 5:27 below). Thus some interpreters have supposed that insiders, Christian prophets or teachers, give this false reassurance.[70] While charismatic

68. Matthew 24 combines Mark 13 and the Q apocalypse. Luke incorporates the Q apocalypse in Luke 17 and the Mark 13 apocalypse in Luke 21.
69. See further Str-B 4:564, 1042, 1067; Georg Bertram, *"Ōdin," TDNT* 9:672–73.
70. So, e.g., Malherbe 2000, 302.

preachers and teachers were active in Thessalonica (see on 5:16–22), those who speak of "peace" and "security" are the outsiders, with whom Christian believers are contrasted in v. 4 (*hymeis de*, but as for you). As in the Q oracles with which Paul may have been acquainted, the general population will be conducting business as usual when the end comes (Luke 17:26–30 par.).

In recent years the claim has often been made that Paul is here quoting a familiar slogan of Roman imperial propaganda. While there is little evidence that "peace and security" was a specific slogan,[71] it does seem evident that Paul is here reflecting a common mind-set in Thessalonica, which had been spared the ravages of the 42 B.C.E. civil war and in the following decades had benefited greatly from the Roman rulership (see intro, "The City"). Many people in Thessalonica spoke with gratitude of the peace and security brought by the order imposed by Roman rule; Paul himself may have been grateful for a peaceful and ordered city in which to preach.

Paul's message cannot be reduced to anti-Roman polemic, nor his mission to establishing cell groups of resistance to imperialism. There can be no doubt, however, that the gospel he proclaimed had political overtones and represented an alternative view of who is in charge of the world, who provides authentic peace and security.[72] Key words of his message represent a challenge to the assumptions of imperial rule as normative for the good life. (See the discussion of *parousia* and *apantēsis* above; the discussion of *kyrios* and *ekklēsia* throughout; and intro, "Religion in Thessalonica.") That Paul immediately follows with a discussion of the believers' "armor" illustrates that such allusions are rarely univocal and that reductionistic approaches should be avoided.

[4–5] The binary perspective inherent in the image of the coming day of the Lord continues with the imagery of darkness and light. The darkness/light contrast is virtually universal in religious language.[73] Modern readers might well remind themselves that, until early in the twentieth century, virtually all of humanity for most of its history had lived in a world without the instant avail-

---

71. Typical is the statement of Weima (2012, 358): "The predominately Gentile believers in Thessalonica would have immediately recognized in Paul's brief phrase 'Peace and security,' a clear allusion not to the warning of the OT prophets who spoke only about false claims of 'peace' but [to] the sloganeering of the Roman state and its claim of providing for its citizens the same two benefactions highlighted by the apostle," reasserted in his 2014 commentary, 349–51. Joel R. White's article (2013) surveys the debate and provides all essential bibliography. After carefully examining all the evidence cited by Weima and others, he concludes, "While there can be no doubt that 'peace' played an important role in Rome's imperial ideology, it is less clear that this was the case for 'security,' and a review of the evidence presented by the proponents of this view calls into question their conclusion that 'peace and security' had the character of a slogan" (382).

72. For full discussion and a nuanced understanding of the alternative that Paul's gospel provides to the symbolic universe of Roman imperial propaganda, see Harrison 47–70.

73. Cf. Lewis; Hans Conzelmann, "*phōs ktl.*," *TDNT* 9:310–58; "*skotos ktl.*," *TDNT* 7:423–45.

ability of artificial light. The sun was the source of life and light; darkness was deep, dangerous, and all-permeating. It is readily understandable that religious experience would express itself in these terms. This deep-seated religious imagery was already familiar to the Thessalonians, as it was to Paul—not only from his life in the Hellenistic world, but also because his own tradition also makes much religious use of the light/darkness contrast. From God's first words in Gen 1:3, "Let there be light," and the separation of light and darkness in 1:4, this contrast appears throughout the Bible and Jewish tradition (e.g., Job 22:9–11; 29:3; Ps 74:20; Isa 2:5; and of course Hanukkah, the Festival of Lights!). Especially in apocalyptic Judaism, light represents the presence of God and darkness signifies God's absence or judgment (e.g., *T. Levi* 19.1; *T. Naph.* 2.7–10; *T. Benj.* 5.3; 1QS 3.14–4.26). The Qumran sectarians had an entire document devoted to the *War of the Sons of Light and the Sons of Darkness* (1QM, *The War Scroll*).

In adopting this darkness/light terminology, Paul skillfully interweaves it with other binary pairs: day/night, waking/sleeping, sober/drunk, and wrath/salvation. This is done with a deft touch, preserving the general contrast between darkness and light, making contact with the religious imagery already ingrained in the Thessalonians' preconversion religious experience, as well as with the well-known nighttime revelry of Thessalonica, including its religious connotations (see intro, "Religion in Thessalonica"). The most important shift Paul makes is the modulation of general darkness/light imagery into the specific night/day paradigm of the day of the Lord; while "sons of light" was fairly common, "sons of the day" is unique to Paul.[74] Thus in v. 5 he specifies that to belong to the light is to belong to the day; Christian believers are not only light-people as opposed to darkness-people; they are also day-people as opposed to night-people. This is not merely a stylistic or terminological shift. Traditional pagan religion had used darkness/light in the sense of two contrasting static realms of being. Without rejecting this, Paul nudges the imagery from the spatial to the temporal. His inherited Jewish apocalyptic worldview, now rethought on the basis of the Christ event, pictures the world as underway from darkness to light. The move is from being to time, from spatial to temporal imagery, from ontology to history. The "day" to which Christians belong is not only the static-ontological realm of light, but also the temporally future day of the Lord.

The complex interplay of imagery expresses the dialectic of Paul's (and early Christianity's) dialectic of already/not yet. Paul thinks in terms of the two ages, the present age and the age to come, but these overlap. They are not merely chronological, but both synchronic and diachronic (see 1 Cor 10:11 and recent commentaries thereon). To be sure, the present age is the age of darkness,

74. Cf. Camille Focant.

dominated by Satan, but the true light is already dawning, not only in the hearts of believers (2 Cor 4:1–6), but also for the world as a whole. Paul is reminding his readers of what he taught when he was present with them. Later, however, in a letter to a church where he had not taught personally, he makes explicit the reality of God's future already impinging on the present (Rom 13:11–14). It is instructive for modern readers to see this for themselves, by comparing the two texts (NRSV, indicating in bold font identical and similar vocabulary in the Greek text):

1 Thess 5:4–10

4 But you, beloved, are not in **darkness**, for that **day** to surprise you like a thief; 5 for you are all children of **light** and children of the **day**; we are not of the **night** or of **darkness**. 6 So then **let us** not **fall asleep** as others do, but **let us** keep awake and be sober; 7 for those who sleep sleep **at night**, and **those who are drunk get drunk at night**. 8 But since we belong to **the day**, **let us** be sober, and **put on** the **breastplate** of faith and love, and for a **helmet** the hope of **salvation**. 9 For God has destined us not for wrath but for obtaining **salvation** through our Lord Jesus Christ, 10 who died for us, so that whether **we are** awake or **asleep** we may live with him.

Rom 13:11–14

11 Besides this, you know what time it is, how it is now the moment for you to wake from **sleep**. For **salvation** is nearer to us now than when we became believers; 12 **the night** is far gone, **the day** is near. **Let us then** lay aside the works of **darkness** and put on **the armor** of **light**; 13 let us live honorably as in **the day**, not in reveling and **drunkenness**, not in debauchery and licentiousness, not in quarreling and jealousy. 14 Instead, **put on** the Lord Jesus Christ, and make no provision for the flesh, to gratify its desires.

For Paul, believers in the Christ event do not merely try to orient themselves by the light already present within and around them in the darkness of the present world. This light, though real, is only the first glimmer of the true light to come. When he says they belong to the day, he pictures them as already anchored in the future day of the Lord, which to all people will vindicate and make manifest the resurrection reality of the new creation that is now dawning. They still live in the nighttime of the dark world, but they know what time it is. By being baptized into Christ, believers already belong to the resurrection that has begun in him and will be completed on the day of the Lord. They are already incorporated into the continuing act of God, looking back to the resurrection of Jesus and forward to the day of the Lord. This was very real both to them and to Paul, for—in contrast to later generations such as our own—when they spoke of the resurrection and the day of the Lord, they looked neither to the distant past for the resurrection nor to the remote future for the day of the Lord.

[6–7] The indicative implies and includes an imperative, but it is not a static, ontological "Be what you are." To be "sons of the day," to belong to the coming day of the Lord, means to lean into the real-but-not-yet future into which their lives are already incorporated, during that between-the-times eschatological existence, between the eschatological king's appointment and his inauguration. Paul thus exhorts them (and himself, shifting to "we" in vv. 5b–10) to avoid being asleep, blissfully unaware of the world-and-life-changing Christ event, as though it were still midnight instead of daybreak. Believers need to be alert and sober, not muddled and drunk, clearheadedly recognizing the dawn, and shape their lives in the light of the new day. Although Paul opposed drunkenness, he is not giving a list of specific vices to avoid.[75] Both sleeping and drunkenness are here metaphors for the lives of those who do not recognize the new location they have been given in Christ. Perceiving what time it is on God's clock calls for a renewed life. Later generations would find appropriate ways to live authentically within the Pauline time frame set by the resurrection and the Parousia, even after the expectation of the near Parousia was recognized as a chronological error. In the two generations after Paul, the Pauline school itself first explored the limited number of options for doing this with integrity (see on 2 Thess 2).

[8] Living such a life involves conflict and struggle, but believers are not on their own. They are already clad in the armor provided by God (they are not urged to put on this armor; see trans. note i above). In contrast to Qumran, such armor is not gearing up for participation in the final eschatological battle, for this battle is already won, and believers have been armor-clad by its results from the time of their conversion. They belong to a community in which God's Spirit is active (1:5–6; 4:8), a community with the resources of faith, love, and hope, on which they can draw (see on 1:3). The imagery of armor would easily come to mind in Thessalonica, where there were Roman breastplates and helmets aplenty. The helmeted goddess Roma was a familiar image on coins stamped in Thessalonica. Paul's metaphor not only conjures up the believer's alternative to Roman power—faith, hope, and love belong to the new age, not to the age of darkness that is passing away, and with it the Roman power—but also is an aspect of Paul's stock of images that portray the Christian life in terms of belonging to God's army (2 Cor 6:7; 10:3–5; Phil 2:25; Phlm 2; Rom 13:12). The specific combination of breastplate and helmet is clearly drawn from Paul's

---

75. Paul's reference to drunkenness may have been triggered by the excesses of the Dionysiac cult, which were well known in Thessalonica. Cf. Vom Brocke 128–29.

Bible (Isa 59:17), as seen from the way Paul must force his threefold faith/love/ hope into the twofold pattern. It was more important to him to maintain the key dynamics and content of his threefold summary of Christian existence than to have a neat metaphorical fit.

Three other changes in Paul's adaptation of the Isaiah imagery reveal aspects of his theology. (1) In that Old Testament prophetic book, the armor is God's armor, the armor that Yahweh dons as he goes forth to engage in the eschatological battle on behalf of his people. Even though the phrase "day of the LORD" is not found in this Isaiah text, it is this day that is described, the day of Yahweh's wrath, when God will establish justice (cf. the whole context of Isa 59:1–21, which has influenced Paul here and elsewhere). As Paul has begun this letter by addressing its readers as those "in God," so here they are addressed as those who have been clad in God's own armor. (2) The context in Isa 59 has nine references to *justice* (*mišpāṭ*) or *righteousness* (*ṣĕdāqâ*), key words in Paul's theology. The verse to which he alludes identifies the breastplate with God's own righteousness, as does the immediately preceding verse. The *righteousness of God*, as opposed to human efforts to attain one's own righteousness, is a key term in what Paul will later explicate as (what has come to be called) his doctrine of "justification by faith." This vocabulary occurs 93 times in Paul's later letters, chiefly in Galatians (13×) and Romans (64×). Yet this terminology does not occur at all in 1 Thessalonians, and in Paul's allusion to a biblical text in which it does appear, he replaces "God's righteousness" with "faith" as the believer's breastplate. Although interpreters should not claim that the "early" Paul had not yet thought about these issues, this topic was not yet in sharp focus or permeating his theology as it would in the controversies reflected in the later letters. (3) In Isa 59:17, the helmet is "salvation"; Paul makes this the "*hope* of salvation." First Thessalonians is a concentrated treatment of the Christian hope (see on 1:3, 9–10; 2:19; 4:13). "Paul's overall descriptive term for the final victory of God in the coming age, when the last enemy shall have been destroyed and God shall reign as the unchallenged Sovereign above all, is *salvation*"[76]—here cast in imagery conveying confident expectation.

[9–10] Paul now makes clear the basis for the preceding exhortations: the twofold act of God in electing believers for salvation (see on 1:2–4, 9b–10; 2:12; 4:7; 5:24), actualized "through our Lord Jesus Christ, who died for us." The imperatives of human responsibility are based solidly on the indicative of God's act. The saving act is theocentric: not "God and Jesus," but "God through Jesus." Virtually all interpreters recognize that Paul is citing part of a creedal formula. That Christ "died for us" is introduced without elaboration,

76. Furnish 2009b, 122.

as a fundamental affirmation with which the new converts are familiar. Jesus' death was God's act for our salvation, but Paul says not a word about how Jesus' death was "for us." In later letters, he will be more expansive, using a variety of images and metaphors, some from earlier Christian tradition, some his own formulation (e.g., Rom 3:21–26; 5:6–8; 8:33–34; 14:15; 1 Cor 15:3–5; 2 Cor 5:14–21; Gal 3:13).

As Paul brings this section to a close, he deftly mentions the "waking and sleeping" imagery again, but this time in the sense of 4:13, thus forming an appropriate frame for the unit and setting it in relation to the Thessalonians' original question that has triggered the discussion. The "waking and sleeping" are no longer the insiders and outsiders, believers and unbelievers, of 5:6, but Christians who remain alive at the Parousia and those who have died. This brings closure, with the assurance that we (believers) will all be together, and all will be with the Lord. Paul has kept their question in his mind's eye the whole time.

[11] These words duplicate 4:18, fusing the disparate elements of 4:13–5:11 into a unity addressed to the Thessalonians' question and its wider implications. *Edification*, "building up," is a key theme of Jeremiah (see the LXX of 1:10; 12:16; 24:6; 37:18 [30:18 ET]; 38:28 [31:28]; 40:7 [33:7]; 49:10 [42:10]). In this letter Paul provides material and means for building up the community, central to his own prophetic mission in continuity with Jeremiah. He expects the letter to be read (repeatedly) to the gathered congregation. But the edification he calls for is not just from apostle to congregation; all the members of the community are also equipped with the Spirit; all can and should encourage and edify one another, as they are indeed already doing. Though there are offices of a sort—positions of leadership—in the new congregation, edification is not allocated to an office but is the responsibility of each member. With these words, Paul turns to a new topic, addressing the life of the congregation and its leadership.

5:12–22 Life Together in the Spirit-led Community

Here as elsewhere, form and meaning are integrally related. Two extreme views are to be avoided: (1) Paraenetic sections are entirely general and only loosely structured if at all. (2) Each item of paraenetic material reflects some corresponding element in the church to which the letter is addressed, which can be identified by mirror reading.

The nature of some of the material in 5:12–22 does suggest that it was not formulated by Paul just for this occasion, but is common Christian paraenesis that could appropriately be recycled. This impression seems to be confirmed by the parallels (indicated in bold font below) in the paraenetic section of a letter written several years later, Rom 12:9–21:

Rom 12:9–18 NRSV

9 **Hate what is evil, hold fast to what is good**; 10 love one another with mutual affection; outdo one another in showing honor. 11 Do not lag in zeal, **be ardent in spirit**, serve the Lord. 12 **Rejoice in hope, be patient** in suffering, **persevere in prayer.** 13 Contribute to the needs of the saints; extend hospitality to strangers.

14 Bless those who persecute you; bless and do not curse them. 15 Rejoice with those who rejoice, weep with those who weep. 16 Live in harmony with one another; do not be haughty, but associate with the lowly; do not claim to be wiser than you are. 17 **Do not repay anyone evil for evil, but take thought for what is noble in the sight of all.** 18 If it is possible, so far as it depends on you, live **peaceably** with all.

1 Thess 5:13–22 NRSV

13 Be at **peace** among yourselves. 14 And we urge you, beloved, to admonish the idlers, encourage the fainthearted, help the weak, **be patient** with all of them. 15 **See that none of you repays evil for evil, but always seek to do good to one another and to all.** 16 **Rejoice always,** 17 **pray without ceasing,** 18 give thanks in all circumstances; for this is the will of God in Christ Jesus for you. 19 **Do not quench the Spirit.** 20 Do not despise the words of prophets, 21 but test everything; **hold fast to what is good; 22 abstain from every form of evil.**

The similarities and points of contact cannot be missed, but the differences in wording and distinctive elements of each passage should also be noticed, including the reversal of order:

	1 Thessalonians	**Romans**
Be at peace.	5:13b	12:18
Do not repay evil.	5:15	12:17a
Rejoice.	5:16	12:12a
Pray without ceasing.	5:17	12:12c
Free the Spirit.	5:19	12:11b
Hold fast to the good.	5:21b–22	12:9b

Such phenomena are best accounted for neither by free composition in each case, nor by literary dependence, as though Paul has 1 Thessalonians before him as he writes Romans, but by a free adaptation of traditional material.

The overarching theme of 1 Thess 5:12–22 is the work of the Spirit in the life of the church, in particular how the work of particular persons in leadership roles is related to the spontaneous guidance of the Spirit in the congregation as a whole. In the preceding section, Paul has been responding to eschatological concerns of the community. This is directly related to their experience and understanding of the Holy Spirit, for the Spirit is an eschatological reality. Since the Messiah has come and since the resurrection has begun, then Christian believers are living through the eschaton-in-progress, and the eschatological Spirit is powerfully at work among them. What is the relationship of this potent dynamic of the Holy Spirit in their midst to the leaders and teachers who are assuming the pastoral care of the community?

With this issue in mind, Paul seems to have shaped some elements of traditional paraenesis to fit, and he has added new directives. Verses 12–14 belong together as two complementary sentences dealing with congregational leadership, instruction, and pastoral care. Verse 15 is a transitional appeal to seek the good of the whole congregation, in view of the church's wider mission to all people. Verses 16–22 are exhortations and directions about the work of the Spirit in the congregation—especially how to respond to prophetic speech.

5:12 We ask[a] you, brothers and sisters, to acknowledge[b] those who are laboring[c] among you, who are leading[d] you[e] in the Lord and instructing[f] you,[e] **13** and to hold them in the highest esteem because of their work. Be at peace among yourselves.[g] **14** At the same time,[h] brothers and sisters, we appeal to[a] you: instruct[f] the disorderly,[i] encourage the disheartened, show solidarity with[j] the weak, be patient with everyone.

15 See to it that no one repays anyone wrong for wrong, but always strive for what is best for each other and for everyone.

16 Rejoice always. **17** Pray without ceasing. **18** Give thanks in every situation, for this is the will of God in Jesus Christ for you. **19** Do not quench the Spirit. **20** Do not treat prophetic messages with disdain, **21** but[k] test everything; hold fast to what is good, **22** but keep your distance from every worthless form[l] [of purported prophecy].

a. *Erōtaō* is a general word for asking a question. In classical Greek, it was distinguished from *aiteō*, to ask for a favor, to request, but in Hellenistic times this differentiation had long since disappeared. Paul uses the word sparingly and as a synonym for the more muscular *parakaleō* (only here, 4:1, and Phil 4:3; see on 2:3). In the precisely parallel structure in 5:14, he uses *parakaleō*.

b. *Eidenai* is the infinitive of the common verb *oida*, and normally means simply "know" (13× in 1 Thessalonians, often with the connotation of reminding them what they were taught during the founding visit, as in 1:4, 5; 2:1, 2, 5, 11; 3:3, 4; 4:2; 5:2). The congregation in Thessalonica was very small; "know" cannot mean "get acquainted with" your congregational leaders, but means *ac*knowledge them: accept them as your actual leaders.

c. *Kopiōntas* is an ordinary word for "work, labor," but became a semitechnical term for "church workers" in early Christianity and esp. in Paul (cf. Luke 5:5; John 4:38; Acts 20:35; Rom 16:6, 12; 1 Cor 15:10; 16:16; Gal 4:11; Phil 2:16).

d. *Proïstamenous* (leaders) is the plural participle of the verb *proïstēmi*, a combination of the preposition *pro* (before) and *histēmi* (stand), thus, lit., "those who stand before" others. In the Hellenistic period, the word had two basic meanings: (1) to exercise a position of leadership, i.e., to rule, direct, to be in charge; and (2) to have an interest in, show concern for, care for, help (see BDAG 870). In the LXX, Paul's Bible, the word occurs 8×, when used of human beings always with the meaning "to be in charge of" and related senses (e.g., 2 Sam 13:17, "in charge of the house"; 1 Macc 5:19, "take charge of this people"; 4 Macc 11:27, "set over"; Dan 14 [= Bel]:8, "leaders" of the temple). So also in later Christian tradition, the word is used of the *presbyteroi* (elders) who are in charge of the Roman church (Hermas *Vis.* 2.4.3). The Pastorals likewise use the word 6×, always for church officers (1 Tim 3:4, 5, 12; 5:17; Titus 3:8, 14). Paul himself uses the word only here and in Rom 12:8, where it occurs, not as the designation of an office but, as here, in a list of the Spirit's functions in the life of the congregation. The majority of English translations favor the first meaning (e.g., NRSV, "have charge of you"; NABRE, "those . . . who are over you"), though a few favor the second meaning (e.g., TNIV and NIV11, "who care for you" [reversing the NIV's "who are over you"]). The translation above takes a mediating position (so also, e.g., REB, NJB, CEV, CEB).

e. The *hymōn* (you) following the participles of the transitive verbs "leading" and "instructing" is not the possessive ("your leaders," "your instructors"), but the direct object, "those who lead and instruct you," as is clear from the LXX usage.

f. *Nouthetountas* is the plural participle of the verb *noutheteō*, derived from *nous* (mind, understanding) + *tithēmi* (put, set, arrange, etc.), thus etymologically = "to arrange (straighten out) someone's thinking." In Hellenistic times the word comes to mean simply "instruct," though often with the overtone of warning or censuring. The word is not frequent or particularly theologically significant in the LXX (13×), where it means both "instruct" (e.g., Job 4:3) and "admonish, warn" (e.g., 1 Sam 3:13). All eight occurrences of the word in the NT are in the Pauline tradition: 4× in the undisputed letters (Rom 15:14; 1 Cor 4:14; 1 Thess 5:12, 14), 4× in later writings associated with Paul (Acts 20:31; Col 1:28; 3:16; 2 Thess 3:15), and always with the meaning "instruct," sometimes with the mild overtone "admonish." Since there are several stronger words for "warn" that Paul could have used (*apeileō, diamartyromai, enkeimai, embrimaomai,* and esp. *epitimaō*), the choice of *noutheteō* suggests a kind of firm instruction, with no connotation of a serious problem. Paul uses the same word in vv. 12 and 14; instruction and encouraging admonition is the responsibility of both leaders and congregation (cf. Rom 15:14).

g. The MS tradition has relatively strong support for the reading *autois* ("with them," i.e., the leaders; so 𝔓³⁰ ℵ D* F G P Ψ 81 104 1505 1881* 2464 and the Old Latin versions), rather than *heautois* ("with one another" = among yourselves, as translated above). Contextual reasons, however, as well as substantial MSS support, point to *heautois* as original: there is little evidence of Paul addressing one group and asking them to be at peace with the other. Paul is not taking sides in a presumed conflict, but addressing the exhortation to the whole congregation.

h. The conjunction *de* introducing v. 14, parallel to the *de* introducing v. 12, is best taken as "a marker with an additive relation, with possible suggestion of contrast, *at the same time*" (so BDAG 213, giving Titus 1:1 as an example).

i. *Ataktos* does not mean "idle." The adjective *ataktos* is derived from the common verb *tassō*, "to bring about an order in things, to arrange," with the prefixed negating alpha privative (= in/un/dis-). The basic meaning is thus "without order, disorderly," which is the only meaning given in BDAG 148; cf. 991, with examples of Hellenistic usage in this sense. The word is found only once in the LXX, 3 Macc 1:19, where it means "disorderly," used of young women who rushed to see a public spectacle without taking time to dress appropriately. There are no examples from Hellenistic Greek authors in which the word means "idle," "loafer," "those who do not work," though there are questionable instances in the papyri that may be so interpreted.[77] *Ataktos* is found only here in the NT, though cf. the related verb *atakteō* (2 Thess 3:7) and adverb *ataktōs* (2 Thess 3:6, 11), where the term is related to those who do not work (see comments there). From the time of Frame's classic 1912 commentary, some commentators adopted the meaning "idle" for 1 Thess 5:14, a translation adopted by the versions MOFFATT in 1922 and GOODSPEED in 1923.[78] Both E. J. Goodspeed and James Moffatt were on the RSV translation committee that in 1946 introduced "idlers" into the mainstream of English renderings of this text, which has been followed by numerous English versions (NRSV, REB, NIV, TNIV, NIV11, TEV, ESV; cf. *The Message*'s typically cute but misleading "warn the freeloaders to get a move on").

j. The Greek language has at least a dozen words that mean "help" in some sense. Paul's word here, *antechō*, means basically "to have a strong attachment to or interest in someone, to cling to, hold fast to, be devoted to" (BDAG 87), i.e., to be in solidarity with. While it includes concrete acts of help in the present context, it is without the slightest trace of condescension.

k. The connecting *de* (but) is omitted in ℵ* A 33 81 and a few other MSS, but present in B and the vast majority of later MSS. Its omission is more readily explained than its addition. It is virtually certain to be original; the variant reading is not even mentioned in UBS⁴. The conjunction shows that vv. 21–22 are not generalizing moralisms, but connected to the preceding: they continue and conclude the instruction about the evaluation of prophetic speech in the congregation.

l. English versions have almost always rendered *apo pantos eidous ponērou* as "from every form of evil," i.e., from evil of every form. This was probably the intended meaning in the traditional maxim Paul is paraphrasing. However, if both words were in the nominative, dative, or accusative, the noun *eidos* followed by the adjective *ponēros* would be translated "evil form." But the preposition *apo* requires that all three of the following words be in the genitive, which creates an ambiguity as to how *ponērou* (evil) is related to *eidous* (form). The phrase can legitimately be translated "form of evil" (i.e., evil in any form), understanding "evil" to be the object of the preposition, or "evil form," understanding "form" to be the object of the preposition. In the latter case, the reader is warned to avoid any form (or prophetic speech) that is evil or worthless. Diagramming

77. See the excursus "On *atakteō* and Its Cognates" in Milligan 152–54.
78. Frame 196–97; see 1 Thess 5:14 in MOFFATT and in GOODSPEED.

the sentence makes these options clear. The parallel construction in 2 Tim 4:18, *pantos ergou ponērou*, "every evil action" rather than "every action of evil," shows that "from every evil form" is a perfectly legitimate translation. In the present context, this construal is to be preferred: Paul is not making general comments about good and evil, but calls for evaluating prophetic utterances. In regard to prophecy, "authentic" and "worthless" are the appropriate terms (see comments on vv. 21–22). On this verse Calvin already points out the two grammatical options, argues for the one taken here, and says it was preferred by Chrysostom and Ambrose.[79]

[12–14] Several considerations argue for vv. 12–14 as a unit revolving around a single theme, the relations of leaders and the congregation as a whole in the ordering of community life. The Greek text of vv. 12 and 14 begin with exactly the same structure, as can be seen in the literal translation:

Erōtōmen de hymas, adelphoi   But we ask you, brothers and sisters
Parakaloumen de hymas, adelphoi   But we appeal to you, brothers and sisters

The renewed address "brothers and sisters" at v. 14 does not necessarily mean the introduction of a new topic. There are several instances in the Pauline corpus where repetition of the address *adelphoi* in the immediate context does not signal a change of subject but introduces the complementary half of the preceding instruction (e.g., 1 Cor 1:10/11; see also 1 Cor 1:26/2:1; 14:20/26; 15:1/31/50/58, all on the same persistently pursued subject; Gal 4:28/31; indeed, Paul has already used this form in 1 Thess 2:1/9). Furthermore, in 4:1, as Paul begins the paraenetic section of the book, he combines the two verbs *erōtōmen* (ask) and *parakaloumen* (appeal), using them virtually as synonyms. Here he uses them singly, to introduce each half of the unit. Moreover, the content of vv. 12–14 has *no* parallels in Rom 12 (except the common word "peace"), while vv. 15–22 are replete with such points of contact. This suggests that 5:12–14 is less dependent on traditional material, more of a Pauline compositional unit. This, in turn, means that the references to "your leaders" in v. 12 and to "the disorderly" in v. 14 are part of the same train of thought and are to be interpreted in relation to each other.

In v. 12 Paul now turns to his readers with a serious request, not a demand or command. He has apparently learned from Timothy (see on 3:1–10) that within the new and growing congregation there is a relatively minor tension regarding leadership. If there has been a serious problem with troublemakers or "opponents," Paul would hardly have spoken in such glowing terms of the congregation throughout the letter (1:3–10; 2:13–14, 19; 3:6–10; 4:1, 9; 5:11). With the familial address "brothers and sisters," he addresses the new community as a whole. All is addressed to the whole congregation; it is not a matter of

79. Calvin 1960a, 376–77.

the regional manager directing local managers to shape things up in their bailiwick. The paragraph will deal with leaders and followers, order and disorder, eventually with "charisma" and "office," with what may be the beginnings of a rift between "charismatic" and "official-traditional" leaders, but Paul does not address some instructions to leaders and some to followers. All are brothers and sisters, but this does not exclude a certain hierarchy. In the Hellenistic family, older brothers are privileged, and in the Christian community of brothers and sisters, some are *leading* brothers (cf. Acts 15:22).[80] Paul calls for the whole congregation to acknowledge their existing leadership. Who are these leaders?

Paul describes them with three active participles (see trans. notes c, d, and f); they are verbal forms that refer to activity and function, not designations of offices. All three are part of one phrase introduced by one definite article, indicating that Paul is referring to one group with three functions, not three different groups. The first designation, "laborers," used for Paul's coworkers in establishing and nurturing churches, is made more specific by referring to their work as "leading" and "teaching." Paul seems to be soft-pedaling the aspect of directive leadership. He does not begin with *proïstamenous*, the most official-sounding word, and qualifies only it with the double-edged "in the Lord": those who have responsible leadership do so only as participating in the reality shared by all believers who are "in Christ" (2:14; 4:16; 5:18), yet they are also not merely operating as leaders on the basis of their own authority. Like Paul and the founding missionaries, the authority of the Lord stands behind their work. As Paul urges that these leaders be acknowledged, he apparently has his eye on the more charismatic types of whom he will speak shortly.

We do not know just what leadership looked like in the early Pauline churches or to what extent it varied in nomenclature and function from congregation to congregation. Yet in regard to the new congregation in Thessalonica, we can be sure of three things: (1) There are no "offices" that go by a generally accepted name; otherwise Paul would have used these terms. If Paul greeted the leaders of the church in Philippi as *episkopoi* and *diakonoi*, he was not talking about bishops and deacons in the later ecclesiastical sense, but using the words in their ordinary meaning of "overseers" and "helpers" (see NRSV mg.).[81] In the next generation the author of Acts will picture Paul as appointing elders in

80. This point is elaborated and documented by Burke 97–127, 230–44, 256, against, e.g., Schüssler Fiorenza (1983, 279), who argues that the original Christian communities were absolutely egalitarian, and that the beginnings of a patriarchal understanding of church leadership began in the later Pastorals. In 1 Thessalonians the situation is more complex: Paul as apostle is father, mother, brother, baby, orphan, and nurse, and there are some *adelphoi* who must command the respect and obedience of others.

81. It may be that Philippians is an editorial combination of more than one letter and that 1:1 is from the editor, who updated the greeting to correspond to the terminology for church leadership of his own later generation. So, e.g., Keck 1979, 17.

every church (Acts 14:23), but the undisputed Letters of Paul never mention them—though if they had existed he could have sorely used their help in his dispute with the Corinthians. Although the function of teaching and instructing the congregation in the tradition was certainly present in the Thessalonian church, neither the verb "teach" nor the noun "teacher" occurs in 1 Thessalonians. (2) Every Pauline congregation had some sort of leadership, or it could not have continued to exist. Paul saw the life of the new congregations as led by the Spirit, given to each member and active in the congregation as a whole. The Spirit energized different people with different gifts, which were expressed spontaneously in the worship, fellowship, and mission of the church, but there was also a concern for structure and order (1 Cor 12–14). (3) In the Pauline churches there was no ordination or commissioning, no distinction between "clergy" and "laity." Although Paul seems not to have formally "appointed" pastors and teachers to direct and instruct the congregations in his absence, he apparently did train a core of teachers and leaders to carry on the work he and his colleagues had begun (see intro, "Church-Founding Visit" and "New Congregation"). We do not know how he selected such local "workers"; in the new congregation, most likely some "natural leaders" emerged who seemed to have competence in teaching, administrative authority, and pastoral care. It is likely that these were often the patron-hosts of the church, in whose houses the congregations met. The story of Jason in Acts 17:5–9, whether or not it is factual in all details, suggests such a pattern for the emergence of local congregational leaders. It must, however, have been at Paul's invitation and encouragement that such people were trained by him so that they could continue to lead and instruct the church in his absence.

Paul would surely have seen the Holy Spirit at work in this process (cf. 1 Cor 12). He did not arbitrarily appoint people to an office, but "acknowledged" their gifts of leadership. Paul encourages the Thessalonian congregation to do the same, to continue to acknowledge these "established" (after a few months of Christian experience!) leaders, and to hold them in the highest esteem because of their work—not because of their "office."

"Be at peace among yourselves" is, in this context, not a general platitude. As Paul will later, in the name of the "God of peace," appeal for order in a more stressful situation generated by charismatic phenomena (1 Cor 14:33), so here he invokes the God of peace to sanctify the community as a whole. He does not instruct one "side" of the "conflict" to be at peace with the other (see trans. note g; on "peace," see 1:1). As in the liturgy of passing of the peace on Sunday morning in many twenty-first-century churches, the Thessalonian congregation is called to actualize among themselves the saving peace of God that has happened, that has become a reality in the Christ event, and to conduct their discussions about congregational leadership and exercise their ministry of pastoral care within the framework of the saving history of God.

The next sentence (v. 14) likewise addresses the whole congregation, urging that, with patience and forbearance, they admonish the *ataktoi* (disorderly). Who are these? Though understood in some recent scholarship and several English versions as referring to recalcitrant members of the congregation with an unwillingness to work induced by expectation of the near Parousia, there is little or nothing in the text of 1 Thessalonians to support this interpretation, which is dependent on a particular understanding of 2 Thessalonians and the centuries-later experiences of the church with millenarian enthusiasts.[82] The only point of contact in 1 Thessalonians for this view is 4:11, which offers little support (see comments there and trans. note i for 5:14). Paul's strong affirmation of the power of the Spirit in the life of the church includes a concern for order. This is clear from his "ranking" of spiritual gifts in 1 Cor 12:27–31 and his directions for the orderly expression of tongues and prophecies during worship in 1 Cor 14:1–19, concluding with "all things should be done decently and in order" (14:40 NRSV). While there may have been other dimensions to the disorderliness Paul calls on the community to address, the most probable view is that those who emphasized the spontaneity of the Spirit were failing to acknowledge the leadership of the less obviously "charismatic" established leaders charged with nurturing the church in the traditional faith delivered to them by the founding missionaries.

The pastoral care with which the community and its leaders are charged is not only admonition for the disorderly, but also encouragement for the disheartened and help for the weak. The exhortation seems to be directed generally, rather than aimed at three specific groups. The disheartened may be feeling the effects of the unexpected deaths within the community, or problems with their relatives, neighbors, employers, or (if they were slaves) their masters, problems generated by their new faith. The "weak" likewise does not seem to refer to a group with a specific profile, as later detailed by Paul when addressing a different situation in the Roman church (Rom 14:1–15:13). In Thessalonica, the weak are members of the community who are struggling with physical or other weakness, who know that they need help, and who can receive it within the new family to which they belong.

---

82. Though the thorough commentary of Rigaux argues for Pauline authorship of 2 Thessalonians, he rightly rejects using the *ataktoi* of 2 Thessalonians as the key to interpreting 1 Thessalonians, since 2 Thessalonians is dealing with a different problem (583). This point is even more important if Paul did not write 2 Thessalonians. So far as I have been able to determine, the connection between the "idle" in Thessalonica and overenthusiastic eschatology was first made by Johann Albrecht Bengel in his 1742 commentary on 2 Thess 3:6: "The Thessalonians . . . seem to have ceased working because of the nearness of the day of Christ," misunderstanding *ataktoi* as "idle" and positing a connection with their eschatology without any basis in the text of either 1 or 2 Thessalonians (*Gnomon,* 2:501).

"Be patient with everyone" is a call for all the acknowledging, laboring, leading, instructing, admonishing, encouraging, and helping to be done in love. The first expression of Christian love mentioned in the hymn of 1 Cor 13—a traditional piece that Paul perhaps already knows when sending 1 Thessalonians—is patience, just as patience is prominent among the "fruits of the Spirit" in Gal 5:22. The biblical understanding of patience to which Paul appeals attributes it to God, who is merciful and compassionate (cf. famously Exod 34:6). The patience for which Paul calls is not a bland "tolerance" that tends toward live-and-let-live indifference, but the patience inherent in the dynamic of *agapē* that facilitates *koinōnia*, especially in a community with budding tensions about congregational leaders.

[15] In this context, the injunction to strive for the good of everyone forms a transition from the preceding exhortation, continuing the series of plural imperatives, but also with the individualizing *tis . . . tini* that concludes with the corporate *pantas* (no one . . . anyone . . . everyone). This dictum, a form of the Golden Rule generally known in various streams of pagan, Jewish, and Christian tradition, is not cited as a teaching of Jesus (see on 4:2). The whole community is summoned to guard against (*orate = see* to it, *watch out* for) individualistic quid pro quo behavior that disrupts community and forces people to take sides. "What is best" is not the Platonic ideal, not a pleasant friendliness, but actions for the concrete good of others, especially in the community. As in 3:12, the love manifest in such behavior is to extend beyond the new little congregational family and be manifest to outsiders, to all. Though the new converts have now experienced the love of God within the community in a special way as they come to understand their new situation in the history of salvation, this same realization necessarily leads them to see their non-Christian neighbors, even their enemies and persecutors, as also embraced in the love of God, as already/not-yet brothers and sisters, and they cannot do otherwise than share this love with them.[83]

[16–18] To a congregation grieving over the death of some of its members and coming to terms with internal tensions, the call for constant joy, prayer, and thanksgiving regardless of the situation is in sharp contrast to the philosophical *ataraxia* (ataraxy), the cool resignation with which the Stoic instructed people to respond to tragedy (see, e.g., the *Discourses* of Epictetus and the *Meditations* of Marcus Aurelius for the serenity of surrendering to irresistible nature, of which death was simply a part). Joy, prayer, and thanksgiving are all manifestations of the presence of the Spirit in the congregation and its individual

---

83. Cf. Barth (1958, 802–9), who finally affirms Paul's statement here (805), while insisting that it cannot be stated as a bland universal love for all people in general, but must always be manifest in concrete acts to the particular neighbor, though not necessarily in the geographical or temporal proximity.

members (Rom 8:26; 14:17; 1 Cor 14:6; Gal 5:22; 1 Thess 1:6; cf. Sir 39:6; Luke 10:21). That such a life is the will of God is the only specific theological grounding of Paul's exhortation in the whole pericope, but all his instruction presupposes the symbolic universe that locates lived experience in the next-to-last act of the unfolding divine drama, between resurrection and Parousia. Such a framework gives bite to what might otherwise sound like the injunctions of conventional piety.

[19–22] The relation of inspiration by the Spirit to established leadership has been the undercurrent of this whole section (vv. 12–22). What has been mostly implicit now emerges in plain view, as Paul turns to give specific instructions on manifestations of the Spirit in the life of the congregation and how they should be evaluated. Paul assumes that the Spirit is present in the life of the whole congregation, that every believer participates in the life of the Spirit (1:5–6; 4:8). Although every Christian has received the Spirit, there are also special manifestations of the Spirit not experienced by every believer personally, but all still participate in the one congregation in which these grace-gifts (*charismata*, graces, results-of-grace) are present. As Paul will point out in later letters, the *charismata* are for the benefit of all, not just the individual (1 Cor 12–14; Rom 12:1–8).

The Thessalonians were familiar with spiritual phenomena prior to their conversion. Glossolalia, oracles, and prophecies were well known in Greco-Roman religion. Wherever people are intentionally religious, there will be some, typically a small minority, who believe they are in direct communication with the deity, and they may speak, not on the basis of common sense, authoritative texts, tradition, or their own experience, but with the direct authority of divine revelation.[84] When the Thessalonians were converted, they brought with them into the church their previous attitudes about such phenomena, and some brought their previous spiritual experiences. They are now learning to rethink all this in the light of their new faith. Paul speaks out of his own view, which was not only influenced by his Hellenistic environment, but also primarily shaped by the understanding of prophecy in his Bible and by his earlier experience of prophecy in the church. He understands himself to be in the line of biblical prophets (see on 5:27) and evaluates the tensions in Thessalonica from that perspective.

The staccato commands of vv. 19–22 are triggered by the phenomenon of charismatic speech that breaks out out in the worship service. We have no description of what transpired at a gathering of the new congregation in Thessalonica (for Corinth, see the more informative 1 Cor 14:26–33). With regard to preaching and teaching, we will not be far off target if we allow our informed imagination to picture two types of leadership, overlapping and in moderate

84. See Aune 1983, 23–80; Boring 1991, 48–57; Forbes 103–217; Nasrallah 2003.

tension. On the one hand, there will be the teachers of the Pauline tradition, informally trained and authorized by him. On the other hand, there will be prophetic figures who speak directly in the name of the risen Lord, who differ in both style and content from the designated leaders. The former group will be tempted to disdain the latter and to restrain what they see as intrusive behavior and to neutralize the effect of their purported revelations. The latter group will understand themselves to be directly inspired to speak in behalf of the Lord, whose presence is experienced as real.

It never occurs to Paul to suggest that they form two separate congregations, with "traditionalists" in one house church and "charismatics" in another. Addressing the whole community, he admonishes them not to quench the Spirit. The instruction is probably directed mainly at the established teachers and their supporters, but also applies to the prophets themselves,[85] who may have been inclined to yield to social pressure and squelch the promptings of the Spirit for them to speak out. Paul knows this is a temptation of authentic prophets (cf. Jer 20:7–9).

In vv. 21–22, Paul makes clear that prophecy is to be accepted in the church, but not uncritically. "Test everything; hold fast to what is good" is, as Paul inserts it into this context, not a stray maxim of generalizing exhortation, but applies specifically to the inspired revelations that emerge in the church's worship. "Keep your distance from every worthless form" is not a general admonition to stay away from all kinds of bad things, but in this context acknowledges that utterances in worship claimed to be under the influence of the Spirit may be useless or worse. The church may indeed be nourished and strengthened by the revelations of inspired speakers, but it may also be harmed. The Holy Spirit is not the possession of a few inspired prophets, however, but is at work in the whole congregation, which is charged to put all such purported revelations to the test.

From the beginning and throughout its long history, the people of God have been guided and warned by prophets sent from God. These prophets did not always agree with each other; some considered their rivals to be insincere "false prophets." In Jer 23:18–40 the prophet (whose work will turn out to be canonical) portrays his rivals as those who have not been sent by God, but speak on the basis of their own dreams and the deceit of their own evil hearts. This was the view that *they* had of *him*, too. Although the Hebrew Bible reports conflicting revelatory claims among Israelite prophets, the terminology of "false prophets/prophecy" does not occur; all are simply "prophets" (though note the caveat in Deut 18:20–22). The LXX, however, introduces the term *pseudoprophētēs* (false

---

85. Elsewhere Paul can speak of prophets as a distinct category (1 Cor 12:28–29). Here he speaks of prophecies, the manifestation of a gift of the Spirit that is not bound to particular people, but, at least in theory, can be spoken by anyone in the Spirit-filled congregation.

prophet) ten times for those prophets who turned out to be in opposition to the canonical prophets (Zech 13:2; Jer 6:13; 33:7, 8, 11, 16 [26:7, 8, 11, 16 ET]; 35:1 [28:1]; 36:1, 8 [29:1, 8]). This gives the reader the impression that they were insincere, intending to lead the people astray with purported revelations they knew were invalid. This terminology and understanding then comes into the New Testament (Matt 7:15; 24:11, 24; Mark 13:22; Luke 6:26; Acts 13:6; 2 Pet 2:1; 1 John 4:1; Rev 16:13; 19:20; 20:10).

Paul does not adopt this conceptuality or vocabulary of true versus false prophets. Although he understands his apostolic office to place him in the line of biblical prophets (see on 5:27 below), and in later conflicts he can speak of "false *apostles*," whom he considers to be insincere and "deceitful workers, who disguise themselves as apostles of Christ" (2 Cor 11:13 NRSV), there is none of that in his instructions to the church in Thessalonica. Those in the congregation who deliver prophetic revelations are considered to be beloved brothers and sisters—the Holy Spirit does not discriminate between men and women, and women too prophesy in the church. But all these prophecies can only be accepted after critical evaluation by the congregation. From his own experience and from such texts as Jer 32:6–8, Paul knows that even the prophets themselves must struggle to discern which prophetic experiences are valid revelations and which are not.

Prophecy is a gift of God for the strengthening of the church, but it is fragmentary and imperfect (1 Cor 13:9). Paul is not warning against insincere "counterfeiters," who knowingly attempt to foist false prophecies on the congregation. Some early commentators aptly connected this text with a directive variously cited as from Scripture, Paul, or Jesus: "Be approved money changers, who reject much, but retain the good" (Clement of Alexandria, *Strom.* 28; Pope Dionysius of Alexandria, *Epistle 7, to Philemon*; *Apostolic Constitutions* 2.4; Pseudo-Clementine *Homilies* 2.51). The money-changer analogy is on target; money changers do not sort out criminals from upright citizens, but focus on sorting out valid currency from worthless. Good people can unsuspectingly circulate a mixture that includes worthless money. So also, the church is not charged with identifying false prophets, but with evaluating prophecies—*all* of them. No charismatic leader may claim that a message must be accepted because the speaker is a true prophet, and that the messages of others must be rejected because they come from false prophets. It is a matter of discerning the prophetic messages themselves. Someone or some group must be charged with sorting out the valuable from the worthless. Paul lodges this responsibility with the whole congregation.

Discernment of prophecies is, in fact, inherent in the prophetic gestalt itself. In the biblical tradition, the prophet is never the lone authoritative individual, but speaks out of and to a community of faith, such that prophecy always functions in the interaction between prophet and community. Paul charges the congregation with this responsibility but provides no criteria. Later, when the issue becomes more intense, Paul will attempt to provide more specific guidance (1 Cor 12–14; 2 Cor 10–13; Gal 1:6–9; 2:11–21; 5:13–26; Rom 12:6; 14:1–15:13).

Any religious community that believes God speaks to it through chosen prophetic messengers must devise some criteria by which prophetic claims can be tested. What criteria can the "money changers" use? Among the numerous criteria that have emerged in the long history of Israel and the early church are these:

- *Miraculous validation.* True prophets are validated by their ability to work miracles and signs (1 Kgs 17–19). But false prophets also work miracles (Deut 13:1–3; Matt 7:21–23; Rev 13:11–18 [cf. 16:13]; 19:20; 20:10).
- *Accurate predictions.* True prophets are validated by the accuracy of their predictions (Deut 18:18–22; 1 Kgs 22:28; Isa 30:8). But, apart from the fact that the bulk of prophecy is not predictive anyway, the hearers must typically decide before this criterion could be helpful.
- *Manner of reception:* True prophets receive their messages in visions, or are caught up into the presence of God to hear the words to be delivered, while the message of false prophets comes through dreams (Jer 23:16–18, 25–28). Yet dreams are also evaluated positively by those who affirm prophetic revelation (Num 12:6–8; Dan 2; 4; 7:1; Matt 1–2).
- *Doom.* The true prophet proclaims doom, the false prophet salvation (Jer 23:17; 28:8; 1 Kgs 22; Ezek 13:10) But some prophets (e.g., Second Isaiah) are entirely positive, and most prophecies contain a combination of judgment and salvation.
- *Loyalty to the covenant, tradition, or creed.* True prophets cannot contradict what has become the normative guiding tradition of the people of God (Deut 13:1–3; Matt 7:15–20; Rom 12:6; 1 Cor 12:3; 1 John 4:1–3; 2 John 7–9; cf. *Did.* 11.1, 8, 10). But what constitutes such fidelity is often a matter of interpretation. Who gets to interpret, and on what basis? Strictly and consistently applied, this criterion means the community always already knows the truth and the will of God, and nothing *new* can ever be revealed.
- *The character of the prophet.* True prophets will be unselfish, willing to suffer for the faith. Those who want to do the will of God will know whether the purported revelation comes from God or not (John 7:17). True prophets will not order meals for themselves in the Spirit, or ask for money for themselves, or want to stay

more than three days (*Did.* 11.9; 12.2). The Montanists had many martyrs (according to Eusebius, *Hist. eccl.* 5.20), but *this* does not validate their prophecy, for "some of the other heresies have many martyrs" too. Here the criteria may be clear enough, but their application will always be ambiguous.

- *Community benefit.* True prophets do and speak that which builds up the community (1 Thess 5:21–22; 1 Cor 14). Yet what constitutes "building up the community" and "good order" is itself a matter of interpretation.

Through the centuries of its history, the believing community has found value in each of these criteria. But no one of them, nor all of them together, form an objective grid through which purported revelations may be sifted, nor does Paul expect that it is or can be so. Paul believes that the Spirit of God dwells among and within the community of believers, and that they are fully qualified, risky though it may be, to accept some prophetic messages as authentic divine word to the particular situation, and reject others as contrary or irrelevant to the will of God—even if they are not able to articulate in a convincing manner *how* they can know this, and even if they mistakenly suppose that they *can* do it.

1 Thessalonians 5:23–24
Concluding Prayer and Affirmation

Just as Paul has concluded the first part of the main body of the letter with a prayer (3:11–13), so now he brings the hortatory second part of the letter to a close with a similar prayer, in each case focusing on the holiness of the congregation at the Parousia.

5:23 May the God of peace himself[a] make you holy through and through; and may your whole being[b]—spirit, soul, and body—be kept blameless at the Parousia of our Lord Jesus Christ. **24** The one who calls you is faithful, and he will do it.

a. *Autos de ho theos*, "God himself." The expression is unusual in Paul (only here and in the parallel 1 Thess 3:11) and found elsewhere in the NT only in Rev 21:3.
b. The grammar is a bit awkward, perhaps intentionally so. Of the several ways to construe the syntax, it is perhaps best to express the apparent parallelism of the two clauses by taking the initial *holoklēron hymōn* (your whole [being]) as the subject, with *pneuma, psychē*, and *sōma* as an appositive phrase.[1] The two clauses are then parallel, with God the acting subject in each, and the whole person the object. Each clause emphasizes the person as a whole, with *holoteleis* (totally complete, through and through) parallel to the similar-sounding *holoklēron*.

[23] This final reference to the Parousia in the letter (8× in total!) is not strategic advice ("Don't let the Parousia catch you doing something you shouldn't"), but illustrates how Paul's whole understanding of the life of faith is within the eschatological horizon. The typical "Peace be with you" at the end of Jewish letters (missing from 5:28) becomes a prayer to the God of peace. During his instruction, Paul has called for peace within the congregation (5:13b; see 1:1 on "peace"). In the letter he has not explicitly addressed the new converts as "holy ones/saints," but that seems to be merely accidental; he regards them as the chosen, elect eschatological community, already in a state of holiness (4:3–8). Some of their members who have died seem to be expected among those

---

1. So Richard 1995, 286.

who accompany the returning Lord at the Parousia (3:13), and now he prays for their continuing sanctification, that God will make them completely dedicated, living holy lives prepared for the coming of the Lord.

"Spirit, soul, and body" is a rhetorical expression for "completely," not a tripartite analysis of human being, as though Paul were here presenting doctrinal teaching on the nature of human selfhood. Nor is he consistent in his ways of speaking about the nature of human being; note the variety of ways in which he uses *kardia* (heart), *psychē* (soul, life, self), *nous* (mind), *sōma* (body), *sarx* (flesh), *pneuma* (spirit), as aspects of human being (e.g., Rom 13:1; 16:4; 1 Cor 16:18; 2 Cor 2:13; 7:1, 5, 13; Gal 6:18; Phil 4:23; 1 Thess 2:4, 8; 5:28; Phlm 25).[2] In contrast to the common Greek understanding, which tended to think of an immortal internal "spirit" or "soul" dwelling temporarily in a material body,[3] Hebrew thinking typically conceived of human being as a unity. As in the Great Commandment to love God with heart, soul, mind, and strength (Deut 6:5; Matt 22:37; Mark 12:30; Luke 10:27), each word expresses one aspect of human being as a whole, and the integral whole with all its "parts" is seen as God's good creation. This is a final reminder that salvation is not the escape of a spiritual soul to the heavenly regions, but redemption of the whole person, including the body, and on that day (of Parousia and judgment) what has been done "in the body" will indeed matter (cf. 2 Cor 5:10).

[24] The complete sanctification for which Paul prays is not that the Thessalonians will all try harder to be more holy as the last day approaches. The preceding paraenesis has reminded them, not without apostolic muscle, of their own responsibility to be faithful to the gospel. The imperative is indispensable, but it does not have the last word. Just as the whole letter, with all its appeals for faithful Christian living, is framed by references to God's call and election (cf. 1:4), so their own actions are all embraced within the gift and call of God, whose faithfulness can be counted on. The new converts at Thessalonica were minding their own business when, through the message of an itinerant handworker-preacher, God took the initiative, disrupting and fulfilling their lives by calling them into the eschatological community that is part of God's eternal plan. The call continues (present participle, "the one who continues to

2. So also Barth, after an extensive discussion of "biblical anthropology" and its history in church conciliar debates and decisions, decides that 1 Thess 5:23 cannot provide any basis for a tripartite understanding of human being (1960, 322–436, "Man as Soul and Body," esp. 355). Still valuable is the extensive discussion of Paul's anthropological terminology in Bultmann 1:191–226.

3. See, e.g., Iamblichus, *Vit. Pythag.* 2.3–5; Philostratus, *Vit. Apoll.* 7.14; Plutarch, *Quaest. rom.* 72 (in *Mor.* 4.20); Plutarch, *Cons. Apoll.* 13; Plato, *Phaedo* 66DE, 67E, and often throughout his works. For further parallels from the Hellenistic world, see Boring, Berger, and Colpe (via index: soul, immortality). This view was sometimes adopted in Hellenistic Judaism (e.g., Wis 9:15; Philo, *Mos.* 1.279), and from there occasionally in the NT (Matt 10:28; contrast the more Jewish parallel in Luke 12:5).

call, whose calling remains valid"). In Paul's next letter, written to the church established just before his arrival in Thessalonica, Paul will write, "I am confident of this, that the one who began a good work among you will bring it to completion by the day of Jesus Christ" (Phil 1:6 NRSV). "The One who calls you is faithful, and he will do it."

1 Thessalonians 5:25–28
Conclusion: Greetings, Adjuration, Benediction

Paul's letters neither end abruptly nor trail off. They combine personal warmth and the awareness that they are to be read forth in the solemn and joyful worship of the community.

> 5:25 Brothers and sisters,[a] pray for us. 26 Greet all the brothers and sisters[a] with a holy kiss. 27 I put you under an oath[b] sworn before God that this letter be read to all the[c] brothers and sisters.[a] 28 The grace of our Lord Jesus Christ be with you all.[d]

a. On *adelphoi,* see comment and trans. note c on 1:4. Paul uses this term 3× in these four sentences, twice with an insistent "all." Several English versions vary the translation, presumably to avoid stylistic monotony, but the repetition and emphasis seem important to Paul and are preserved here.

b. *Enorkizō* (adjure, to place under a legally binding oath, to "swear in") is found only here in the NT, not at all in the LXX, but the noun *enorkion* is found once, in the dangerously solemn procedure of Num 5:21.

c. Although the letter strongly emphasizes the holiness of the new community, Paul never explicitly addresses the new converts as *hagioi* (holy ones, saints). This was "corrected" by numerous scribes, who added the word at this point. *Hagiois adelphois* (holy brothers, brother saints) is found in numerous late MSS and became the accepted reading. Thus the earliest English versions (Wycliffe, Tyndale, Bishops, Geneva, Douay) all read "holy brethren" or "brethren, the saints," which was followed by the KJV (retained in the NKJV, but not in most other modern English versions).

d. Most MSS, including some of the better and more ancient ones, include the liturgical *amēn* as the last word of Paul's Letters. Only at Gal 6:18, however, do NA[28] and UBS[4] consider it original with Paul. While most of the occurrences undoubtedly reflect the liturgical practice of the later church, the practice of reading Paul's Letters in worship began with his earliest letter (see v. 27), and the later additions are appropriate to his intention.

[5:25] In concluding his letters, Paul never uses the conventional *errōsthe* that originally meant "farewell," "be strong," but had become a functional word without actual content (as "God be with you" became "Good-bye," then "Bye-bye"; cf. Acts 15:29). He typically includes a prayer request, blessing, greetings to the congregation (sometimes individual members or groups by name) from his coworkers and the congregation(s) where he is presently working, and sometimes other liturgical expressions appropriate to the worship setting in which the letters would be read. Presumably he is writing from Corinth (see intro, "Context of Paul's Life"). His colleagues who are with him there have already greeted the congregation in 1:1. Apparently Paul is in the early days of the Corinthian mission, and so there is not yet a congregation who can join him in greeting the church in Thessalonica. Paul knows the letter will be read out in the worshiping, praying congregation, and he asks that he and his fellow missionaries be remembered in their prayers. The church in Thessalonica is thereby involved in the continuing mission elsewhere.

[26] Kissing was a common enough greeting in the Hellenistic world, but it was not for everyone, not the equivalent of a handshake. There was no general practice of public kissing, which was regarded differently in various urban and rural settings, among Jews and Gentiles, and in various strata of Greco-Roman society.[1] Lovers kissed on the lips (Song 1:2), family on the cheeks, brow, or shoulders (Luke 15:20). Superiors were kissed on the hands or feet as a mark of respect and honor (Exod 18:7; Ps 2:12; Sir 29:5; Luke 7:45), but superiors, at their own initiative, kissed subordinates on the cheek ([1 Sam 20:41?]; 2 Sam 15:5; 19:39; [20:9?]; 1 Esd 4:47). Paul's understanding of the church as family made greeting with a kiss an appropriate act within the new congregations he founded. Four of the seven undisputed letters refer to it in the closing lines, in each case as something with which his readers were familiar (Rom 16:16; 1 Cor 16:20; 2 Cor 13:12; 1 Thess 5:26). It is continued in the Pauline tradition reflected in 1 Pet 5:14 and Acts 20:37.[2] We cannot be sure just how conventional the greeting kiss would have been in the various circles in which Paul and the new converts in Thessalonica moved, but so far as we know there is no analogy in ancient society, Jewish or Gentile, to the sacred kiss as practiced in the Pauline churches. While Paul is not initiating a new ritual in the closing lines of his letters, the repetition of the command suggests that the readers may have needed some encouragement to continue with this new practice. Did he intend that Christians greet each other with the holy kiss whenever they met in public? Possibly, but since the command is pointedly directed to *all*, men and women alike, it seems improbable that he would promote a practice so easily

1. See Klassen.
2. Apart from Luke 7:38, 45, 15:20, the only kisses in the Gospels are the references in the Synoptics to Judas's betrayal of Jesus with a greeting kiss. We cannot be sure whether this is historical memory of an actual event. The Judas kiss is missing from John; Matthew and Luke are dependent on Mark, so Mark is the sole originating source for such a greeting. Did early Christian practice continue the custom of Jesus' inner circle of disciples, who thought of themselves as brothers and sisters in the family of God? Or does the betrayal scene in Mark reflect early Christian practice read back into the pre-Easter narrative, with Judas perverting something that had become sacred to the Christian community?

misunderstood by the very outsiders he wants the church to impress favorably (see on 4:12). More likely, the holy kiss is a sign of group identity, perhaps already a part of the liturgy, a ritual that solidifies their sense of belonging and marks them off from outsiders.[3] With this kiss they greet each other. It is not merely a sign of greeting from Paul—"Give them a kiss for me"—but an expression of greeting, welcome, and acceptance of each other (made explicit in Rom 16:16; 1 Cor 16:20; 2 Cor 13:12; cf. 1 Pet 5:14). It is a *holy* kiss, which does not merely contrast it with erotic kisses, but also identifies the ritual as belonging to the holy community (1 Thess 3:13; 4:3, 4, 7; 5:23), in which the Holy Spirit is the driving force (1:5, 6; 4:8; 5:19). Whether a formal ritual or not, it is in any case not casual.[4]

[27] The voice of the apostle, who has been gentle as a mother nursing her children (2:7), now becomes somewhat stern, though not distancing and professional, as a serious reminder that the apostolic letter is not chatty communication. Paul insists that the letter be read to *all* (aloud, of course, in the common gathering for worship; the letter is to be read *to* all, not *by* all). For the first time since 3:5, he switches to the first-person singular and speaks with an apostolic authority that, while present, has remained subdued throughout the letter. Why this insistent tone? Several house churches may have been formed in and around Thessalonica during and since the founding visit, and Paul wants the letter read in each of them, or at a plenary meeting. Though he does not say so explicitly, it is likely that Paul assumes the letter is to be read repeatedly. Such regular readings, in community gatherings, would allow the hearers to pick up the subtleties and allusions of Paul's communication they might have missed in the initial reading; the readings would allow the more informed members to help others grasp the depths involved in the letter. Such repeated, communal reading would gradually reshape their mind-set more into conformity with Paul's own. These circumstances, however, hardly account for the insistent placing of the readers under solemn oath. Two reasons may plausibly be gleaned from the letter itself.

1. Just as Paul pointedly greets *all* the brothers and sisters, so his emphasis that the letter be read to all indicates that he is pastor and apostle to the whole congregation, that he is not taking sides in any budding disputes, that what he has to say applies to those whom he knows personally, has baptized, and has instructed during the founding visit, and also to those who have been added

---

3. By the middle of the 2d cent. C.E., the holy kiss is associated with the eucharistic liturgy, a sign of mutual love and forgiveness in preparation for receiving the sacrament (Justin, *1 Apol.* 65.2). This is, of course, a century after 1 Thessalonians and thus is only minimal evidence for the practice of the Pauline churches. Some interpreters see a liturgical, eucharistic context reflected in 1 Cor 16:20–24.

4. PHILLIPS's paraphrase is off target in rendering the Greek as "Give a handshake all round," as is the CEV's "Give the Lord's followers a warm greeting."

to the congregation since his departure. Paul has no favorites; none are to be neglected or ignored. His apostolic commissioning applies to all, not just those who know him personally. It is a matter of ecclesial authority, not personal charisma.

2. Yet there is very likely another reason for this solemn insistence, related to Paul's understanding of his prophetic-apostolic role on the model of the prophet Jeremiah.

Paul as prophet. It has been increasingly recognized that Paul understood his own vocation in prophetic terms.[5] To be sure, Paul—who regards prophecy as one of the spiritual gifts that God gave to the church in these latter days, in which the power of the Spirit is again at work in the people of God—never refers to himself as a prophet. As external pressures increased for Paul to clarify and defend the authority by which he carries out his ministry, *apostle* becomes the key term (see intro, "Context of Paul's Life" and "Apostolic Letter"; and on 1:1; 2:5–8, 15–16). As indicated by the variations in his lists of charismatic gifts (1 Cor 12:4–11, 28–31; Rom 12:6–9), Paul does not have an understanding of "the" spiritual gifts that crisply distinguishes one from another. He could never say, for example, "I have the gift of apostleship, not the gift of teaching or prophecy." Being called and equipped to be an apostle includes other gifts as well. As an apostle, he teaches; as an apostle, he can speak in tongues; as an apostle, he can and does prophesy (cf. 1 Cor 14:1–19). As apostle-prophet, he writes an authoritative and encouraging letter. Among the biblical prophets, Jeremiah is Paul's primary model.

Excursus 3: Paul and Jeremiah

Jeremiah was the only canonical prophet reported to have written a letter. Like Paul as he writes 1 Thessalonians, he could never have imagined that his writing would become canonical Scripture. Yet he founds a tradition of prophetic communication through letter writing.[6] Jeremiah is in Jerusalem. The faithful community is in hostile Babylon. But though there were prophetic figures among the Jewish groups in Babylon, God speaks to Jeremiah in Jerusalem, and he sends his prophetic message in a letter (Jer 29:1–23). This model influences Paul as he formulates the new genre of "apostolic letter" (see intro, "Apostolic Letter"). Like Jeremiah, Paul writes not only to the leaders, but directly to "all the people" (Jer 29:1). Like Jeremiah, Paul is aware of other prophetic activity within the distant congregation, and sends his own prophetic message as norm and guide (though Paul does not speak of "false prophets" in Thessalonica as Jeremiah had in Babylon, in the LXX of Jer 6:13; 33 [26 ET]:7, 8, 11, 16; 34 [27]:9; 35 [28]:1; 36 [29]:1, 8). Like

---

5. See, more extensively and with further bibliography, Boring 1991, 30–36; Rigaux 154–70.

6. The image of Jeremiah as letter writer is preserved in the apocryphal Letter of Jeremiah (see Bar 6:1 = Ep Jer 1) and in *2 Bar.* 78–86. In 2 Chr 21:12 the image of Elijah is adjusted to this tradition by having him address the king in a letter.

Jeremiah's letter (Jer 29:23), Paul's prophetic letter focuses on sexual ethics as the focal instance of faithfulness to God (see on 4:3–8). Like Jeremiah's letter, 1 Thessalonians reassures the congregation of the future hope, but in the meantime he encourages them to settle down and live in a manner respectable to outsiders (4:12). Jeremiah incurred the wrath of the revolutionaries by claiming that imperial power was under the sovereignty of God, who would deal with it in due time, but in the present God's people should "seek the welfare of the city [Babylon!] . . . and pray to the LORD on its behalf" (Jer 29:7 NRSV). So also Paul, who knows that in the near future, publicly visible sovereignty will pass from Rome to the kingdom of God, will later instruct Christians in the imperial capital to conduct themselves appropriately in their present context (Rom 13:1–7). This does not mean, of course, that 1 Thessalonians is a prophetic oracle in epistolary form. It is a real letter, but written by one with a prophetic self-consciousness whose new epistolary form is influenced by a model he finds in his Bible.

Several other indications point to Jeremiah as Paul's model:

- Like Jeremiah, Paul considers himself to have been separated by God for his prophetic vocation before he was born, then called as a young man (Jer 1:5//Gal 1:15).
- Paul was from the tribe of Benjamin; Jeremiah, a priest of the tribe of Levi, lived in Benjamin (Jer 1:1//Rom 11:1: Phil 3:5).
- Of the canonical prophets, only Jeremiah links his prophetic vocation directly to the nations/Gentiles; Paul considers himself the apostle to the Gentiles (Jer 1:5//Gal 1:15–16).
- Jeremiah was rejected by his own people, whom he was trying to serve; he was beaten and imprisoned as one who had betrayed the cause for which the nation had been called. Paul also sees his own experience in these terms (Jer 26; 37–45//1 Cor 4:8–13; 2 Cor 11:22–29 [also with the "boasting" motif from Jer 9:23–24 = 1 Cor 1:31; 2 Cor 10:17]).
- Jeremiah contrasts his prophetic ministry with false prophets who get their messages from each other, and insists that his orders come directly from the LORD. Paul has a similar self-understanding, expressed in a context that uses the images of Jeremiah's call to express his own (Jer 23:18–22; 1:5–9; Gal 1:11–16).
- The canonical prophets typically have wives and families, understood this to be entirely normal and in accord with the command of God, and incorporate aspects of their family life into their prophetic ministry—Isaiah and Hosea famously so. Of the canonical prophets, only Jeremiah sees celibacy as inherent in his prophetic vocation. Paul, too, affirms life with spouse and family to be a divine blessing, yet regards himself as called to a life of celibacy. Both Jeremiah and Paul related this not to any view that sexuality itself is somehow tainted, but to the crucial times in which they carried out their ministry (Jer 16:1–4; 1 Cor 7:8; 9:5).
- In 1 Thessalonians Paul never cites Jeremiah or even clearly alludes to Jeremiah or any other biblical text, but elsewhere he cites texts from Jeremiah as formative for his thinking. These include "circumcision of the heart" in Jer 4:4 (Rom 2:25–29); "edification" or "building up" as

inherent in the prophet's vocation in Jer 1:10 (13× in Paul, including 1 Thess 5:11); "wrath" as expressing God's coming judgment (eighteen times in LXX Jeremiah, often in Paul; cf. 1 Thess 1:10; 2:16; 5:9); "vessel" as a metaphor for the human body (Jer 18:4; 19:11; cf. 1 Thess 4:4); false assurances of "peace" in Jer 5:31; 6:14; 8:11; 23:14–32 (cf 1 Thess 5:3); *dokimazō*, testing prophetic experiences, including one's own, in Jer 6:27; 12:3 (1 Thess 5:21–22); "boasting" as excluded in Jer 9:24 (1 Cor 1:31; 2 Cor 10:17); "new covenant" in Jer 31:31–33 (2 Cor 3:6; Rom 11:27). Moreover, the Pauline neologism "Godtaught" (1 Thess 4:9) is likely dependent on Jer 31:34.[7]

[28] This first apostolic letter closes not with the conventional *errōsthe* typical of Hellenistic letters, but with a blessing on the congregation. With minor variations, "The grace of our Lord Jesus Christ be with you" is included in every later letter. These words were likely a typical concluding benediction in the worship of the Pauline churches, another indication that the letter was intended for liturgical reading.

Despite his casting himself in a somewhat Jeremiah-like prophetic role—Paul would say that God has cast him in this role—he by no means sees himself as composing a document that will function as Holy Scripture for the church at large and through the centuries. Nor is such a claim presented in the concluding adjuration that the letter be read to all members of God's new family. But in giving this solemn charge that his lengthy, carefully composed apostolic letter be read to the congregation as a whole, presumably repeatedly, and alongside the Scriptures in a worship service, Paul in fact provides a written norm for the life of the church, and he starts the young church on the road that will lead to the New Testament canon. "Paul, as a child of his age, addressed his contemporaries. It is, however, far more important that, as Prophet and Apostle of the Kingdom of God, he veritably speaks to all [people] of every age."[8]

---

7. See the careful argument of Witmer re *"Theodidaktoi* in 1 Thessalonians."

8. Barth 1933, 1. Though Barth, writing in the present, would doubtless replace "all men" with "all people" (as would Barth's 1932 translator), I think Paul would affirm Barth's summary of what he saw himself doing in 1 Thessalonians.

INTRODUCTION TO
2 THESSALONIANS

2 Thessalonians as an Interpretation of 1 Thessalonians

Second Thessalonians is a significant text in its own right, both as a document of the New Testament canon and as an important text in early Christian literature. One dimension of its importance is that it is the earliest specific interpretation of 1 Thessalonians. If by Paul himself, the letter was written shortly after 1 Thessalonians and represents Paul's understanding and clarification of what he wanted to say in 1 Thessalonians. If, as argued here, the document is by a teacher in the Pauline school who sets forth his understanding of Paul for a new time and place, the letter addresses the network of Pauline churches sometime after Paul's death. In either case, 2 Thessalonians can be understood only with reference to 1 Thessalonians. It presupposes that the readers (i.e., hearers) are familiar with 1 Thessalonians and are pondering its meaning. Thus 2 Thessalonians is among the very first commentaries on 1 Thessalonians.

Particularly those interpreters who consider 2 Thessalonians pseudepigraphical are in danger of having the arguments about authorship bleed into the exegesis, which tends to take on the flavor of contrasting 2 Thessalonians with the authentic Paul, and judging that it exhibits something of a decline from the apostle's vigor and theological depth. However, once having accepted 2 Thessalonians as deuteropauline, the interpreter's task is to hear the text as a document of canonical Scripture, with its own message to its own time, and to allow the contemporary reader to come within hearing distance of *this* message.

2 Thessalonians as Deuteropauline

I began to read the Bible in late childhood with the assumption that Paul wrote all the fourteen letters attributed to him in the titles of the King James Version. In my earliest serious academic work on the New Testament, an M.A. thesis on Paul's theology while still in seminary, I had already become convinced that Ephesians and the Pastorals, while still Holy Scripture, are best understood as deuteropauline, but regarded Colossians and 2 Thessalonians as written by

Paul. Sustained, more careful study in later years has convinced me that both letters are products of the vigorous debate among Christian teachers in the two generations after his death on how to interpret Paul's gospel. In my opinion, there are two compelling lines of evidence: (1) The letter can be more plausibly located in the setting of the Pauline school tradition than in Paul's own mission. (2) In the work for this commentary, the exegesis of the letter's text makes more sense on the presupposition of deuteropauline than Pauline authorship. The first set of evidence is briefly sketched below. The second is represented by the commentary itself. Prior to these discussions, however, I will sketch the classical types of evidence that have led many scholars to interpret the letter as deuteropauline.

Many interpreters who continue to affirm Pauline authorship start with the details of the text of 2 Thessalonians and ask if they can be understood as written by Paul—in other words, assuming Pauline authorship and placing the burden of proof on the challenger. My approach is to postulate the two possible backgrounds—Paul writing to the new congregation in Thessalonica around 50 C.E., or a teacher in the Pauline school composing the letter a generation or two later—and ask which reading better illuminates the content of the letter.

The following is an abbreviated sampling of the kinds of evidence that have convinced many scholars that 2 Thessalonians is deuteropauline.[1]

Relation to 1 Thessalonians: Structure, Topics, Template

Second Thessalonians closely follows 1 Thessalonians in both structure and content, as evident in the following parallel outlines:[2]

---

1. Already in 1988, Raymond F. Collins (1988, 209–41) could report that most contemporary critical scholars tended to regard 2 Thessalonians as pseudepigraphical, supported by the fact that among the 38 contributors and 175 participants at the Leuven Colloquium of that year devoted to 1–2 Thessalonians, there was "near universal agreement as to the pseudepigraphical character of the text" (cf. R. Collins and Baumert 1990, xiv). In 2004, I. Howard Marshall, a British scholar who continues to affirm Pauline authorship himself, reported his impression that the majority opinion of international scholarship favors post-Pauline authorship (236). By contrast, a later informal survey indicates that slightly more than half of the 110 members of the British New Testament Society surveyed regard 2 Thessalonians as by Paul (Foster 2012).

A full discussion of the issue, with a history of the study of the problem, objections, and counterarguments, requires a monograph. For more extensive treatments and bibliography, see Trilling 1972; R. Collins and Baumert.

2. Adapted from Bailey 133. For more detailed analysis of the parallel structure, see Wrede 1903, 247–56, showing the Greek texts in parallel. A detailed tabulation by Holland (78–79) shows that the exact parallels are formal and that where the author is developing his own themes, there are the fewest parallels.

1 Thessalonians		2 Thessalonians
1:1	Prescript (Greeting)	1:1–2
1:2–3:13	Thanksgiving/letter body	1:3–2:17
2:13–3:10	Second thanksgiving	2:13–15
3:11–13	Benediction	2:16–17
4:1–5:22	Paraenesis: The life to which Christians are called	3:1–15
5:22–28	Letter close	3:16–18
5:23–24	Peace wish	3:16
5:26	Greetings	3:17
5:28	Second benediction	3:18

Every section of 2 Thessalonians is related to a corresponding section of 1 Thessalonians, and in the same order. The reverse relationship, however, is not true. Extensive sections of 1 Thessalonians have no counterpart in 2 Thessalonians. The absence of some themes is striking. There is no concern for church life as such (sexual ethics, holiness). Second Thessalonians introduces no new topics or themes but is entirely devoted to three themes taken from 1 Thessalonians: persecution, eschatology, and the "disorderly." In 1 Thessalonians, Paul has deviated from the standard outline of a Hellenistic letter in only two major ways, not repeated in any undisputed letter: a second thanksgiving formula at 2:13, and a second benediction at the end of the main body of the letter, 3:11–13. Precisely these deviations are found in 2 Thessalonians (2:13, 16–17).

The variety of explanations boil down to two basic types: (1) Paul wrote both letters, so a personal, pastoral, or psychological explanation for his compositional procedure must be found; or (2) a later author wrote 2 Thessalonians and consciously imitated 1 Thessalonians, closely following the form of his template, but elaborating its content in terms of his own agenda.

The first explanation assumes that Paul wrote 2 Thessalonians while the structure and content of his previous letter was still in his head. This is an impressionistic response, not based on detailed analysis of the parallels. This response to the problem is reminiscent of early attempts at dealing with the Synoptic Problem by claiming that various eyewitnesses remembered essentially the same events and sayings, but differed in the details. The intense study of the details of actual parallels in order and wording convinced virtually all interpreters that the interrelations of the Synoptic Gospels required a literary solution: the later author(s) used the earlier as a source. Thus some scholars held on to Pauline authorship of 2 Thessalonians by imagining that Paul himself had kept a copy of 1 Thessalonians, which he studied carefully before composing 2 Thessalonians some months later. This accepts the necessary literary relationship of the two texts, but attributes it to Paul.[3] Why Paul would use an earlier, failed letter as the template for a second letter remains unexplained, as does the absence from 2 Thessalonians of any reference to the first, to the intervening history, or to the experience he has shared with the addressees. We have, of course, undisputed instances in which Paul himself writes a second letter responding to the reception of an earlier one (the Corinthian correspondence), and letters in which a later letter treats themes introduced in an earlier one (Romans and Galatians). These letters show how Paul himself handles such situations; they manifest little of the phenomena that connect 1 and 2 Thessalonians. Neither do the letters of Ignatius, all written within a brief period and with several overlapping themes, provide an analogous case. The closest analogy is Ephesians' use of Colossians, in which a later member of the Pauline school tradition uses an earlier letter as a model for both form and content.

In the second explanation, a post-Pauline author utilizes 1 Thessalonians as the template for his own composition. We need not think of this as the scissors-and-paste industry of a "forger," who patiently studies the structure and content of 1 Thessalonians (and other Pauline letters), including Paul's vocabulary and style, in order to imitate him precisely.[4] Instead, we should think of a member of the Pauline school,[5] a teacher in the network of Pauline churches of the second or third generation who has steeped himself in the emerging collection of Pauline letters as inherent in his vocation as a Christian teacher. He may well have the text of 1 Thessalonians before him, as well as other Pauline Letters, but he has them thoroughly in mind, virtually memorized. He does not intend to write a commentary on Paul in the sense that distinguishes his interpretative comments from the original text, but to write *as* Paul, to allow the voice of Paul to continue to guide the churches of his own day.

---

3. So Zahn et al. 1:242, 249–50. Others have imagined more complex and subtle aspects of Paul's psychology to account for the similarities and differences. Josef Wrzoł, e.g., argues that Paul wanted to enhance the authority of 1 Thessalonians, which had been disputed in Thessalonica, so he made 2 Thessalonians sound very much like it, only more authoritarian. And Josef Graafen (12) argues that Paul wrote 1 Thessalonians immediately upon receiving Timothy's positive report but shortly thereafter, without receiving any new information and "perhaps on the same day," had second thoughts and wrote the more stern 2 Thessalonians to address eschatology and the "disorderly." For further examples and documentation, see Trilling 1972, 20–42.

4. Contra Friesen (207), who thus considers the author "the first New Testament scholar, the first specialist in New Testament studies"! Gordon Fee (237–41 and often) is among interpreters who point to such similarities as evidence that the letter must be by Paul, since no "forger" would have had the skill or motivation to imitate Paul so closely.

5. I use "Pauline school" in the broad sense of an informal network of Pauline teachers with varying points of view, in dialogue and sometimes debate with each other. I do not intend a localized, institutionalized organization (see Müller 321). Despite its variety, this school tradition was held together by its admiration for Paul and commitment to his theology, not always understood in the same manner by his later advocates. The beginnings of this school tradition go back to the extensive circle of Paul's coworkers in his own lifetime.

Why choose to model his letter so closely on 1 Thessalonians? The author was presumably free to address his letter to any church or individual within the fictive world of the Pauline churches, and to use any literary form. The author of Acts opted to expand the gospel form rather than compose a letter in Paul's name; the author of the *Didache* chose neither the narrative nor the letter form to set forth apostolic teaching for postapostolic generations. The author of 2 Thessalonians, like the authors of Colossians, Ephesians, and the Pastorals (to name only the canonical examples), adopted the form that Paul had already made the standard genre of Christian instruction, and for which a slot in the worship and catechetical life of the church already existed. Having decided on the letter form, the author could have looked over his collection of Pauline Letters, authentic and deuteropauline, and decided to compose a new letter without any previous model. He would have been free to include whatever topics he deemed appropriate and to structure it according to his own intentions. This is presumably what the author of Colossians had done earlier and what the Pastor would do later for the Pastorals. Alternatively, he could have composed a letter to the (Pauline) church at large, but based on a letter already circulating among the Pauline churches. This is what the author of Ephesians did, adopting Colossians as his template, following its structure, content, and style closely, and expressing his distinctive message by strategic omissions, additions, expansions, and modifications.

The author of 2 Thessalonians adopted the second model and chose 1 Thessalonians for his template. He does not choose an individual as fictive addressee, as the later author of the Pastorals will do. This would have tended to confirm the developing paradigm of hierarchical, clerical, official leadership, which he wants to oppose (see on 3:6–15). Instead, he chooses a church. Why Thessalonica? A close retrospective observation of what he has actually done suggests that 1 Thessalonians provided the structure, points of contact, and elements of content that he wanted to develop in allowing the continuing voice of Paul to address the Pauline churches of his own time. *Heresy*, internal threats posed by defective understanding of the faith, was not his main concern. He has no "opponents" to refute.[6] He is not trying to present a comprehensive reinterpretation of the whole of Pauline theology, to write a Pauline summa for the post-Pauline period. He has two main pastoral concerns: response to persecution and development of leadership structures. These concerns are related to each other, and both are related to the reinterpretation of eschatology that was necessary in the second and third generations of the Pauline tradition. First Thessalonians is very appropriate to this agenda. It is Paul's most apocalyptic letter, clearly assuming the nearness of the end. It is also a short letter, appropriate to the

6. See esp. the methodologically rigorous work of Sumney (1999, 214–28), who concludes, "We find, then, no opponents combatted in 1 Thessalonians" (227).

author's limited purpose. Once the author has chosen 1 Thessalonians as a template, the original letter exercises its own formative energy in shaping what 2 Thessalonians becomes.

Tone, Style, Language

Tone of Voice

While there is always an element of subjectivity involved,[7] discerning readers have frequently noticed the different tone of 2 Thessalonians when compared not only to 1 Thessalonians, but also to the undisputed Letters of Paul in general. The letter has a somewhat official, impersonal, and authoritarian tone. Already 1 Thessalonians had a certain liturgical style; Paul intended it to be read aloud to the congregation in the context of worship. This tendency is extended and intensified in 2 Thessalonians. For instance, 2 Thess 3:17 is not an actual greeting, but rather a comment on "Paul's" customary mode of epistolary greeting (the contrast with the holy kiss of 1 Thess 5:26 comes easily to mind). This tendency to step back and comment on his own composition, looking over his own shoulder as he writes, is unique in the Pauline corpus. It lacks the spontaneity of one addressing new converts whom the author knows personally and thus appears to be the composition of one writing for the church in general on the basis of Pauline tradition and letters already in circulation for some time.

Second Thessalonians thus contains no greetings to the congregation, no personal data whatever about Paul or his readers, nothing about "Paul's" present location, situation, or future plans. Except for the address in 1:1 (copied verbatim from 1 Thess 1:1), nothing connects the letter specifically to Thessalonica; it could be understood and heard as personal address in any church in the Pauline network of churches in the decades after Paul's death. It carries the didactic tone of the teacher addressing a general readership personally unknown to him rather than the warm tone of 1 Thessalonians addressing fellow believers he has recently converted and whose sufferings he shares. First Thessalonians expresses a personal relation of love and trust, while 2 Thessalonians operates on the basis of authority and command. The tone of "we are obligated to give thanks for you . . . as is appropriate" sounds too formal to be the composition of one addressing a beloved congregation in which Paul has not flouted his apostolic authority (2 Thess 1:2–3; see comments there and notes throughout). Paul argues with his readers, attempts to persuade them, while 2 Thessalonians operates on the basis of apostolic authority and commands

---

7. Though such shifts in tone are difficult to quantify, hearers and readers do detect them. Transcripts of class lectures purportedly from the same professor to the same class, but which make a midsemester shift from first names to last names, or from *Du* to *Sie* when addressing class members, suggest a different teacher and/or a different class.

(though the author avoids this terminology). Despite the common outline and overlapping contents, the letters manifest two different kinds of rhetoric: epideictic rhetoric in 1 Thessalonians, deliberative rhetoric in 2 Thessalonians. This is not a manifestation of Paul's purported "authoritarianism," but the view of Paul within the second- and third-generation Pauline school, where Paul was admired and various teachers struggled to be the representatives of his authority. This authority was everywhere assumed in the postapostolic network of Pauline churches; it did not need to be imposed or argued for. The commanding tone of 3:6–15, for example, is different from the familial tenderness of 1 Thessalonians, but it is like the deuteropauline Pastorals. The difference of tone between 1 and 2 Thessalonians seems to be best explained as a matter of two different authors in two different situations with two different goals, not by positing mood swings in Paul.

Style

Second Thessalonians has its own style, only distantly related to Paul's characteristic manner of thinking and writing. Like tone of voice, observations on style necessarily include a subjective element yet cannot be reduced to mere impressions. The following notes are illustrative samples derived not only from my having diagrammed every sentence in the Greek text of 1–2 Thessalonians, but also from the long tradition of critical study analyzing the literary style of the two texts.[8]

- *The longer sentence structure* of 2 Thessalonians contrasts with the shorter sentences of 1 Thessalonians and is more like the deuteropauline Colossians and Ephesians. For example, compare 1 Thess 1:2–10 to its structural counterpart 2 Thess 1:3–12. This needs to be done in the Greek text; English translations break up long sentences in the interest of readability (see the translations in this commentary, closer to the structure of the Greek sentences). This is a feature of the liturgical use of Paul's Letters in the Pauline churches of the second and third generations, in which such solemn extravagance is not artificial pomposity but appropriate liturgy.
- *Fullness of expression* bordering on excess is characteristic of 2 Thessalonians. Intensifying prefixes are added to words: thus Paul's *auxanō* (grow, increase; 1 Cor 3:6, 7; 2 Cor 9:10; 10:15)

8. Already the 1903 monograph of Wrede analyzed and tabulated stylistic differences between the two letters. Wrede's work has been refined by the studies of Dobschütz and Bornemann 28–36; Frame 46–51; Rigaux 76–93; and Trilling 1972, 46–66, who offers the latest, most precise, and most complete catalog of stylistic differences between the two letters.

becomes *hyperauxanō* in 2 Thess 1:3. A generalizing *pas* (all) is often added, as in the post-Pauline tradition in general. Sometimes two verbs or nouns stand for a single act or reality ("epiphany and Parousia," 2:8; "persecutions and afflictions," 1:4; "wicked and evil," 3:2; "command and exhort," 3:12). All writers, including Paul, occasionally do this; however, there is a notable increase in such expressions in 2 Thessalonians.

- *Synonymous parallelism* is characteristic of 2 Thessalonians. While Paul himself, in 1 Thessalonians and all his other letters, mostly has antithetic parallelism, this stylistic feature is virtually absent from 2 Thessalonians, which instead prefers synonymous parallelism. Thus 2 Thess 1:3, "Your faith is growing abundantly, and the love of every one of you for one another is increasing" (NRSV) is amplified in the author's characteristic style from the analogous text in 1 Thess 1:3, in which Paul mentions faith, love, and hope. See also 2 Thess 1:6, 8, 9, 10, 11, 12; 2:1, 3, 8, 9–10a, 12, 16, 17; 3:1–2, 3, 8, 9.[9]

- *Figurative language* recedes in 2 Thessalonians. Paul's Letters in general are rich in pictorial language. While the author of 2 Thessalonians can also use figurative expressions (e.g., the word of the Lord "runs" [*trechē*, translated "spread rapidly"] in 3:1), he is not creative in this regard and sometimes omits the figurative language from parallel passages in 1 Thessalonians. One not only thinks of the plenteous family imagery of 1 Thessalonians, robust and tender (see on 1 Thess 2:7–11), which is entirely absent from 2 Thessalonians; one also notices how some images—such as the day of the Lord coming as a thief in the night (1 Thess 5:4), and believers being protected by the breastplate of faith and love, with the hope of salvation as their helmet (1 Thess 5:8)—dramatically recede. The point is not that these particular images are not repeated in 2 Thessalonians, but that the author does not express himself with the same imaginative power as does Paul in the undisputed letters.[10]

- *Particle and preposition usage* is different from Paul's authentic letters. The data assembled by Dobschütz, Rigaux, and Trilling[11] document such differences as the reduced use of *gar*, the increased frequency of *de*, and the virtual disappearance of *kathōs* (13× in

9. See Weiss 1897, 175–81.

10. Even Rigaux (90), who finally decides for Pauline authorship, thoroughly documents this difference, stating that on this point, "One is struck by the disparity between the two letters."

11. Cited in Trilling 1972, 56.

1 Thessalonians; 2× in 2 Thessalonians). The particle *men* ("on the one hand," etc.) is frequent in the undisputed Letters of Paul (55×), but is rare in the Deuteropaulines and not found at all in 2 Thessalonians.[12]

- *Repetition* of the same word instead of varying the vocabulary for style indicates a certain poverty of expression. For such a short composition, a remarkable number of words occur two or more times. Notable among these: "God our Father and the Lord Jesus Christ" (1:1, 2; cf. 1:12; 2:16), "We must always give thanks to God for you" (1:3; 2:13) and the "work" vocabulary (*ergon, ergazomai,* 1:11; 2:17; 3:8, 10, 11, 12).
- *Absence or rarity of characteristic elements* of Paul's style have been cataloged by several interpreters. These include the short lively sentences of spoken Greek characteristic of dictation, brief parenthetical comments or imperatives, diatribes, and rhetorical questions. These are conspicuous by their absence in 2 Thessalonians.
- *The ostensibly plural authorship* represented by the repeated "we" and "our" of 1 Thessalonians is mostly retained, but with a different function. In 1 Thessalonians, the authorial "we" is sometimes the equivalent of Paul's "I" (e.g., 1 Thess 2:18; 3:2, 5), but in 2 Thessalonians the "we" is intended more literally: it is the network of some teachers in the Pauline school that speaks (e.g., 2 Thess 2:15).

Vocabulary, Terminology, Word Usage

The author sometimes copies the wording of his template exactly, sometimes uses words not in 1 Thessalonians but found in later Pauline Letters. He also has numerous words that do not appear in Paul's undisputed letters, omits characteristic Pauline words, and sometimes uses Paul's vocabulary in a non-Pauline sense. Space limits prohibit extensive lists and discussions; a few samples of the various types demonstrate the extent of the data to be explained.[13]

---

12. The Greek particle *men* is found only once in 1 Thessalonians (2:18). Does the author of 2 Thessalonians consciously or unconsciously imitate his template? Or is this simply a coincidence?

13. Frame 28–37; Rigaux 80–85. Trilling (1972) provides no analysis of the vocabulary and is correct in arguing that the vocabulary data themselves are no independent argument for or against Pauline authorship. However, while the vocabulary and word usage are not probative, taken with other evidence the data seem to be better explained in terms of deuteropauline authorship, or at least to illustrate post-Pauline usage when this is supported on other grounds. Cf. the argument illustrated by the use of *pistis* (faith, faithfulness), *agapē* (love), and *pneuma* (Spirit) in Holland (87–88).

- The greeting in 1 Thess 1:1, found nowhere else in the undisputed Pauline Letters, is reproduced verbatim in 2 Thess 1:1–2. Numerous other close echoes of the vocabulary and wording include "our labor and hardship; working night and day so as not to burden any of you" (1 Thess 2:9; cf. 2 Thess 3:8).
- "The Lord be with you all" (2 Thess 3:16b) seems to be extracted from the full proto-Trinitarian form in 2 Cor 13:13, but as such is found nowhere else in Paul.
- The *apokalyptō* (reveal, revelation) vocabulary, frequent in Paul's undisputed Letters (19×), is missing from 1 Thessalonians but does emerge in 2 Thessalonians.
- The *epiphaneia* (epiphany) vocabulary, though appearing often (5×) in deuteropauline letters, is not found at all in the undisputed Letters of Paul, who consistently uses *parousia* (coming, advent) instead. Second Thessalonians has both, thereby showing that it draws from Paul and also the current vocabulary of the Pauline school.
- *Kyrios hēmōn Iēsous Christos* (our Lord Jesus Christ) is a set formula in Paul, mostly with a characteristic word order. In 1 Thessalonians, the formula occurs five times, always in the fixed order except the opening greeting formula of 1:1. The shorter 2 Thessalonians has the formula eight times, a fourfold increase in relative frequency, but only four of the instances in 2 Thessalonians include the characteristic Pauline *hēmōn* (our).
- As in the deuteropauline Pastorals, the characteristic Pauline phrase "in Christ" is missing from 2 Thessalonians (see comments on 1 Thess 1:1; though cf. 2 Thess 3:4, 12).[14] This is in contrast to the undisputed letters and especially to Colossians and Ephesians, where this terminology is multiplied.
- Some words, rare in Paul, are used with increased frequency in 2 Thessalonians as in the deuteropauline letters (e.g., *axios* and *axioō* [adj., "worthy"; verb, "count worthy"]).
- Second Thessalonians has by far the highest relative frequency of the word *kyrios* in the whole Pauline corpus, tending to replace the *theos* (God) of 1 Thessalonians with *kyrios* referring to Jesus Christ (2 Thess 2:16//1 Thess 3:11; 2 Thess 3:16//1 Thess 5:23). Of the thirteen occurrences of Jesus and/or Christ in 2 Thessalonians, none are without "Lord." Virtually every christological reference in the letter either explicitly uses the title *kyrios* or associates Jesus

---

14. The variation *en Christō Iēsou* is found twice in 1 Timothy, and 7× in 2 Timothy. The trademark Pauline *en Christō*, though found in every undisputed letter, is entirely missing from 2 Thessalonians.

with that title.[15] Old Testament attributes of God are increasingly attributed to Christ. This corresponds to the developing Christology within the postapostolic Pauline churches and their neighbors in the contemporary Johannine community, where the address "Lord and God" is used of the risen Jesus (John 20:28; cf. John 1:1, 18; 1 John 5:20b–21).

- In 2 Thess 1:10, both instances of the verb *pisteuō* (believe) are in the aorist. In the undisputed Letters of Paul, by contrast, the present tense of *pisteuō* is characteristic (26×). On the other hand, its present tense is never found in 2 Thessalonians. Parenthetically: while this is indeed different from Paul, it need not signal a decline from the more dynamic Pauline usage. For the author, becoming a believer meant accepting the truth of the Christian faith as testified to in the Pauline gospel, but also holding on to that faith under duress (see comments on 1:3 below).

- For "evidence," Paul uses *endeixis* (4×); the author of 2 Thessalonians uses the related synonym *endeigma* (1:5, only here in the NT).

- Though Paul refers often to judging and judgment, he mostly uses the verb *krinō*, and when using the noun he employs *krima*. Like the deuteropauline 1 Timothy, the author of 2 Thessalonians uses *krisis* for God's eschatological judgment, a word never found in the undisputed letters (2 Thess 1:5; 1 Tim 5:24).

- *Anesis* is used three times by Paul for this-worldly relaxation and refreshment (2 Cor 2:13; 7:5; 8:13), but never for eschatological salvation, as in 2 Thess 1:7.

- In Paul's usage, *paradosis* (tradition) always refers to firm tradition he has received and is passing on, with Jesus or the Lord as the source; Paul himself is a link in a chain that does not begin with him (e.g., see the related verb *paradidōmi* in 1 Cor 11:23–26; 15:3–5). The two usages of the noun in 2 Thessalonians refer to Paul's own teachings (2:15; 3:6) and look no further back than the beginnings of the tradition with Paul. This fits the thought world of the later Pauline school, but it is not Paul's own view of his ecclesiological role.

- The interest in *alētheia* (truth, 2 Thess 2:10, 12, 13), absent from 1 Thessalonians but frequent (15×) in Colossians, Ephesians, and the Pastorals, also points to a second-generation Pauline school context, where such topics were in the air. The neighboring Johannine community also made intensive use of the term (45×).

15. Of the 24 such references, 2 Thess 3:5 ("the steadfastness of Christ") is the only exception (see Donfried 1993b, 94–95).

Post-Pauline Date

Significant evidence has persuaded numerous scholars to regard a post-Pauline date as more plausible than the alternative.

- The earliest allusion to 2 Thessalonians is found in Polycarp's *Letter to the Philippians* 11.4, which exhorts the readers to restore an erring presbyter, not regarding such people as enemies but as sick and straying members (cf. 2 Thess 3:15). Since this part of Polycarp's letter has been preserved only in a Latin translation, it is not possible to compare its Greek text with that of 2 Thessalonians. If this is indeed an indication that Polycarp (and the Philippians) knew 2 Thessalonians, it would mean that the letter was in circulation by about 130, but it is no help in knowing how much earlier it might have been written.[16]
- Second Thessalonians contains numerous words and phrases that several scholars, including the present author, consider to be allusions to later Pauline texts, but none can be considered certain (e.g., 2 Thess 1:8//Rom 10:16; 2 Thess 3:9//1 Cor 9:6; 2 Thess 1:4//2 Cor 1:24; 7:4, 14; 8:24; 9:3; 2 Thess 1:5//Phil 1:28; 2 Thess 2:12//Rom 1:18, 32; 2 Thess 2:10//1 Cor 1:18; 2 Thess 3:2//Rom 15:31; 2 Thess 3:13//Gal 6:9; see comments on 1:3–12 and on each of the above texts). If Paul is the author, in such cases he is anticipating language that will later appear in his letters. It seems more likely that the author is familiar with Paul's later Letters.
- The author presupposes that readers are aware of other letters circulating in Paul's name (2 Thess 2:2; 3:17). Individual letters and/ or a variety of small collections seem to be circulating among the churches. We do not know when firm collections of Paul's Letters emerged. The situation presupposed in 2 Thessalonians does not suggest that the Pauline corpus was already a fixed protocanonical list. By Marcion's time (mid-2d cent. c.e.) a fixed collection was emerging, and a new letter would have to contend for a place. In the period 90–110, however, the appearance of a new letter from Paul among the churches would occasion no surprise; there was as yet no firm idea of how much Paul had written.
- The author presupposes that some letters in circulation are falsely attributed to Paul (2 Thess 2:2; 3:17). This state of affairs is very difficult to imagine during Paul's early Aegean mission in 50 c.e. Such a presupposition seems realistic only after Paul himself

16. Polycarp's letter (*To the Philippians*) is generally dated shortly after the death of Ignatius, but this is itself disputed, the range being ca. 110–138 c.e.

became a recognized authority and disputed interpretations of his legacy emerged in the form of pseudonymous letters. There is no known instance in the Hellenistic world of a pseudonymous letter being written in the name of a contemporary person. Second Thessalonians thus seems to be written at a time when it is commonplace that letters bearing Paul's name are in circulation among the churches, which must distinguish letters that represent an authentic understanding of Pauline theology from false efforts to represent Paul's teaching. The author claims that his own letter belongs to the former category.

• The author seems to be aware of issues that only became prominent in the generation or two after Paul: how to come to terms with the delay of the Parousia, how to deal with ongoing hostility and persecution, whether and how to restructure the church and its ministry for the long-term mission. Although each of these issues will be dealt with at length in the commentary, by way of anticipation we might, with some oversimplification, note that 1 Thessalonians reflects a situation in which members of the community have unexpectedly died before the Parousia, which had been expected very soon; 2 Thessalonians addresses readers whose flagging hopes for the Parousia are, in the author's view, falsely shored up by announcements that the day of the Lord is already present. The new congregation addressed by 1 Thessalonians has already experienced hostility and persecution, and it needs to be reassured that this should be no surprise; 2 Thessalonians speaks to a church in which such hostility and persecution are a given, and believers need encouragement for the long pull. First Thessalonians already manifests the rudiments of church structure and designated leaders; 2 Thessalonians speaks to a more developed situation in which claims for an emerging "institutional clergy" are being made.

• While 2 Thessalonians can thus be contrasted with 1 Thessalonians on each of the above points, 2 Thessalonians appears to be aware of the issues that generated Colossians, Ephesians, and the Pastorals—which do not seem to know 2 Thessalonians. In particular, Ephesians shows familiarity with all the undisputed Letters of Paul, and especially with the probably deuteropauline Colossians, but not with 2 Thessalonians.[17]

---

17. Exhibited in Mitton 280–315, who presents the Greek text of Ephesians with all NT points of contact in parallel columns. All the undisputed Pauline Letters are copiously represented. Verbal parallels exclusive to 2 Thessalonians appear only in the two words *tou ponērou* of Eph 6:16 = 2 Thess 3:3.

- Some items in the letter's content fit better into the struggles of the postapostolic period than the time of Paul's own ministry. These include a declining appreciation for new revelations by the Spirit, an increased interest in tradition, the increasing tendency to represent the church's faith as "truth" and as "the faith" (i.e., a body of material to be believed), and the shift of "faith" in the direction of "faithfulness" (see Excursus 1: "Persecution," below). The Pauline school was sometimes against *other* traditions as "merely human traditions" (e.g., see Col 2:8), but, like Paul, was not against tradition as such.
- There are no references to current events or realities that would place the letter in Paul's own time. The reference to the temple is not an exception in this regard, and it is not an argument for Pauline authorship (2 Thess 2:4; see comments there). While it could be merely an indication of the fictive world represented by the letter, since the temple was still standing in Paul's time, it is more likely a traditional element of the apocalyptic worldview adopted by the author without regard to the historical reality of the temple, as happens, e.g., in the works of Josephus and the Revelation of John, both written long after the temple had been destroyed.
- The narrative world of 2 Thessalonians fits the post-Pauline period, but not Paul's own time (see intro to 1 Thessalonians, "Narrative World"). While 1 Thessalonians is replete with personal allusions that correspond to the history shared by Paul and the congregation in Thessalonica in 50 C.E., 2 Thessalonians has only the data that could be gleaned from 1 Thessalonians itself, and it retrojects the author's own understanding of tradition into the time of the founding visit. Elements of this presumed tradition actually conflict with 1 Thessalonians (see, e.g., on 2 Thess 2:5). When the author is not following and adapting 1 Thessalonians as his template, no new events in Thessalonica are mentioned or alluded to. All the events of the narrative world of 2 Thessalonians supposed to have occurred between the founding visit and the time of writing fit the world of the Pauline churches in general in the second and third generations; nothing in the letter distinctively fits into the world of the congregation in Thessalonica in 50 C.E.[18]

Thus the deuteropauline 2 Thessalonians could have been written any time between 80 and 120 C.E. At present there is no way to ascertain its date more precisely. It was written at the same time as some of the other deuteropauline

18. Cf. the similar comments of Marxsen 12–14, though he has made no detailed analysis of the respective narrative worlds of 1 and 2 Thessalonians.

letters and the traditions that were incorporated in them, after the Gospel of Mark, and in the same general period as Matthew, Luke–Acts, Hebrews, and 1 Peter, during the time the Johannine literature was developing in neighboring Christian communities. The letter seems to make most sense when set about the turn of the century, when these canonical documents were being composed and/or the traditions they contain were being circulated, a time reflected in *1 Clement* and the letters of Ignatius, in a situation described a bit later in Pliny's letter to Trajan.

There is no way to determine the provenance of the letter. It was likely written somewhere in the broad range of the Pauline Aegean mission. Since the author is in communication with the theological discussion within and among the Pauline churches, a location in Achaia, Macedonia, or Asia would be a likely guess. There seems to have been a concentration of Pauline traditions associated with and perhaps emerging from Ephesus, where Pauline teachers would also have had opportunity to be in communication with Johannine and other streams of second- and third-generation Christianity.

Theology

Significant theological differences exist between 2 Thessalonians and the undisputed Letters of Paul, especially differences from 1 Thessalonians, the author's template.[19] These point to different authorship and a later date. Such differences are best discussed in the context of the letter itself.

Reading 2 Thessalonians within the Pauline School Tradition

Interpreters have mostly focused on the author and sought his intention and meaning in composing 2 Thessalonians. This aspect of the interpreter's task cannot be neglected in responsible historical study. Yet it is equally important for the modern reader to identify with the ancient reader, asking how the letter was heard and understood in the second and third generations of the Pauline churches. In pseudepigraphic writings, not only the author but also the addressees belong to the fictive world.[20] We should not think of a lone individual writing in Paul's name to adroitly foist his interpretation of Christian faith and

19. For summaries, see Laub 1990, 413–14; Holland 90.

20. On the Pastorals, some scholars speak of a "double pseudonymity" as not only Paul but also Timothy and Titus receive new personifications. Both author and addressees belong to the fictive world of the text. Since these letters were not written by Paul, neither were they written to Timothy and Titus, but to the Pauline churches in general. This is not always recognized in studies of Colossians and 2 Thessalonians, which sometimes continue to use the historical Colossae and Thessalonica as part of their discussion. But if 2 Thessalonians was not written by Paul, neither was it written exclusively to the church in Thessalonica. The modern reader should hear it against the background of the network of Pauline churches of the second and third generations and not try to fit it into a distinctively Thessalonian context.

responsibility on others. The writing, circulation, reception, and understanding of the letter was a community transaction, an event within the network of the Pauline congregations. Much work has been done on the sociology of networking in the Hellenistic world of the first century.[21] It is clear that such networks were in place and provided a pattern for new groups, but just how this applied to teachers and leaders in the Pauline tradition is not yet clear. That they existed is clear from the existence of the Pauline corpus and New Testament canon, but the steps by and through which this came into being require informed historical imagination, with large gaps in what is known and can be known.

We know the beginning and end of the track that led to the New Testament canon.[22] At the beginning stands Paul the active missionary, who writes to new converts he knows personally and whose history he has shared. At the end stands the Pauline letter corpus incorporated into the New Testament. A combination of data and historical imagination yields the following plausible sketch.

Stage 1: Paul and his coworkers. Paul, often in consultation with his coworkers (see on 1 Thess 1:1), writes to a particular congregation or group of house churches. The apostolic letter is not a casual communication and is not received as such. It is repeatedly read in the worship and instruction of the church. In the weeks and months after the letter's reception, new members are added to the congregations, people who have not known Paul personally and did not experience the original founding events. If these new members are to understand the Scriptures read in the churches, and Paul's letter(s) to the congregation read alongside them, teachers and other members of the congregation must supply the needed interpretation. Thus even *First* Thessalonians, with its *particular* address to the new converts in Thessalonica, was already read by some in the first generation, within the church in Thessalonica, with the hermeneutical dynamic of "not written to us" / "written to us" (see intro to 1 Thessalonians, "Canonical Context").

After Paul's death, Paul's coworkers continue in various settings as representatives of the Pauline gospel; they are not new figures on the scene who must defend their legitimacy but are already involved in the ongoing life of the churches. Their names have been joined with Paul's in sending letters that are now read regularly in the Pauline churches.

Stage 2: Letters exchanged. Already during Paul's lifetime, congregations would receive letters from Paul that had not been delivered directly to them, but to some other congregation that shared them with sister congregations. This would have been the case with house churches in the same city, and it was probably the point of Paul's solemn insistence that 1 Thessalonians be read to *all* the brothers and sisters (1 Thess 5:27). Likewise it seems more probable

---

21. See the bibliography in Ascough 2003, 2014, 79.
22. A comprehensive historical perspective would, of course, include para- and postcanonical texts reflecting Paul's influence.

that the plurality of congregations in a region would receive copies of a letter delivered to one congregation in the region rather than that the original letter was carried from church to church (see 1 Cor 1:2; 2 Cor 1:1; Gal 1:2). If Colossians was written by Paul, it was already understood and expected that believers in the Pauline churches were to read letters written to other congregations, and to share the letter written to them with others (Col 4:16). If, as is more likely, Colossians is deuteropauline, the author assumes this practice as already standard in the first generation.

Stage 3: Network of Pauline teachers continues. The informal connections and lines of communication established in the first generation continue and grow. Mainly as a result of Paul's influence, letters as such become a major vehicle of instruction in the churches. The sharing of letters, informal at first, begins to jell into small collections that are circulated as a corpus. We have no hard data at all from the first two generations after Paul's death, the likely time of the composition of 2 Thessalonians. While some collections, with varying contents, probably circulated in the 80s and 90s C.E., there was as yet no firm list. Thus the view that the author of 2 Thessalonians intends his letter to "replace" 1 Thessalonians is anachronistic; when he writes, there is no collection from which 1 Thessalonians is to be dropped and "replaced" by his own work. He launches his own writing into a complex interchange of oral tradition and written documents that includes Letters of Paul, deuteropauline letters, and other genres of early Christian writing.[23]

By the end of the first century, there seem to have been seven-letter collections. Revelation's "seven letter" corpus (Rev 2–3) and the almost immediate collection and circulation of Ignatius's letters as a seven-letter corpus may well reflect a pattern already present in collections of Pauline Letters.[24]

Stage 4: Letters interpreted, edited, and amplified. The presence of letters, regularly read in worship and used in instruction, has become a given not only in the Pauline churches, but also in other streams of early Christian tradition. The "not-written-to-us" / "written-to-us" dynamic becomes paradigmatic for transmitting, forming, and norming the content of the faith. It becomes standard procedure that a letter written earlier to a particular congregation, as to Corinth,

---

23. Contra, e.g., Lindemann (1977), who follows Hilgenfeld's 1862 theory in arguing that the author wrote specifically to replace 1 Thessalonians, the letter "purportedly from us" of 2:2. This theory has convinced few. Not least of its problems is that the author himself adopts 1 Thessalonians as his template and borrows much of its phraseology, which he would hardly do if he considered his model as not itself written by Paul. Although in 2:2 a letter purportedly from Paul can convey error or misunderstanding, in 2:15 the authentic tradition from Paul is represented by a letter; thus the church is in a situation where it must discern the authentic tradition from within a multiplicity of letters circulating in Paul's name.

24. The Muratorian Fragment documents that by the end of the 2d cent. C.E. it was understood that Paul's Letters were addressed to seven churches, with seven considered a symbolic number representing the "one church spread throughout the whole extent of the earth."

is now understood to address the wider church of a later time. The present text of 1 Cor 1:2 addresses the letter not only to believers in Corinth, but along with them to "all those in every place who invoke the name of the Lord Jesus, their Lord and ours."[25] Christians of the second and third generations learn about Paul by reading what he has written. This image is projected back into the framework of Paul's life, so that even in the deuteropauline Ephesians the readers know about Paul's insight into the gospel only from his *letters* (Eph 3:4–8).

The meaning of some parts of the letters had not always been clear even to their original readers. When the letters were heard and taken seriously by later readers, in a different situation, they required interpretation. In the second and third generations, this interpretation was not given by composing commentaries that distinguished between what Paul had originally said to "them" and later comments explaining what Paul's letter now means to "us," but instead by amplifying Paul's Letters themselves—by editing, glossing, and composing new letters in his name. Just as individual letters had been amplified by non-Pauline insertions, so the emerging corpus of Pauline teaching as a whole was amplified by composing new letters in his name. In 2 Thessalonians and other deuteropauline letters, the living voice of Paul, in concert with the collection of Paul's own letters, continues to instruct the churches.

Structure and Summary of the Argument of the Letter

Since the author of 2 Thessalonians is using 1 Thessalonians as his basic template, 2 Thessalonians has aspects of the structure of 1 Thessalonians. He does not copy this structure mechanically but adapts it to his own agenda.

This agenda comprises three interrelated items: (1) persecution, (2) eschatology, and (3) the structure and leadership of the congregation. The reinterpreted eschatology of the central section is not abstract doctrine, but has a pastoral concern; it is the theological basis and center for the two hortatory concerns: persecution and leadership. These two are also interrelated. The community's response to persecution is not just an individual matter; it also concerns the believer's relation to the community. The community's continued existence and mission depend to some extent on its structure and internal cohesion and its sense of mutual responsibility. How best to do this was a matter of intense discussion in the Pauline school. In some streams of post-Pauline Christianity, the firming up of leadership structures was in order to resist false teaching.

---

25. This text could have given a powerful impetus to the general circulation and reception of Paul's Letters, or could be the result of it if it was not part of the original wording but added in the process of collecting and editing the Pauline corpus. There is no MS evidence for this conjecture (of addition), so if these words are not originally from Paul, they must have been added very early in the collection and editing process. Weiss (1925, ad loc.) and others consider the phrase to be an editorial addition. Conzelmann (1975, 22) reviews the discussion and considers the phrase original.

This was the internal threat. The author of 2 Thessalonians is only moderately concerned about this, only at the point of eschatology—and even here, it is not a matter of combating heretical opponents who were a threat to the core understanding of the faith. The author is more concerned about the external threat and the church's remaining faithful under the duress of harassment and persecution. His reformulation of eschatology is not a matter of correct doctrine, but rather is intended to disabuse the church of a false hope that the end is near, thus enabling it to make a realistic response to external pressures. The author calls Christian believers to resist the social and political pressures of the church's non-Christian context. Such harassment and persecution was carried on by those who considered themselves to be the insiders of responsible society and regarded the Christian believers as outsiders. The coming judgment will show who are the real insiders (ch. 1). But this will not be soon (ch. 2). The churches need to sustain a cohesive community to resist the external (as well as internal) pressures, but this does not mean they are to have a separate class of salaried leaders (ch. 3). These are the author's own concerns, inserted into the matrix of 1 Thessalonians, the Pauline letter he found most congenial for his purpose.

The author adopted 1 Thessalonians as his template for the reasons given above, and he superimposed upon its outline his own thematic structure. The structure of 2 Thessalonians thus represents the merging of two different compositional patterns and their respective dynamics and emphases. The relation of the structure of 2 Thessalonians to 1 Thessalonians is somewhat analogous to the structure of a house built on the foundation of an earlier house; though it has a different floor plan, it follows the constraints of the earlier structure, some elements of which can still be seen, whether as built into the new house or as protruding from the later construction without having their original function.

These considerations result in the following structure:

1:1–2	Prescript (greeting)
1:3–2:17	Thanksgiving/body
1:3–12	Thanksgiving
1:3–4	Thanksgiving as obligation
(1:5–10	*First insertion: Ultimate justice despite present injustice)*
1:11–12	The author's prayer
(2:1–12	*Second insertion: The day of the Lord)*
2:13–17	Second thanksgiving and benediction
3:1–16	Paraenesis: The life to which Christians are called
3:1–5	Prayer for the missionaries
(3:6–16	*Third insertion: The "disorderly")*
3:17–18	Conclusion: Authentication and benediction

COMMENTARY ON
2 THESSALONIANS

Title

To the Thessalonians B′

See commentary on the title to 1 Thessalonians.

1:1–2 Prescript (Greeting)

1:1 Paul, Silvanus, and Timothy, to the church of the Thessalonians in God our Father and the Lord Jesus Christ. 2 Grace to you and peace from God our Father and the Lord Jesus Christ.

[1:1–2] The greetings of the seven undisputed letters all have the same basic elements, but no two of them have such close verbal agreement as 1 and 2 Thessalonians. The author reproduces the greeting in 1 Thessalonians virtually verbatim, only adding "our" to the first "Father" and appending "from God our Father and the Lord Jesus Christ." The additions do not change the meaning but represent assimilation to the developing manuscript tradition of Paul's Letters, bringing the greeting into conformity with the standard form found in all the undisputed letters. This assimilation also results in a ponderous duplication of the phrase "God our Father and the Lord Jesus Christ," not found in Paul's undisputed Letters, reflecting editorial rather than spontaneous composition. This does not mean that the author is only a mechanical repeater of Paul's original lively discourse, but suggests that, after a generation or two of usage in the liturgy and instruction in Pauline churches, Paul's language has now become somewhat sonorous and liturgical (see at 1:3).

At the beginning we notice that the modern reader's understanding of the text will vary depending on whether it is read as from Paul to people he knows—to whom he has preached and whom he has baptized, with whom he has worshiped and celebrated the Eucharist—or read as a teaching document in the Pauline churches composed for people who know Paul only as the heroic founding figure of the churches, whose letters are read in worship alongside the (Jewish) Scriptures.

When Paul wrote his letter to Thessalonica in 50 C.E. (1 Thessalonians), he had expected to live to see the Parousia and had not reckoned with an apostolic authority that would need to be continued into later generations. By reproducing almost verbatim the greeting of 1 Thessalonians, the deuteropauline author expresses his intent to extend the authority of the earlier letter into his own time. Here the plural authorship—"Paul, Silvanus, and Timothy"—reflects the network of teachers in the Pauline school.

As was typical of such teachers, they address their readers as those who have never "seen me face to face" (Col 2:1) and who are hearing the voice of Paul in letters written to churches to which the authors do not themselves belong. The letter thus makes real to the reader the fictive world of both author and reader and allows them to appropriate it as a word from Paul spoken to them (cf. esp. Col 2:1; even if Colossians is regarded as written by Paul himself, such texts indicate that the deuteropauline letters are in continuity with Paul's intent and practice).

One might reasonably ask why the title "apostle" does not appear here, as in Paul's own later letters, and in the first line of all the other deuteropauline letters. While there can be no doubt that the author affirms Paul's apostolic authority, it may well be that one of the reasons he has adopted 1 Thessalonians as his template is that it lacks explicit claim to hierarchical authority, and he does not wish to add this claim to his adoption of 1 Thess 1:1 as the beginning of his letter. The inclusion of Silvanus and Timothy, and the continuation of the "we"-address of 1 Thessalonians, reinforces this collegial understanding of authority. The Pastorals will present Timothy as the next link in the hierarchical chain below Paul; here he is presented as Paul's colleague. We probably already have an anticipation of the author's resistance to the developing monarchial episcopate (see on 3:6–13). Readers are invited to hear the letter as directly representing the authoritative voice of Paul to their own time, unmediated by "clerical" authority. In their troubled situation, they continue to hear and receive the apostolic mediation of grace and peace.

The letter begins (1:2) and ends (3:16, emphatically) with the pronouncement of "peace," *shalom*, the ultimate well-being provided by the grace of God. The content of the letter itself is filled with references to the violence the readers are suffering for their faith, and the threat/promise of eschatological violence that will establish the justice of God's kingdom. These two pronouncements of the peace of God to the worshiping congregation (the only references to "peace" in the letter) may simply be following the Pauline convention, but more likely they point to the reality that present suffering and eschatological judgment are finally embraced within the framework of the peace of God, thus relativizing the statements about present and future violence by placing them in their ultimate context.[1]

1. So Bassler 1991, 71–85.

2 Thessalonians 1:3–2:17
Thanksgiving for the Coming Judgment and Salvation of God

1:3–12 Thanksgiving

This rich, dense, one-sentence paragraph is not merely a preface to the author's "main concern," as though the substance of the letter begins with the revision of eschatology that first appears in 2:1–12. Such readings reverse horse and cart, dog and tail, and regard steadfastness under persecution as a prelude to the purported real theme of eschatology. In fact, the deuteropauline author, like Paul himself, is concerned to focus on the real situation of the community, with eschatology as the necessary theological support and framework for his pastoral instruction. Caring for distressed believers, not teaching correct eschatology, is the author's concern. He does this, however, by introducing the theme of the Last Judgment and the coming visible glory of Christ early on, integrating his call to resistance to cultural pressure into the eschatological framework. The following format suggests the solemn, somewhat poetic structure of this long, complex sentence.

1:3 We should always give thanks to God for you, brothers and sisters,
    for it is right that we should do so,
because your faithfulness[a] is becoming stronger and stronger,
    and your love for one another, each for all, is growing greater and
        greater,
4 so that we ourselves boast about you in the churches of God
    for your steadfast endurance, that is,[b] your faithfulness
    in all the persecutions and sufferings you are enduring
5 —clear evidence for[c] God's coming righteous judgment,
    which will result in your being declared worthy[d] of the kingdom of
        God,
    for[e] which you are in fact suffering,
6 since, after all, in God's sight it is only right
    to repay those who are causing your suffering by making them suffer
        themselves 7 and
    to grant relief to you who are suffering, along with us,

when the Lord Jesus is revealed from heaven in fiery flame,^f
with the angels of his power^g **8** meting out justice^h to those who do not
  know God,
that is, those who do not obey the gospel of our Lord Jesus,ⁱ
9 who will pay the penalty of agelong^j ruin
away from the presence of the Lord and his powerful glory^k
10 on that day^l when he comes
  to be glorified^k by his saints,
  to be praised for his majesty by all those who have become
    believers^m—
  for in fact our testimony to you has been believed^m—
11 for all of whichⁿ we are always praying for you,
  that our God will make^o you worthy of his call
  and will fulfill every good resolve^p and faithful deed by his power,
12 so that the name of our Lord Jesus will be glorified^k by^q you,
  and you by^q him,
  according to the grace of our God and Lord, Jesus Christ.^r

a. *Pistis* can be rendered as "faith" or "faithfulness." See on 1 Thess 3:2; and the discussion below, in Excursus 1: "Persecution." On the translation of *hypomonē* by "steadfast endurance," see on 1 Thess 1:3.

b. The two nouns *hypomenē* (steadfast endurance) and *pistis* (faithfulness) are objects of the single preposition *hyper* and are united by a single article; the repeated possessive pronoun "your," necessary for English syntax, represents a single pronoun, *hymōn.* The *kai* (and, also, even) is thus best taken as epexegetical: the two terms joined by the conjunction are not two different items, but the second explicates the first; cf. *charin kai apostolēn*: "grace, that is, the apostolic office" (Rom 1:5). *Kai* could also, as in some translations, simply mean "also"; i.e., "you too are suffering for the kingdom—you are not the only ones but are included in the suffering ecumenical church." This same note was struck often in second- and third-generation churches related to the Pauline tradition (cf. 1 Pet 4:12; 5:8; Heb 11:1–12:3; Revelation passim).

c. A syntactical difficulty is created by the absence of a verb, which must be understood or supplied, and by the rare form of *endeigma* ("clear evidence," only here in the NT and not in the LXX), which can be either nominative or accusative. *Endeigma* can be either the subject of an understood "which is," or an appositive referring to something in the preceding clause. In the latter case, this could be the persecution, the readers' endurance, or both. "For" represents the Greek genitive case and can mean that the present evidence points toward the coming judgment, or that the persecution and the believers' response is evidence that will be introduced in the coming judgment to show that God's judgment is just. The translation above, though awkward, stays close to the original text and retains the ambiguity.

d. *Eis to* + infinitive often means purpose but can also mean result (e.g., 1 Thess 2:12, 16; 2 Thess 2:11). *Kataxioō* can mean to make worthy, but elsewhere in the NT it always means "declare worthy," "deem worthy." Thus four different combinations of these meanings are theoretically possible. The context calls for the translation rendered above.

e. The preposition *hyper* (here = "for") can have a variety of functions. This is one of several ambiguous elements in the syntax of this long, complex sentence. Here the meaning can be "for" in the sense of "in order to obtain"—suffering now in order to enter the kingdom later, so that suffering is God's way of making the believer worthy of the coming kingdom. Alternatively, *hyper* as "for" can interpret suffering as the result of one's confession of Jesus as the true Lord and representative of God's kingdom.

f. The Greek syntax is ambiguous, so that the fire could conceivably go with either "revealed from heaven" or "meting out justice." The verse division is unhelpfully located, and some English versions compound the misunderstanding by placing a comma between vv. 7 and 8. The long association of fire with theophany provides strong, though not compelling, evidence that the fiery flame describes the appearance of the Lord, not the punishment of the condemned (see comments).

g. *Dynamis* (power) modifies Jesus, not the angels; *autou* (his) modifies *dynamis*, not angels: his *power*, not his *angels* (so NJB, contra most modern English versions). "His powerful angels" understands the phrase in terms of Hebrew grammar, not Greek. Though the phrase is awkward, it is clear that the reference is to Jesus, who returns in power and has angels in his charge, not to his being accompanied by powerful angels.

h. *Ekdikēsis* has been consistently translated "vengeance" in the tradition that extends from Wycliffe through Tyndale, the Bishops' Bible, Douay, the Geneva Bible, and into the KJV, then into the RV, ASV, RSV, and NRSV. Most other English versions have rendered it as "punish(ment)" (REB, NAB, TEV, CEV, and the whole NIV tradition), "retribution" (NAS95), "penalty" (NJB), or "justice" (CEB). See comments on vv. 6–9.

i. In the Greek text, each of the two phrases ("those who do not know God" and "those who do not obey the gospel of our Lord Jesus") has its own article, which in Greek grammar would often signal that they refer to two distinct groups.[1] In this case, however, the repetition of the article is a matter of biblical parallelism, not two different groups, which would be called for by standard grammar. See Jer 10:25a, which has two phrases, one of which is "those who do not know you [viz., God]," but both obviously refer to the same group.

j. *Aiōnios* has frequently been translated "eternal," reflecting the Greek philosophical distinction between time and eternity, becoming and being, space-time existence and transcendent being. This distinction is unknown to the Hebrew biblical tradition, which thinks in terms of this-worldly time and manifests no interest in metaphysical endlessness. The standard lexicon of biblical Greek thus lists "a long period of time" as the first meaning (BDAG 33). Here the author is not speculating on whether divine punishment is endless, but he is placing it in the age to come rather than in the present world. Though I have sometimes retained "eternal" in the commentary, it is always meant in this biblical sense. Thus such expressions as "eternal life" refer primarily to the quality of life of the age to come, not to the chronological quantity of endless time.

---

1. The use of the Greek article is more subtle than often assumed. See Wallace (270–77), whose full discussion shows the fallacy of too-simple application of such "rules."

234

2 Thessalonians 1:3–12

k. The vocabulary of glory/glorify (*doxa/doxazō*) is found here three times (vv. 9, 10, 12, plus 2:14; 3:1). *Doxa* does not occur in the section of 1 Thessalonians the author is using as his template, but is used thrice by Paul elsewhere in the letter (1 Thess 2:6, 12, 20). Some English versions (e.g., CEV, CEB) render this with "praise" or "honor," as more in accord with both modern speech and ancient understandings of honor/shame. Such translations miss both the power of the author's repetition, which the English reader can no longer hear, and the theophanic majesty of the divine glory resonant in *doxa* and its cognates (see comments on v. 9).

l. *Hēmera* (day) here retains and sums up the image of the coming future Day of Judgment, the imagery of the courtroom scene in which evidence is weighed and judgment is pronounced (cf. *hēmera* in 1 Cor 4:3). In the Greek text, *en tē hēmera* concludes v. 10, at the climactic end of a long series of clauses, referring to everything in vv. 5–10. To express the same point in English syntax, it is better to move the phrase to this earlier position, though something of the dramatic impact is lost.

m. These aorists are not the typical style of Paul, who uses the present tense in such instances. A few MSS "correct" *pisteusasin* to the present *pisteuousin* (Ψ 33 630 2464 and parts of the Syriac and Coptic MS traditions), but both MS evidence and the author's consistent usage elsewhere indicate that the aorist is original.

n. Some editions of the Greek New Testament place a period here and begin a new sentence with v. 11. However, v. 11 begins with a dependent prepositional phrase, and there is no independent subject or predicate in vv. 11–12, which continue the one long sentence that began at v. 3. The neuter relative pronoun *ho* refers to the whole preceding constellation of the future judgment scenario.

o. *Axioō* may be either "make worthy" or "declare worthy." The related form *kataxioō* in v. 5 is best rendered "declared worthy," but here the context seems to call for "make worthy."

p. *Eudokian agathōsynēs* (mechanically and lit., "goodwill of goodness") refers to one's good intentions. There is no possessive pronoun, so it is not clear whether the reference is to the intent of God (so KJV, NKJV) or the believer (virtually all other English translations).

q. The *en* in the parallel phrases *en hymin // en autō* could be translated "in" (locative) or "by" (instrumental). For Paul, whose thought was profoundly shaped by his "in Christ" theology (see on 1 Thess 1:1), the translation might well be "in you" // "in him." The deuteropauline author is not deeply influenced by this theology, however, and intends the pair of phrases instrumentally and reciprocally: at the Parousia, Christ will be glorified *by* believers, and believers will be glorified *by* Christ.

r. *God* and *Lord Jesus Christ* are united by a single article, resulting in the translation above. Only a few English versions so translate (e.g., NAB, TNIV mg., NIV11 mg.). Most insert an extra "the" to distinguish God and the Lord Jesus. While grammatically possible, this seems to be influenced by what the translators regard as Paul's theology (see comments on v. 12).

The author omits all the autobiographical particulars of 1 Thessalonians and goes directly to the first theme related to his own agenda, the persecution threatening the readers. Before proceeding with the exegesis, we bring this aspect of the letter's context into sharper focus with a consideration of persecution in that period.

Excursus 1: Persecution in the Second and Third Generations

In 1 Thessalonians, Paul has already repeatedly declared that those who have become Christian believers will inevitably face persecution (see intro to 1 Thessalonians, "New Congregation," and comments on 1 Thess 1:3, 6; 2:13–16; 3:3–7). This is one reason the author of 2 Thessalonians chose 1 Thessalonians as the template for his own letter. He attaches his own discourse to Paul's statements in such a way that persecution becomes a central focus of the author's exhortation and his first topic. Immediately he incorporates his praise for readers' endurance into the initial words of thanksgiving, referring to persecution more frequently and making the theme more prominent than in 1 Thessalonians. The references to persecution are not part of the fictive world of Paul, but belong to the present, experienced world of the author and his readers. The community of Christian believers was no longer faced with one last battle, but with a war of attrition, and the line between acceptable accommodation to the culture and faithful resistance had become blurred and debated.

First Thessalonians pictures persecution as inherent in the life to which its first-generation readers had been converted, an inevitable component of their initial break from and clash with their culture, in the prospect of the near Parousia—persecution to be faced in the power of the Spirit and the new life to which they have been converted. For Paul, persecution has been part of the *eschatological* events. In the world projected by the deuteropauline letters, where many Christians have been born into believing families and have grown up in the faith (e.g., 2 Tim 1:5; 3:14–15), persecution was a reality of continuing *history*, and the church is settling in for the long pull, thinking through how to come to terms with a hostile world that is not going away soon.

The initial readers of 2 Thessalonians knew, of course, the threats and problems of their own social situation. The letter does not need to spell this out. In order to come within hearing distance of what the letter has to say, the modern reader needs to enter imaginatively into the world directly experienced by its first readers. This can only be done indirectly, by overhearing descriptions of the Christian community as perceived by outsiders, and by a close reading of other Christian texts of the same period.

The Roman view from outside. How should we picture this world into which 2 Thessalonians is launched? We might best begin by pondering the following excerpt from a letter of Pliny the Younger, new governor of Bithynia, to the emperor Trajan, around 111 C.E. Since Pliny refers to similar events as long as twenty-five years earlier, his description spans the time in which 2 Thessalonians was presumably written.

> I have never been present at the interrogation of Christians. Therefore, I do not know how far such investigations should be pushed, and what sort of punishments are appropriate. I have also been uncertain as to whether age makes any difference, or whether the very young are dealt with in the same way as adults,

whether repentance and renunciation of Christianity is sufficient, or whether the accused are still considered criminals because they were once Christians even if they later renounced it, and whether persons are to be punished simply for the name "Christian" even if no criminal act has been committed, or whether only crimes associated with the name are to be punished.

In the meantime, I have handled those who have been denounced to me as Christians as follows: I asked them whether they were Christians. Those who responded affirmatively I have asked a second and third time, under threat of the death penalty. If they persisted in their confession [Latin *perseverantes*, related to *hypomonē*, "endurance"; cf. 2 Thess 1:4; 3:5], I had them executed. For whatever it is that they are actually advocating, it seems to me that obstinacy and stubbornness must be punished in any case. Others who labor under the same delusion, but who were Roman citizens, I have designated to be sent to Rome.

In the course of the investigations, as it usually happens, charges are brought against wider circles of people, and the following special cases have emerged:

An unsigned placard was posted, accusing a large number of people by name. Those who denied being Christians now or in the past, I thought necessary to release, since they invoked our gods according to the formula I gave them and since they offered sacrifices of wine and incense before your image, which I had brought in for this purpose along with the statues of our gods; I also had them curse Christ. It is said that real Christians cannot be forced to do any of these things.

Others charged by this accusation at first admitted that they had once been Christians, but had already renounced it; they had in fact been Christians, but had given it up, some of them three years ago, some even earlier, some as long as twenty-five years ago. All of these worshiped your image and the statues of the gods, and cursed Christ. They verified, however, that their entire guilt or error consisted in the fact that on a specified day before sunrise they were accustomed to gather and sing an antiphonal hymn to Christ as their god and to pledge themselves by an oath not to engage in any crime, but to abstain from all thievery, assault, and adultery, not to break their word once they had given it, and not to refuse to pay their legal debts. They then went their separate ways, and came together later to eat a common meal, but it was ordinary, harmless food. They discontinued even this practice in accordance with my edict by which I had forbidden political associations, in accord with your instructions. I considered it all the more necessary to obtain by torture a confession of the truth from two female slaves, whom they called "deaconnesses." I found nothing more than a vulgar, excessive superstition.[2]

This is the earliest extant source in which we have a window into the Roman world's view of the early church. For our purposes, we need to keep in mind two complementary aspects of the picture projected by Pliny's letter.

2. Pliny the Younger, *Ep.* 10.96–97; cited from Boring 1989, 14–15, ET by Boring.

1. Eighty years after the Roman condemnation and crucifixion of Jesus and the beginning of the church, there was no general or official persecution of Christians. Pliny was a well-informed career officer in the Roman government, acquainted with the historians Tacitus and Suetonius, who had made brief references to the early Christian movement.[3] He did not know who the Christians were, whether they were to be considered criminals, or how to deal with them. We should not picture the world in which the addressees of 2 Thessalonians lived as always and officially persecuting the church. The first official, systematic, empire-wide persecution of Christians occurred under the emperors Decius and Diocletian, more than a century after 2 Thessalonians was written.

2. Pliny's letter reveals that the new Christian group lived under constant threat and pressure, not so much from the government but from the suspicious populace. This pressure could be expressed in harassment and discrimination, and it could sometimes erupt into mob violence, arrest, torture, and death. From the underside of society, Christians learned the arrogance of power. They could be arrested and tortured as a matter of intimidation or to obtain information about their group. They could be subjected to arbitrary tests to determine their loyalty to society and the government. And they experienced the disdain of neighbors, community leaders, and government officials. No doubt there was considerable variety, depending on place and time, but the potential for active persecution was always there. Since the execution of James, one of the original apostles, by Herod Agrippa I in the 40s (Acts 12:2), the killing of James the brother of Jesus by the Jerusalem Jewish authorities in the early 60s (see Josephus, *Ant.* 20.9), and the arrest, condemnation, and gruesome executions of Roman Christians in 64 C.E. under Nero, Christians throughout the empire knew that they always lived in precarious circumstances.

The believers' view from inside. The shift from an eschatological view of persecution to a historical perspective is illustrated by Matt 10:17–22, written at approximately the same time as 2 Thessalonians. The author of Matthew transfers the persecutions from Mark's apocalyptic discourse (Mark 13:9–13), which portrays the extraordinary events of the end times as including terrible persecutions, to the mission discourse, the "ordinary" life of the church carrying on its mission in history, no longer in the shadow of the coming end (see also Matt 24:10–12, in which persecution is the "normal" ethos of the church; and 24:15–22, which resists seeing persecution in terms of "realized eschatology"). In a striking way this corresponds to the reinterpretation of apocalyptic troubles by second- and third-generation Christianity, illustrated as 2 Thessalonians reinterprets the persecution in 1 Thessalonians: it is not a onetime-only climax at the end of the world but is woven into the warp and woof of ongoing history.

3. Tacitus (*Ann.* 15.44.2–5) reports that Nero blamed the great fire in Rome (64 C.E.) on the Christians and had them arrested and killed. Suetonius (*Claud.* 25.4) briefly mentions that Claudius expelled the Jews from Rome, apparently in 49 C.E., because they were making disturbances at the instigation of a certain "Chrestus." This is probably his misunderstanding of problems caused in the synagogues of Rome by Christian Jews evangelizing in the name of Christ (Chrestus, a Greek name common among Romans, was pronounced the same as *Christos* = Christ).

The variety and fragility of the church's situation into which 2 Thessalonians is launched are illustrated by the letters of Ignatius, bishop of Antioch. Ignatius was arrested, condemned, and en route to martyrdom in Rome about the same time Pliny is exchanging letters with the emperor on whether Christians should be actively prosecuted. On stopovers at various points during the journey to Rome, the prisoner Ignatius is visited by numerous other Christians and leaders of their congregations, who seem not to be endangered by their association with the condemned criminal. Ignatius's guard of ten soldiers makes no attempt to interfere with the visits or to arrest other Christians or their leaders. Ignatius writes to them without any indication that they are in legal danger from the state. Yet all know that at any time they could find themselves in the same situation as Ignatius.

The Paul of the Deuteropaulines declares that being persecuted is the cost of discipleship for all believers, not just prominent leaders who attract public and official opposition (2 Tim 3:12), and not just for the terminal generation living in the glow of the near Parousia. It is instructive to closely read the deuteropauline and associated literature, including Hebrews, the Catholic Letters, and Acts, with this one question in mind: what picture(s) of the persecuted Christian community of the second and third generations do they project, the world in which the readers of 2 Thessalonians lived? Such a reading opens up numerous vistas helpful to a historical understanding. For example, warnings against the greed and love of money that cause some to wander away from the faith may not always be general condemnations of avarice, but responses to the economic deprivations suffered by those who persisted in the faith, a sacrifice not all were willing to make (e.g., 1 Tim 6:10). The language of 2 Thessalonians often resembles the vocabulary and imagery of other letters to churches in the Pauline tradition facing persecution. First Peter, for example, portrays Christians as suffering various *trials*, for the sake of the *name* of Christ, tested by *fire*, with an *endurance* that results in *glory* at the *revelation* of Jesus Christ, which will result in a *reversal of present circumstances* by the *righteous* Judge who *judges each one impartially* (1 Pet 1:6–17; 4:2–12). All these motifs are found in the opening section of 2 Thessalonians (1:3–12). Such references apply not only to the particular readers addressed in the fictive world of each letter; according to 1 Pet 5:8, this same experience of suffering is required of all Christians throughout the world. Already in the readership addressed by the Gospel of Mark (ca. 70 C.E.), 4:17 can take it for granted that "trouble or persecution arises on account of the word" and is a reality in the missionary churches generally. To explore this approach thoroughly would be a monograph-sized undertaking,[4] far beyond the scope of a commentary, but a sampling of the results of such a close reading is illuminating.

---

4. For summary discussions, see Potter; Oster; and their bibliographies. For more extensive treatments, see Frend; and the relevant essays in Mitchell, Young, and Bowie. Moss (2013) rightly rejects the oversimplified view that from the beginning all Christians were persecuted by evil Romans; she warns against a "martyr complex" in the later church (though this is not a danger prevalent in modern American Christianity), but hardly does justice to the realities of social problems faced by the church of the first two centuries.

Prison, judge, judgment imagery. As a consequence of his missionary work, Paul himself was imprisoned several times, experience referred to almost incidentally as a "normal" part of church life (2 Cor 6:5; Rom 16:7). It is only in the sarcastic and ironic "fool's speech" of 2 Corinthians, however, that imprisonment becomes a (reversed-value) authentication of legitimate apostleship (11:23, 32). Of the seven undisputed letters, Philippians and Philemon were actually written from prison, probably about the same time, from the same situation. The Letter to Philemon emphasizes the identity of Paul as "prisoner for the cause of Christ Jesus" (CEB; v. 1 and then four other times in the brief letter). It is no accident that the actual setting of Philemon became the fictive setting for the earliest deuteropauline letter (cf. Col 4:10–18), and that "Paul the prisoner" becomes a dominant image in the deuteropauline letters (Col 4:10, 18; Eph 3:1; 4:1, 8; 6:20; 2 Tim 1:8, 16–17; 2:9). Already in the 90s, Clement of Rome can refer to Paul as having been "seven times in chains" (the complete, symbolic number; *1 Clem.* 5.6). In the later stage of this tradition, Acts portrays not only Paul but also other church leaders and Christians as suffering imprisonment, which they endure not only with courage but even with joy (Acts 4:3–31; 5:18–41; 8:3; 12:1–17; 16:19–34; 20:23). In the entire final quarter of the Acts narrative (21:24–28:31), Paul is in Roman custody, detained in prisons in Jerusalem, Caesarea, and Rome. Hebrews and Revelation, though not deuteropauline, also have contacts with the Pauline tradition and presuppose that imprisonment of some members is a standard feature of church life (Heb 10:34, 36; 13:3; Rev 2:10). The exhortations to remember, visit, and care for those in prison are not only, or even primarily, humanitarian compassion for prisoners in general, but indeed express concern for fellow church members who have been arrested (e.g., Matt 25:36, 43, 44). The moving depiction of Paul in prison (2 Tim 4:9–18, 21) is to encourage the readers to follow the Pauline model, to fight the good fight, to keep the faith, to suffer when necessary, to visit and attend those in prison, to "come before winter."

The image of standing before judges and being condemned in human courts became integral to the self-understanding of the faithful community, as did the sure hope of a reversal of these verdicts in a Last Judgment that will reveal the justice of the Ultimate Judge. This is one factor in the pervasive language of judgment that permeates the Christian texts written in the same general period as 2 Thessalonians (and the traditions they incorporate; e.g., Matt 10:14–16, 26–28; 11:22–24; 12:41–42; Luke 18:1–7; John 5:28–30; 7:51; 8:15–16; 12:46–48; 16:7–11; Acts 10:42; 17:31; 23:1–3; 24:10, 25; 1 Tim 5:24; 2 Tim 4:1, 8; Heb 4:12–13; 6:2; 9:27; 10:26–27, 30; 12:23; 13:4; Jas 2:13; 4:12; 5:9; 1 Pet 1:17; 2:12, 23; 4:5–6, 16–17; 2 Pet 2:9; 3:7; 1 John 4:17; Jude 6, 15; Rev 6:10; 11:18; 14:7; 15:4; 16:5, 7; 18:10, 20; 19:2; 20:4, 11–15).

In what I regard as the earliest deuteropauline letter, the hearers are addressed by the voice of Paul-the-prisoner, a voice that continues throughout the later Pauline tradition (Col 4:10). The greeting in his own hand refers to only one thing: his imprisonment (4:18). The first words of Colossians address the readers as those who are *pistoi* (faithful-under-pressure), which represents a semantic shift in key Pauline vocabulary.

Semantic shift from faith to faithfulness. Paul's "faith" terminology includes the verb *pisteuō* (to believe), the noun *pistis* (belief, faith), and the adjective *pistos* (having-faith, believing, faithful). The vocabulary cluster is multilayered, with the three overlapping meanings of personal trust, the content of what is believed, and faithfulness (see on 1 Thess 3:2). Paul uses this vocabulary with all three meanings, as does the deuteropauline tradition. However, a discernible semantic shift takes place between the seven undisputed letters of the first generation and the six deuteropauline letters addressed to the Pauline churches of the second and third generations.[5]

	pisteuō, to believe	*pistis*, faith	*pistos*, faithful
Paul, seven letters	42× in 6 letters 1.74× per 1,000 words	91× in 7 letters 3.78× per 1,000	9× in 4 letters .37× per 1,000
Deuteropaul, six letters	12× in 5 letters 1.45× per 1,000	51× in 6 letters 6.15 per 1,000	11× in 6 letters 1.33× per 1,000

Paul manifests a more dynamic understanding of believing, of faith as obedience-in-personal-trust, for which the verb is more appropriate; of 142 occurrences of the faith vocabulary, 42 are the verbal *pisteuō* (= 30%), 26 of these in the present tense (which never occurs in 2 Thessalonians). For the Deuteropaulines, the 74 occurrences of the faith vocabulary include only 12 uses of the verb (= 16%). There is a corresponding dramatic increase in the use of the noun and adjective in the Deuteropaulines (as indicated by the data in the table above). Moreover, not only is there this significant shift to the noun and adjective; the meaning of each also clearly shifts from "faith" toward "faithfulness" in these letters. Thus, for example, in the opening words of the earliest deuteropauline letter, the readers are addressed as *hagioi kai pistoi adelphoi* (Col 1:2, "holy and faithful brothers and sisters"), which not only means "believing" (the Christian faith), as assumed, but also "faithful," holding on to the faith under duress. What defines the identity of the readers is not a contrast between believers and unbelievers, but between faithful and unfaithful. This phrase is then picked up and intensified in Eph 1:1, "to the saints who are also faithful." Paul rarely uses *pistos* (faithful); when he does, it is mostly for the faithfulness of God or for human faithfulness, only in Gal 3:9 as a designation for Christian believers per se.[6] The dramatic increase in frequency and the shift in meaning of both *pistis* and *pistos* in the Deuteropaulines indicate that in the second and third generations being a believer comes to mean holding on to the faith under the pressure of developments within the church judged to be heretical, as well as external pressures to apostatize.[7]

5. These data are presented in full awareness that the database is not large enough, nor the statistical methodology sophisticated and rigorous enough, for such comments to be probative, but they nonetheless add strands to the web of evidence and illustrate the deuteropauline character of the six disputed letters accepted on other grounds.

6. The only other instance, 2 Cor 6:15, is found in the section 6:14–7:1, which may be a non-Pauline interpolation (cf. commentaries on 2 Cor 6:14–7:1).

7. Space does not permit analysis of the usage in Hebrews, Acts, the Catholic Letters, and the Apostolic Fathers, but analogous linguistic shifts can be detected in much of this later literature that had continuing interaction with the Pauline tradition. In Hebrews, *pistis* is not so much

Interaction with society. Several common themes recur as the network of post-Pauline teachers view the relation of the church to its social context.

1. *Concern for what outsiders think.* This is a matter of strategy in the church's evangelistic mission, but it also expresses a concern not to unduly upset outsiders in the interest of avoiding unnecessary harassment and persecution. Other deuteropauline texts show a concern to act and speak so that outsiders do not misunderstand the nature of the Christian community (e.g., Col 4:5–6; 1 Tim 3:7; cf. also 1 Pet 3:15). The qualifications for church leaders have an eye on how they are viewed by outsiders (1 Tim 3:7). Even the instructions to women that moderns find so objectionable are given "so that outsiders will have no occasion to revile us" (1 Tim 5:14). In Eph 6:18–19, Paul in prison models Christian existence, asks prayer that he might speak boldly and clearly—that is, presents encouragement to the threatened and persecuted church neither to be silenced nor to unnecessarily provoke persecution by lack of clarity concerning what the Christian community and its relation to the dominant society are about. Believers are encouraged to speak up appropriately as witnesses to the faith, but not to pose unnecessary or false stumbling blocks in its communication nor to kindle opposition for the wrong reasons.

2. *Concern for regular assembly.* Letters from the generation or two after Paul express the importance of regular worship and instruction but also reflect and resist the temptation to keep a low profile, to avoid being seen in the Christian assembly in order to avoid harassment and persecution (Heb 10:25; Ign. *Eph.* 5.3; 13.1; Ign. *Pol.* 5.2).

3. *Longing for tranquillity.* The post-Pauline literature sometimes reflects the yearning for normal, business-as-usual life in which ordinary human values can flourish (1 Tim 2:2). This longing is rooted not only in human nature, but also in Paul himself and in his Bible (e.g., 1 Thess 4:11; Deut 28:1–14 and often; Isa 17:2; Jer 29:7; Ezek 34:28; 39:26; Mic 4:4; Zeph 3:13). Christian literature of the second and third generations is sometimes maligned for betraying Paul's call to Christian life as eschatological existence that resists the pressures of the dominant culture, and for reverting to "bourgeois morality," the conventional values of middle-class culture.[8] A reading more in tune with the precarious situation of the original readers (cf. Pliny's letter quoted above) might

---

"faith" as trust or content, but rather as "faithful endurance," enabled by grasping the reality of the transcendent and future world (10:38–39; 13:7; and famously 24 times in Heb 11). Clement of Rome uses the word 3× as often as Paul, predominantly as "faithfulness" (*1 Clement*). Ignatius is particularly significant in this regard, since his route to martyrdom in Rome went through the Pauline mission territory to which the deuteropaulines were also directed. He is concerned with the same issues as the developing Pauline tradition: internal heresy, external pressures that must be resisted even to the point of martyrdom, and (like Clement of Rome) encouraging a church structure that would help the church resist both internal and external threats. He uses *pistos* with twice the frequency of Paul, always in the sense of "faithfulness."

8. So, e.g., Bultmann 2:111–18, 203–30, esp. 226 for "bourgeois morality." Bultmann himself presented this with a nuanced historical and theological understanding and some appreciation of the post-Pauline development. Later scholars have sometimes treated the deuteropauline authors, especially the Pastor, with a superior disdain, exhibiting little effort to actually understand them. Conzelmann (1969, 289–317), appreciative student of Bultmann, shows that even his teacher did

gather more understanding for a community already experiencing great tension with its culture, having yearnings and prayers for a more tranquil situation in which life, liberty, and the pursuit of happiness could thrive—the kind of life often enjoyed by modern critics of the deuteropauline writings.

Composition of 1:3–12

By placing 2 Thessalonians alongside 1 Thessalonians and noticing additions, omissions, and modifications, modern interpreters can precisely observe how the author has used his template and gain insight into the meaning and purpose of his composition, much as redaction critics study Matthew's and Luke's use of Mark as template and source. Such a procedure should not be misunderstood as merely the imposition of modern analytical methods on an ancient text, using a living, dynamic communication as grist for the scholar's mill. Such a redaction-critical reading is in step with the dynamics of the initial readers' hearing of the text. Like the author, the readers were familiar with the repeated reading and hearing of Pauline Letters in the worship and instruction of their congregations. They would therefore notice the additions, omissions, modifications, and shifts of emphasis and nuance that gave "2 Thessalonians" its distinctive place in the Pauline Letters. Close attention to such features of the letter helps bring the modern reader within hearing distance of the letter as it was originally heard. As is also the case in redaction criticism of the Synoptic Gospels, this does not mean that every minute change is fraught with theological significance; but before judgments can be made as to what is significant and what is merely incidental, all the data from such a reading must be observed and clearly perceived.

Following the form of the Hellenistic letter adopted and adapted by Paul, and the template of 1 Thessalonians, the author begins the conventional thanksgiving. The sentence begun at 1:3 continues through v. 12 and concludes with a prayer (vv. 11–12) that corresponds to the conclusion (1 Thess 3:11–13) of Paul's much longer thanksgiving (1 Thess 1:2–3:13). Then 2 Thess 2:1 clearly begins afresh. Thus 1:3–12 is a single unit, the thanksgiving section of the letter; in Greek it is one long sentence, with several complex turns.[9] For the sake of readability, translators and editors break the section into smaller units, so that it appears as a number of shorter sentences in English and other modern languages.

---

not evaluate the post-Pauline situation carefully enough and value its contribution highly enough. See also Dibelius and Conzelmann 8–10 and passim.

9. This compositional style has often been unappreciated and contrasted with Paul's. The sentence has been berated as "a real monster" (Holtzmann 1901, 98); as "bombastic, overloaded, campy, pompous" (Trilling 1980, 39–40); and as "a long, poorly constructed Greek sentence" (Richard 1995, 312).

The author uses the template of 1 Thessalonians but reconfigures it to fit his own structure. In 1 Thessalonians, the thanksgiving vocabulary is sustained from 1:2 through 3:13, modulating en route into the body of the letter (see intro to 1 Thessalonians, "Outline and Structure"). In 2 Thessalonians, the thanksgiving ends at 1:12, but thanksgiving terminology recurs at 2:13 because the author is following 1 Thessalonians, though the macrostructure of the template no longer corresponds to the composition of his own letter. The recurrence of thanksgiving terminology in 2 Thess 2:13 is no longer integral to the larger structure and indeed formally (and awkwardly) begins a "second thanksgiving."

The author's thanksgiving that begins at 1:3 immediately focuses on the faithfulness and love of the readers. The author has nothing that corresponds to virtually all of 1 Thess 1:4–10, with its gratitude for the Thessalonians' election manifest in the way they have responded in the power of the Spirit to Paul's initial proclamation of the gospel in Thessalonica. Instead, he picks up on Paul's reference to persecution (*thlipsis*, 1 Thess 1:6) as the point of contact for his own theme and elaborates it into the main topic of this section. Although Paul exulted in not needing to tell others of the Thessalonians' faith, for others tell Paul about them (1 Thess 1:8), the Paul of the fictive letter now boasts to all the churches about the readers' faithfulness. The author takes up the picture in 1 Thess 1:10 of the readers' waiting for the Parousia as the point of contact for an extended portrayal of the coming judgment that will reveal the ultimate justice of God despite the persecutions of the present.

Three major movements are thus held together in this one complex sentence:

1:3–4	thanksgiving as obligation
1:5–10	ultimate justice despite the seeming injustice of the present
1:11–12	the author's prayer

Form-critical analysis suggests that the middle unit is the core and high point of this complex sentence. The first and third sections are more dependent on 1 Thessalonians; in the middle section the author elaborates his own agenda. This corresponds to the structure of the letter as a whole, in which the eschatological section 2:1–12 is the pivot about which the rest of the letter turns, preceded by the warrant for faithfulness in persecution (ch. 1) and followed by his concern for proper church structure (ch. 3). The correspondence to the Pauline thanksgiving is primarily formal. In contrast to the lively and personal thanksgivings typical of Paul's Letters, this thanksgiving morphs into an indirectly hortatory text: boasting about the fictive Thessalonians' faithfulness functions as a call for continuing faithfulness on the part of the actual hearers, bolstered by an inserted didactic text about the Parousia. The effect is no longer the living *address* to a concrete community, known and beloved by the writer, but his letter nonetheless allows the voice of Paul to address, instruct, and encourage them as they face the trials of their own times.

The manner in which the author utilizes the vocabulary of previous letters in the Pauline tradition, especially from his template 1 Thessalonians, is (approximately) manifest in the following:[10]

1:3 *We should always give thanks to God for you,*	1 Thess 1:2
brothers and sisters, for it is right that we should do so,	
because *your faithfulness* is *becoming stronger* and	1 Thess 1:3; 2 Cor 10:15
stronger, *and your love for one another, each for all,*	
is *growing greater* and greater, **4** so that we ourselves	1 Thess 3:12; 5:15
boast about you in *the churches of God* for your	1 Thess 2:14, 19; 2 Cor 8:4
steadfast endurance, that is, your faithfulness *in all the*	1 Thess 1:3, 6
persecutions and *sufferings you are enduring* **5** —clear	1 Thess 2:15, 1 Cor 4:12;
evidence for God's coming righteous judgment, which	Rom 8:35
will result in your being declared worthy of *the kingdom*	
of God, for which *you are* in fact *suffering,* **6** since, after	1 Thess 2:12, 14
all, in God's sight it is only right to repay those who are	
causing your *suffering* by making them *suffer* themselves	1 Cor 1:7
7 and to grant rest/relief to you who are *suffering,* along	1 Thess 1:10; 3:13
with us, *when the Lord Jesus is revealed* from *heaven*	1 Thess 4:16
in fiery flame, with the *angels* of his power **8** meting out	1 Thess 4:5–6; Rom 10:16
justice to *those who do not know God,* that is, *those who*	1 Thess 3:2; 5:3
do not obey the gospel of our Lord Jesus, **9** who will pay	1 Thess 5:2
the penalty of agelong *ruin* away from the presence of the	1 Thess 2:12, 20; 3:13; 5:2
Lord and his powerful *glory* **10** on that *day* when *he comes*	1 Cor 1:6
to be *glorified* by *his saints,* to be praised for his majesty	1 Thess 1:7
by all those who have become believers—for in fact our	1 Thess 1:2; Eph 4:1;
testimony to you *has been believed*— **11** for all of which	1 Tim 5:17
we are always praying for you, that our God will make	1 Thess 2:2, 12; 3:9;
you *worthy of his call* and will fulfill every good resolve	1 Cor 1:2
and *faithful deed by* his *power,* **12** so that *the name of our*	1 Thess 1:5; 2:12, 20
Lord Jesus will *be glorified* in/by you, and you in/by him,	1 Thess 1:3; 2:12, 5:28
according to the *grace* of *our* God and *Lord, Jesus Christ.*	

10. Precise analysis requires work with the Greek text and making distinctions between exact and approximate correspondence. See the more sharply exact analysis in the tables of Wrede 1903, 4–12, 24–28; and an English-language approximation of the data in the table of Richard 1995, 313–14.

1:3–4 Thanksgiving as Obligation

[3] "We should always give thanks" (1:3, repeated in 2:13) sounds less personal and more distant than (what became) Paul's typical "We give thanks. . . ." For Paul, the opening thanksgiving was an opportunity to look back on his close personal experiences with the readers and give thanks for them, a thanksgiving in which the readers are included. This perspective is completely missing from 2 Thessalonians. The act of thanksgiving has become instruction on the Christian duty to give thanks. This long sentence could apply just as well to any church in the Pauline tradition as to Thessalonica. The difference is not to be explained with reference to Paul's psychology or presumed disruption in his personal relations with the Thessalonians, but in terms of the developing liturgical practice of the church.[11]

So also, the declaration "For it is right that we should do so" is not found elsewhere in the thanksgiving section of a letter in the Pauline tradition, and it seems a bit more officious than Paul's customary greeting. Such language is not impersonal and cold, but the language of liturgy (cf. "It is meet and right so to do" of the Anglican *Book of Common Prayer*). To speak in this somewhat formal manner is an acknowledgment that the language of worship is not everyday language, spontaneously invented on the spot, but that it is interwoven into the traditional and worldwide language of the church. Although there was to be no missal or prayer book for centuries, we already see in the Pauline tradition of the second and third generations a developing sense of tradition: when one joined in worship with the Christian community, the language of worship was not ad hoc, but expressed the experienced reality of joining a chorus of previous and widespread voices. The liturgically fulsome copiousness (cf. the comment on 1:1–2) is of one piece with "forever and ever, world without end," "amen and amen," "for all generations forever and ever." This fullness of liturgical expression is characteristic of the later Pauline tradition, as evident in 1 Tim 1:17 and in the baroque style of the benediction in Eph 3:14–21. First Thessalonians is warmhearted and personal because Paul is addressing people he knows and has baptized, with whom he has suffered and worshiped. Second Thessalonians is written by a teacher in the Pauline school, addressing a wider audience in the Pauline churches of the second or third generation, believers who hear the letter as the voice of the revered apostle of an earlier time, couched in the language

---

11. The phraseology here fits in with the liturgical solemnity and fullness throughout the letter. See the detailed study of Aus, who illustrates such language from the worship practice of Hellenistic Judaism. At the same time, he handily eliminates other, unsatisfactory explanations: Paul's personal coolness, his response to their objections that they are not worthy of the praise/thanksgiving for them in 1 Thessalonians (F. F. Bruce), 2 Thessalonians as intended for solemn oral reading to the assembled community (so Dibelius), as though Paul's other letters were not.

of the church's instruction and developing liturgy. This is the reason it lacks the personal familiarity of Paul's own letters.

Those who defend Pauline authorship and want to explain the presumed "cool tone" of 2 Thessalonians point to the "warmth" of the repeated *adelphoi* ("brothers and sisters," 1:3; 2:1, 13, 15; 3:1, 6, 13). It is true that the warmth of Christian family language is expressed in this address, but it is not the personal closeness of an author who knows his readers directly, as in 1 Thessalonians. This simply represents the common address to members of the Christian community preserved in the later epistolary tradition by Hebrews (4×), James (15×), 2 Peter (1×), *1 Clement* (16×), *2 Clement* (15×), the letters of Ignatius (6×), *Martyrdom of Polycarp* (3×), *Epistle of Barnabas* (6×), and *Shepherd of Hermas* (7×). That is, it represents what had become the liturgical language of the worshiping Christian community, with all its warmth, but does not connote that the (purported) author knows the addressees personally or has shared their experience.

We have noticed the shift in the center of gravity from *pistis* as obedient trust in God, moving in the direction of the truth that is believed and faithfulness in holding on to this truth (see Excursus 1: "Persecution," above). Some interpreters have been critical of this shift, as though it represents a dilution of the authentic understanding found in Paul.[12] Such critiques often fail to notice the reality of persecution with which this letter deals, treating the issue as though it were a theological understanding of faith that is at stake, not pastoral address to suffering people.

Faith and *love* (v. 3) are taken from the Pauline template, but here faith means primarily faithfulness under the pressure of persecution, and love refers to the mutual help of a persecuted community. It thus is true that, in comparison with 1 Thessalonians, love is limited to insiders, but this is not a regression toward theological shallowness or a denial that Christian love also includes outsiders. In this context, love is focused on members of the community giving concrete help to fellow members in distress. This need not be seen as a theological shift toward a sectarian limitation of love to insiders, but reflects their actual situation as members of a harassed community who need to help each other, and are increasingly doing so, for which they are commended. The author begins by boasting of their love, and he ends by praising their endurance in persecution. This is not a shift of subject matter but indicates community-internal *agapē* is expressed by caring for persecuted brothers and sisters. Thus the author does not just repeat faith and love from 1 Thessalonians as a way of making contact with the previous letter, and then launch into his own agenda that calls for remaining steadfast in persecution; he also interprets *pistis* and

---

12. E.g., Trilling 1980, 48; Furnish 2007, 149. See above, Excursus 1: "Persecution," and comments on 1:10 below.

agapē as speaking to the present situation. There is no disconnect or shifting of agendas between v. 3 and the following; the faith and love of v. 3 are paralleled by the endurance and fidelity of v. 4.

That *hope* is missing from the traditional triad (as found in 1 Thess 1:3; 1 Cor 13:13) is probably intentional and would also have been noticed by the original hearers. Perhaps the author regards them as still too focused on the hope for an eschatological climax soon to come. In place of the anticipated "hope," the author will immediately speak of "steadfast endurance and faithfulness," and in the following section he will explicate the kind of hope he thinks they *should* have (2:1–12).

[4] The author reflects the imagery found in his template, but he reverses it. There, the other churches brag on the Thessalonians to Paul because of the *eisodos* (founding visit and response), without Paul's having to say anything (1 Thess 1:8). Here, with an emphatic "we ourselves," the deuteropauline author, in Paul's name, brags on the Thessalonians to other churches, citing their steadfastness in persecution. This is difficult to understand if written by Paul a few months after 1 Thessalonians, but not if here, a generation or two after Paul's time, we have a different function for a different situation and set of addressees. The deuteropauline letter allows Pauline Christians of a later generation to hear the voice of the apostle commending them to their fellow believers, who are also remaining steadfast in suffering. As in the deuteropauline Col 1:5–6, the letter reminds the hearers that they belong to an ecumenical community in which the faith is growing and abounding (cf. Col 1:23, which envisages the Christian message already "preached to every creature under heaven"). As in the roughly contemporaneous book of Revelation, the readers in small, scattered congregations need to ponder the immense size of the church to which they belong (Rev 7:4, "144,000"; 7:9, "a great multitude that no one could count" NRSV). The reference to persecution in 2 Thessalonians is general: one cannot tell who the persecutors are, of what kind and intensity, or what the charges and reasons are. Such references are not specific as in 1 Thessalonians, but they are appropriate to the various situations in the network of Pauline congregations of the second and third generations. The commendation in the indicative mood is sincere, not merely a veiled imperative. The Pauline churches of the second and third generations were indeed enduring, and even flourishing despite resistance. But such commendation also has a paraenetic function: this is what they should be doing. "Paul's" praise not only commends them for their faithfulness; the assumption challenges them to live up to the praise they are receiving. "The individual becomes what [one] is addressed as."[13]

---

13. P. Berger and Luckmann 152; cited in Petersen 165.

1:5–10 First Insertion into the Template: Ultimate Justice Despite Present Injustice

This first insertion into the template of 1 Thessalonians is bracketed by dashes. The outline headings here inserted into the flow of the author's text are intended to help the modern reader follow the thought but should not be interpreted didactically, as though the author were saying, "Now I'm switching to another topic and will provide a few clauses about God's judgment." The eschatological imagery is still part of one long sentence, in which the coming judgment is integrated into the thanksgiving period.

[5] When the author declares that the readers are suffering for the kingdom of God, this does not mean that suffering is the price they pay for later entrance into God's kingdom ("suffer now, heaven later"). This is the only reference to God's kingdom in 2 Thessalonians and reflects 1 Thess 2:12, which also refers to the divine *doxa* (glory), to be elaborated in 2 Thess 1:9–12 below. While there is no precisely uniform theology of the kingdom of God shared by the churches represented by the deuteropauline letters, in a variety of ways they preserve the Pauline conviction that the future kingdom of God is already impinging on the present (see Eph 5:5; Col 1:13; 4:11; 2 Tim 4:1, 18). Readers are addressed as belonging to the church (2 Thess 1:1), the community that affirms the present sovereignty of God over this world, a sovereignty already manifest in the transcendent world, hidden in the present world but real to eyes of faith, a sovereignty to be fully revealed to all at the Parousia. The Pauline churches affirm the claim of God's present sovereignty over this world—a claim also expressed in the confession of Jesus as *kyrios* (Lord)—and live in tension with the claims made by this-worldly sovereigns. They suffer *because* they belong to the church that makes this claim, not *so that* they can enter the heavenly kingdom.

As part of his encouragement, the author casts the readers' situation as a courtroom drama, with evidence, judge, and judicial condemnation, a scene some of them had personally experienced. For those who believe in the one God, the suffering of innocent people at the hands of the powerful is always a theological problem, raising the issue of a *just God.* The judgment is not what is happening in the present, in which some Christians are being unjustly charged before human judges: the real judgment is yet to come. The author declares that something in the present situation is "clear evidence" (*endeigma*) of God's coming righteous judgment, but the grammar does not make clear whether such evidence is the readers' steadfast endurance of sufferings, or the sufferings themselves. Jouette Bassler argues that the sufferings themselves are the evidence, appealing to a "theology of suffering" current in Hellenistic Judaism. In this view (to offer an oversimplified summary), God chastises his own people for their sins during their lifetime, so that they can be admitted to the coming kingdom of God, while outsiders will need to pay for their sins in the age to come. Present suffering of God's people is thus evidence of the love and justice of God.[14] While one text associated with the Pauline tradition does have something like this view (Heb 12:5–11), it does not seem to fit the context in 2 Thessalonians. An alternative view represented by Earl J. Richard is probably closer to the author's intended meaning: some readers mistakenly believe that they are living in the few last days before the end, and thus they misunderstand their present sufferings as part of the end-time sufferings, the "messianic woes."[15] The author declares that the unjust sufferings of the present point to the future justice of God.

Such explanations are probably more systematic than the author himself. As the context suggests, the fundamental point is that although the readers' present suffering seems to be unjust—unbelievers who do not know God oppress the faithful community—the situation will be rectified (indeed, can only be rectified) when God, the righteous Judge, establishes the final justice of the kingdom of God.[16] The evidence pointing to the future just judgment is the readers' faithfulness in the midst of persecutions; this retains the character of the thanksgiving begun at 1:3 and affirms the faithfulness of God, whose justice will be manifest to all at the Parousia. The Parousia is here virtually reduced to a judgment scene. The coming of the kingdom of God is reduced to the establishment of justice by the righteous judge, who will condemn the oppressor and vindicate the innocent. The thought is thus similar to Phil 1:28, probably known to both author and readers, which combines "evidence" (there *endeixis*, here the related form *endeigma*), eschatological "destruction" (there *apōleia*, here *olethros* [in 1:9]; cf. 1 Thess 5:3 and 2 Thess 2:3 for the interchangeability of these terms), the eschatological reversal of the Last Judgment, and the assurance of God's faithfulness, which will make it happen—the affirmation with which the author of 2 Thessalonians concludes this long sentence (1:11–12).

[6–7] The author's primary point is that the coming judgment will reveal that those who are dishonored now will be vindicated by God in the Last Judgment, as in the eschatological reversal declared in the preaching of Jesus (as represented, e.g., in Luke 6:20–26; 16:19–31). This imagery of the coming reversal by the just Judge is common in the Pauline school. Thus 2 Timothy rings the

---

14. Bassler 1984. In a variation of this view, Nicholl (125) argues that "their persecutions are a sign of God's future just judgment, a guarantee that those persecuted would be counted worthy of the kingdom, since persecution functioned to purify God's people in preparation for the kingdom."

15. Richard 1995, 317.

16. See Holland 92–94.

chimes on the same themes found in 2 Thessalonians—persecution, prison, that Day, the Lord, the righteous Judge—and makes it clear that the picture of the suffering-and-vindicated Paul is not just Paul's own destiny, but also for "all who have longed for his appearing" (2 Tim 4:8 NRSV). The author of 2 Thessalonians takes up the *epiphaneia* vocabulary of the contemporary Pauline school and refers it to the coming judgment (*epiphaneia* is not found in the undisputed Pauline Letters, but six times in the Deuteropaulines).

The present suffering of the readers will be shown to be unjust, and God will be shown to be just. For God's own honor as the final court of appeal for a just world, it was important in apocalyptic thought not only that justice finally be done, but that it be *seen* to be done.[17] This hope and expectation need not be seen as an expression of personal vindictiveness, though it can be so regarded. It can also be seen in the same light as the imprecatory psalms and the liturgical materials of Revelation. Such calls for vengeance/justice, uttered not in the private recesses of one's heart but publicly and in the presence of God, occur in the worship of Israel and the early church. They are not presented as models for how we should be, but acknowledge who and what we are—an acknowledgment made before God and fellow worshipers that we not only harbor feelings of vengeance but at the same time also long for the coming justice of God. The Psalter, Revelation, and 2 Thessalonians, as well as apocalyptic judgment imagery in general, can express this human dimension of biblical revelation, not all of which is to be taken as a model for contemporary Christian conduct. It can be understood, even in a sense appreciated, without suggesting that it be emulated, and without forgetting that it is found in the same Bible as the Lord's Prayer, Luke 6:27–36, and Luke 23:34.

It is axiomatic for Paul and his successors that there will be a final judgment in which the injustice of the present, which is surely real, will be seen for what it is, when God establishes justice at the last day, rewarding the righteous and punishing the guilty.[18] Throughout the Bible, this forensic conception of God's nature and actions rests in uneasy dialectical tension with the idea of God's ultimate mercy and forgiveness for all. The author of 2 Thessalonians continues to affirm the Pauline theology, but without the subtlety of Paul's dialectic, which is relaxed in a way that allows his language and imagery of judgment to be taken here more univocally, as objectifying, matter-of-fact language (see on 1 Thess 1:9–10). Here and elsewhere, 2 Thessalonians has its own valid message, but it cannot be appropriated in abstraction from the rest of the Pauline and biblical corpus, nor was it written to be so appropriated.

---

17. D. S. Russell 380.

18. The lex talionis was a firm part of the biblical imagery of justice. Cf. the biblical scenes in which the tables are finally turned and the oppressed get to repay their oppressors in kind: at the exodus, Israel despoils the Egyptians, celebrated through history and today; in Ezek 39:10, Israel at the eschaton will plunder those who plundered them; etc.

The coming judgment will bring just repayment for present crimes, but repayment is left to the justice of God. Believers are passive; God is the actor. That Christians are not to take vengeance into their own hands but leave it to the justice of God is part of Paul's theology (Rom 2:6–8; 12:19; 2 Cor 5:10; 1 Thess 5:15; cf. Col 3:25), as well as the theology of Jesus as represented in the Gospels (e.g., Luke 16:25; Matt 5:38–48). While it could be interpreted then, and still today, as the kind of consolation that encourages those presently suffering unjustly to look forward to the day when their oppressors will get what's coming to them, it need not be. The point can be heard as an appeal to leave retribution in the hands of a just God, as already in Paul and the biblical text he cites (Rom 12:19; Deut 32:34–43).

Salvation as future. The center of gravity of the saving event has been shifted to the future, away from the past event of Jesus' death and resurrection (neither of which is mentioned in 2 Thessalonians) and the believers' present experience of life in the Spirit (minimally present in 2 Thessalonians). Paul's dialectic of already/not yet has faded yet has not completely disappeared. There is no clear Pauline "overlapping of the ages" (1 Cor 10:11).

The Parousia as revelation. The verb *apokalyptō* (reveal) and cognate noun *apokalypsis* (revelation) were used by Paul both for the act of disclosing the will of God or a divine message to prophetic figures (e.g., Gal 2:2; 1 Cor 14:26) and for the actual appearance of the eschatological realities at the end of history (e.g., Rom 2:5; 8:18; 1 Cor 1:7; 3:13). Second Thessalonians uses these terms only in the latter sense (1:7; 2:3, 6, 8). The Parousia will be an unveiling (the literal meaning of *apokalypsis*), a disclosure of the true identity of Jesus to the world, which has mostly misjudged and rejected him. The Lord Jesus is present and active (1:12; 3:18), and the mystery of lawlessness is already at work (2:7). Both will be *revealed* for what they truly are, however, at the eschaton. Thus there is an already/not yet dimension to the author's theology. The point is not abstractly christological, but directly pertains to the present experience of the readers: Jesus is presently rejected by most, but in reality is already the Lord; likewise the readers presently experience rejection and persecution, but the reality of their status, the injustice of their condemnation, will be revealed at the Parousia. The author wants the readers in the Pauline churches to live their lives not in terms of present appearances, but in the light of how things truly *are*. What is presently hidden will be ultimately *revealed*. This is in continuity with Paul's own theology (Rom 8:18–19), and is found in other branches of the Pauline tradition (see Col 3:4, 6, which also includes the imagery of the wrath [*orgē*] and glory [*doxa*] to come).

The Parousia as the revelation that Jesus is the true *kyrios* of the world was against the stream of the Roman propaganda from Vespasian through Domitian: the Flavian emperors struggled to present themselves to the Roman world as the true successors of Nero's world rule. Not just local officials, but also much of the grassroots public, may well have decided to proceed with rigor against dissidents who hesitated to participate in the Caesar cult. This would have been particularly the case in Thessalonica, which had historically tried to demonstrate its loyalty to the empire. Even if, as here argued, 2 Thessalonians was not written exclusively to Thessalonica and may be dated later than the conflicts in the late 60s C.E. about the legitimate successor of Nero, a fictive letter to Thessalonica addressing the situation in that city would be particularly appropriate and would address the situation of Pauline churches of the second and third generations generally—particularly at the end of the first century, with the intensification of Roman propaganda under Domitian, the last of the Flavians, which generated such apocalyptic responses as found in Revelation.[19]

Incorporation of traditional apocalyptic imagery. The mosaic of imagery in 1:7–12 reflects a variety of LXX texts (lit. ET corresponds to parallels between the Greek NT and the LXX text):[20]

v. 7b	at the revelation	*2 Bar.* 29.3
	with the angels of his power	*T. Jud.* 3.10 (cf. *4 Ezra* 7.28; 13.32; *1 En.* 61.10)
8	in a flame of fire	Exod 3:2; Isa 66:15 (cf. Isa 4:4; Sir 21:9; 45:19; Dan 3:49; 7:9; *2 Bar.* 48.39; 49.2; 85.13)
	bringing vengeance on those who do not know God and who do not obey	Isa 66:15 (cf. Ezek 35:14; esp. Deut 32:35); Jer 10:25; Ps 58:6; Isa 65:12; 66:4
9	agelong destruction from the face of the Lord and from the glory of his power	4 Macc 10:15; *1 En.* 84.5; *Pss. Sol.* 2.35 Isa 2:10; cf. 2:19–20
10	when he comes to be glorified in his holy ones and marveled at	Ps 88:8 [89:7]; cf. Exod 14:14; Ps 67:35 (68:34)
12	in that day in order that the name may be glorified	Isa 2:11, 17; Zeph 1:7 Isa 44:3; 65:5

Although some have argued that the author is inserting a collage of pre-formed material,[21] the style is the same as that of the rest of 2 Thessalonians.

---

19. Roh (110–15 and passim) argues that the Flavian propaganda in the 70s, specifically in Thessalonica, is the historical setting for 2 Thessalonians, which represents a Christian response to the new ruler Vespasian. The perspective is important even if 2 Thessalonians was written later and for a wider readership.

20. See the more detailed charts in Rigaux 624; Fee 257, 259, 261.

21. So, e.g., Wanamaker 232.

It is better to see these clauses as the author's own composition, but the echoes of biblical and extracanonical apocalyptic language show that the author was at home in the apocalyptic tradition. Beginning with the image of God-the-judge, the figure who actually executes judgment morphs into the image of Christ, as is characteristic of the author himself, but not necessarily of his tradition. The ambiguity of the "holy ones" who accompany Jesus at the Parousia, in the imagery of 1 Thess 3:13 (see comments there), is resolved on the later, non-Pauline side. Paul's own aversion to the imagery of angels is relaxed in the post-Pauline tradition, and the "holy ones" become angels, more appropriate as the agents of God's punishment (e.g., Matt 13:39–41, 49; 16:27; Rev 15:1, 6; 16:1; 17:1). The indications of general persecution, apocalyptic reversal, and agelong punishment are reminiscent of the imagery of Revelation, thus suggesting some interaction between the Pauline and Johannine traditions circulating in the environs of Ephesus at the end of the first century.

[8–9] Verses 8–9 bring the fate of unbelievers into sharp focus. Israel, the people of God, are those who "know the Lord." By contrast, "those who do not know God" is a biblical expression for the Gentiles that could also be used of those who are nominally Israelites but do not share Israel's faith in Yahweh, and who stand condemned before God's judgment (e.g., Exod 5:2; Job 18:21; Ps 76:1; Isa 19:21; Jer 31:34; Hos 5:4; 6:6; 13:4; Wis 2:13). Paul appropriated this conceptuality and vocabulary from his Bible and Jewish tradition in the light of his new Christian faith: Gentiles who have come to believe in Christ are also those who know God, but others do not (Gal 4:8–9; 1 Thess 4:5). The distinction is between those who have been incorporated into the people of God—the elect—and those outside the covenant community, not between persons who have had the individual experience of coming to "know the Lord" and those who have not. For the author of 2 Thessalonians, those who know the Lord are those who "obey the gospel of our Lord Jesus" (see trans. note i above).[22]

Paul himself did not dwell on the fate of unbelievers. His pictures of eschatological judgment and salvation portray the destiny of insiders, but his confessional language does not draw logical inferences about the fate of outsiders. The author of 2 Thessalonians does not seem to be as aware of this use of language as was Paul and here does take this additional step; the reference to "agelong ruin" in 1:9 is the only such reference in the Pauline corpus. Even here, however, these clauses are not "instruction" in an abstract "doctrine" about "eternal destiny." It is confessional language to a suffering church (even if the author

---

22. Differently Richard 1995, 308: the two phrases refer to two different groups: (1) the outsider Gentile persecutors who do not know God; (2) the insider Christians who yield to them, not obeying the gospel. He elaborates somewhat persuasively, using *hypakouō* in 3:14, and references to 2:3, 10, 12.

does not consciously deal in confessional, nonobjectifying language). Insiders are addressed, for their own edification; though outsiders are "described," they are not addressed, and insiders cannot construct objectifying doctrinal systems from such nonobjectifying lumber. The author is both encouraging and warning the insiders of the Pauline churches. Though in the form of a description of what will happen to outsiders, the words in fact warn those actually addressed, the insiders who are tempted to leave the community, to join the outsiders, who will be condemned in the future judgment. As is typical of the language of oppressed communities, all believers are lumped together, not differentiated as to quality and quantity of their works or the depth of their faith. As in Revelation and Mark 13, oppression intensifies a dualistic perspective in which distinctions within each group disappear. All that counts is that they have remained believers, faithful to the end, as in Rev 2:10 and Mark 13:13. This shift to insider confessional language becomes explicit in the prayer that concludes this section (2 Thess 1:11–12).

The flame of fire is a standard element of theophany, like God's appearance on Sinai, which has a long biblical tradition (see Exod 3:2 [cf. Acts 7:30]; Exod 19:18; Deut 33:2; Ps 18:8; Ezek 1:13, 27; Hab 3:4; Dan 7:9, 10; Isa 66:15–16). The consequence of disobedience to the gospel is agelong ruin away from the presence of the Lord and his powerful glory—the very opposite of "being with the Lord," the salvific destiny of the saints, according to 1 Thess 4:17. Unbelievers are not actively punished but are in a passive state that is described negatively, as what it is *not*: they are "away from the presence of the Lord and his powerful glory." The returning Lord is not portrayed as inflicting fiery torment on unbelievers. Though the judgment is severe, the fire is the theophanic and fiery presence of God, not the hellfire of punishment. The author's confessional language focuses on what happens to the believers whom he is addressing. In the author's logic, unbelievers do not receive this.

Vengeance? Or justice? From the earliest days and through the whole KJV tradition (KJV, ASV, RSV, NRSV), the noun *ekdikēsis* has been translated "vengeance," as has Paul's language in 1 Thess 4:6 regarding unethical practices of Christians (see comments there). Such language is related to the Bible's language for justice.[23] For Paul, believers too will stand before God's judgment (2 Cor 5:10; Rom 14:10). The author of 2 Thessalonians uses this language, but not in the Pauline sense. Here all unbelievers are condemned by God's *ekdikēsis*. Sensitive modern liberals should not *too* quickly abandon the biblical language of "vengeance," if such there be, in understandable haste to "correct" biblical theology. Honest hermeneutics must let the Bible be what it is. In the prayers for

---

23. Linguistically and theologically, the "vengeance" terminology is related to justice; *ekdikēsis* is a cognate to other vocabulary from the *dik-* root of 1–2 Thessalonians (*dikaiōs* in 1 Thess 2:10; *ekdikos* in 1 Thess 4:6; *dikaios* in 2 Thess 1:5, 6; *dikē* in 2 Thess 1:9; *adikia* in 2 Thess 2:10, 12).

vengeance in the imprecatory psalms and Revelation (Pss 35, 55, 69, 109, 137; Rev 6:10; cf. 18:6), we hear a community that feels itself pushed to the edge of society and the edges of its own endurance, a community that, in its worship, gives vent to the natural feelings of resentment, even revenge, as it anticipates the eschatological turning of the tables. Acknowledging that the Bible contains such human cries need not mean that they are a model for our own conduct. Even in such passages, cries for "revenge" are not personal, but a plea for the justice of God to be manifest publicly.[24] Even so, this is in contrast not only to Jesus' own response to his persecutors (Luke 23:34), but that of his followers as well (e.g., Acts 7:60). In both Paul and the deuteropauline tradition, judgment or "vengeance" is the prerogative of God. The New Testament contains nothing like the apocryphal saying of Jesus quoted by the Crusaders, "There will yet come the day when my sons will come and revenge [*sic*] my blood."[25]

[10] The focus in v. 10 returns to the eschatological destiny of believers. *Doxa* (glory; cf. "doxology") is a fulcrum word on which the imagery turns (v. 9, "his powerful glory"; v. 10, "to be glorified by his saints"; v. 12, "our Lord Jesus will be glorified by you"; cf. also 2:14). It may seem strange to the modern reader to find this concentration on the glory of God embedded in a section of the letter centering on judgment and "vengeance." Not so in biblical theology, in which the glory of God, God-as-God, is primary, and offense against this glory is not taken lightly. The essence of judgment scenes has to do with who God is, not quid pro quo punishment. The presence of God is the presence of glory. Especially in the Psalter, the worship of God is to glorify God, to acknowledge God as God and to give God the glory due his name (Pss 3:3; 8:1, 5; 19:1; 21:5; 22:23; 24:7–10; 26:8; 29:1, 3, 9; 45:3; 50:15; 57:5, 11; 63:2; 66:2; 71:8; 72:19; 79:9; 85:9; 86:12; 90:16; 96:3, 7, 8; 97:6; 102:15, 16; 104:31; 106:20, 47; 108:5; 113:4; 115:1; 138:5; 145:11, 12; 148:5, 13). When the ark of the covenant, the throne on which the glorious Presence of God is manifest (Shekinah Glory), appears before the temple gates, the choir sings of the "King of Glory" (= glorious King) who enters (Ps 24:7–10). The departure of God from the temple at the time of the exile is the departure of glory, and the return to the purified temple when the deportees are regathered in Jerusalem is the eschatological vision of the radiant glory of God over the whole earth (Ezek 10:18–19; 11:22–23; 43:1–12).

As a Hellenistic Jew, Paul's vocabulary was partially shaped by the honor/shame values of his Greco-Roman culture, but on this point his theology was steeped in the biblical language and conceptuality of the glory of God.[26] For

24. See Schüssler Fiorenza 1985; A. Collins 1984; Boring 1989, 112–18, "Interpreting Revelation's Violent Imagery."

25. Cf. R. Brown 1994a, 2:981.

26. Harrison (201–70) places this in contrast to the "Roman Ideal of Glory."

Paul, all creation—including humanity—once shared God's glory, at present falls short of God's purpose in creation (Rom 3:23), but looks forward to participating in this glory when, with all creation, human beings will join in glorifying God (e.g., Rom 5:2; 8:18, 21, 30). This emphasis is sometimes missed when *doxa* and its cognates are translated by "honor." The seven undisputed Letters of Paul use this vocabulary fifty-six times (e.g., Rom 1:21, 23; 2:7, 10; 3:7, 23; 5:2; 6:4; 8:18, 21, 30; 9:4, 23; 11:36; 15:6, 7, 9; 16:27; 1 Cor 2:7, 8; 10:31; 15:43; 2 Cor 3:7–11, 18; 4:4, 6, 17; 6:8; 8:19, 23; Gal 1:5, 24; Phil 1:11; 2:11; 3:21; 4:19; 1 Thess 2:6, 12, 20).

Already in Paul, God's glory is shared by the Lord Jesus (e.g., 1 Cor 2:7; 2 Cor 4:6). The author of 2 Thessalonians extends this dimension of Pauline theology, making more explicit that Christ's return in power will be the final manifestation of the true God, who establishes the kingdom of justice. The glory of the Lord is presently hidden, seen only by eyes of faith. Believers suffer in the conviction that their Lord, presently reviled and disdained as they are, in reality shares the glory of God, even as they themselves are already "in God . . . and the Lord Jesus Christ" (1:1). This hidden reality will become manifest to all at the Parousia. The Lord will receive the glory due him: his name will be glorified; believers will glorify him, acknowledging his rightful praise; and the fateful error of unbelief will be revealed. In pale demythologized language, the ultimate future will disclose the justice of God, the hidden reality that is already present, for which the readers already suffer. Their suffering will be vindicated since it corresponds to the reality of things already revealed in the Christ event, ultimately to be revealed to all.

Just as the author's description of the outsiders does not include a portrayal of actual punishments, so the destiny of the insiders is not described as specific good things they receive. The Lord returns in divine glory; they glorify him and participate in this eschatological glory, but it is Christ-centered, not going-to-heaven self-centeredness. In Paul, believers participate in the glory of Christ at the Parousia, but this glory is already partially experienced in the present life (see Phil 3:21; 1 Cor 15:43; 2 Cor 3:4–11; Rom 8:18, 30). In 2 Thessalonians, however, present experience is overshadowed by the author's emphasis on eschatological glory.

His saints. Although 1:7 has portrayed the returning Lord as accompanied by angels, the *hagioi* (holy ones) of 1:10 are not angels who come from heaven, but believers who wait on earth, as indicated by the parallelism (made clear by diagramming the sentence in Greek): "his saints" are identified with "those who have become believers." Both instances of the verb *pisteuō* (believe) in this verse are in the aorist tense.

In contrast to Paul, for whom the present tense of *pisteuō* is characteristic (26× in the undisputed letters), the verb "believe" in the present tense is not found in 2 Thessalonians. While this is indeed different from Paul, it need not signal a decline from the more dynamic Pauline usage. For the author, becoming a believer means accepting the truth of the Christian faith as testified to in the Pauline gospel, and holding on to that faith under duress (see comments on 2 Thess 1:3 above). This faith means believing the testimony of Paul, phrasing that reflects 1 Thess 2:13, where Paul's preaching is identified with the word of God, further identified with the gospel (2 Thess 1:8), truth (2:10–13), and tradition (2:15; 3:6). As in other deuteropauline writings, the Pauline understanding of faith is tending toward "the faith" as a body of teaching, the Christian truth to be believed and held on to (Col 1:23; 2:7; 2 Thess 2:13; 3:2; Eph 4:5, 13; 1 Tim 1:2, 19; 3:9, 13; 4:1, 6; 5:8; 6:10, 21; 2 Tim 1:13; 2:18; 3:8; 4:7; Titus 1:4, 13; 2:2; 3:15; cf. 2 Pet 1:1, 5; Jude 3, 20).

On that day. The Greek sentence has withheld the climactic "on that Day" to this point (see trans. note 1 above), which reflects 1 Thess 5:2 and points ahead to the argument about the day of the Lord that immediately follows.

1:11–12 The Author's Prayer

The lengthy sentence that began with the liturgical "We should always give thanks . . . for it is right" (v. 3), after long affirmations of the readers' faithfulness and future vindication, winds its way back to the language of worship with which it began. Verses 5–10 then cast the spotlight on human responsibility. Those who respond in faith are saved, those who refuse to believe the truth are condemned, and the future judgment will reveal this. Now the perspective shifts. The focus in vv. 11–12 is not on human responsibility, but on the One who called them and who himself takes responsibility to fulfill his promise. The author is mindful of the template he is following, and his prayer, a prayer of gratitude, reflects the way Paul ended his long thanksgiving with a prayer at 1 Thess 3:11–13 and also echoes Paul's promise in 1 Thess 5:24.

The prayer will be answered. This will happen gracewise, as gift, *kata charin* (v. 12). The confessional language of prayer and praise gives glory to God and incorporates human responsibility within the promise of divine faithfulness. The Pauline dialectic of the believer's striving and God's action (e.g., Phil 2:12–13) has not been entirely lost in the deuteropauline tradition.

[11] The language of being counted or made worthy (*axioō* and its compounds) is never found in the undisputed Letters of Paul. Its ten occurrences in the New Testament are all found in various later streams of the tradition that look back to Paul as their source (5× in Luke–Acts; 2× each in 2 Thessalonians and Hebrews; 1× in 1 Timothy). The language of justification is absent from 2 Thessalonians, as it had been absent from 1 Thessalonians. Here in 2 Thessalonians, the language of deem worthy/make worthy functions in a way analogous to the language of justification in Paul's Letters composed later than 1 Thessalonians (esp. Galatians and Romans), and with something of the

same overlapping of "deem/make righteous" in the undisputed letters—again preserving something of the Pauline dialectic.

We are always praying for you may be simply historicizing, reflecting the fictive world of Paul and the Thessalonians, or it may express an unfocused affirmation of the communion of saints: Paul still belongs to the church, the readers belong to the same community as Paul did, and the communion has not been severed by Paul's death. Just as Paul can continue to speak to them in the letter, he can speak for them to God. The author does not take this as objectifying language on which a doctrine can be constructed, but neither does he consider the saints who have died as no longer part of the Christian community. The letter as a whole, in a real but nonfocused way, embraces past and present believers in the one church of God.

Although the perspective is shifted toward the eschatological future, God's call through Paul's preaching in the past (2 Thess 2:14) continues in the present: the God who called continues to be the Caller (cf. Isa 6:4). The readers have heard and responded to that call, and the Caller himself will vindicate both their good intentions (always imperfectly carried out) and their faithful deeds.

[12] Confessing the *name* of Jesus as Lord was already important in Paul's time (e.g., Rom 1:5; 10:13; 1 Cor 6:11; Phil 2:9–10). By the time of the deuteropauline letters, persecution of Christians sometimes focused on the name, which was dishonored by unbelievers but exalted and magnified by believers (Eph 1:21; 1 Tim 6:1; Heb 1:4; 13:15; Jas 2:7; 1 Pet 4:14, 16). Pliny the Younger inquired of the emperor whether Christians were to be prosecuted only for specific crimes, or if *the name itself* was sufficient warrant for punishment (see discussion of Pliny's letter in Excursus 1: "Persecution," above). The author of 2 Thessalonians addresses Pauline churches that live in a world in which the Christian name is dishonored and reviled; a dimension of the eschatological reversal is that this name will be glorified, will be seen to belong to the one God whose glory also belongs to the Lord Jesus. Those who now wear the dishonored name will be vindicated and participate with him in the eschatological revelation of the divine glory.

In this context, does the author use God-language for Jesus? In the undisputed letters, there are no places where Paul clearly uses "God" for the Lord Jesus. Depending on punctuation, Rom 9:5 is the only candidate.[27] Certainly there is no God-language for Jesus in 1 Thessalonians. But 2 Thessalonians is launched into a world in which Christians are beginning to blur the distinction between God and the Lord Jesus Christ, and sometimes they clearly refer to Christ as "God" (e.g., John 1:1, 18; 20:28; 1 John 5:20; Titus 2:13; Heb 1:8–9;

---

27. Cf. R. Brown (1994b, 182–83) concludes, "Personally, I am swayed by the grammatical evidence in favor [of the interpretation in which] the title 'God' is given to Jesus. But one may claim no more than a plausibility."

2 Pet 1:1). By the early second century, Pliny could characterize Christian worship as including the singing of "an antiphonal hymn to Christ as their god," and Ignatius of Antioch could unabashedly refer to Christ as God (Ign. *Eph.* 1; *Trall.* 7; *Rom.* 1, 3, 6; *Smyrn.* 1, 10; *Pol.* 8). Thus, if 2 Thessalonians is by Paul, it is likely that he intends to distinguish between "God" and "the Lord." If by a Pauline teacher of the second or third generation, the letter is launched into a context in which this distinction is being blurred, and it may well be that God-language is here used of Christ. While there is, of course, no systematic doctrine of the Trinity in the New Testament, the earliest texts already provide materials for this later doctrine. The church represented by the author of 2 Thessalonians has taken a further step toward Nicaea than had Paul.

2:1–12 Second Insertion into the Template: The Day of the Lord

This section is the second insertion into the template provided by 1 Thessalonians. The chapter break is intrusive, interrupting the flow of the author's thought. The author does not now turn to a new subject, in a discrete "eschatological section." He has cast the whole discourse in an eschatological framework since 1:5. The discussion does take a new turn, though, rejecting a false understanding of eschatology. The author is not paraphrasing or interpreting his template, but inserting new material. Yet he is not composing spontaneously but incorporating prior apocalyptic traditions, which he reshapes according to his own interpretation and purpose. His purpose is not didactic, as though he now decides to instruct his readers about some features of the eschatological drama; rather, he encourages steadfastness in view of the long-term future for which the church must be prepared.

The opening sentence appeals to the readers to think through the issue calmly (vv. 1–2). Then follows the author's own correction of their mistaken apocalyptic timetable (vv. 3–12).

2:1 Now, brothers and sisters, concerning the Parousia of our Lord Jesus Christ and our being gathered together to him: we ask you 2 not to be too quickly rattled out of your minds or alarmed by a claim that "the day of the Lord has come"[a]—even if this claim comes by a prophetic revelation,[b] by teaching or preaching,[c] or by a letter purportedly from us.[d]

3 Let no one deceive you in any way, for before that day comes, the apostasy[e] must come first,[f] and the Man of Lawlessness[g] must be revealed, the Son of Destruction,[h] 4 the Adversary[g] who exalts himself above every so-called god or object of worship, so that he even takes his seat in the temple of God, proclaiming that he is God. 5 Don't you remember that I used to tell[i] you all this when I was still with you?[j] 6 And you already know[k] what is restraining him[l] now, so that he may be revealed in his own

time. 7 For the mystery of lawlessness is already active, and will continue
until God removes the Restrainer.[m] 8 And then the Lawless One will be
revealed, whom the Lord Jesus[n] will destroy with the breath of his mouth
and eliminate just by *his* epiphany and Parousia.

9 The Lawless One, too, has a parousia, which functions by the power
of Satan, the power to do deceitful signs and miracles, 10 with every
kind of evil deception that misleads those on the way to destruction who
refused to love the truth and so be saved. 11 This is why God sends[o] them
a powerful delusion, and so[p] they believe the lie, 12 so that all may be
judged[q] who have not believed the truth but approved what is wrong.

a. *Enestēken* is the perfect tense of *enistēmi*, a verb that identifies a set of circumstances in a temporal sequence, but with two basic meanings: to be *present* or to be *imminent, impending* (see BDAG 337; LSJM 568). The perfect tense refers to an event that has happened and whose effects continue into the present, "has come." The LXX uses this verb almost entirely in the sense of "to be present"; its appearances 7× in the NT (Rom 8:38; 1 Cor 3:22; 7:26; Gal 1:4; 2 Thess 2:2; 2 Tim 3:1; Heb 9:9) are all in the perfect tense except 2 Tim 3:1 (future, clearly meaning "will be present in the future," not "will be about to happen at some future time"). All NT instances thus refer to something being present, sometimes explicitly contrasting it with the future (Rom 8:38; 1 Cor 3:22). There are no instances in which the perfect of *enistēmi* means "be imminent, be impending."

b. *Pneuma*, i.e., a prophetic revelation presumably inspired by the Holy Spirit, as in 1 Thess 5:19.

c. *Logos*, i.e., a message given orally in the church's teaching and preaching, here contrasted with the written medium of a letter, *epistolē*.

d. In terms of grammar and syntax, *hōs di' hēmōn* (purportedly from us) could theoretically modify *pneuma*, *logos*, and *epistolē*, so that the reference is to a misinterpretation of something Paul has said or written (so translated and punctuated in NIV, TNIV, NIV11, NRSV).[28] This more easily allows the statement to be read as from Paul himself. It is more likely, however, that "purportedly from us" refers only to letters circulating in Paul's name (so KJV, RSV, REB, NABRE, ESV, CEB). It is difficult to think that oral sermons and teaching, and especially prophetic messages, circulated as purportedly from Paul.

e. *Apostasia* has two basic meanings: (1) rebellion, the defiance of established authority (e.g., Josephus, *Life* 43 [against Nero]); and (2) abandoning the faith (e.g., 1 Macc 2:15; Acts 21:21 [in each case abandoning the law of Moses]). The two choices are to see the Lawless One as leading a general revolt against all established authority, i.e., against God as the One who establishes order in the world, or a general falling away from the faith, in which believers in the one true God represented by Jesus Christ abandon their faith under pressure from the Lawless One.

f. More lit., "unless the apostasy comes first." "Before that day comes" is not in the Greek text but is implied by the context and supplied by virtually all modern transla-

28. E.g., Marshall 1983, 187.

tions. "First" refers to the day of the Lord: that Day cannot come until the apostasy has occurred. It is not entirely clear whether the apostasy also comes before the parousia of the Man of Lawlessness, or is coincident with it, or is the result of his appearing, but context and grammar support the order: first comes the apostasy, then the Man of Lawlessness.

g. The vast majority of later MSS read *hamartia* (sin; followed by AV) instead of *anomia* (lawlessness; followed by virtually all modern translations), but *anomia* is read by ℵ B 0278, as well as several later minuscules and the entire Coptic tradition, and is undoubtedly original, as both MS evidence and transcriptional probability indicate. Both *anthrōpos tēs anomias* (Man of Lawlessness) and *ho antikeimenos* (v. 4, lit., "the one who opposes," "the opponent," "the adversary," as, e.g., in Luke 13:17; 21:15; Phil 1:28) seem here to refer to specific, well-known, figures in the traditional apocalyptic drama and so are capitalized.

h. *Ho huios tēs apōleias*, lit., "son of destruction," a semitizing Greek idiom for "one doomed to destruction." The apocalyptic tradition loves archaic, Semitic expressions such as "Son of Destruction," "Man of Lawlessness," and "Lawless One." They sound more mysterious, more grandiose, than ordinary terms with the same content and meaning. The translation above attempts to preserve these overtones by capitalization and by partly preserving the archaic phraseology, while rendering them in comprehensible English.

i. *Elegon*: the iterative use of the imperfect tense here refers to customary and repeated action in the past.

j. The rhetorical question beginning with *ou* (no, not) assumes a positive answer and is thus a way of declaring something with which the readers are expected to agree.

k. The *nyn* (now) could theoretically go with either "you know" or "what restrains." English versions are about equally split. The syntax favors "you know," as does the context, continuing the emphasis of the preceding verse. Thus the meaning is "now know," not "now restrains," though the context also makes clear that what restrains is doing so in the readers' present time.

l. The neuter participle *to katechon* in v. 6 (what is restraining) is identified with the masculine participle *ho katechōn* in v. 7 (the Restrainer, here capitalized to indicate the titular character of the word). The verb can be either intransitive (the ruler, the controller) or transitive (the one who rules or controls something or someone). If transitive, as translated here, an understood "him" (for Man of Lawlessness in vv. 3–4), not in the Greek text, must be supplied.

m. The strange expression *ek mesou genētai* (lit., "comes out of the midst") is an idiom in which *ginomai* functions as a passive verb and means "is removed" [BDAG 199, 635]). The passive voice points to divine action, the divine passive. The author intends God as the active subject (see comments).

n. The MS evidence is evenly balanced between "Lord" (the majority of late MSS, but also in B K L* 630 1175 1505 1739 1881, some MSS of the Coptic, and Irenaeus) and "Lord Jesus" (ℵ A D* F G Lᶜ P Ψ 0278 33 81 104 365 1241 2464 latt sy co; Irˡᵃᵗ Or Did), and good arguments can be made for scribal omission as well as addition. The author uses "Lord" both with and without "Jesus" and/or "Christ." Since he emphasizes that the eschatological judge will be Jesus, it is perhaps slightly preferable to include the name here.

o. The present tense *pempei* is supported by the original reading of ℵ and D, as well as A B F G 6 33 1739 1881 and MSS of the Old Latin, Vulgate, and Coptic, as well as some MSS of Irenaeus. It may be understood as either the readers' present or a futuristic present pointing to the eschatological times. The majority of later MSS have the exclusive future reference, and scribes "corrected" some earlier MSS to read the future-tense verb *pempsei*. It is much more probable that the present *pempei* is original and the future *pempsei* the "correction" than vice versa.

p. *Eis to* followed by the infinitive here does not indicate purpose, its more common meaning, but the general result of the action, as in 1 Thess 2:12, 16; 2 Thess 1:5.

q. *Krithōsin* may be either neutral, to be called into court for judgment, or negative, "condemned," presupposing that the accused will be found guilty and punished.

2:1–2 Addressing a False Understanding of the Parousia

In continuity with the preceding encouraging paraenesis, the author now turns to address a general problem faced by the Pauline churches of the second and third generations: "the Parousia of our Lord Jesus Christ and our being gathered together to him." Some of his readers are "too quickly" (*tacheōs*) accepting a misunderstanding, accepting wrong ideas without adequately thinking them through. The author asks them to think, appealing to tradition, experience, and reason. Using the same phrase as 1 Thess 5:12, the author asks; he does not "urge," "order," "command," or "insist." In this context (the judgment scene introduced in 1:5–12), the phrase *episynagōgēs ep' auton* may have the overtones of the lawcourt, picturing a summons to appear before the judge. Primarily, however, this way of characterizing the hoped-for coming of the kingdom of God reflects the biblical hope that had become living Jewish tradition. As part of the eschatological fulfillment in which God reasserts the divine sovereignty over the alienated and rebellious creation, God would regather the scattered people of God and remake them into the one united people they were called to be (e.g., Isa 27:12; 52:12 LXX; Sir 36:13–16; *Pss. Sol.* 17.26–28, 2 Macc 1:27; 2:7, 18; *T. Naph.* 8.3; *T. Ash.* 7.7; Mark 13:27//Matt 24:31). These words also reflect the specific hope of 1 Thess 4:15–17 (though without the imagery of being caught up into outer space). Paul and his contemporaries had expected this to happen soon, in their own lifetimes. Several crises had seemed to signal the near Parousia: Caligula's attempt in 40 C.E. to install his statue in the Jerusalem temple, Nero's brutal persecution of Christians in Rome in 64 C.E., the unthinkable destruction of Jerusalem and burning of the temple by Roman legions in 70 C.E. All this came and went, and the first generation passed away without the advent of the Lord from heaven. There is no evidence that this was a particularly intense crisis of faith for the Christian community, but the eschatology of the first generation could not simply be repeated in ensuing generations. It had to be rethought. As the author writes, a vigorous discussion is underway within the Pauline churches.

Rethinking Eschatology in the Pauline Tradition

There were five possibilities that believers needed to weigh:

1. *Abandon the faith.* Some might decide that the new Christian community was based on an erroneous faith, as the nonappearance of the Parousia proves. Apostasy would later become the technical term for this stance.[29]

2. *Abandon eschatology.* Rethink the faith in such a way that there is no longer a hope for the redemption of creation and history, but a deliverance of individual souls to the heavenly world at death. Some gnostics of the second century interpreted Paul in this way.

3. *Internalize, individualize, and spiritualize eschatology.* The original hope that the end is coming soon was true and right, and the end did come as promised. However, "end" is reinterpreted so that it is not the end of the world and of history. The eschatological events happen in the spiritual life of the believer: Jesus comes back to dwell in the believer's heart, and the resurrection is the internal, personal event of the new life in the present. This approach is exemplified by some streams of earlier Johannine theology, though this is tempered in the canonical forms of the Gospel and Letters.

4. *Renew the imminent hope.* Second- and third-generation readers of Paul understand "soon" to refer not to the first generation, but to their own time, allowing Paul's Letters to speak directly into their situation. John the seer writes Revelation about the same time that 2 Thessalonians is written, in the same geographical area, with an extensive cast of eschatological characters in the final apocalyptic drama. His message is, in effect, "Now [in the 90s C.E.] the time *is* near, and the troubles we are enduring are the prelude to the end; we need to hold fast to the faith, but the trials are only for a short time."

5. *Rethink the chronology of the end.* The end will come in God's own time, but not soon. Christian responsibility is to be faithful for the long pull. This view is variously represented by Luke–Acts, 2 Peter, and the Pastoral Letters.

Sources and Authorities for Theological Reconstruction

All these views were advocated and vigorously discussed in the Pauline school tradition of the second and third generations. What sources were available to inform and deepen the faith for those teachers who wanted to be faithful to the teaching of their founder Paul? The author of 2 Thessalonians lists three, all

---

29. *Apostasia* (2:3) is the noun for the cognate verb *aphistēmi*, the basic meaning of which is simply "leave," as in exiting a building (e.g., Luke 2:37). In second- and third-generation Christianity, including its Pauline streams, both noun and verb came to mean "abandon the faith, leave the Christian community," a meaning the terms had already developed in Judaism. Thus Luke 8:13 adds to the parable interpretation of Mark 4:13, "and in the time of testing they apostatize" (AT). See also Acts 15:38; 21:21; 1 Tim 4:1; Heb 3:12.

valid sources of instruction, all potentially problematic: prophetic revelation, oral teaching and preaching, and letters ascribed to Paul.

Prophetic revelation (*pneuma*, spirit) had been a regular phenomenon within the Pauline churches of the first generation (Rom 12:6; 1 Cor 11:4–5; 13:2, 8–9; 14:1–39; cf. Eph 2:20; see comments on 1 Thess 5:20). Christian prophets continued to be active in the Pauline churches of the second and third generations (Eph 3:5; 4:11; 1 Tim 1:18; 4:14; Acts 2:17–18; 13:1; 15:32; 19:6; 20:23; 21:4, 9–10). Such prophets claimed not only (or mainly) to foretell the future, but also (and primarily) to speak the direct word of the risen Lord, giving his will for the present. Such prophets could interpret the present troubles of the church as the beginning of the eschatological events, the arrival of the day of the Lord, as in Revelation. Paul had respected such claims but insisted that they be evaluated by the community as a whole. The author of 2 Thessalonians no longer encourages the congregation to hear and evaluate such revelatory claims (contrast 1 Thess 5:19–21). Authoritative tradition trumps charismatic spontaneity.

Teaching and preaching (*logos*, "word") did not claim direct inspiration by the Holy Spirit but were based on the teacher's or preacher's own interpretations of Scripture and the Pauline traditions handed on within the Spirit-led community, and they could lead to authentic new insights regarding Christian understanding and responsibility. They could also be mistaken. In John 21:23, the supposed promise that the beloved disciple would not die before the Lord returns, that the Parousia would occur in the first generation, is called a *logos*, and it is considered a misunderstanding that needed to be corrected.

Letters ascribed to Paul (*epistolē hōs di' hēmōn*, a letter as written by us) would include both those written by the apostle himself and circulated within the later Pauline congregations and letters written in his name by the continuing line of teachers in the Pauline school.

The specific issue the author of 2 Thessalonians is addressing is that some are advocating, in his view mistakenly, that "the day of the Lord has come." Rather than a direct quotation, this may be the author's expression, in his own vocabulary, for what he understood their interpretation of Pauline eschatology to be. He does not regard this as merely an acceptable difference in theological opinion, but as impacting the way believers should live their lives, how they should relate to each other and to others outside the Christian community, and even how the church should be structured. Whoever has a mistaken idea of the eschaton—namely, that it has already come or that the final events are already beginning—empties the time remaining before the end of its significance. The issue is not merely apocalyptic timetables, but rather the significance of present life with its decisions and responsibilities.[30] The troubles the readers are expe-

---

30. A similar situation is addressed in Mark 13, where mistaken belief in the nearness of the end discourages the Christian mission to the world. The author of Mark insists that the end is not

riencing are causing some to apostatize, others to endure persecutions by interpreting them as the apocalyptic woes, the beginning of the end. The view the author is opposing does not mean that there is a specific group of "opponents" or "false teachers" he is refuting, but a mistaken view circulating among the Pauline churches, a view with a variety of advocates and rationales.

Day of the Lord

The "day of the Lord" has already been foreshadowed in the pregnant reference in 1:10 to "that day" when the Lord will come. The author now addresses the issue directly. We do not know how the (various) advocates of the false view expressed their theology (or theologies). If the letter had been written by Paul, it would have addressed a (presumably small) group within the Thessalonian congregation that likely would have shared a uniform view. However, if, as argued here, the author circulates his letter among numerous congregations in the post-Pauline era, he would be engaging a broad spectrum of views. Thus the issue is not whether the author opposes a superrealized or superimminent expectation, as though these were the only two options. By summing up the idea(s) he opposes under the motto "The day of the Lord has come," the author addresses a spectrum of reinterpretations of Paul, not necessarily just one. He does not describe the opposing view as claiming "the Parousia has already happened," "the Lord has already come," "the Last Judgment is already happening," or "the resurrection has already happened" (cf. 2 Tim 2:18). The false view the author opposes is not that Jesus, the resurrection, or a false Messiah has already appeared, but that the apocalyptic countdown has already been triggered. However the advocates of the views the author opposes would have described their own theologies, the writer sums them up in the generalizing "the day of the Lord has come," using a phrase that embraces the whole eschatological drama: final troubles, Parousia, resurrection, judgment. *His* point: this day is *not* already here.

In any case, "day of the Lord" is the author's term for what they are talking about, which had become traditional in the Pauline school (see comments on 1 Thess 4:16; 5:2). "Day," of course, does not refer to a period of twenty-four hours, but, as in the Scripture and in Jewish tradition, the period of the end time that includes the eschatological events. (For "day" as an extended period, see, e.g., Job 38:23, "the day of battle and war"; Ps 137:7, "the day of Jerusalem's fall"; Eccl 7:14, "the day of prosperity"; and such texts as Luke 19:42; Heb 4:8.) In Isa 61:2, the "year of the LORD's favor" is identified with the "day of

---

so close; there is still time for the world mission (Mark 13:7–10). So also in Luke–Acts, gazing *up* into the sky, expecting the Lord to appear soon, prevents the disciples from looking *out* into the world mission to which Christ has called them (Acts 1:6–11; cf. Luke 19:11–26; 21:8).

vengeance." For the deuteropauline author of 2 Thessalonians, the day is not identical with the Parousia but refers to the cluster of events that comprise the end of this world and this-worldly history.

Already Come?

What did the claim that the day of the Lord "has come" mean for those who advocated it? There are three main possibilities:

1. *Jesus' counterimperial reign already inaugurated.* After the tumultuous days that followed the death of Nero in 68 C.E., in which there were three emperors in less than two years and the empire was in chaos, order was restored by Vespasian, and a new line of emperors was inaugurated, the Flavians, who represented themselves as the legitimate successors of Nero's world rule. The emperors claimed the title *Kyrios* (Lord); their propaganda, widely welcomed and celebrated, represented their arrival as a new day of peace and prosperity. Christians in the Pauline tradition proclaimed Jesus as already the heavenly *Kyrios* and expected his kingdom to arrive in the near future, as the successor to Nero's world rule. This would have brought them to the attention not only of the Roman authorities, but also of their patriotic neighbors, and it would have led to harassment and potentially even persecution. The "day of the Lord" had arrived with the enthronement of Jesus as heavenly Lord. Jesus is Lord; Caesar is not. While there were undoubtedly political overtones to the Christian proclamation that brought them into conflict with the prevailing ideology, it is difficult to confine the disputed meaning of the conviction that "the day of the Lord has come" to this one issue, and few interpreters have done so.[31] Nevertheless, teachers in the Pauline churches of the latter half of the first century who advocated this view would have been challenged by 2 Thessalonians.

2. *Day of the Lord a present, spiritual reality.* A second approach argues that 2 Thessalonians addresses the mistaken view of Christians who believed that the day of the Lord had come in an internal, spiritualized sense (option 3 for the rethinking of early Christian eschatology, sketched above). Some gnosticizing interpretations of Paul followed this path, proclaiming that the resurrection has already happened (the view advocated in the *Gospel of Thomas* and opposed in

---

31. The most substantial argument for this view is presented by Roh, who sees 2 Thessalonians as written in the 70s, the time of Vespasian, addressing the question then in the air, "Who is the successor of world rule after Nero?" Roh associates the letter specifically with Thessalonica, a city that would have encouraged increased loyalty to the emperor to forestall any suspicions and to maintain their favored status. City officials may have decided it was a good thing to proceed with vigor against dissidents who were reluctant to participate in the Caesar cult. This situation need not be limited to Thessalonica nor to the reign of Vespasian; it continued, with varying degrees of intensity, into the time of Domitian at the end of the century, and in other cities of the Pauline churches' mission in Achaia, Macedonia, Asia, and elsewhere.

2 Tim 2:18). This view was alive in the Pauline tradition of the second and third generations. The deuteropauline authors of Colossians and Ephesians interpret the resurrection as something that has already happened in the experience of believers. Indeed, Ephesians portrays Christian existence as not only already "risen with him," but also "ascended with him" (Col 3:1–3; Eph 2:6)—but without abandoning future eschatology (Col 1:27; 3:4, 6; Eph 1:21; 4:4). One side of Paul's own already/not yet dialectic provided a point of contact for this misunderstanding, already in his own lifetime (see 1 Cor 4:5–13, esp. v. 8). Some streams of Johannine Christianity leaned toward this view, not abandoning futuristic eschatology but shifting the center of gravity to the realization of eschatological hopes in the present. The appearance of the antichrist, the return of Christ, the defeat of Satan, the resurrection, judgment, and eternal life—all these are counted as matters of present experience (1 John 2:18–22; 4:3; 2 John 7; John 3:18–19, 36; 6:47; 11:21–26; 12:31, 48, chs. 14–16; 17:3). During the middle and late twentieth century, the influence of gnosticizing ideas in the formation of early Christianity was often (over)emphasized. It was sometimes argued that the view "the day of the Lord has come" represented a gnosticizing realized eschatology. This approach to interpreting 2 Thessalonians has now receded.[32] Nonetheless, Pauline teachers advocating a realized eschatology would have felt themselves targeted and challenged by this letter circulating in the name of Paul.

3. *Eschatological events already begun.* The majority of current interpreters, myself included,[33] understand the author to be addressing primarily teachers within the Pauline churches who maintain that the Parousia of the Lord Jesus will occur very soon, and who mistakenly interpret the present distress of the churches as signs that the eschatological events are already underway. It is clear that the Greek phrase *enestēken* [perfect tense of *enistēmi*] *hē hēmera tou*

---

32. That the problem addressed by 2 Thessalonians was some type of realized eschatology has been argued in various ways by, e.g., Schmithals 1972b, 123–18, esp. 202–8; Jewett 1986, 176–78, who connects the realized eschatology of the "opponents" with their intense charismatic experiences; Hughes 1989, 87–91; Malherbe 2000, 429: "On the basis of 1 Thess 5:1–11, they would have claimed that they had escaped the judgment of the day of the Lord and that they were living in the light of the Day. Fully clad with faith, love, and hope, they were already in possession of salvation, which they had attained at his Parousia, which they presumably understood as a spiritual event. It is not difficult to see how such a view could raise problems for believers confronted by continuing persecution and tribulation." Cf. also 455: "The eschatological error mentioned [in 2:1–2] is not an imminent futuristic expectation, but an already realized eschatology."

33. Trilling (1972, 124–25) lists advocates up to 1972. Among more recent advocates are Koester 1990, 456; Furnish 2007, 153–62; Richard 1995, 323–54. My own earlier views tended to see the author as opposing some version of realized eschatology, as seen in Colossians and Ephesians. It now seems to me more likely that both the author of 2 Thessalonians and the proponents of the primary view he opposes were apocalyptic thinkers; he differs from them primarily on the location of the present on the apocalyptic clock.

kyriou must be translated "the day of the Lord has come/is here," not "is dawning" or "is imminent." Such language, however, is often used when something
expected is seen to be arriving, even if not yet literally present.[34] The vocabulary
used (*saleuthēnai hymas apo tou noos mēde throeisthai*, not be rattled in your
thinking nor alarmed) is the language of apocalypticism, as is all of the author's
response in vv. 3–10 (cf. Mark 13:7; Matt 24:6—the only other instances of
throeō in the NT). Aspects of the view he opposes can probably be seen in the
Revelation to John, written as "what the Spirit says to the churches" (Rev 2:7,
11, 17, 29; 3:6, 13, 22) about the same time as 2 Thessalonians and circulating
in the same area. The present threats and suffering of the faithful community
are indeed the leading edge of the final events; believers must remain faithful
and are encouraged to do so because the persecution will last only a short time,
then the end will come (Rev 6:11; 17:10). Thus Rev 6:17, with the persecutions
of the writer's time in view, asserts that "the great day . . . *has* come."

Whatever the view or views the author opposes, it is clear that he reaffirms
the apocalyptic hope—neither has the Lord already returned in the experience of
believers, nor is he about to come in the immediate future. This is the point of the
apocalyptic scenario depicted in the ensuing verses. His interest is not in drawing up an apocalyptic calendar as such, but in refuting false expectations about
the present. The argument, based on a combination of traditional apocalyptic
imagery that was again becoming current in Christian circles in Asia in the 90s
(cf. Revelation), is that certain signs must precede the end. Since these have not
yet happened, the end cannot have come already in some spiritual sense, nor can
it be imminent in a literal sense. The author's eschatology focuses sharply on
these points: not now and not imminent, but future; not private and subjective,
but public and cosmic. This primary emphasis is clear and does not depend on
identifying the details of the apocalyptic scenario that follows.

The author does not itemize the eschatological events in chronological order,
as though he were teaching new ideas, but refers to the eschatological drama
as though the readers are already familiar with it (or should be; see 2:5). From
the plotted order of the presupposed narrative, the referential order can be
abstracted as a summary of the author's apocalyptic scenario, stretching from
the readers' present to the ultimate end:

- The "mystery of lawlessness" is already at work in the readers'
  present, but there is something or someone that restrains its full
  operation (2:6–7). During this period, from the present through
  the historical future, the church is to continue in good work and
  word (2:17). The present is not already determined but can be

---

34. One seated in the restaurant of a train station will not misunderstand if a friend, waiting
outside, sees the train approaching and rushes to announce, "Your train is here."

determined by the readers. They have some responsibility to shape the present; it is not already shaped. The anticipated length of this period is not given.

- At the end of this period, the eschatological events will begin: the Restrainer will be removed (2:7), the "apostasy" will come, the day of the Lord will arrive (2:3), the false parousia of the Lawless One will occur (2:3, 6, 8, 9). The Lawless One will take his seat in the temple of God, declaring himself to be God, exalting himself above every so-called god or object of worship (2:4).
- Then the true Parousia will come (2:1), when the Lord Jesus will be revealed from heaven in flaming fire, in charge of his angelic host (1:7–8). He will destroy the Lawless One with the breath of his mouth (2:8). Believers will be delivered from the persecution they have been experiencing (1:7) and "gathered together to him" (2:1). They will glorify the returning Lord, whose name will then be honored (1:10, 12). The Lord will glorify them (1:12), they will be made worthy of their calling, and their good intentions and faithfulness will be fulfilled (1:11).
- A different destiny awaits unbelievers. God will justly repay with affliction those who are afflicting the believers and have not obeyed the gospel of the Lord Jesus, those who do not know God and have not loved the truth, but have taken pleasure in unrighteousness (1:6, 8, 9; 2:12).

Interpreting Apocalyptic Language

The identification of the characters in the cast of this apocalyptic drama has generated a variety of interpretations and an enormous bibliography.[35] A helpful oversimplification may be to first divide all proposed interpretations into two groups, depending on whether they regard the apocalyptic language as nonreferential or referential, roughly corresponding to "subjective" and "objective." In nonreferential language, the author is not actually talking *about* anything that is real (even if he supposes that he is), but using apocalyptic imagery to express his own hopes and self-understanding. Referential language, on the other hand, refers to a reality outside the speaking subject, points to an *extra nos* (outside ourselves), nonsubjective reality. Such language intends to point to the restraining power, the Lawless One, and the future advent of the Lord Jesus as realities in their own right, not projections of the author's imagination. This

---

35. For a sketch of the history of interpretation, delineation of the major interpretations, and bibliography, see Wanamaker 250–52. For thorough bibliographies, see Rigaux xxii–xxix; Bruce 159–61; Roh 131–36. Already in 1912, Frame could report "the literature is enormous" (276).

is true whether or not these realities actually exist; I am referring to a linguistic category, not necessarily an ontological one.

These two types of language cannot be reduced to "symbolic" and "literal." Referential language itself must be divided into objectifying and nonobjectifying language. Objectifying language supposes it is talking about particular realities that fit into an objective system, like the parts of a machine that are geared together. A change in one then affects the whole system in a predictable, logical way. Necessary inferences can be made from one element of the system about its other parts.

Construing the language of 2 Thess 2:1–12 as objectifying language understands the Restrainer and the Lawless One to be particular figures the author expected to appear at the end of history. This view has led to the plethora of attempts by interpreters to identify them. Other interpreters, while operating with the same view of the kind of language at work, have decided that these attempts are both futile and unimportant. The original author and readers knew who or what these images referred to, but they have not given enough information for later readers to identify them. The quest is fruitless and should be abandoned.

There is another category of referential language that is nonobjectifying. In this view, the language does indeed refer to eschatological realities, but not in a way that allows them to be particularized and identified with specific objects or persons. In the nature of the case, finite human language cannot express the nature of transcendent realities. They are indeed realities, and human language can point to them, actually referring to something beyond itself, but is incapable of designating them in an objectifying way. This is the nature of all God-language, which indeed points to the Ultimate Reality but can never contain the reality in the space-time categories of the human thought world or in the logic of human linguistic systems. In this view, not only God, but also heaven, the Last Judgment, the second coming, and—in the case at hand—the Restrainer and the Lawless One are expressed in referential but nonobjectifying language. This means it is pointless to inquire what or whom they refer to in particular, for there is nothing or no one in the space-time material world to "identify" for either the author or the readers, ancient or modern.

Does the author himself suppose he is referring to objective realities that will occur in the space-time world sometime in the future? Some interpreters argue that the mysterious, veiled nature of this whole section is an intentional feature of the author's strategy of communication. Like Jesus' parables, the author's apocalyptic scenario points to an ultimate reality that cannot be communicated except in this-worldly imagery, and he was fully aware that the dramatic apocalyptic scenario he projects does not refer to objectifiable persons and events that will someday unfold just as he describes them.[36] Perhaps. More

36. So, e.g., Trilling 1980, 89–90.

likely, the author adopts elements of traditional apocalyptic thought that allow him to make his primary point—the end is neither present nor imminent—and he does this without reflecting on how the imagery is related to ontological and historical reality. In any case, the modern reader should not necessarily suppose that the author thinks his readers actually know all these details, that he claims to know them himself, or that understanding and believing what he wants to say means attempting to identify the characters in the apocalyptic drama.

2:3–12 Correcting the Apocalyptic Timetable

Three preliminary points are important for understanding the function of this material in the present context.

1. *No innovation.* "Paul" had already taught the apocalyptic program set forth in 2 Thessalonians. The author does not cite Paul and then interpret him for a later generation, but writes *as* Paul, in the fictive setting of the first generation, claiming he has always taught that certain events must occur before the eschaton, so the day of the Lord cannot be dawning in the present. What is in fact a new understanding of eschatology is presented as what the Pauline churches have always been taught.

2. *No revelation.* Such material is the result of prophetic revelation, of the kind found in the Apocalypse of John. It is not the kind of information that can be derived from historical observation or biblical exegesis, but must have been revealed to some prophet or seer. But unlike the prophetic author of Revelation, the author of 2 Thessalonians does not claim he himself has received the revelation. It is traditional material, the common property of various streams of second- and third-generation Christianity in Asia and the Aegean, which some congregations and church members may understand in varying degrees, and others may find quite strange.

3. *No explanation.* The author introduces traditional apocalyptic material circulating in the second and third generations without explaining the terminology or dramatis personae. Whether or not the actual readers are familiar with the cast of apocalyptic characters, the author addresses them as though these figures are well known. The definite articles (*the* Man of Lawlessness, *the* apostasy, *the* Restrainer) are broadly anaphoric,[37] meaning they refer to things that are well known and can be assumed, as a modern writer might refer to "the capital," "the civil war," "the civil rights movement." In fact, the actual readers of the second or third generation may have only a vague idea of such things. They can hear the letter as though from Paul to the Thessalonians of a previous generation, and they can assume that both Paul and they knew what these terms referred to. The

---

37. On this use of the Greek article, see BDF 131–32 (§252); Wallace 225, with numerous illustrations.

letter can have its intended effect on the actual readers without their needing to identify the particular characters and events in the apocalyptic scenario. They likely did not know what these images stand for, and the author himself may not have had particular referents in mind. Readers are simply to understand that the day of the Lord has not come, that the "mystery of lawlessness" is already at work (the present is not empty waiting, treading water; see on 2:13–17), that the end-time events are still in the future and will be clearly recognizable when they appear. These will be visible, public, community events. They cannot be invisible, private, individual experiences. So Pauline tradition shows that the day cannot have already come (against realized eschatology). Before the author begins his explicit refutation, he indirectly calls both tradition and the experience of his readers to his side; what he is talking about is not merely a matter of *doctrine*, but of (their common) *experience*.

[3] In 2:3–4, on the apostasy and advent of the Lawless One, the author proceeds to describe the eschatological events, with the goal of showing that they are neither present nor on the immediate horizon. He does not do this as though he were instructing the readers, proceeding step by step in chronological order, but weaves their present into past and future events.

The admonition "Let no one deceive you in any way" does not indicate that there is a group of "opponents" who are intentionally trying to mislead the congregations. The Pauline tradition can use "deceive" (*exapataō*) of intentional deceit by false teachers (2 Cor 11:3), but also of self-deception, accepting plausible but misleading ideas (1 Cor 3:18). The latter is the case here.

"The apostasy must come first." The Pauline school tradition included the topos that in the last days there would be widespread departure from the faith, and that almost all would abandon the faith as taught by Paul, including even some who had been faithful believers (1 Tim 4:1–3; 2 Tim 3:1; 4:3–4, 10–11; cf. Jude 17–19; Heb 3:12; *Did.* 16.3–4). This corresponds to a general apocalyptic pattern in which not only will believers be tested and tempted to apostatize, but also a great cataract of evil will engulf the world, which will be characterized by *anomia* (lawlessness; cf., e.g., Matt 24:12). The reference is not only to abandonment of the law of Moses by Jews, but also to a general breakdown of an orderly world as history approaches its denouement. The pattern appears: a final spasm of evil, one last outburst in which rebellion against God comes to a head before it is finally smashed. Thus, for example, in *1 En.* 91.5–7:

> 5 For I know that the state of violence will intensify upon the earth; a great plague shall be executed upon the earth; all (forms of) oppression will be carried out; and everything shall be uprooted; and every arrow shall fly fast. 6 Oppression shall recur once more and be carried out upon the earth; every (form of) oppression, injustice, and iniquity shall infect (the world) twofold. 7 When sin, oppression, blasphemy, and injustice increase, crime, iniquity, and uncleanliness shall be committed and increase. (*OTP* 1:72; cf. *Jub.* 23.14–25; *2 Bar.* 27)

The many points of correspondence to the picture in 2 Thessalonians 2 are obvious.

After the apostasy comes the Lawless One, the author's term for the eschatological figure often called the "antichrist." The particular term "antichrist" is found in the New Testament only in the Johannine Letters (1 John 2:18, 22; 4:3; 2 John 7), where, as with "Man of Lawlessness" here, it is presumed to be common knowledge, and a correction of misunderstandings is attempted. From ancient times a pattern had existed in which evil would appear in concentrated, superhuman form just before the fulfillment of God's purpose; then God or God's agent would appear and destroy the evil power, and God's act would bring salvation. In Gen 15:16 Yahweh explains to Abraham that the oppression in Egypt will last a long time, that God's redemption will not take place until "the iniquity of the Amorites . . . is complete." So also in the Ezekiel tradition, as prophecy morphs into apocalyptic, the final redemption does not occur when a relatively few returnees from the Babylonian exile resettle in Judea, but only after "Gog, of the land of Magog" brings the quasi-mythical hordes from the Far North against the people of God. The final forces of evil are destroyed not in a historical battle, but by fire from heaven (Ezek 38–39). The attempt to sit in God's place in the temple is also an old, biblical pattern (the king of Babylon, Isa 14:4–14; the prince of Tyre, Ezek 28:2).

The tumultuous Jewish history during the period 168 B.C.E.–70 C.E. provided several occasions to sharpen the imagery and fill in some of its details. In 167 B.C.E. Antiochus IV Epiphanes desecrated the Jerusalem temple so that it became unholy and could not be entered by pious Jews (the "abomination of desolation" = "the desecrating sacrilege"; see 1 Macc 1:54; 2 Macc 6:1–5; Josephus, *Ant.* 12.316–322; Dan 8:13; 9:27; 11:31; 12:11; this imagery is also adopted in Mark 13:14 par.). In 63 B.C.E. the Roman general Pompey intervened in a civil war in Judea between Hyrcanus and Aristobulus, thereby establishing Roman power there that continued through the entire New Testament period. A three-month siege of the temple in Jerusalem ended in Roman victory. It was never forgotten that Pompey, called the "Lawless One," had evoked apostasy, scattered the covenant people, and even entered the holy of holies (*Pss. Sol.* 17.11–22; Josephus, *Ant.* 14.71–72; *JW* 1.152–53). In 40 C.E. the emperor Gaius Caligula, claiming divine honors for himself, attempted to set up a statue of himself in the Jerusalem temple, which would have provoked terrible riots and slaughter if he had not been killed before the command was carried out (Josephus, *Ant.* 18). In 64 C.E. Nero, claiming divine honors, had accused Christians in Rome of arson and inflicted terrible punishments on them. This imagery, in a variety of fluid combinations, was alive in the imaginations of Jews and Christians throughout the first century.

With the image of a "Lawless One," the author of 2 Thessalonians makes no attempt to signify a particular figure. His allusions instead evoke a stylized combination drawn from various apocalyptic images that were circulating in the Pauline churches. His intention is not to spur his readers to attempt to identify the Lawless One, but to insist that the whole eschatological program has not yet begun. Nonetheless, later church interpreters, misunderstanding the kind of language being used, tried to identify the antichrist figure in the Pauline tradition with their own opponents.[38]

The author's point is clear. Even as he introduces the Man of Lawlessness, he designates him the Son of Destruction, meaning the one already condemned to be destroyed. To be sure, the power of lawlessness is already at work, a reality the readers are experiencing. The readers are not called to join a campaign to destroy the Evil One. They may live in the confident hope that the ultimate power of evil will be destroyed as an integral part of the eschatological victory of God (see v. 7). But the ultimate victory cannot come until the ultimate Opponent appears. This has not yet happened, so the readers cannot be living in the eschatological last days, and their troubles are not the eschatological woes.

[4] The reference to the temple (*naos*) in v. 4 has sometimes been taken as evidence that the author is Paul, writing before the destruction of the temple in 70 C.E. However, that the antichrist would enthrone himself in the temple and claim divine honors was a firm part of the traditional imagery, which the later deuteropauline author could assume without reflection, or simply adopt as part of the fictive framework within the lifetime of Paul. Even some advocates of Pauline authorship do not rely on this argument nor suppose that even Paul expected this as an actual event; instead, they relegate the reference to the traditional repertoire of apocalyptic imagery.[39] Contemporary interpreters who affirm Pauline authorship and do take the language as referring to an actual event must face the difficulty that Paul predicted an event that did not happen. Thus some modern dispensationalist interpreters insist that the temple will have to be rebuilt so that "Paul's" "prophecy" can be fulfilled. This argument was already made by some ancient interpreters, though without the modern dispensationalist framework (e.g., Hippolytus, *Dan.* 4.49; cf. *Barn.* 16.4–5). Other attempts to deal with the problem that have emerged in the course of church

---

38. Rigaux (259–80) offers an extensive history of interpretation yet rightly says it would take a whole monograph to trace the history of exegesis of this one word. Even before the Reformation, some Roman Catholic exegetes (including the Cathari, Joachim of Fiore, and the Franciscan spirituals) considered the papacy to be the antichrist. This became the "standard" view of Protestantism until the rise of historical criticism. Rigaux explains that, thereafter, exegetes of all traditions who interpreted the text historically considered any view incorrect that could not have been understood and affirmed by the original readers.

39. So already Irenaeus (*Haer.* 5.25.4), for whom it was unproblematic. More recently: Rigaux 661; Malherbe 2000, 421; Bruce 169, 183. A good parallel text is Rev 11:1–2, written after the temple's destruction, about the same time as 2 Thessalonians, but using imagery that pictures the temple as still standing in Jerusalem (cf. Wrede 1903, 110–12).

history—such as claiming that the temple refers to the church or to the heavenly temple—are rarely found today. From the perspective that the letter is deutero-pauline and the language is traditional and nonobjectifying, all such attempts represent a genre mistake in terms of both the document and its language.

[5] The author is no innovator. He interrupts his depiction of the Lawless One to remind the readers that they already know this, for it has been a matter of authentic Pauline tradition from the beginning. This tradition takes priority over any prophetic revelations, sermons, or teachings that do not conform to it. Thus the author's reinterpretation of Paul is presented as the true Pauline eschatology handed on in oral tradition. The imperfect tense *elegon* ("I used to say"; see trans. note i above) refers not to what Paul once said to a particular group of Thessalonians, but to Paul's typical, customary preaching: "This is what Paul used to say, as you remember." This means that the author is not introducing this apocalyptic tradition for the first time, but is using oral apocalyptic tradition that has been circulating in the Pauline churches as an alternative to both a near expectation and also a hyperrealized eschatology. The author may or may not have thought that it actually went back to Paul, but he insists that he is not composing ad hoc; he has already accepted it as authentic Pauline tradition before he ever composes the letter. The Johannine Letters and Revelation show that such ideas were already circulating among the churches of Asia in the 90s. He appeals over the head of other letters circulating in the Pauline churches under Paul's name to his own "apostolic" letter.[40]

The very manner of presenting the drama assumes that the readers "already know." It is not done straightforwardly, diachronically, as though the author were instructing them in a step-by-step apocalyptic program, but weaves back and forth among past, present, historical future, and apocalyptic climax, in an allusive way that assumes familiarity. The author imputes such familiarity to his readers, whether or not they are actually aware of these events and characters. The real readers have never been in Paul's presence and heard him teach such things.[41] This is part of the fictive world of the deuteropauline letter, for, as Wrede has detailed, if Paul had really taught the eschatological program of 2 Thessalonians while with them, then he must have forgotten it while writing 1 Thess 5:1–4. The Thessalonians must also have forgotten it, for their supposed knowledge of the eschatological program does not prevent them from being "rattled out of their minds" by the claims that the Lord has in some way already come or that his Parousia is imminent. The author is not an innovator

---

40. Cf. Laub 1990, 407.

41. The *oidate* (you know) of 2:6 was frequent in Paul (25× in the undisputed letters, including 9× in 1 Thessalonians; see comments on 1 Thess 2:1; 4:13). The author of 2 Thessalonians never repeats the "you know" statements of 1 Thessalonians, but only adds the appeal to what he has "already" taught them in the two areas that have become controversial (2:6, eschatology; 3:7, financial support of a special class of ministers).

in the sense of introducing something absolutely new, for the views he advocates have been circulating among the Pauline churches alongside the views he opposes. He is in fact innovating, however, bringing Paul up to date in the light of recent and current developments, though he does not want to be understood as an innovator. He actually sees himself opposing innovation and appealing to the original tradition (see on 2:15 below).

[6–7] Now the author returns to the present of the actual readers. None of the things described in vv. 3–4 have happened. This is the point—not to describe what will happen someday, but to make clear that they have not happened and are not happening. Nothing in the readers' situation signals that the day of the Lord has arrived or is arriving.[42] Why have the promised events of the last days not begun? Because something and/or someone restrains them. The *katechon*, the restraining power at work in the present, is otherwise unknown in apocalyptic tradition and seems to be the deuteropauline author's own interpretation. Whatever—if anything in particular—the author has in mind, God is the Lord of history and Director of the eschatological drama that will bring history to a worthy conclusion, and thus ultimately the one who is holding back the final events until their divinely appointed time.[43] Other post-Pauline New Testament authors also struggled to reinterpret the expectation of the first generation, whose hopes for the near consummation of history had turned out to be unfulfilled. One approach was to reassert the sovereignty of God, who is not bound to apocalyptic schemes and who can even change the timetable of the final events. In Mark 13:20, for example, God the Creator shortens the days of eschatological tribulation for the sake of the elect. In 2 Pet 3:9–10, history is extended in order to grant more time for repentance. This contrasts with such apocalypses as *4 Ezra*, in which even God seems bound to a previously announced apocalyptic scheme (*4 Ezra* 4.35–37).

The author of 2 Thessalonians himself probably did not have in mind a specific power, principle, or person that was presently restraining the advent of the Lawless One. He likely intended his depiction to be provocatively obscure. I thus consider it fruitless to rehearse once again the numerous attempts to identify him or it.[44] If the author of 2 Thessalonians had anything definite in mind,

42. The contemporaneous author of Revelation also has an apocalyptic theological understanding of the troubles the church is experiencing in his time. The harassments are expected to intensify, and martyrdoms are to increase, for they are only the leading edge of the eschatological woes the faithful people of God must endure in the last days. The author of 2 Thessalonians affirms the faithfulness called for but presents an alternative theological base. In terms of the chronology of God's plan, his theology has turned out to be the more enduring.

43. The LXX of Isa 40:22 refers to God as *ho katechōn*, the same term as 2 Thess 2:7, the Controller who has appointed the rulers of the earth.

44. Already Augustine candidly acknowledged, "I frankly confess I do not know what he means. I will nevertheless mention such conjectures as I have heard or read" (*Civ.* 20.19.2). Among

whatever or whoever it was indeed is subject to God, who is in charge of present and future. If one insists on trying to identify some historical institution or person as "the Restrainer," interpreters can probably do no better than the ancient interpretation of the Roman Empire as embodied in the Roman emperor. This would again position the writer as opposing some views promoted by the author of Revelation that were circulating in his day and claiming: we are *not* in the last days, and the Roman Empire is *not* the evil beast/Lawless One, but instead (at present at least) that power of law and order holds back the forces of chaos and creates a stable world in which the Christian mission can be carried out. This would be a nuanced view of Roman power, somewhat like the views circulating in the Pauline churches that would later be inscribed in 1 Peter, the Pastorals, and Luke–Acts. The exhortation the author will make in 2 Thess 3:12–13 fits this ethos.

The "mystery of lawlessness" is already at work. The day has not come, has not even begun, but the present is not empty, not ordinary, normal time (see on 2:13–17). The ultimate concentration of evil that will be revealed at the eschaton is already at work in a subterranean way in the present. Only believers, however, see it. This understanding was current in various ways in the Pauline school tradition (e.g., see Eph 2:1–3). The author is not interested in merely offering interesting eschatological instruction; instead, he wants to mobilize his readers to be alert to the evil already present and to resist it (2:15, 17; 3:3, 5). Their present troubles are not the beginning of the end, but they are an anticipation, a foretaste of the satanic power ultimately to be revealed and destroyed. Such ideas were circulating in the Pauline tradition. The author of Ephesians likewise does not regard the present as the beginning of the end, but does see the spirit of the ultimate Evil One already at work in those who have not accepted the gospel (Eph 2:2). This is the counterpart of the "mystery of our religion" already energizing the believing community (1 Tim 3:16). In such contexts, *mystērion* does not connote a riddle or enigma difficult to understand,

---

possibilities that have endured into the present discussion are the following: (1) A view prevalent since Tertullian is that the Roman Empire (thus the neuter form *to katechon*) and emperor (the masculine *ho katechōn*) maintain law and order in the world until the final breakdown of the world's structures. (2) Another ancient view (Theodoret), revived by a few scholars in the 20th cent., is that the preaching of the gospel, especially as embodied in Paul and the Pauline mission, must be accomplished before the end can come (cf. Mark 13:10, featuring *prōton* ["first"] as in 2 Thess 2:3). (3) God or a deputized angel restrains the evil powers until they are unleashed at the end (cf. Hab 2:3; Rev 7:1–3); Nicholl (230–46) argues extensively for the archangel Michael, though Michael is never designated "the Restrainer." (4) A Christian prophet in the community, "seized" (understanding *katechō* to mean "seize") by the Spirit, has mistakenly predicted that the Lord is coming soon, but the end will not come until the misleading prophet "is removed"; so Giblin 224–42. (5) A power or principle hostile to God, embodied in some evil person, will continue to rule until the end comes; so Frame 259–62. For more detailed descriptions and documentation, see Best 295–302; Trilling 1980, 94–102; Marshall 1983, 196–200; Wanamaker 250–52.

but a matter of revelation: a reality hidden to unbelievers, but already revealed to eyes of faith, like the kingdom of God in the Synoptic Gospels, already at work in the present in a hidden manner, ultimately to be revealed to all (e.g., Mark 4:11; Matt 13:10–17). As in Mark 13, the end in 2 Thessalonians 2 is not yet, but present troubles are not just ordinary historical troubles. The trials and tribulations experienced by the readers are indeed manifestations of the evil power that is to be fully *revealed* at the end, an evil power that is already mysteriously at work in the present. The harassment and persecution the readers are enduring are not to be mistaken as signs of the end, but neither are they merely the evils of everyday life or the result of a society that misunderstands and abuses them. They represent a *mystery*. Believers know what is already at work, know it will be revealed for what it is at the Last Judgment, know that it is already defeated and that this will be made manifest to all at the Parousia. But their present troubles do not mean that the end is already beginning. They have the wrong chronology.

[8] The restraining power will not hold back the final revelation of evil forever. God will remove this restraining force, and the eschatological drama will begin (see trans. note f above). The author returns to a fuller description of the Lawless One, which he has saved until this point, not so that he could give additional, curiosity-satisfying details of what the Lawless One will be like when he finally comes, but to relate his characterization to an important dimension of present discipleship: the love of the truth (emphasized in vv. 10, 12, 13). Identifying Christian faith as "the truth" was a developing theme in second- and third-generation Pauline churches, as it was in the contemporaneous Johannine tradition (see, e.g., Eph 1:13; 4:21; 6:14; Col 1:5, 6; 1 Tim 2:4, 7; 3:15; 4:3; 6:5; 2 Tim 2:15, 18, 25; 3:7, 8; 4:4; Titus 1:14; 67× in the Johannine tradition, as in John 1:17; 5:33; 8:32; 16:13; 17:19; 1 John 2:21; 2 John 1, 4; 3 John 3, 4, 8).

The first thing said about the arrival of the Lawless One is that he will be destroyed. The powers of evil are already a defeated enemy; believers are not called to be faithful in order to help God beat the devil. The author has no interest in identifying the Lawless One or portraying the lurid details of what he will actually do. Nor is there a final battle. The returning Lord will destroy the final manifestation of evil effortlessly, simply by his advent and the "breath of his mouth," fulfilling the biblical hope of the powerful Messiah who will establish justice by his divine power (Isa 11:4; cf. Rev 19:11–16). The image of the divine "breath" (*rûaḥ*, which also means "wind" and "Spirit") does not mean the Lawless One is a pushover, easily blown away. Far from it—yet the Lord's breath/wind/Spirit is much more powerful, the original creative force that drove back the powers of chaos (Gen 1:2). The earlier Pauline *parousia* vocabulary is retained but fades into the *epiphany* language current in the second- and third-generation Pauline school (see on 1 Thess 4:15).

[9] While not cast as a fake messiah, the Lawless One imitates the Messiah. As in the apocalyptic traditions preserved in Revelation, roughly contemporary with 2 Thessalonians, the final representative of evil is a perverse reflection of the Christ. Both have a parousia, both are revealed, God-language is used of both, both are agents of transcendent power: the Messiah's ultimate opponent works by the power of Satan;[45] the Messiah represents the true God. They are related to each other as the truth is related to the lie. Just as the Parousia of the Lord is for those who are to be gathered to him, so the parousia of the Lawless One is for those who believe the lie. Apocalyptic thought tends toward (penultimate) dualism. There is no middle ground, but only truth and lie. "Everything is in pairs" (*T. Ash.* 1.4).

As in Rev 13:13, Satan's final representative and his agents work miracles, but neither 2 Thessalonians nor Revelation portrays Christian believers as exhibiting miraculous powers. The imagery of "deceitful signs and miracles" does not mean that the miracles are fake but that they deceive. The final revelation of the Lawless One will bring a spate of miraculous phenomena supporting his claims. Yet in the author's and readers' present, miracles are already appealed to in support of various theologies—including the view that the end is already breaking in. The author is not merely asserting that the readers have a faulty chronology, as though he wanted to defer their present excitement to the future, leaving the present blank. He could have said simply, "You are wrong to believe that 'the day of the Lord is already here,' because such and such must happen first; since these things have not happened, the Great Day is not yet here." Rather, the reference to the deceitful miracles of the Lawless One is contemporizing, interpreting the present, in which the mystery of lawlessness is already at work. The author opposes both a superheated apocalypticism, in which the end-time events are seen as already happening, and an indifference that in practice abandons eschatological thought entirely. Both views fail to understand the present as the believers' time for responsible action.

The author's own eschatology does not merely postpone the end to the indefinite future; instead, his eschatology also affects the present. The *katechon* has a retarding function in the eschatological drama, giving a positive dimension to the present that is not mere waiting, for the mystery of lawlessness is already at work (like the spirit of antichrist in the Johannine Letters [1 John 4:3!]). Faith and unbelief are matters of present decision, and the only options are Christian truth and satanic lie. The author thus has his own way of affirming the Pauline already/not yet. In a situation where the "delay of the Parousia" is already beginning to be a problem evoking a variety of responses within the

---

45. For the image and language of Satan, see on 1 Thess 2:18.

Pauline churches, he does not reduce everything to the future hope, but calls for faithfulness in a present seen as already shaped by the eschatological reality.[46]

[10–12] The author's understanding of the responsibility for belief and unbelief also preserves something of the Pauline dialectic. Those on the road to destruction did not welcome the truth and are themselves responsible. Since they have so decided, God sends them a powerful delusion. The end is pictured dualistically, but as in all biblical apocalyptic thought, the dualism is penultimate and relative, while trust in the sovereignty of the one true God is ultimate and absolute. The advent of the Lawless One and his deceitful miracles is future, yet it already casts its shadow back on the present, and miraculous phenomena of the present can already represent the final evil power to be revealed in the eschatological future. Being a believer now, in the present, amounts to living in the presence of two force fields. Each person must decide, but the decision is not a matter of autonomy. After the decision has been made, it is seen to have been "determined" by transcendent powers; human beings are not autonomous, individual beings who exercise their right of decision as peers with God. The author himself does not, of course, reflect on any of this, but operates within this assumed view of reality, which the modern reader can unpack and interpret.

The unreflective, confessional-language dualism of this paragraph is not objectifying doctrine about outsiders or addressed to them. It is not informational language at all, but the language of paraenesis, addressed to insiders—not to inform them about particular apocalyptic events, but to encourage them to live in a particular way. The background is still the courtroom scene, present human courts contrasted with the eschatological judgment. The judicial vocabulary of *krinō, alētheia, pseudos* (judgment, truth, lie) pervades the whole section. As in Revelation, which is also severe on liars (14:5; 21:8), those who lie may get off easily in this-worldly courts, while those who confess the truth are condemned. The eschatological judgment, however, will reverse the judgment of human courts. Those who are presently the judges—not just court officials—will themselves be judged. They have given the wrong verdict in human courts, approved what is wrong (note the contrast of *alētheia* not only with falsehood, but also with "wrong" in the ethical sense, *adikia* [vv. 10, 12]). The concentration on *alētheia* (3× in this letter [2:10, 12, 13], absent from 1 Thessalonians, but strong in the Pastorals, Ephesians, and in the neighboring

---

46. So rightly Trilling 1980, 90–91, against numerous other interpreters, who too quickly classify the author as having failed to grasp Paul's understanding of the present as eschatological existence. Bultmann's description of post-Pauline Christianity has been strong and pervasive. Though Bultmann had some appreciation for the contributions of Colossians, Ephesians, the Pastorals, 1 Peter, Hebrews, and Luke–Acts, he barely mentions 2 Thessalonians, which is entirely absent from the index of his comprehensive *Theology* (see esp. 2:111–16, "The Transformation of the Church's Self-Understanding," and 2:119–236).

Johannine school; see list at v. 8) also points to a second- or third-generation Pauline school context, where such topics were in the air. The "power of delusion" that God sends on the wicked is almost parallel to the Spirit of truth, which the contemporary Johannine school emphasizes as God's gift to believers ("truth," 45× in the Johannine writings, combined with "Spirit" 17×; e.g., see John 14:17; 15:26; 1 John 4:6; 5:6). As in the Johannine school, which also is concerned with the relation of miracles and truth, the truth of God is not validated by miracles but is recognized by those who love the truth and want to do God's will (cf. John 7:17).

In the final sentence of this section (v. 12), the author explicitly returns to the courtroom imagery and points to the future judgment that—with the justice of God's coming kingdom—will reverse the decisions of human courts and vindicate those who have been faithful in their confession to the Christian truth (1:5).

2:13–17 Second Thanksgiving and Benediction

Following the corrective insertion on eschatology in 2:1–12, the author returns to the template provided by 1 Thessalonians, with a second thanksgiving section that concludes with a second benediction (see intro to 2 Thessalonians, "Structure and Summary").

> 2:13 But we should always give thanks to God for you, brothers and sisters beloved by the Lord, because God has chosen you as the firstfruits[a] of those who are being saved, [a salvation] that comes through sanctification by the Spirit and belief in the truth, 14 for which [salvation] God[b] called you through our proclamation of the gospel, so that you may participate in the glory of our Lord Jesus Christ.
>
> 15 So then, brothers and sisters, stand firm and hold fast the traditions that you were taught by us, whether through oral preaching and teaching or through a letter from us.
>
> 16 Now may our Lord Jesus Christ himself, and God our Father, who in grace[c] has loved us and given us the encouragement and good hope that belong to the salvation of the age to come,[d] 17 encourage your hearts and strengthen you in every good work and word.[e]

a. The MS evidence is about evenly split between *ap' archēs* (from the beginning; so ℵ D K L Ψ and most later MSS) and reading the text as a single word *aparchēn* (firstfruits; so B F G P 0278 33 81 323 326 365 1505 1739 1881 2464 vg sy[h] bo). The comments below give reasons why "firstfruits" is the more probable original reading.

b. The thought is continued elliptically into the next clause by a neuter relative pronoun that refers to the whole process of salvation for which God is responsible, as diagramming the Greek sentence makes clear.

c. Most translations take *en chariti* (lit., "by grace"), which comes at the end of the Greek clause, as modifying only the second participle, "given," but this seems to be mainly in the interests of smooth English syntax. The phrase is better taken as modifying both participles: it is the grace of the Lord Jesus/God our Father that erupts in both loving and giving. Richard's translation also captures this: "God loved us and so through grace has given us . . ."

d. More lit., as in most versions, "eternal salvation." On the translation of *aiōnios*, see note j for 2 Thess 1:9. On the difficulty of rendering the rich NT term *paraklēsis* by a single English word, see on 1 Thess 2:3.

e. *En panti ergō kai logō* could be rendered more colloquially as "in everything you do and say" or the like, but the author points not only to the individual believer's everyday behavior and conversation—though no less than that—but also to their collective service to God in the work of the Christian mission and its preaching and teaching. This combination, already used by Paul (Rom 15:18; 2 Cor 10:11), was tending to become a fixed phrase in the Pauline churches of the second and third generations (Col 3:17; Luke 24:19; Acts 7:22).

Composition of 2:13–17

These three sentences constitute the concluding section of the thanksgiving/ body that began at 1:3, and thus they play the same role, and have the same form, as 1 Thess 3:11–13. In v. 15, the author interrupts his thanksgiving with a brief but firm exhortation to maintain the tradition. The *oun* (therefore), which typically occurs at the transition from the indicative "theological" to the imperative "paraenetic" sections of a Pauline letter (Rom 12:1; Gal 5:1; 1 Thess 4:1; cf. Eph 4:1; Col 3:1) should not be taken as the beginning of the paraenesis at 2 Thess 2:15. Rather, in 2 Thessalonians the paraenetic section begins at 3:1, where the *to loipon* that opens the verse corresponds to the *loipon* of 1 Thess 4:1, which begins the paraenesis of the author's template (see trans. note a on 1 Thess 4:1). Here in 2 Thess 2:15, though the author shifts briefly to the imperative, the formulaic *oun* is expanded to *ara oun* (so then), an expression common in Paul and Pauline tradition, but never used in this crucial transitional function between the two major parts of the letter (e.g., Rom 5:18; 7:3, 25; 8:12; Gal 6:10; 1 Thess 5:6; Eph 2:19). The reference in 2 Thess 2:15 to *logos* (oral preaching and teaching) and *epistolē* (letter), with the striking omission of *pneuma* (spirit), forms an inclusio with v. 2 and thus joins this sentence to the preceding, rather than beginning a new section. The verse is a minor structural interruption of the thanksgiving period, important to the author in that it allows him to pull together the argument of 2:1–17. This then allows 2:16–17 to come at the appropriate place as the benediction that concludes the first main part of the letter, as in the structure of 1 Thessalonians he is following.

The deuteropauline author continues to mine 1 Thessalonians for both vocabulary and themes, drawing material from other Pauline Letters as well (2 Thess

2:13 = 1 Thess 1:2, 4; 2 Thess 2:14 = 1 Thess 1:5; 2 Thess 2:15 = 1 Thess 1:5 and 1 Cor 11:2; 2 Thess 2:16 = 1 Thess 3:11, 12; 2 Thess 2:17 = 1 Thess 3:13 and 2 Cor 9:8). This does not mean that he is utilizing Paul's Letters in a cut-and-paste procedure, but that he is familiar with Pauline phraseology from repeated reading and hearing them in church liturgy and school discussion. Nor does he merely repeat Paul; instead, he creatively integrates materials from the Pauline tradition into his own composition for a new situation.

[13–14] These two verses are one closely packed sentence, whose structure is maintained in the translation above. The meaning is clear, with six distinct yet interrelated affirmations. (1) God has chosen you. (2) You are the firstfruits of the harvest of those who are being saved. (3) This salvation comes through the sanctifying action of the Spirit. (4) This salvation comes by your belief in the truth. (5) God called you through our preaching the gospel. (6) The goal of salvation is participation in the glory of Christ to be revealed at the Parousia.

Both the emphatic "we" with which the thanksgiving begins and the disjunctive conjunction *de* (but) contrast the life and destiny of the believing hearers with that of those who have been deluded by Satan, have believed the lie, and are on the way to destruction. The focus of confessional language on insiders continues. The author is grateful to God for those in the Pauline churches who continue steadfast in the tradition they have received, who are neither swept away by the false eschatological excitement nor drift carelessly into apostasy. The thanksgiving is the standard Pauline form, adjusted to the author's later situation, in which the language has become more liturgical (see on 2 Thess 1:3). Though the form is conventional, the thanksgiving is real. As the letter is read aloud in the worship of the Pauline churches, the author wants the audience to hear not only the thanks given to God in the voices of Paul, Timothy, and Silvanus, the original founders of the mission, but also the praise given to God by their fellow worshipers, too—in the second- and third-generation setting, the "we" has become ecclesial, and all the worshipers participate in the thanksgiving. Again, in contrast to Paul, though formally a thanksgiving, the address is to the Pauline churches generally; there is no personal note or tone, nothing that indicates a particular group of addressees in Thessalonica or any other single congregation.

Thanksgiving for the saving act of God in the past. The thanksgiving expresses the gratitude of both author and congregation that they have been incorporated into the people of God and belong within God's saving purpose. By adjusting the language of 1 Thessalonians ("beloved by God" [1:4] is modulated to "beloved by the Lord" here), the author allows it to resonate with Deut 7:7–8 LXX, where this language is used of God's choice of Israel. Worshipers in the predominately Gentile churches of the Pauline mission hear themselves addressed in the biblical language for the chosen people. The thanksgiving continues as praise to God, who has chosen them for salvation, continuing to affirm the Pauline theology of election (see on 1 Thess 1:4), though not in Paul's characteristic vocabulary (*haireō* is found in Paul only at Phil 1:22, and not—as in 2 Thess 2:13—in the sense of election to the people of God, for which Paul uses *eklegomai* and *eklogē*). The author celebrates the status of the insider addressees not because, in contrast to the outsiders who chose the lie, they chose the truth, but because *God* chose *them*. This is the retrospective confessional language of faith, not the objectifying language of inferential logic. The God who chose them called them into the Christian community through the preaching of the Pauline gospel. In the present post-Pauline context represented by the letter, this does not refer only to the founding mission of the church in Thessalonica by Paul and his associates, as in 1 Thessalonians, but also (and primarily) to the preaching of the Pauline gospel in the Aegean mission and beyond that called the Pauline churches into being. The point here is not just that the readers belong within the Christian community as the result of God's act and call, but also that this call came specifically through the preaching of Paul's gospel, even if this was done by later preachers in the Pauline tradition.

Thanksgiving for the continuing saving act of God in the present. The readers' conversion was through the work of God's Spirit, which called them into the holy community. This was their sanctification, their being-made-holy (see on 1 Thess 4:3, 4, 7, 8). The readers are reminded that the Spirit is at work in the church as a whole and all its members, not only in those who claim to give new revelations by the Spirit. In contrast to outsiders, who believe the lie, their conversion meant and means believing the truth, which is identical with Paul's testimony and the Pauline gospel (cf. 2 Thess 1:10 and 2:14). In 1 Thessalonians, Paul had spoken often and passionately of the present work of the Holy Spirit in the life of the church (see 1:5, 6; 4:8) and had insisted that the congregation not quench the Spirit (5:19). In 2 Thessalonians, the author refers to a deceitful spirit once (2:2) and only once to the Holy Spirit (2:13)—where he links sanctification by the Spirit with "belief in the truth." Paul himself, of course, spoke of the truth of God and the truth of the gospel (e.g., Rom 1:18, 25; Gal 2:5, 14), but for Paul, faith was never in "the truth," but in God or Christ. In the post-Pauline tradition's struggle to maintain the truth of the Pauline gospel, however, the combination "faith/belief" and "truth" is often found, with "faith" tending to become "the faith," identified with "the truth" (see Eph 1:13; 4:21; 6:14; Col 1:5; 2 Thess 2:12, 13; 1 Tim 2:4, 7; 3:15; 4:3; 6:5; 2 Tim 2:15, 18, 25; 3:7, 8; 4:4; Titus 1:1, 14), as in other streams of second- and third-generation Christianity (e.g., John 8:45–46; 1 Pet 1:22; 2 Pet 1:12).

In the present, the saved community of believers constitutes the firstfruits of God's saving act for the world. It is not that the Thessalonian believers are firstfruits of their province,[47] but the scattered Pauline churches, and through them the church as a whole, are the firstfruits of God's redemptive plan. This usage of the image of firstfruits is represented also in Rev 14:4–5, 14–15, where the worldwide church is contrasted, in a fashion similar to 2 Thess 2, with those seduced by "the lie." Throughout this section, the author has been in dialogue with the kind of apocalypticism represented by the imminent expectation of Revelation, and he shares some of its conceptuality and terminology, though not its chronology. Both the author of 2 Thessalonians and the author of Revelation understand the church to be the firstfruits of humanity, those who already belong to the saved community, awaiting their ultimate salvation. Thus the author of 2 Thessalonians does not entirely project the reality of salvation into the future, but sees believers as already experiencing the meaning of salvation in the present.

Thanksgiving for the salvation to be realized in the future. The author opposes any view that reduces salvation to present experience. As in the theology of the contemporaneous author of 1 Peter, salvation is real but incomplete (1 Pet 1:5, 9). The coming eschatological reality can be summed up in the word "glory" (see on 2 Thess 1:10).

The Pauline dialectic faded but preserved. Paul's soteriology was expressed in a robust dialectic. Salvation was ultimately future, but truly experienced in the present as the believer is transformed from one degree of glory to another en route to eschatological fulfillment (e.g., 2 Cor 3:18). Our author has shifted the center of gravity of salvation toward the future, yet without abandoning its present reality. The reality of salvation is grounded in God's act and election of the believers, but not without human responsibility and decision. Salvation is not parceled out quantitatively between God's initiative and human response— "God's part" and the "believer's part"—but can only be expressed in a series of affirmations in which God chooses, humans believe, and the Spirit sanctifies. The Pauline dialectic is also preserved in the way the readers' conversion is portrayed: God called, and Pauline preachers proclaimed the Pauline gospel— a single act in which God's word comes through human testimony. It is God who calls, but not without the human act of preaching and response. This is the author's version of the Pauline dialectic (cf. 1 Thess 2:13; Phil 2:12).

[15] At this point the author's need to contrast faithfulness to the Pauline tradition with the misleading teaching that has shaken the readers out of their wits generates this minor interruption of the second thanksgiving (see above, "Composition of 2:13–17"). He is not only thinking of the false apocalypticism

---

47. If 2 Thessalonians is by Paul, he more likely wrote *ap archēs* (see trans. note a on 2:13). *Aparchēn* would not fit the congregation in Thessalonica because the Philippian church had been founded before Paul's mission in Thessalonica and would have been the first converts in Achaia (cf. Paul's usage of *aparchē* in Rom 16:5; 1 Cor 16:15).

he has opposed in 2:1–12, but is already thinking ahead to his resistance to particular innovations in church structure and authority (3:6–12). Here the author
follows, extends, and concretizes Paul's own positive view of tradition. In the
first generation, Paul had repeatedly challenged his congregations to stand fast
in the faith, in freedom, or in the Lord (1 Cor 16:13; Gal 5:1; Phil 4:1; 1 Thess
3:8). Nonetheless, he had already seen the importance of tradition despite his
expectation of the near Parousia (see intro to 1 Thessalonians, "New Congregation"; comments on 1 Thess 1:9b–10; 2:13; 4:1–2, 14–17; 5:1–11; cf. 1 Cor
4:17; 11:2, 7, 23–26; 15:3–5).[48] The author of 2 Thessalonians concentrates this
Pauline exhortation into a charge to stand fast in the *tradition*. This represents
a concern of the Pauline school of the second and third generations, where
various views struggled with each other as to what it meant to be faithful to
the Pauline gospel in their own time. Colossians, too, commends the churches
for continuing faithfulness to the truth of the Pauline gospel that they had not
learned directly from Paul (Col 2:1) but that had come to them via one of his
followers, in which they are to "continue securely established and steadfast,"
not "shifting from the hope promised by the gospel that you heard," "just as
you were taught" (NRSV: Col 1:5–7, 23; 2:7, hence rejecting "human tradition," 2:8). The author of Colossians cites traditional material that had been
handed along and around in the oral tradition (e.g., 1:15–20; 3:18–4:1), and he
encourages his readers to attend not only to his letter but also to other Pauline
letters in circulation (4:16). Likewise the author of Ephesians warns against
being tossed about by every new wind of doctrine and encourages adherence
to the truth revealed to the apostles and prophets of the first generation (2:20;
3:5; 4:14–15) and now available in Paul's Letters (3:4). This is the way they
have "learned Christ" (4:20). The Pastorals, too, are concerned to pass on the
authentic tradition of which Paul is source and norm (1 Tim 1:3–4; 2 Tim
2:2; Titus 1:1–4). Strangely enough, though, the vocabulary of tradition (verb,
paradidōmi; noun, *paradosis*) is virtually absent from the other deuteropauline
writings, found only in the negative sense in Col 2:8 and not at all in Ephesians
or the Pastorals. The author of 2 Thessalonians is unique in the deuteropauline
tradition in emphasizing the specific terminology of tradition (2:15; 3:6). He

---

48. There is a contrast with, and perhaps misunderstanding of, Paul's own view of tradition.
Paul saw himself as a link in a chain of tradition that began with the Lord and other apostles before
him, a tradition shared with other apostles. After citing the tradition of 1 Cor 15:3–5, he insists,
"Whether then it was I or they, so we proclaim and so you have come to believe" (v. 11 NRSV). He
resisted any tendency to an exclusive "Pauline" tradition or theology (1 Cor 1:10–17). The author
of 2 Thessalonians, like other teachers in the Pauline school (Ephesians is an exception: 2:20; 3:5;
4:11), tends to see Paul as *the* apostle, himself the source and norm of the faith. From Colossians
and the Pastorals, one would never guess that there are other authoritative apostles; apostolic faith
is Pauline faith. The author of 2 Thessalonians leans in this direction (the sole reference to apostles
[plural!] in his template is omitted [1 Thess 2:7]).

regards the new interpretations of eschatology and church order that appear in Ephesians and the Pastorals to be innovations. In the name of Paul, he resists innovation and appeals to tradition.

The readers are assumed to know this tradition by having been taught, not in person by Paul and his colleagues, but through oral preaching and teaching and by Pauline letters.[49] The reference in 2 Thess 2:2 to new oracles of the risen Lord spoken through the Spirit is conspicuously absent elsewhere in the letter. Even in 2:2, such prophetic oracles are classified with teaching and epistles falsely claiming to represent the Pauline gospel. Though frequent in 1 Thessalonians, the author is hesitant to speak positively of the dynamism of the Spirit in the life of the church (only 2:15 is unambiguously positive). The author, like the Pastor (i.e., author[s] of 1–2 Timothy and Titus), is suspicious of purported new revelations, which probably had contributed to the superheated eschatological expectation that he considers illegitimate and unhealthy. Not new revelation, but firm tradition from the past, is norm and content for the church's faith. Paul's own letters have already become integral to this tradition.

The author uses the singular *epistolē* (letter) in v. 15, but without the definite article, indicating that the reference is not to a particular letter, but generic, referring to the Pauline corpus that is being formed among the Pauline churches ("every letter," 3:17; cf. 2 Pet 3:16). The author insists the readers were "taught by us," though absent, in the oral Pauline *logos* and the written corpus of letters (so also Col 2:1, 5; cf. 2 Thess 2:15 [contrast 2:2]). This whole concept is appropriate to the second generation, not to Paul's letter a few months after the founding of the church in Thessalonica. They are not taught by apostles in general, but by Paul-the-apostle. We hear the voice of a living tradition, a network of Pauline churches and teachers, engaging in lively interchange of news and a sense of koinonia of a persecuted minority contrasting itself with outsiders, but sure of its ultimate vindication.

[16–17] After the interjected exhortation to hold fast to the tradition, the author returns to his template of 1 Thessalonians. The concluding benediction comes in the same place in the outline, has essentially the same form as the model in 1 Thess 3:11, and reproduces some of its wording. Like its model, the sentence has a dual subject (the Lord Jesus Christ and God our Father), but the two verbs are in the singular; the unity constituted by the Lord Jesus and God the Father "has loved us and has given us the encouragement and good hope that belong to the salvation of the age to come," as they are both addressed by the prayer to strengthen the readers in every good work and word. Moreover, the dual adjective participles "who . . . has loved . . . and given" need

---

49. The expression is general, without the definite article, and can hardly refer to 1 Thessalonians alone, which would be the case if Paul were the author. Paul in 50 C.E. would have said, "through my previous letter," or some such. See Marxsen 10–11.

not be restricted to God the Father but in this sentence modify both "the Lord Jesus" and "God our Father." This is not to suggest that the author is specifically making a christological or proto-Trinitarian theological point but only to call our attention to how easily and unreflectively he speaks of Father and Son as a unity (see comments on 2 Thess 1:12). Nor is this mere pious verbiage. The encouragement (*paraklēsis*, see on 1 Thess 2:3) is general and universal, but also focused on the situation of persecution. Though "hope" (*elpis*) is a muscular term of Pauline theology, "good hope" is not a Pauline formulation, but the conventional expression for a happy future in both classical and Hellenistic Greek. This does not mean it is trivialized, but, like "work and word," is an everyday term that might encourage the readers to turn away from too-enthusiastic apocalyptic hopes for the immediate present, not to settle for an understanding of Christian responsibility as passive endurance, but rather to settle in for the long pull and the task of being disciples of Jesus in a world that is not going to go away soon.

2 Thessalonians 3:1–16
The Life to Which Christians Are Called

Some interpreters have argued that the author has now made his main point, his reinterpretation of Paul's eschatology, and that he is ready to end his letter here. The remainder of the letter would then be regarded as merely following the pattern of 1 Thessalonians and adding a few general exhortations to conform to the pattern of a Pauline letter. It is supposed that, while Paul had asked his congregations to pray that he would be delivered from specific situations that he names (2 Cor 1:8–11; Rom 15:30–31), the author of 2 Thessalonians speaks only in generalities, reflecting the idealized picture of Paul in a later generation (cf. 2 Tim 3:10–13; 4:16–18). So also, it is pointed out that the assertion "Not everyone has faith" (3:2) is general, almost trivial.

This reading of chapter 3 does only minimal justice to the author's intent. What might appear to be unfocused and miscellaneous is to be explained by the author's situation, writing a generation or two after Paul, to a number of churches not known to him personally. True enough, the letter lacks personal detail and concern for specific problems of a particular congregation, but it does address issues faced by the church in general in the author's time. Moreover, the issue of the *ataktoi* (disorderly), which forms the core of the paraenesis (3:6–13), is a particular concern, the third main item of the author's agenda.

3:1–5 Prayer for the Missionaries

3:1 As for what remains to be said,[a] dear brothers and sisters, pray for us that[b] the word of the Lord may spread rapidly and be honored,[c] just as it has been among you, 2 that we may be delivered from those[d] evil people who are out of line,[e] for not everyone has [the] faith.[f] 3 Faithful is the Lord;[g] he will strengthen you and protect you from the Evil One.[h] 4 Moreover, in the Lord we have confidence in you,[i] that you are doing and will continue to do what we have commanded. 5 May the Lord direct your hearts to the love of God and the steadfastness of Christ.

a. For the translation of *loipon*, see trans. note a on 1 Thess 4:1; for *adelphoi*, see trans. note c on 1 Thess 1:4.

b. Here the *hina* signals not the purpose of the prayer, but its content; cf., e.g., 1 Cor 14:13; Col 1:9; BDAG 476.

c. *Doxazō* here does not mean "glorify," but "honor" (as in Acts 13:48), where the Christian message is honored rather than disdained.

d. Here the article has the force of a demonstrative pronoun (as, e.g., 1 Thess 5:27, *tēn epistolēn* = "this letter." Cf. *BDAG* 686; Wallace 221). So understood, the author has a definite group in view.

e. *Atopos*, the word for "place" with the prefixed alpha privative, lit., "out of place" (rendered "out of line" above). The word can mean "unusual, dangerous" (Acts 28:6), or simply "wrong, evil" (Luke 23:41; Acts 25:5). See the comment on vv. 2–3 below.

f. *Hē pistis* (with the article) can be either *fides qua creditur* (the faith with which one believes) or *fides quae creditur* (the faith that one believes; see on 1 Thess 3:2), as it can mean either "faith" or "faithfulness" (see on 2 Thess 1:3). An alternative translation, taking *pistis* as "faithfulness," would thus be "Not everyone is faithful. *Faithful* is the Lord." In the Greek text, the last word of v. 2 corresponds to the first word of v. 3, and there is a serious wordplay on "faith/faithfulness" that can be expressed only awkwardly in English.

g. The somewhat awkward English word order is chosen in an effort to retain the rhetorical punch of the Greek text, which ends v. 2 with *pistis* (faith) and begins v. 3 with *pistos* (faithful).

h. *Tou ponērou* in the genitive can be either neuter, hence "from evil" (so KJV, RSV; CEV, "harm")—or masculine, thus "from the evil one" (so NRSV and most versions). The same translation issue in Matthew arises in 6:13, the final petition of the Lord's Prayer. Paul does not refer to Satan as "the Evil One," but it is common in post-Pauline texts (see Matt 5:37; 6:13; 13:19, 38; John 17:15; Eph 6:16; 1 John 2:13; 3:12; 5:18).

i. The meaning is that the author has confidence in the readers, and this confidence is a matter of both author's and readers' existence "in the Lord." Paul's "in Christ" terminology is absent from 2 Thessalonians (see trans. note d on 1 Thess 1:1, intro, "Vocabulary, Terminology, and Word Usage," and trans. note q on 2 Thess 1:12).

This is a transitional section, blurring the Pauline distinction between the didactic and paraenetic sections that form the bipartite body of the typical letter (see intro to 1 Thessalonians, "Hellenistic Letters").

[1] The author has taken the appeal "dear brothers and sisters, pray for us" from 1 Thess 5:25, slightly adjusting the word order to allow the sentence to begin with *to loipon* (as for what remains to be said), which signals the beginning of the second major part of the letter. For Paul, the request for prayer came at the end of the letter, addressed to real people he knew personally and expected to see again (see, e.g., 1 Thess 5:25; Phlm 22). The deuteropauline letter is addressed to a wider, more general readership, and the prayer request is located in a different context and given a different content, with the focus now on the church's mission and congregational practice. The readers in the Pauline churches hear the voice of Paul asking for prayers for the missionaries, those

who in their time continue to preach and teach the Pauline gospel, founding new congregations and nurturing those already begun. In the Pauline school, the regular object of prayer requests is the progress of the gospel (Eph 6:19–20; Col 4:3–4). The post-Pauline readers heard such requests the same way as those of 1 Corinthians, for example, not as addressing them directly, but still positioning them to hear the voice of Paul exhorting them (not just speaking to the original Corinthians or Thessalonians). They are thus encouraged to pray for the missionaries of their own time, who are also enduring hardship and opposition. The section is not filler material but addresses the situation of the church as it waits for the Lord's return, which must not be mere idle waiting: instead, it is the time of the Christian mission (as in Mark 13, esp. v. 10). The expansion of the mission and founding of new churches is pictured in biblical language as the spread of the word of the Lord, which "runs" (cf. Ps 147:15) and is the generative power that calls new believers and congregations into existence (cf. 1 Thess 1:8; 2:13).

[2–3] The readers are to pray that the missionaries will be delivered from those who oppose the mission, for "not everyone has faith." At first this statement may seem to be trivial or mildly sarcastic, but it is apparently intended seriously, constituting the basis of the prayer request. The meaning is not obvious. *Pistis* can be translated as "faith" or "faithfulness"; the presence of the definite article can indicate either "faith/faithfulness" as the believer's trust and commitment to God, or "the faith" as the content of the Christian faith, what is believed (see comments on 1 Thess 3:2). These considerations lead to the following three major possibilities, each of which has its strong advocates and can be supported with plausible arguments.

1. In the first option, those who lack *faith* are the outsiders, either those who explicitly oppose the Christian mission as such, or those who have not yet heard the gospel and might become believers if they had the opportunity to hear.[1] If this is the clue, the general meaning is "pray for us that we will be delivered from those who are impeding the mission—and are out of line, aligned with the evil powers in doing so—for there are still many who do not believe" (lit., "not everyone has [the] faith," litotes rhetoric, which understates for effect). This view would be supported by its similarity to Rom 10:16–17: "Not all have obeyed the gospel; . . . faith comes by hearing" (AT). The Romans text would have been known by the author (probably also by the readers), reflecting the missionary mandate of the church, which is also the topic here.

---

1. If 2 Thessalonians was written by Paul in 50 C.E., the ones afflicting the missionaries would be those in Corinth who are opposing the mission. It is difficult to see this general description as intended to describe the problems of Acts 18. Such a reading calls for Paul to switch subjects in the next verse, from the unbelief of outsiders to the faithfulness of insiders and of God (so, e.g., Rigaux 695).

2. In the second option, those who lack *the faith* are insiders who are out of line in opposing Paul's law-free Gentile mission. "The" faith is not personal commitment and trust (*fides qua creditur*), but neither is it the orthodox body of traditional doctrine; it refers to faithfulness in holding on to the Pauline theology of the Gentile mission, which would still be opposed by Jewish Christians who advocated circumcision and adherence to the torah. Interpreted this way, faith/faithfulness means "holding the line," "staying in line with the Pauline tradition," and the meaning is "Pray for us to be delivered from out-of-line, evil people who are unfaithful to the gospel, for not everyone is faithful." In this view, author and readers are looking back on the situation of conflict that had not yet occurred when 1 Thessalonians was written. Later in Paul's mission, as reflected especially in Galatians, 2 Corinthians, and Romans, well-meaning believers (who in Paul's perception were in fact unfaithful to the gospel) were impeding its progress. Such people, represented in the author's situation by those who are yielding to cultural pressure and persecution, exacerbated in some way by Jewish Christian believers, in fact belong to the "other side," those who are opposing the spread of the gospel. Theoretically, this could be the case, but we have little evidence that opponents of the sort resisted in Galatians are still active in the churches addressed by 2 Thessalonians. Furthermore, neither of these first two exegetical possibilities lines up with the next sentence, which affirms the faithfulness of God in contrast to human faithfulness.

3. In the third option, those who lack *faithfulness* are insiders who are not remaining true to their confession under the cultural pressures, thereby impeding the mission. The article indicates that "Paul" has a definite group in mind (see trans. note d), which the readers already know about. On this reading, "Not everyone is faithful" is hardly the bland generalization "Not everyone believes," but a reminder that within the church's own ranks some people are inhibiting the Christian mission by their lack of steadfastness in standing up publicly for the faith. Though the expression may have overtones of all these three listed meanings, this sense seems to be the author's primary meaning. This reading is supported by the next sentence (v. 3), in which human unfaithfulness is contrasted with God's faithfulness. In the Pauline school, *pistis* is coming more and more to mean "faithfulness" (e.g., see 1 Tim 5:12; and the chart in Excursus 1: "Persecution" at 2 Thess 1:3 above). This is the case in other Christian texts of the second and third generations (e.g., Rev 2:13, 19; 13:10; 14:12—every reference to *pistis* in Revelation!). The contrast between human unfaithfulness and divine faithfulness is the same as Rom 3:3–4, which may be in the author's mind: not all humans have *pistis*, some are wavering and apostatizing, but God is unwavering (see also 1 Cor 1:9; 10:13; 2 Cor 1:18; 1 Thess 5:24).

Verse 3 makes clear that the danger is not evil in the abstract, but the Evil One, Satan, whose power is already at work in the mystery of lawlessness (2:3–4, 8–10). The "evil people" of v. 2 are the unwitting agents of the Evil One of v. 3. The troubles experienced by the church are not signs that the day of the Lord has begun and eschatological terrors are already present, but they are real enough, the actual difficulties with which the churches must contend. Nevertheless, God's faithfulness is also already at work and will preserve the believers.

[4] The author expresses confidence in the readers, that they will endure the trials they are experiencing; they are doing and will continue to do what he commands. Such commendation is a rhetorical device, bragging on the addressees as a way of encouraging them to do what they are already being commended for doing. This is not necessarily manipulative or phony: the author does in fact celebrate the faithfulness of the Pauline churches of his time in being faithful to the gospel, churches that are growing and winning many converts. His confidence is "in the Lord," but *en kyriō* here does not mean "We have confidence in the Lord" in the conventional sense that the Lord is the one in whom we trust. The author's confidence in his readers is not a matter of human, commonsense judgment, but of his (and their) being "in the Lord" in the Pauline sense. Unlike Colossians and Ephesians, but like the Pastorals, the author is aware of Paul's usage, but he does not easily appropriate the unself-conscious way in which Paul uses "in Christ," "in the Lord," "in him"; instead, he uses it rarely (only here and in v. 12; see on 1 Thess 1:1).

[5] The preceding sentence had been something of a disruption in the author's train of thought, anticipating and preparing for the stern commands he will give in the next paragraph. Now he returns to the mode of prayer, reflecting the language of his model, 1 Thess 3:11, 13. In 1 Thess 3:11, the prayer is for God to direct Paul back to the Thessalonian congregation, a petition that does not fit the author's purpose here. The author of 2 Thessalonians instead adopts the language of "directing the heart," not found in Paul (or elsewhere in the NT), but common in the LXX (9×; e.g., Sir 49:3; Prov 21:2).

Both "love of God" and "steadfastness of Christ" can be understood as either subjective or objective genitives. Paul rarely speaks of the believer's love for God (objective genitive), but often of God's love for human beings (subjective genitive).[2] So also here, the readers' hearts are directed to God's love for them (not their love for God), to remember God's election of them as *agapētoi* (beloved by God; cf. 1 Thess 2:8; 2 Thess 2:13, 16), and the Lord as himself the active preacher in the spread of the gospel.

---

2. Of 84× the word group for "love" is used in Paul's undisputed letters (*agapaō, agapē, agapētos*), only Rom 8:28; 1 Cor 2:9; 8:3 refer to human love for God.

Likewise "steadfastness of Christ" (a somewhat strange expression here) may be understood as a subjective genitive parallel to the love of God, meaning Christ's own steadfastness, not human steadfastness given by Christ (as in Heb 12:3; cf. comments on 1 Thess 1:6). The expression would then be understood as "the steadfastness of the risen Lord who continues to be the faithful preacher of the gospel in and through the missionary efforts of the church." The author prays that God will direct readers' hearts to God's own initiative, election, and love, which generated the church and empowers its mission. Corresponding to this is the missionary word in which the risen Christ faithfully speaks. This in turn would mean that the author is a faithful follower of Paul in his understanding of mission. If the author has been thinking of Rom 10:16–17, which seems to be echoed here, this would be a powerful appropriation of Paul's own mission theology. So construed, "Paul" prays that God will guide their hearts into a deeper understanding of God's love and Christ's dependability, as they are active in the church's mission.

Yet all this may be too subtle. Though possible, it is a somewhat unlikely understanding of *hypomenē*, which normally means endurance and fortitude in the face of difficulty. This is the meaning of the word elsewhere in 2 Thessalonians (1:4) and in its only occurrence in the author's template, 1 Thess 1:3. Thus the expression *tou Christou* (of Christ) is probably best taken as a descriptive or possessive genitive, denoting a quality possessed by Christ that is commended to the readers. The prayer here is thus similar to the exhortation of 2 Cor 10:1, where Paul exhorts the readers by "the meekness and gentleness of Christ," pointing to qualities of the earthly Jesus that are now to be manifested in Christian missionaries and other believers. On this reading, the "steadfastness of Christ" points to Jesus' own faithfulness under duress, and the author prays that God will direct their hearts to the same steadfastness. In the author's template, too, Christ is model for the believer's faithfulness (1 Thess 1:6).

3:6–16 Third Insertion into the Template: The "Disorderly"

This section borrows extensively from the wording of the 1 Thessalonians template—language the author expects the readers to recognize and respect—but the topic itself is developed in the author's own way and oriented to the readers' post-Pauline situation. Expansions and modifications indicate that the section is not merely filling in the traditional pattern of a Pauline letter: its tone shows that it deals with a very serious matter.[3] The section is not a separate topic, "the

3. Contra, e.g., Marxsen (98–99), who argues that at 3:5 the author has finished what he wants to say and could conclude the letter here, except that this would be too short for a letter written in the name of Paul.

idlers," but one of three interrelated themes that constitute the letter as a whole: response to the harassment and persecution faced by all the Pauline churches of the second and third generations (ch. 1), as they settle down for the long-term mission in a world not hastening to its end (ch. 2), but do not need a salaried and institutional ministry in order to cope (ch. 3).

3:6 Now we command you, brothers and sisters, in the name of our Lord Jesus Christ, to keep your distance from any brother[a] whose way of life is not in line[b] with the tradition they[c] received from us. **7** For you yourselves know that it is necessary to follow our example; when we were living among you, we did not conduct ourselves in this irregular way, **8** nor did we eat anyone's bread[d] without paying for it, but in labor and hardship we worked night and day so as not to burden any of you. **9** This was not because we do not have that right, but in order to give you an example to follow. **10** In fact, when we were still with you, we gave you this command: "Anyone not willing to work may not eat." **11** For we hear that some are practicing a way of life that is out of line, busybodies who are not doing any actual work.[e] **12** Such persons we command and encourage in the Lord Jesus Christ to earn their own living, working without disturbing others.[f] **13** As for you, brothers and sisters, do not be discouraged as you continue to do what is right. **14** But note well if anyone does not obey what we say in this letter. Do not get involved with him, in order to put him[g] to shame. **15** Do not consider him an enemy, but admonish him as a brother. **16** And may the Lord of peace himself always give you peace in every way.[h] May the Lord be with you all.

a. Although *adelphos* elsewhere generally includes all believers and is appropriately translated "brother or sister" (see trans. note c for 1 Thess 1:4), in second- and third-generation Pauline Christianity leadership was mostly restricted to men. In the exegesis pursued here, those who advocated an emerging class of ordained ministers were primarily male.

b. *Ataktōs peripatountes*, more lit., "walking [in a] disorderly [way]." See trans. note h on 1 Thess 2:12, trans. note i on 5:14, and comments below. The verb *peripateō* represents a way of life, as also in v. 11.

c. Though most MSS read *parelabete* (you received), corresponding to the second-person plurals of vv. 1, 4, 7, 13, 14, 15, this instance of the third-person plural (and in the unusual dialectical form *parelabosan* instead of *parelabon*) is found in ℵ* A 0278 33. As the more difficult reading and the reading that best explains the other readings, *parelabosan* (they received) is more likely original. The author's point: the "disorderly" received the apostolic tradition as did the Pauline churches in general, but they are not following it.

d. *Esthiō arton* (eat bread) is a biblical, Semitic idiom that means "earn one's living," "support oneself" (as translated in v. 12; cf. Gen 3:19; 2 Sam 9:10; Amos 7:12). The more literal image is retained here, since the imagery of eating is basic to the instruction and has overtones of the Eucharist and church fellowship meals.

e. The serious Greek wordplay *ergazomenous/periergazomenous* is difficult to retain in English. It means, lit., something like "not working but concerning oneself with other people's work." The NIV, TNIV, and others follow the suggestion of MOFFATT: "not busy but busybodies."

f. More lit., "eat their own bread" (see trans. note d above and the comment on v. 8) "in quietness" (*meta hēsychias*), i.e., without disturbing others.

g. On the male terminology, see trans. note a on v. 6. *Entrapē* is here understood not subjectively, "feel shame" (and so be moved to repentance), but objectively, "put to shame" (as in NAB, NAS95, CEV), i.e., to reveal to others that they are advocating a shameful arrangement.

h. The vast majority of MSS read *topos* (place), which would fit the post-Pauline situation of a letter addressed to numerous churches scattered about the Aegean and beyond. However, the strong support of ℵ, B, and numerous other ancient witnesses tips the balance in favor of *tropos* (way). The later variation *topos* probably reflects the copyists' accommodation to 1 Cor 1:2; 2 Cor 2:14; 1 Thess 1:8; 1 Tim 2:8.

In no part of 1–2 Thessalonians is the presumed historical context more important than in this text. There are three basic options:

1. In 50 C.E., according to the first view, in the *real world of Paul and the Thessalonians*, the problem is the same disorderly persons as in 1 Thess 5:14 (see comments there). The people of 2 Thess 3 who "are practicing a way of life that is out of line" (3:11; NRSV, "living in idleness") are understood to be a group within the congregation at Thessalonica whose superheated eschatology has caused them to quit their jobs, or who are just lazy and expect to be supported by the church. Yet this connection between mistaken eschatological expectations and the "idle" is never made in either letter, but once "found" in 2 Thessalonians, it is then read back into the interpretation of 1 Thessalonians.

2. In the second or third generation, around 80–100 C.E., in this second view 2 Thess 3:6–12 is understood as addressing the *fictive world of Paul and the Thessalonians* as in the preceding paragraph; thus it is only indirectly relevant to the readers' own situation. No longer do the scattered postapostolic congregations in the Pauline tradition each have a group of "idlers." The words are present only to complete the letter from the model the author is following. As when reading 1 Corinthians, the real readers "overhear" Paul's address to a particular congregation of a previous generation, and they may derive lessons for their own time from it—though the situation that supposedly once existed in Thessalonica is not a general problem in the real world of the actual readers.

3. In the interpretation pursued here, a Pauline teacher addresses a real situation faced by the actual readers of the letter in the network of Pauline churches of the second or third generation. These congregations are struggling with the options of how the tradition from Paul is to be actualized in their own situation.

The problem is no longer, if indeed it ever was, that some members of the congregation refuse to work and expect to be supported by their fellow church members. Rather, a vigorous discussion is underway regarding what sort of structure and leadership the church needs, both inside and alongside the network of Pauline congregations.

Excursus 2: Emerging Patterns of Church Leadership

The Pauline churches would have been aware of several options for emerging leadership patterns among non-Pauline congregations and were perhaps in dialogue with them.

The Matthean churches, presumably in Syrian Antioch or its environs, would have had some interchange with the Pauline churches. There are no presbyters, bishops, or deacons; such titles as "rabbi," "teacher," "father," and "instructor" are opposed (Matt 23:8–10). The risen Christ sends prophets, sages, laborers, and scribes as leaders of the church (9:37–38; 23:34). How these are authorized and supported is not clear, but the mission charge to the disciples, transparent to the situation of the post-Easter church, insists that the laborers deserve their food, which they receive *dōrean* (Matt 10:8–11, "freely," the same word as in 2 Thess 3:8, "without paying for it").

Hebrews, probably written within a Roman context in the same general period as 2 Thessalonians, sees a close connection between leaders who watch over the faith(fulness) of the community, who are responsible for it, who will give account, and who are to be obeyed (Heb 13:7, 17, 24). The community is called to be faithful under persecution, to go outside the camp and share the reproach of Jesus. The addressees are social outsiders, as was Jesus, but are now insiders within the authentic community. There is a specific class of ministers charged with preaching and teaching the word, with specific responsibilities. Nothing is said about how they are supported. These themes are all echoed in 2 Thessalonians.

The Johannine writings, including Revelation, reflect a developing struggle over a period of some decades in which a predominately charismatic community suspicious of institutional leadership struggles with the values and problems of developing structures. *Revelation*, about the same time as 2 Thessalonians and in the core area of the Pauline churches, knows only of charismatic prophets as church leaders. *Presbyteroi* (presbyters, elders) are mentioned often (5× in chs. 4–5; 7:11, 13; 11:16; 14:3; 19:4), but they are in heaven, not the leaders of earthly congregations. Yet there seems to be no direct polemic against developing institutional ministries. In the Farewell Discourses of the Gospel of John, the risen Jesus, through the promised Spirit-Paraclete at work in the community as a whole, will be the churches' sole guide, with no need of a specialized clerical class. The Johannine Jesus proclaims himself the Good Pastor, in contrast to hirelings who do not care for the sheep and leave them at the mercy of wolves (John 10:11–18). Yet the Johannine Letters reveal an authoritative *presbyter,* probably representative of an emerging class of church leaders, whose claims are resisted by others. By the time John 21 is written, the Johannine churches are encouraged to acknowledge pastoral oversight from leaders authorized by the risen Jesus himself.

The Didache represented some churches presumably in the same general area as the Matthean churches, in Syria around 100 C.E. It reflects local congregations that are in the process of developing structures, but also must decide how to respond to traveling fellow believers in need of hospitality as well as assess the legitimacy and support of traveling missionaries and teachers who claim authority in the congregations they visit. The following quotation gives some insight into the problems, though much remains unclear:

> **11:3** Concerning the apostles and prophets, conduct yourselves according to the ordinance of the gospel. **4** Let every apostle who comes to you be received as the Lord; **5** but he shall not abide more than a single day, or if necessary, a second day; but if he stays three days, he is a false prophet. **6** And when he departs, he is to receive nothing except bread to supply him until his next station; but if he asks for money, he is a false prophet. . . . The false prophet can be distinguished from the true prophet on this basis. **9** No prophet ordering a table in the Spirit shall eat of it; otherwise he is a false prophet. **10** And every prophet teaching the truth, but not living according to his own teaching, is a false prophet. . . . **12** And do not listen to anyone who says in the Spirit, "Give me silver" (or anything else); but if he tells you to give on behalf of others that are in want, then he is not to be judged. . . . **12:2** If the new arrival is a traveling missionary, assist him, so far as you are able; but he shall not stay with you more than two or three days, and then only if it be necessary. **3** But if he has his own trade and wishes to settle with you, let him work for and eat his bread. **4** But if he has no craft, according to your wisdom provide how he shall live as a Christian among you, but not in idleness. **5** If he is not willing to do this, he is making Christ into a cheap way of making a living. Beware of such people. (*Did.* 11.3–12.5 AT)

First Clement indicates that in the mid-90s C.E. a firm structure of bishops (elders) and deacons is being put into practice in some churches and resisted by others (*1 Clem.* 42). The order is hierarchical, analogous to the chain of command in the army (37.2). This order has been established by God and is affirmed in the Scripture, which, in Clement's reading of Isa 60:17 LXX, predicted that God would establish bishops and deacons in the church. Within two more decades, Ignatius in his *Letters* portrays an organized church with a firm monarchial episcopate, though it is not clear whether the ordered ministry he projects is already in place or whether he is still struggling to secure a wider acceptance of this pattern.

These differing views of how second- and third-generation churches should be structured for mission are also reflected in the deuteropauline texts, where the issue is focused specifically on how Paul's teaching is to be understood in the post-Pauline situation.

Colossians has nothing specific to say on ministerial offices, but it also manifests a pronounced lack of interest in Paul's understanding of charismatic leadership. Already in the earliest deuteropauline letter, good church order is a guard against both heresy and apostasy. Colossians 2:5 makes a direct connection between the *taxis* ("good order," RSV) and the *stereōma* of their *pistis* (firmness of their faithfulness). Colossians is for good order, but it has no clerical hierarchy to propose, only the presence of Paul among them via the letter (Col 2:1–5). This also seems to be the approach of 2 Thessalonians.

In *Ephesians,* the apostles and prophets of the first generation are succeeded by evangelists and pastor-teachers as the gifts of the risen Christ to the church to equip congregations for their ongoing ministry (Eph 4:1–16, esp. vv. 11–12; cf. 2:20; 3:5).

Apostles and prophets belong to the first, founding generation and to the whole church. As in Paul, there is no indication of a distinction between clergy and laity, but there are still different gifts. Though "ordained ministry" is not the author's focus, and the author does not see it as a major problem, Eph 4:28 does encourage "working with your own hands," and 4:19 discourages "greed," which could have the emerging salaried ministry in view. The epistle is directed to the congregation as a whole (i.e., to the scattered network of Pauline churches), in which the Spirit is active, not to a special group within the church as bearers of the Spirit.

The Pastorals are somewhat later, but the traditions that are jelling in them did not emerge from a vacuum and may have already been known to the author of 2 Thessalonians. The Pastor advocates a firmly established class of ministers (*episkopoi, presbyteroi,* and *diakonoi*; see 1 Tim 2:2; 3:1–13; 4:6, 14; 5:1–2, 17–19; Titus 1:5–7) who receive and hand on authentic Pauline tradition, who rebuke false teaching and regulate an orderly church. Titus 1:10–12 seems to reflect the same kind of problems as in 2 Thessalonians, but from the side of those supporting the new order of clergy. The Pastor affirms a paid ministry, but he also sees its problems and opposes those "who are teaching for base gain what is not right to teach" (Titus 1:11). The congregation is no longer directly addressed as in Paul, but through its officers. Yet it is still the congregation that is addressed; they overhear "Paul" speaking to "Timothy" and "Titus." The instructions may correspond to the wishes of the author rather than to a uniform reality already existing. Like the author of 2 Thessalonians, the Pastor launches his letters into the situation of second- and third-generation Pauline churches, but in contrast to him, the Pastor wants to show that his understanding of the developing clergy is rooted in Paul's own instruction.

In all this a key point for understanding 2 Thess 3:6–15 is that some of these emerging patterns of church structure and ministry seem to involve "full-time" ministers who do not do "secular" work and are *paid* for their services (1 Tim 5:17; cf. 1 Pet 5:2; Acts 14:23; 20:33–35).[4] The problem is not "idlers" or "laziness," but the developing distinction between amateur lay ministers and a class of full-time ministers who for the most part are industrious and sincere and want to devote their whole time and energy to preaching and teaching the faith (cf. Acts 6:1–7). The author of 2 Thessalonians opposes this development and appeals to Paul for support. The *ataktoi* (disorderly) of 1 Thess 5:14 (see comments there) have become the *peripatountes ataktōs* of 2 Thess 3:6, 11, "those who live in a disorderly fashion," meaning the new class of "clergy" who have

---

4. See, e.g., Dibelius and Conzelmann 80; Achtemeier 326. Whether any of these texts establish that already in the NT period anything like a salaried clergy had developed is a disputed point among exegetes and historians of early Christianity—as the original emergence of such a class of ministers was controversial. This is illustrated by the references to *presbyteroi* in Acts. Though unknown in Paul's undisputed Letters, such a class of ministers is taken for granted in Acts. The exhortation not to covet silver or gold, with Paul himself as the model (Acts 20:32–35), can be taken as warning against the emerging class of paid clergy or (more likely) as warning against greed among those who are in fact paid by their congregations.

quit their "secular" jobs and expect to be supported by the churches.[5] What is at stake here is the transition from one form of church leadership to another, from "lay ministry" to "clergy," in a gradual process that proceeded in different ways and at varying rates across the spectrum of Pauline congregations.[6]

This hypothesis is illuminated and supported in the following exegesis.

[6] The phrase "brothers and sisters," though written within the fictive framework of a letter of Paul to the church in Thessalonica, does not address a

5. This interpretation is not entirely new, though to my knowledge it has never been fully explored. Some ancient interpreters did not see the problem addressed as "idleness" among Christians in general, but applied this text to the problem of slothful ministers or monks (e.g., Augustine, *Op. mon.*, in *NPNF*[1] 3:503, 508). John Wycliffe (*Pastoral Office* 9 [1953, 39]) and John Hus (*On Simony*) applied the text to bishops, priests, cathedral canons, and other clerics who receive large incomes from the church but do little work, not to problematic lay "idlers" within congregations. Luther (1973, 324) defended ministers who worked full-time in preaching and teaching and did no secular work, and he rejected the current use of this text against the practice of a paid ministry. In contemporary scholarship, E. Earle Ellis (1971, 450–51) regarded 2 Thessalonians as written by Paul, but not to the whole congregation, and saw the addressees as "Christian workers . . . who are receiving financial support." Holland (1988, 52–53) interprets 2 Thessalonians as deuteropauline, but sees the "disorderly" as "false prophets of the 'day of the Lord'" who "claim spiritual authority [and] the right to be supported by the congregation." He rightly sees that the disputed point is "a conflict over leadership" (127). Bengt Holmberg (1978, 159) briefly notes that the author of 2 Thessalonians opposes charismatic leaders who claim their authority entitles them to financial support. Donfried (1993b, 100, 111) endorses this view but sees it as confined to the situation of the one church in Thessalonica in the immediate aftermath of Paul's ministry there. So also Sumney 1999, 236–37, 239, 244. Klaus Berger (1994, 389) rightly interprets 2 Thess 3 in the context of the Pauline and post-Pauline discussion and disputes on the relation of "eating and working" in providing for ministers and missionaries. In a brief article P. Day (1963) argues that 2 Thess 3 is best understood as from someone writing in Paul's name and opposing the establishment of a paid "professional" clergy.

The major alternative, the traditional interpretation still represented late in the last century by, e.g., Best (361 and passim), still argues, "In Thessalonica we have seen that eschatological over-excitement did lead to neglect of one ordinary duty—working for a living." This view, which originated in the effort to find a satisfactory interpretation in terms of Pauline authorship, has become the default position even for authors who consider the letter deuteropauline. Thus recent interpreters such as Earl Richard (1995, 390–91 and passim) regard the *ataktoi* as "idle, . . . misguided, . . . boisterous" people "who do nothing but discuss the end-time events." Fee (324–25) continues to affirm Pauline authorship and see the *ataktoi* as a group of "idlers" in the single congregation in Thessalonica to whom the letter was addressed, but abandons the eschatological argument. He concludes, "We simply do not know why some of them chose not to work," and lists the alternatives, with bibliography: disdain for work itself, expecting the rich to take care of the poor, eschatological understanding, Paul's attempt to break up patron-client relationships, or "just plain laziness."

6. Such terms are necessarily anachronistic, used here only for convenience. By "lay ministry" I refer to those who served in the church as volunteers, called and guided by the Spirit, who worked in their lives and in the lives of the congregations who accepted and respected them; these volunteers served without specific ordination or other authorization and without financial remuneration. By "clergy" I refer to those who were authorized by some sort of "official" ordination, who served as ministers more or less full-time, and who received financial support for their work.

single congregation, but the scattered churches in the Pauline tradition where letters attributed to Paul are respected as guidelines for their current and emerging life and work. There are no recognizable particulars of the Thessalonians' situation or that of any other particular congregation. Everything remains quite general, but not bland: the author is truly engaged, speaking with passion and authority. Though he has harsh words for some who are "out of line," the author does not consider the new developments a church-splitting issue and speaks to all as brothers and sisters in the family of God.

The author commands, in the name of the Lord Jesus Christ. To disobey him is to disobey the Lord. In comparison with the parallel passage in 1 Thess 4:1, the language is insistent; this is not exhortation, but authoritative apostolic tradition (prepared for in 2 Thess 3:4). Church structure was established at the beginning by Paul and by the Lord, handed on by tradition, and confirmed by written letters; it does not evolve to fit changing circumstances.[7] "Apostles," mentioned only once in 1 Thessalonians, are never mentioned in 2 Thessalonians (see on 1 Thess 2:7). The author seems to avoid the idea of *apostolic succession*, the transmission of specifically *apostolic* authority, perhaps as a reaction to its developing use in other parts of the Pauline tradition. He is interested in the authority of *Paul*, not in Paul the *apostle*. Paul appears as *teacher* of the church, not as apostolic authority. The authority of oral tradition is fading into authority of written word from the teacher.[8] The author thus composes a document that can be circulated in the churches and read alongside the other letters and the Scriptures; in a generation or two they will themselves be considered Scripture (2 Pet 3:16).

The author understands proper church order to be that established by the teaching and example of Paul at the beginning. The "disorderly" are those who disregard this tradition. If the advocates of the newer and more structured forms of ministry are using the language of "order," there may be a bit of sarcasm and irony here: the advocates of a clerical order are actually fomenting disorder. The use of the third person to designate the *peripatountes ataktōs* (in my translation: "[any brother] whose way of life is not in line") in a passage that mostly employs second-person forms may indicate a separate group, some of whom are coming to the congregations from outside, no longer simply a part of the congregation as such, but distinct from them. The warning to "keep your distance" from such people and not to "get involved" with them (v. 14) is stronger than in 1 Thessalonians ("admonish," "be patient") and may point to a distinctive group, not merely to problematic behavior. The admonition to follow Paul's

7. This is in contrast to another admirer of Paul in a later generation, the author of Acts, who traces the story of the church's adapting to new situations as it moves through the decades from Jerusalem to Rome (note, e.g., the establishing of new structures, officers and ministers in Acts 6:1–6; 13:1–3; 14:23; and Paul's speech to the Ephesian *presbyteroi* in Acts 20:17–35).
8. Laub 1990, 411.

example is more appropriate to missionary teachers than to resident members of the congregation. So also the *hymeis de* (as for you) of 3:13 distinguishes the primary addressees of the letter from the *ataktoi*.

[7–8] The author presents Paul as offering himself (and the other missionaries of the first generation) as an example of the style of ministry he commends and commands. When he says that he did not conduct himself in a disorderly or irregular way and that it is necessary (*dei*) to imitate him, he is not thinking in terms of disruptive boisterousness, but of only one feature of his missionary activity: he earned his own living while evangelizing and pastoring among them. This was a striking exception in the Hellenistic world, in which the expectation was that traveling preachers and teachers would be paid. Borrowing the language of 1 Thess 2:9 almost verbatim, "Paul" states that as a traveling missionary he supported himself while preaching. This is the one point of orderliness by which Paul himself lived; it is the innovative new clergy who are out of line. Though as an apostle he had the right to financial support from the congregations he established, he did not exercise this right but worked with his own hands to support himself. In 1 Thessalonians, Paul declared that he did this in order not to burden the new congregation. That motive remains valid for Christian ministry, but here, a generation or two later, the deutero-pauline author has Paul say that his motive was to establish a pattern that must be followed in later generations (v. 9). The earlier letter had also called for imitation of Paul, but on the point of enduring suffering, a model that extended from the Lord through Paul to the Thessalonians themselves (1 Thess 1:6–7). That model is now reinterpreted and applied to the issue of financial support of ministers, omitting the reference to "the Lord" (no longer appropriate to the matter at hand). For the author, this model is not optional. For the first and only time in the letter, he declares what must (*dei*) be done. Paul had also used the *dei* imperative only once in 1 Thessalonians (4:1), but there it was in reference to pleasing God; in 2 Thessalonians this has become the imitation of Paul.

[9] First Thessalonians does not speak explicitly of the right (*exousia*) of apostles to support from the congregations they have established (yet cf. 1 Thess 2:5–9). In his later debate with the Corinthian church, Paul's refusal to accept pay for his preaching and teaching in Corinth had become a major issue treated at length (1 Cor 9:1–18, intensified in 2 Cor 11:7–15). As part of the emerging Pauline corpus, 1 Corinthians (though perhaps not 2 Corinthians) had been circulated among the Pauline churches by the time 2 Thessalonians was written. The advocates of the emerging class of "clergy" may have appealed to this right of financial support claimed by Paul, as well as other Pauline traditions that could be used to support the concept of a paid ministry (1 Cor 9:14; Gal 6:6; the tradition behind 1 Tim 5:17). In 1 Corinthians, Paul declares his right to financial support because his apostolic status has been challenged, and his point is that he has *not* appealed to this right. In 2 Thessalonians, the situation

seems to be that the author is opposing ministers who do not earn their own living and do appeal to their right as documented in 1 Corinthians and other traditions in circulation in the second and third generations of the church. The author opposes this with a reaffirmation of Paul's own practice, now made "canonical" by the present letter. Paul's practical instructions, conditioned from case to case by the situation at hand, had from the beginning contained a spectrum of responses. Thus from earliest times, the emerging Pauline corpus did not present one consistent theology and practice, but contained conflicting interpretations of Paul in dynamic tension. This is the nature of canonical authority, also illustrated by the inclusion of four Gospels. From the beginning, the canonical collection functioned by the principle of a limited plurality: "more than one thing, but not just anything" (see intro to 1 Thessalonians, "Canonical Context").

[10] The phrase "For when we were [still] with you" is almost verbatim from 1 Thess 3:4. There it refers to Paul's personal presence with the actual readers during the founding visit. Here the author looks back a generation or more to the time of Paul and affirms that what he is now saying is what Paul said from the beginning, while he was still alive. The statement "Anyone not willing to work may not eat" has a proverbial ring to it. The sentiment is often found in both Jewish and pagan tradition, but the saying itself has not been documented elsewhere and may be the author's own coinage. Though it is cited as a command given by Paul during the initial mission preaching in Thessalonica, it is difficult to envision a situation in that setting where it would have been appropriate. So also, it is difficult to imagine just what this dictum would actually mean on the traditional interpretation in which the "idle" are barred from eating. Are they excluded from church fellowship meals? From the Eucharist? Should we imagine some sort of soup kitchen run by the church for the needy, to which the presumed eschatological enthusiasts who have quit their jobs are forbidden access? If they do resume earning their own living, why would they want to eat from the church's table? Are they supposed to return to their regular jobs? Is this even possible? One can more readily picture the saying as a battle motto against what the author sees as an emerging class of clergy, which would mean "those 'full-time ministers' who do not earn their own living cannot expect to be supported by the church."

[11] "We hear . . ." sounds like an introduction to the issue for the first time, as though "Paul" has heard about the "disorderly" as new information received since the founding visit, but the preceding sentence portrays such conduct as already having become problematic when Paul was with them, against which he issued this sharp mandate. The author does not try to keep the fictive time frame of the real Paul strictly separate from that of his own time, nor does he attempt to synchronize them. His purpose is instruction in the nature of ministry, not a consistent picture of the situation in the time of the historical Paul. The

statement of v. 10 claims that Paul already settled the issue in his own time, and that his pronouncement is now passed on as authoritative Pauline tradition. The statement of v. 11 reflects the experience of the author's time, in which reports of various attempts to introduce new forms of ministry are circulating in the Pauline churches. Here is the first and only clear statement of the problematic conduct of those *ataktōs peripatountes*: they themselves are not working, and they interfere with the work of others. *En hymin* (in/among you), heard in the fictive framework of Paul's own time, refers to Paul's church-founding visit to Thessalonica and would refer to insiders of one particular congregation, meaning some people *in* the little group of new converts in Thessalonica. In the actual author's time, the phrase is better heard as "among you," within the network of Pauline churches, which could include both members of a particular congregation, who now aspire to quit their regular jobs and become "full-time" ministers supported by their own congregation, and traveling prophets, preachers, and teachers who claim the right of financial support from the churches they visit.

[12] The whole of the previous discussion has been addressed to the church at large; the issue of the "disorderly" is a church problem, an ecclesiological issue of church structure and the nature of Christian ministry, not merely an issue between the historical Paul and a few disruptive individuals in Thessalonica in 50 C.E. Nor was it instruction concerning a general social problem, discouraging financial support for people unwilling to work. Now for the first time, the author addresses the "disorderly" themselves, with a combination of authoritative command and pastoral-theological encouragement and appeal taken from 1 Thess 4:10–11 (*parangellomen kai parakaloumen*; see comments on 1 Thess 2:3 for the overtones of the Pauline *paraklēsis* word group). Yet even here, the address is not direct, as the third-person forms indicate. Paul does not speak directly to the *ataktoi*, but addresses the church about them and how to deal with them. Once again, the interpreter is faced with a clear choice. If the historical Paul is dealing with a problem within the membership of the congregation at Thessalonica, this is a matter of "congregational discipline," as in 1 Cor 5:1–13 (cf. Matt 18:15–17).[9] In that case, however, why not speak directly to the troublemakers? But if this is a general church issue that congregations in the Pauline tradition are facing after Paul's lifetime, the discussion is better understood as addressed to the network of Pauline churches as a whole, not to a few loafers among the new converts in Thessalonica, instructing these congregations how to deal with persons who claim financial support for their ministry.

---

9. This has long been considered the proper interpretative approach. Already Dobschütz and Bornemann (309, 317–18) note that Paul addresses the church as a whole, not the "idle," and have an excursus on "Paul's Congregational Discipline," which only serves to point out the difficulties of this interpretation.

[13] From the perspective of form criticism, the conjunction *de* and the renewed address "brothers and sisters" might signal the beginning of a new (sub)section, but the content relates this injunction to what precedes, forming its conclusion. The admonition "Do not be discouraged as you continue to do what is right" is taken almost verbatim from Gal 6:9. Here the injunction is not a platitude (as it was not also in its original, different context in the Galatians controversy) but has a specific focus: restrictions against an emerging salaried clergy should not be an excuse for failing to help the genuinely needy.[10] The specific historical interpretation argued for here means that the text (esp. 3:10, 12) has nothing to say to or about the complex situation of people in later centuries, including our own, who are jobless or underemployed due to the shifting pressures of industrialized global economics. The text addresses a particular problem in the emerging "institutional church" and presents no basis for opposing social welfare programs and other supportive structures for those unable to find enough work to support themselves and their families. On the contrary, the repeated call to love and care for all people, found in both 1 and 2 Thessalonians, communicating God's own love for each and all, is the identifying mark of God's people (1 Thess 1:3–4; 3:12; 4:9–10; 5:8, 13; 2 Thess 1:3; 2:13, 16).

[14–15] These instructions do not begin a new, general topic but continue the author's main concern with the "disorderly."[11] The author's own instruction has been mainly negative, resisting the emerging practice of salaried ministers. He gives no specific directions, however, for the actual functioning of church leadership. He does not repeat or reaffirm the admonition of 1 Thess 5:12–13 and even appears to back away from the encouragement given by Paul for the beginnings of structured church leadership. The author affirms the work of the Spirit in the life of the church but is suspicious of purported new revelations (2 Thess 2:2); otherwise there is no reference to charismatic gifts or prophetic revelations. The church is to be guided by Paul's own example and instruction, continued into the present by Paul's Letters (esp. the present letter, which presents an updated version of 1 Thessalonians) and the Pauline tradition, but the author gives no hint as to how this is actually implemented, or by whom. Far more than any other authors of his own time, he is concerned to establish right practice by means of adherence to written Pauline *letters*. (Not yet written are the Pastorals, which in the following decades will follow this lead and provide *epistolary* authorization *for* the new forms of ministry the author of 2 Thessalonians is opposing.)

10. See *Did.* 12–13, where these twin concerns are also dealt with together, though with different instructions.

11. In this section the vocabulary borrowed from 1 Thess 5:12–14 indicates that the topic is the same: leadership, the status, role and provision for church workers: *adelphoi* (brothers and sisters), *en kyriō* (in the Lord), *ataktos/ataktōs* (disorderly), *noutheteō* (admonish), *hēgeisthai* (consider), *ergon* (work), *eirēnē/eirēneuō* (peace/be at peace).

Those who persist in deviating from the Pauline model in which local ministers and traveling preachers and teachers earn their own living are to be identified and avoided. The directive *sēmeiousthe* (note well) does not refer to a procedure within the congregation by which some of their own members are labeled for shunning; it is rather a warning to congregations to identify preachers and teachers who claim the right to be paid. Congregations are not to enter into arrangements with them that incur financial obligations. Even though the author presumably takes the term *synanamignymi* (get involved with) from Paul's instructions to the Corinthian congregation on dealing with the flagrant immorality of a church member (1 Cor 5:1–13, esp. vv. 9, 11; the only other NT instances of this word), the author's instructions here should not be understood as a matter of congregational discipline such as that portrayed in 1 Cor 5. Neither does it correspond to the instructions for ironing out conflicts between church members in Matt 18:15–17. Here the problem is not a matter of immorality, false teaching, or personal conflicts within a congregation, but an issue of church structure and leadership that affects both the internal dynamics of congregational life and the relations between different congregations, as well as preachers and teachers traveling among them.

The new "clergy" are not to be considered outsiders, not to be excommunicated. They are still "brothers," though they are not to be accepted as ministers by individual congregations. The goal of avoiding such involvements is not (on the analogy of 1 Cor 5:4–5) that such aspiring "clergy" should feel shame and be moved to repentance (see trans. note g on v. 14 above). Rather, their program is shameful in that it rejects the Pauline model and tradition, and so it is to be rejected. Thus the author does not call on the *ataktōs peripatountes* to repent, but addresses the community on how to respond to their claims. In contrast to the *Didache* and the later Pastorals, for example, the author leaves it to the congregations of his own time to implement "Paul's" instruction, but basically he insists that they preserve the status quo and resist the new patterns of leadership.

[16] A benediction concludes this section, but not yet the letter as a whole. "The God of peace" of 1 Thess 5:23 (cf. Paul's later use of the formula in Phil 4:9; Rom 15:33; 16:20, always in the closing greetings) characteristically here becomes "the Lord of peace" (see intro to 2 Thessalonians, "Vocabulary, Terminology, Word Usage"; and comments on 1:12). This reflects not only the author's tendency to change "God" to "Lord," to substitute the Lord Jesus Christ for God the Father, but also the wording of the LXX form of the priestly benediction of Num 6:26: *kyrios . . . dōē soi eirēnē*, "the Lord . . . give you peace." The prayer and benediction are not merely general and conventional, but surely sincere and contextually focused: the author prays for the health and unity of the churches as they face the task of mission in the long-term future within a hostile world.

2 Thessalonians 3:17–18
Conclusion: Authentication
and Benediction

17 This greeting is in my own hand, Paul's, an authenticating mark in every letter; it is the way I write.
18 The grace of our Lord Jesus Christ be with you all.ᵃ

a. Most later MSS add the conventional liturgical *amēn*, but not ℵ, B, and other early witnesses. The earliest MSS subscript only *PROS THESSALONIKEIS B* (To the Thessalonians B). Later variations and additions include "written from Athens" and "by the holy apostle Paul."

[17] The concluding lines refer to a greeting, but there is no greeting in the proper sense. In contrast to Paul's own concluding greetings, filled with warmth and personal details of a common history, the deuteropauline author uses the greeting formula to make a final insistent declaration that the letter represents the authentic instruction of Paul.[1] The words are taken verbatim from 1 Cor 16:21 (cf. Gal 6:11; Phlm 19; Col 4:18). Most letters in the Hellenistic world were dictated by the author and written by scribes (cf. Rom 16:22). While not customary, neither was it unusual for a literate letter writer to take pen in hand and write the closing words in the writer's own hand, sometimes calling attention to this personal touch, but mostly allowing the difference in penmanship to speak for itself (cf. Gal 6:11).[2] Paul too sometimes adopted this practice (1 Cor 16:21; cf. Gal 6:11; Phlm 19), which was imitated by the deuteropauline author of Colossians (4:18). Paul himself had only made it a matter of adding a personal dimension to his communication, not as evidence of authenticity. The occasion for such authentication did not exist in Paul's own lifetime. The author

1. See esp. Holland 57–61. It has often been documented that such "personal" notes were part of the paraphernalia of pseudepigraphy. Cf. the pseudepigraphical letters of Diogenes in Malherbe 1977; and the data in Donelson 7–66. A clear example is from the Deutero-Platonic Letter 13: "Let this greeting not only commence this letter but serve at the same time as a token that it is from me" (cited from Fowler et al. 360a; cf. also 363b, and the first lines of Letter 3).
2. See the photograph in Deissmann 1927, 170. Likewise, letters of Bar Kokhba (ca. 132 C.E.) conclude with his signature in his own hand, obvious from the difference in handwriting (Doering 75).

of 2 Thessalonians, however, writes in a post-Pauline situation in which the identity of authentic Pauline tradition was a live issue and letters were written in Paul's name to advocate particular interpretations of Paul's legacy (see on 2 Thess 2:2 above). The author's claim that Paul personally signs every letter presupposes a historical context in which a corpus of Pauline letters is available, in a post-Pauline situation. These closing words make a final claim that his letter represents the authentic voice of Paul. It is important to see that the *claim* being made is the point, not its actual probative value. Even in Paul's own situation, the letter would have been read aloud, and in any case the handwriting would not have been visually compared with samples of Paul's authentic penmanship. Likewise the "proof" would have functioned only for the original document. Later copies, of course, could not preserve the original handwriting and thus would have preserved the claim, but not the "evidence." In the post-Pauline situation of the actual author and hearers/readers, it is the claim that is functionally important, not the readers' interest or ability to verify it empirically.

Without concern for logical or material proof, then, but in all good conscience and with considerable skill, the author launches his letter into the arena of discussion and debate on the way forward for the network of churches in the Pauline tradition. Christian believers will continue to suffer harassment and persecution. They should not be deceived by the false idea that Jesus is coming soon, but settle into the mode of faithful mission for the long term, guided by the authentic Pauline tradition as represented in this and other letters. They do not need salaried leaders who no longer earn their own living, but teachers who live by the model of Paul himself. As the sociology of religious movements and the wisdom of other canonical documents would have it, on this latter point the author was laboring for a lost cause. A special class of ordained, salaried clergy became the norm, celebrated as God's provision for the ongoing life of the church. Documents affirming that conviction were accepted by the church as canonical. But so was 2 Thessalonians. The voice raised here did not win the day institutionally, but it has tempered the way both ministers and congregations have regarded "professional clergy."

[18] The concluding benediction is taken almost verbatim from 1 Thess 5:28 (see comments there), the only change being the addition of *pantōn* (all) to "with you," which accords with the demonstrable tendency to increase the usage of a generalizing "all" (see intro to 2 Thessalonians, "Tone, Style, Language"). The letter closes with the one word that best sums up the theology of the Pauline school, *charis* (grace), and the pronouncement that it is extended to all who hear.

INDEX OF SCRIPTURE
AND OTHER ANCIENT SOURCES

INDEX OF SUBJECTS AND AUTHORS

Lampe, Peter, 37n50
Langlands, Rebecca, 145n23
language, theological
  confessional language, 63, 71, 76–77, 104,
    174, 176, 184, 283–84
  election as, 62–63
  family language for church, 62, 76, 86, 90,
    108, 110, 134, 149, 216, 301
  gender-inclusive language in translation,
    58, 295
  God-language for Jesus, 259, 271, 279
  Gospels as nonliteral, nonreporter language,
    107
  language and rhetoric of apocalyptic, 107,
    157, 253, 261, 268, 270, 276
  liturgical language and tone of 2 Thessalo-
    nians, 214–15, 229, 246, 283
  objectifying and nonobjectifying language,
    63, 104, 130, 173–74, 254, 258, 270–71,
    284
  referential and nonreferential language,
    130, 269, 270
  Revelation, language and symbolism of, 107
  symbolic universe, new language of, 29
  worship, language of, 246–47, 258, 284
  wrath, language and rhetoric of, 63, 71, 76,
    104, 174, 184
  See also confessional language
Latin
  in Philippi, 16
  in Thessalonica, 16
Laub, Franz, 223n19, 276n40, 301n8
law
  Christian ethic not new law, 39, 99, 292
  enslaving power of, 75, 130
  as halakah, 134
  Jewish, 22, 104, 261, 273
  and order, 30, 277–78
  secular, 89, 143, 263
  works of, 10, 60
Lawless One, 260–61, 269–70, 272–73,
  275–76, 278–80
leipō (leave), 171
letters
  1 Thessalonians as, 33, 37
  distinctive in New Testament, 38
  form and structure, 35, 39–40, 41
  genre, 32–33, 37–38
  Hellenistic, 32, 34–35, 45, 49, 55, 208, 211,
    242

Jewish, 34–35, 40, 61, 200
literary and real, 33
mediates person and presence of author,
  33–34
orientation to community, 43
Pauline, 36, 37, 38
theological perspectives on, 44
Lewis, Scott, 180n73
lex talionis (law of retaliation), 250
Lieu, Judith, 21n31
Lindblom, Johannes, 169n59
Lindemann, Andreas, 225n23
Lindsey, Hal, 107n71
liturgy
  effect on English translations, 97
  effect on Paul's writings, 50–51, 56, 125,
    229
  elements in Pauline corpus, 26, 28, 165,
    204–5, 215
  factor in language and tone of 2 Thessalo-
    nians, 214–15, 229, 246, 283
  letters intended for liturgical reading, 8
  not yet formalized, 26
  Pauline letters intended for liturgical read-
    ing, 208, 283
logos (word, message), 93, 96, 164, 260, 264,
  282, 287
Lohse, Eduard, 164n49
loipon (remainder), 133, 282, 289–90
Longenecker, Bruce, 42n60
love
  agape best translated as "caring," 126
  believers mediators of God's love, 60, 87,
    126, 151
  believers, for each other, 76, 86–87,
    120–21, 124–26, 139, 151, 153, 194, 247
  believers, for God, Christ, Jesus, 122, 293
  believers, for the neighbor and all people,
    122, 124–26, 139, 150–52, 194, 247
  concrete acts, not feeling, ideal, or general
    principle, 122, 150
  God's, for humans, 53, 102, 151, 289, 293,
    305
  Paul's, for the Thessalonians, 112
  Pauline vocabulary for, 149, 150
  truth, believers' love of, 260, 279, 281
  unconditional, 53, 150
  work and, 57–58, 60, 154
  See also hope: "faith, hope, love" triad
LoVullo, Steven, 139n10

Pastorals
  concerned with transmitting the authentic
    tradition, 287, 305
  deuteropauline authorship of, 209, 213, 215,
    218, 293
  do not reflect 2 Thessalonians, 221
  emerging church offices in, 299, 306
  epistolary form, 213
  eschatology of, 287
  moderately positive view of Roman power,
    278
  not found in 𝔓⁴⁶, 31
  positive image of Timothy and Titus, 47, 230
  relaxing of eschatological hope in, 160
  vocabulary of, 188, 218–19, 281, 287
Paul
  Aegean mission, 12, 25, 28, 38, 49, 86, 116,
    220, 223, 284
  Antioch period, 10–14, 28, 47, 85–86, 99,
    102, 138, 165, 179
  apostolic self-understanding, 39
  birth and early life, 10, 23
  chronology of his life, 9, 14, 27, 47, 114
  conversion/call, 10, 23, 85
  death of, 209, 214, 224–25, 258
  "early Paul," 108, 126, 160, 184
  Jerusalem Council, 11, 21, 50
  "missionary journeys," 12, 13
  as Pharisee, 10, 29
  prophetic self-understanding, 39, 172
  as zealot and persecutor, 10, 106, 157
Pauline school
  and angels, 131
  designation already used in nineteenth
    century, 29
  eschatology in, 183
  prayer in, 291
  represented by 2 Thessalonians, 128, 209,
    210–12, 286
Pauline tradition, 52, 82
pax Romana, 54
"peace and security," 18, 175, 179–80
Pearson, Birger, 91n50
peirazō (test, try, tempt), 114, 118
pempō (send), 262
peri de (now as for), 150, 154, 176
periergazomai (be a busybody instead of
  working), 296
peripateō (walk, live one's life), 78, 132, 134,
  295

peripoiēsis (receiving, attaining), 176
perissoterōs (more/most abundantly), 109
persecution
  faith as faithfulness under persecution, 247
  of believers in Thessalonica, 13, 30, 61,
    95–96, 117, 153, 158, 171
  of Christians by Jews, 101
  integral to Christian faith, 98, 117, 221, 237
  of Jesus, 95
  in Judea, 96, 98
  for "the name" (of Christ), 236, 238, 259
  part of eschatological scenario, 171, 265,
    268–69
  of prophets, 95, 97
  in second and third Christian generation,
    235, 237, 239, 241–42, 295
  a theme of 2 Thessalonians, 211, 213, 226,
    231, 250
Peter
  Antioch church and, 12
  confrontation with Paul, 11
  eyewitness of Jesus' ministry, 137
Petersen, Norman R., 42n60, 247n13
Peterson, Erik, 173n63
Pharisee
  Paul as, 10, 29
philadelphia (family love), 149–50, 152–53
Philemon
  addressed to a congregation, 43
  no appeal to apostolic authority, 27
  vocabulary of, 48
  written from prison, 239
philikos (friendly), 32
Philippi
  as destination of 2 Thessalonians? 8
  episkopoi and *diakonoi*, 191
  first church of Aegean mission, 86
  Jews in? 19
  mission center, 12
  Paul received financial support from, 20,
    22, 25, 88
  Paul's letter to, 47
  Paul's mission in, 12–13, 20, 47, 81
  Roman battle of Philippi, 15
  Roman prominence in, 16
Philippians
  letter of gratitude, 59
  literary unity of, 191
  no appeal to apostolic authority, 27
  relative date of, 160